D1179455

MINING
IN THE
EAST MIDLANDS
1550 — 1947

MINING IN THE EAST MIDLANDS 1550–1947

ALAN R. GRIFFIN, B.A., Ph.D., M.B.I.M.

*Special Lecturer in Industrial History
and Industrial Relations in the
University of Nottingham*

With a foreword by Lord Robens

FRANK CASS & COMPANY LIMITED
1971

First published in 1971 by
FRANK CASS & COMPANY LIMITED
67 Great Russell Street, London WC1B 3BT

ISBN 0 7146 2585 X

Printed in Great Britain by
Clarke, Doble & Brendon Ltd.
Plymouth

Contents

List of Illustrations

Preface

This book is based on my Nottingham Ph.D. Thesis which was submitted in 1963. However, whilst the work remains substantially the same in outline, many changes have been made in detail.

The draft as submitted to the publishers was unfortunately too long; and some parts have therefore been abridged. In particular, Part I has been reduced to less than half its original length.

The title requires some explanation. The book is mainly about Nottinghamshire, but not exclusively so. Nottinghamshire is, in any case, an ambiguous expression. Some parts of the geographical county (e.g. Shireoaks) have always been regarded as belonging to the South Yorkshire coalfield. On the other hand, many border areas which are actually in Derbyshire have for a long time been regarded as part of Nottinghamshire. This is true, for example, of Pinxton, South Normanton and Somercotes. Again, the Erewash Valley, which is for some purposes a sensible geographical unit, lies either side of the County border. A further justification for the title is that there is a great deal of similarity between the four wages districts (Nottinghamshire, Derbyshire, Leicestershire and South Derbyshire) which make up the East Midlands. Many things which apply to Nottinghamshire therefore apply, *mutatis mutandis*, to the other districts.

However, for a detailed appraisal of the Derbyshire coalfield, the reader is referred to *The Derbyshire Miners* by Dr. J. E. Williams which is, in many ways an excellent study. Leicestershire and South Derbyshire are similarly covered by Mr. C. P. Griffin in his Nottinghamshire Ph.D. Thesis which is to be submitted later this year.

For a detailed consideration of the history of mining Trade unionism in the locality, reference should be made to my book *The Miners of Nottinghamshire 1914 to 1944*. The present volume contains an abbreviated account only.

Many people have helped me to find material for this book. In particular, I am indebted to various colleagues employed by the National Coal Board including Mr. R. Storer, Mr. R. Shelton, Mr. A. Hendy, Mr. E. Williamson, Mr. A. Morley and other members of the N.C.B. Survey Staff; to former colleagues, Mr. O. B. Lewis, Mr. W. Day, Mr. J. B. Plummer and Mr. E. A. Barlow; to Mr. P. Elliot who, when Company Secretary and Director of the

Butterley Company, made material from the Company's archives available to me; and to Mr. Albert Martin and his fellow officials of the N.U.M. (Nottingham Area) who have always been most co-operative. Others who have helped include Mr. Herbert Booth, whose personal recollections were invaluable, Mr. T. A. Hollyoak who provided information on coal distillation, the Nottingham County Archivist, (Mr. W. R. Sargent), and his staff, the late Mr. H. Hepworth, Librarian of Sutton-in-Ashfield (who let me use John Dodsley's Skegby Colliery Account Book) and the Reference Librarians of Nottingham, Mansfield and Ilkeston. Much of the material concerning Pinxton was obtained for me by Miss L. Walvin. Similarly, Mr. Colin Oakley supplied material relating to the Boot family. Some of those whose personal recollections were helpful have since died. They include Mr. G. A. Spencer, Mr. J. Eyre, Mr. Les Ellis and Mr. Bert Wynn. Others, who are happily still alive, include Lord (Bernard) Taylor, Mr. Owen Ford and Mr. Frank Smith of Pinxton.

I would also like to thank my son Mr. C. P. Griffin, whose B.A. dissertation and subsequent research have been most useful; Mr. P. L. Stevenson of the Railway and Canal Historical Society; and Prof. A. W. Coats for his advice and encouragement.

There are, I know, others who have helped in various ways but whose names do not come readily to mind. My thanks are due equally to them all.

ALAN R. GRIFFIN.

Department of Economic History,
University of Nottingham.
May 1970.

Foreword

by the Rt. Hon. Lord Robens of Woldingham, P.C., D.C.L., Ll.D.
Chairman of the National Coal Board

D r. Griffin is the Area Industrial Relations Officer for the North Nottinghamshire Area of the National Coal Board and a Special Lecturer in Industrial History and Industrial Relations at the University of Nottingham. He has spent almost the whole of his working life in the mining industry.

His academic career really commenced in his late twenties after a number of years spent working at two collieries in Nottinghamshire. Perhaps not unnaturally he chose as a thesis for his Ph.D. at Nottingham 'The Development of Industrial Relations in the Nottinghamshire Coalfield.'

The capacity for reseach is well balanced by the obvious interest the author has in his subject, and the wealth of experience obtained by Dr. Griffin at first hand in the mining industry well equips him to treat this topic with great care and understanding.

He followed his academic success at the University with experience at the Board's East Midlands Divisional Headquarters; then an appointment in the South Derbyshire and Leicestershire Area with particular responsibility for the retention and recruitment of industrial workers at the pits and for their welfare. Subsequently he moved to the Alfreton Area which had collieries in both Derbyshire and Nottinghamshire—there he was responsible for the wages and conditions of service for industrial workers and later became Industrial Relations Officer. For a period just before the major reorganization of the industry in 1967 he was Industrial Relations Officer for the Edwinstowe Area, which later became the Headquarters for the new style North Nottinghamshire Area.

He can therefore be said to be truly a man of the Midlands with personal experience of the problems confronting the men in our industry in these counties.

Industrial Relations are probably the most challenging feature of our time generating problems and opportunities for management and men alike. Increasingly there is an awareness of the part human engineering plays in creating a worthwhile life of fulfilment and a viable national economy. At this time the whole theory and practice of Industrial Relations are under the microscope, as I very well know from the time spent on the Donovan Commission and as most people will recognize from current events. If we seek to answer the vexed industrial questions of today we need to understand yesterday's problems which have formed the context from which the new strains and stresses emerge. It is of the utmost importance to be able to stand back and look objectively at the continuity of our history and thus trace the development of the present difficulties which cloud the industrial horizon.

It is generally left to our academic friends to undertake the painstaking work required to trace back the record of events, and to portray them for current consideration. There is, however, a special contribution that can be made by people with practical experience, but rarely are there those with sufficient dedication prepared to give up evenings and their limited free time for this kind of research work.

Dr. Griffin combines the ability with the willingness and chooses an industry which is richer than most in its story. I am therefore very pleased to have the opportunity of contributing this Foreword to what I feel is a significant historical document.

PART I

PART 1

CHAPTER I

Getting the Coal

1. INTRODUCTION

According to the late Prof. Sir Ian Richmond, traces of Nottingham-shire coal have been found on Roman camp sites in the Lincoln-shire fens.[1] The earliest written evidence of coal mining in the district, however, dates from the later middle ages.[2] All the early coal-mines were on the outcrop between Wollaton in the South of the County and Teversal in the North. The mines at Wollaton, and the neighbour-ing villages of Strelley, Bilborough and Cossall, had the advantage of proximity to the River Trent, the only navigable water-way in the County until canals were cut in the late eighteenth century. They were also close to Nottingham.

From about the middle of the sixteenth century the demand for coal rose rapidly, largely because of the increasing scarcity and dear-ness of wood. Nef estimates the average annual output of the Trent Valley collieries at 10,000 to 15,000 tons in the middle of the sixteenth century, 30,000 to 50,000 tons at the beginning of the seventeenth; and 100,000 to 150,000 tons a century later.[3]

This quickening in demand stimulated technological developments such as the long sough driven at Wollaton in 1552 which was said to have cost £20,000.[4] 'Rag and chain pumps', driven by horses (and occasionally by windmills) were also used for drainage there, from about the same date.[5]

It would seem that Wollaton was also the site of Britain's first railway. This was constructed by Huntingdon Beaumont in 1604 to carry coal from Strelley to Wollaton lane end. Subsequently Beaumont tried, unsuccessfully, to extend his rails to the Trent.[6] Beaumont has also been credited with introducing boring rods which took much of the uncertainty out of searching for coal.[7] He also appears to have made early use of a horse-driven winding device, probably the 'cog-and-rung gin' which replaced the simple hand windlass at large pits in the early seventeenth century.[8]

But Beaumont was not merely the pioneer of mining engineering: he was also the prototype colliery entrepreneur. He took a lease of Sir Percival Willoughby's coal-mines at Wollaton in 1601, and in 1603

3

leased the rival Strelley and Bilborough mines from Sir John Byron. Subsequently, he tried to take over the smaller collieries to the North of Nottingham with the intention of restricting their output, thus forcing up the price of his coal. His adventure proved unsuccessful, and in 1618 his creditors had him jailed for debt.[9] Later monopolists had rather more success.

2. MINING SYSTEMS AND ROOF SUPPORT

Coal was first won from outcrop workings. Where the coal outcropped on to a hillside, the colliers burrowed into the seam for a short distance. Where the ground was level, as in Nottinghamshire, small shafts rather like wells were sunk down to the seam. The coal was extracted from around the pit bottom until the sides were in danger of collapsing when the pit was abandoned and another one sunk nearby. A sectional diagram of such a pit resembles a bell in shape. An aerial photograph of a field at Wollaton shows dozens of these 'bell pits'.[10]

At the next stage of development, where the depth of the coal made the bell-pit method intolerably wasteful of labour, headings were driven into the seam from the pit bottom, and side headings (usually known as stalls) were driven from the main heading.[11] There is evidence of early 'post and stall' workings in the Skegby and Swanwick districts,[12] and at Coleorton in Leicestershire the outlines of 'Stall and Pillar' work can be clearly seen on the surface of a shallow mine. The last privately-owned colliery in Nottinghamshire (Harpur Hill) which closed in 1967, used a similar method.[13]

The stall-and-pillar system and its variants gave way to the long-wall system throughout the Midland coalfields, at some time prior to the nineteenth century. With long-wall working, all the coal along a face is extracted leaving a space called the 'gob', 'goaf' or 'waste' which is then partly packed with debris to support the roof.[14] The actual working faces and the roadways also need support and in the eighteenth and ninetetenth centuries this was provided by wooden puncheons.

The support given to the roof was, however, inadequate and falls of roof caused many accidents. Christopher Hardy, who was buried at Teversal Church on 8th May 1619, was 'slayne in a Coal Pit Road',[15] most probably by a fall. However, falls are undramatic. Unlike explosions, they occurred daily. Sometimes a man would be crushed by 'a great quantity of coal', as was Amos Beardsley of Cotmanhay Colliery in March 1870,[16] but for each fatal accident caused by falls, there were many non-fatal ones. Employers sometimes failed to supply sufficient timber; but often, as Matthew Hayes observed in 1871, workmen were themselves to blame for refusing to set supports at proper intervals.[17]

3. DRAINING THE WORKINGS

For the colliery owner, drainage was an even greater problem than roof control. Before the introduction of steam driven pumps, the most satisfactory way of dealing with water was to drive an underground drainage level (an 'adit' or 'sough') through the field and to connect the pits to the sough.

Long soughs were expensive. The Willoughbys claimed that the sough driven in 1552 cost £20,000, and almost two centuries later, the partnership of Barber and Fletcher (which developed into the Barber, Walker Company) similarly claimed that they had spent £20,000 on driving soughs at Kimberley, Denby, Loscoe and elsewhere.[18] This was almost certainly an exaggeration because the partnership's pits were very small in this period: their total sale in 1750 only amounted to £2,600.[19] Between 1761 and 1766, Lord Middleton spent £2,043 on sinking pits and driving a sough at Wollaton, but his profits were correspondingly high.[20]

In the North of the coalfield, Sir John Molyneux commenced the construction of a sough in 1703, which eventually reached about five miles in length. The work was done piecemeal, being completed up to the village of Hucknall Huthwaite (with financial assistance from the Duke of Newcastle) by 1761 and being completed by the Duke of Devonshire about 1774.[21] The slow rate of progress was dictated by the comparatively small scale of the mining operations in the district.

In some cases, a group of small pits which were below the level of free drainage were connected to a 'sump' pit, that is a shaft sunk to a lower level than the seams being worked. The water was then drawn from the sump pit by a pump of some kind. With very small pits, a 'waller'[22] (i.e. a hand windlass drawing a bucket on the end of a rope) might do: there were still some of these in the foothills of the Pennines in the 1840's. With larger concerns, a pumping 'engine' would be necessary.

During the eighteenth century, horse-driven pumps gave way to steam engines. For example, the sough constructed by Middleton at Wollaton in the 1760's was drained by a Newcomen engine; and the same owner's Trowell Field Colliery had a Newcomen engine in 1733 and a second one three years later.[23]

The Newcomen engine overcame the endemic flooding of pits in the winter which had so worried Huntingdon Beaumont,[24] but the haphazard development of coalfields introduced the danger of inundation from old workings. Such an inundation occurred at Molyneux

Colliery, Teversal, in 1869. The plans of the mine, kept by John Boot as agent for Lady Carnarvon the owner of the coal, were defective. Some old waterlogged workings in the Top Hard Seam, bounded by a water level, were known to Boot but were 70 yards nearer to the Molyneux workings than he had supposed. For all that, the lessees, Eastwood and Swingler, ironmasters of Derby, had a duty to bore for water knowing that they were working close to old pits, but they had failed to do so. Consequently, at 8.30 p.m. on 2nd April 1879, men working on 'A' face broke through into the old workings and four were drowned. Three other men who managed to reach the pit bottom were saved but were fortunate to be so. At Molyneux it was still the practice (as it had been at many local pits thirty years earlier) to have only one winding engine man who went home after winding the day shift men out and the night shift men in the pit. Had the shouts of the three men in the pit bottom not been heard by a pump attendant who happened to stroll in the direction of the shaft, they would have drowned.[25]

4. VENTILATION AND ILLUMINATION

Soughs and water pits fulfilled a secondary function: they acted as airways. In a pit having only one shaft, ventilation was uncertain. In cold weather the temperature underground would be higher than that on the surface and convection currents in the shaft would ensure a flow of air. In hot weather, however, the temperature might well be as high on the surface as underground and no air would flow. Under these circumstances, 'black damp' (or 'choke-damp') could build up. This gas is a mixture of carbon dioxide and nitrogen, is colourless and odourless, and it extinguishes both light and life.

The presence of the gas was usually detected by its effect on the flame of the candles used for illumination underground, but this might be altogether insufficient warning. In summer, the seventeenth-century collier is said to have tested the air by lowering a dog down the shaft. If the dog howled, then gas was present, but if not then it was safe for the men to go down.[26] Where accumulations of gas were detected during the shift, they were cleared by shaking a jacket about vigorously.[27]

Wyllyam Poole, writing in 1620, had a recipe for the prevention of danger from gas. This reads:

'For the dampe. Take a bushell of unslaict lyme, and lett hyme send yt downe and sett yt in the places as neare as the workmen wyll and let yt contenewally remayne tell suche tyme as the moystnes of the dampe begyne to sleake the lyme, and then let hyme renewe yt contenewally. Yt wyll all somer last. Let them take hyd that the do not let any watter come to yt. Yf the dampe be very stronge, let hyme put to the lyme ij d. of camphyre; yt wyll drawe yt awaye the soner.'[28]

Matching this recipe is the treatment for those affected by black-damp as described by Mr. Jessop of Yorkshire to the Royal Society in 1675:

'I never heard of any great inconvenience which any one suffered by it, who escaped swooning. Those that swoon away and escape an absolute suffocation are, at their first recovery, tormented with violent convulsions; the pain whereof, when they begin to recover their senses, causeth them to roar exceedingly. The ordinary remedy is to dig a hole in the earth and lay them on their bellies, with their mouths in it; if that fail, they tun them full of good ale; but if that fail, they conclude them desperate.'[29]

Having two shafts connected together (or a shaft and an adit) ensured a flow of air. The shaft having the heavier column of air became the downcast, although under certain circumstances the direction of the air current could be reversed. In the eighteenth century, fire was widely used to improve the flow of air. Pilkington noted the use of firebaskets hung in the subsidiary upcast shaft in Derbyshire in 1789. Two years earlier, the first proper ventilation furnace had been constructed at the bottom of the upcast shaft at Wallsend Colliery and this became in time the standard system of ventilation throughout the country.[30]

In Nottinghamshire (and at least the Erewash Valley area of Derbyshire) ventilation furnaces were still not in use in 1841, nor were fire baskets used very often. Natural ventilation was still thought to be adequate at all but two or three pits. The Children's Employment Sub-Commissioner, J. M. Fellows, noted a number of fatal accidents which had occurred through inadequate ventilation. At one of the small Babbington (village) pits, a boy named Thomas Neds had been overcome by black-damp whilst riding the shaft and had fallen to his death. Several witnesses said that the pits at which they worked were sometimes forced to stand, because of accumulations of black-damp. Boys at Barber Walker's Beggarlee mine complained that black-damp swelled their bellies and gave them headache—a complaint echoed elsewhere—whilst at the same Company's Trough Lane pit, Watnall, they were not allowed to come out until the gas had extinguished their candles.[31]

Black-damp, it appears, was universal in the district. It caused shortness of breath ('miners' asthma') and must have lowered the efficiency of the labour force, quite apart from the few who were killed by it, but it caused no damage to the owners' property.

Fire-damp, which does damage property, was not much of a problem at most collieries; though those at the Pinxton end of the coal-field were more prone to it than others. Even here, the frequent eruptions were minor ones, although they were frightening enough to those involved. For example, Matthew Hayes encountered fire-damp as a boy at the Old Pinxton Colliery (this would be about 1836). He was in a heading away from the main air stream when he saw a mouse. 'With the naked candle in one hand, and grabbing at the mouse with the other, he was suddenly wrapped in a sheet of flame. . . . This was the first time in his life that he had been burnt with wild fire, but he had heard the men say that the only chance for a fellow was to throw himself face downwards, bury his hands and face in the dust, and wait until the flame died out.[32] On this occasion, he was only lightly injured, but in a similar explosion ten years later he was badly burned and was away from work for thirteen weeks.[32]

A more serious explosion at Crick's pit, Old Pinxton, occurred in the early hours of 22nd March 1825 when 'Pinxton was shaken to its very centre' and two men (Charles Braddow and his son, both leading Methodists) were killed. On Braddow's gravestone in Pinxton church-yard was the epitaph: 'The wild fire proved my fatal destiny.'[34]

A similar explosion on the level between Nos. 1 and 2 Pits at the same colliery occurred shortly before it closed in 1844 when at least one person, a boy named Stocks, was killed.[35] Other explosions occur-ring about 1840 were reported to the Children's Employment Sub-Commissioner. At Kirkby Fenton's Colliery at Bagthorpe (Selston) the explosion had 'blazed out of the headstocks' and killed 13 asses; four men and two boys were burnt in an explosion at Barber Walker's Willow Lane pit; whilst 17-year-old George Peach of Selston, whose family were to become leading trade unionists for four or five genera-tions, was badly burnt in another explosion.[36]

With better ventilation, these minor explosions would not have occurred. Further, with Davy lamps, the presence of gas could at least have been detected, but at all local collieries naked lights were still used and even where a Davy lamp was provided for gas detection, it was employed very sparingly, if at all. The Cokes of Pinxton, for example, kept a Davy lamp in the office but it was rarely taken down the mine, although some of their pits (particularly Carnfield No. 2) were notoriously fiery by Nottinghamshire standards.[37]

After 1843, when the large new colliery at Cinderhill of Thomas North was completed, the use of ventilation furnaces was quickly adopted at all the sizeable mines in the district. Even so, the District Mines Inspectors, first appointed in 1850, complained repeatedly about explosions needlessly caused by inadequate ventilation. For example, in his Report for 1864, the Inspector described fatal explosions at Cinderhill, at High Park and at Mexbro' (Selston) each caused by faulty ventilation. At Cinderhill, Davy lamps were in use, but these introduced a new danger. As the Inspector said:

'I pointed out at this inquest the impropriety and danger of continuing to work with a safety lamp in an explosive mixture. The feeling among some, is that when gas is discovered, and men are furnished with safety-lamps, all is done that is necessary; that it is safe to continue to work with a lamp, which in fact means nothing more nor less than sub-stituting these instruments in lieu of ventilation, a practice most danger-ous to life and property. Directly gas is seen, men ought at once to discontinue working; this is done in all well-regulated collieries; and I was very much surprised to hear an opinion expressed that this was not the custom in some parts of Nottinghamshire.'[38]

These explosions killed few people. Annesley was the site of the most serious explosion in Nottinghamshire in the nineteenth century. This killed seven men as against the 95 killed at Haswell Colliery, Durham, in 1844: by no means the worst North-country example. At Annesley, the seven men killed in 1877 were overcome with 'after damp' (i.e. carbon monoxide) the most prolific cause of death, follow-ing explosions of fire-damp.[39] The Haswell disaster is important be-cause the Committee of Inquiry which investigated it exposed the explosive potential of coal dust, previously unsuspected by most mining engineers.[40] Indeed, there were still some sceptics who insisted that fire-damp was the only explosive agent even in the early twentieth century.[41] By the date of the Annesley explosion, most large collieries in Nottinghamshire had gone over to fan ventilation, but Annesley still employed a furnace.[42]

Some collieries were also now insisting on the use of flame safety lamps, although cheap paraffin lamps with a naked flame were popular in Nottinghamshire between 1847, when a spring of petroleum was discovered at James Oakes's Riddings Colliery,[43] and 1880 when the Mines Inspector insisted on the discontinuance of such lamps, follow-ing a fatal accident to a boy at Wollaton Colliery.[44] The chief opposi-tion to flame safety lamps now came from the men, because they gave a poorer light than candles or ordinary paraffin lamps and this affected the pace at which the men could work. Consequently, their use was by no means general until after 1900. Flame safety lamps introduced a new hazard—miners' nystagmus—which reached the proportions of a scourge between 1880 and the 1920's when electric lamps having a higher standard of illumination became common.

5. GETTING THE COAL TO BANK

So far we have said little about drawing the coal out of the shaft. In the early eighteenth century, the simple cog-and-rung gin gave way to an improved device, the whim-gin. Here, a rope drum was mounted horizontally some distance away from the shaft, and the rope was carried down the shaft over pullies. The spindle on which the rope drum was mounted was rotated by horses (usually two at a time) thus drawing the rope up and down the shaft.

On the end of the rope, hazel baskets (or 'corves') were hung on hooks: there might be one, or several of these, according to the size of colliery. This description relates to a large colliery in Durham, but the system is exactly the same as that in use in Nottinghamshire:

'Instead of a cage, a long chain was attached to the rope, on which at equal intervals were placed three hooks. From each hook was suspended a large basket made of strong hazel rods, closely interlaced and twisted round, as they were firmly fastened to an iron bar. Such baskets were called "corves" and could carry from twenty to thirty pecks of coal. Generally, when men and lads were to ascend and descend, the corves were taken off and the hook was passed through a link of the chain, thus forming a large loop, in which each of two men placed a leg. They grasped the chain with their arms, and a little boy was then sat astride their knees. He grasped the chain with both hands, and they held him to themselves with their free arms. Then they were lowered a little till the loops above were similarly occupied, and sometimes the space be-tween filled with lads clinging with arms and legs to the chain. Above the top hook ten to twenty more lads would catch the chain, till fathoms of rope and chain, covered with human beings, dangled over the dark abyss.'[45]

In Nottinghamshire, with its smaller collieries, the usual 'bantle' (number of men and boys riding on one draw) averaged eight to fifteen. The introduction of the steam winding engine in the later eighteenth century speeded up the winding of men and coal, but did not otherwise change the system.

Most of the early steam winders were Newcomen-type engines with open-top cylinders.[46] The General Manager of the Barber Walker Company claimed that his Company's Willey Lane Colliery was the first in the district to use a Watt 'condensing winding engine' in 1838 or thereabouts.[47] His assertion that all earlier winding engines in the district were 'atmospheric type—open top cylinders' was undoubtedly an exaggeration, but nevertheless many local coal owners did prefer the atmospheric engine. A local engineer of note, Francis Thompson of Ashover, built a number of small Whimseys or atmospheric engines adapted to rotative motion, for winding at collieries.[48]

By 1841, steam engines of one sort or another had replaced whim-gins, for winding mineral at almost all local collieries. The one notable exception was at Swanwick where two coal pits owned by Palmer Morewood were still worked by whim-gins. Whim-gins were also still used at two of Butterley Company's iron pits at Somercotes.[49] Many collieries, however, still had whim-gins at shafts not currently used for drawing coal. For example, in 1848, John Dodsley bought a 'whimsey' from a local builder and carpenter, Abraham Wass, for use at Skegby Colliery for the sum of £10 18s. 6d.[50] This use of the expression 'whimsey' reminds us of its original use as a synonym for 'whim-gin'.

Whim-gins were still used for sinking new pits: this may, indeed, have been the primary purpose of Dodsley's purchase. One whim-gin used for sinking at Langton Colliery (completed 1844) was subsequently re-erected at Old Pinxton No. 1 Shaft where it remained until 1965. This shaft, usually called the Green Shaft, was kept open for drainage when Langton replaced Old Pinxton.[51]

Whim-gins were often used also as emergency winders when the steam engines broke down. Henry Walker's description gives some idea of how primitive the early steam winders were:

'The beam of wood; fly-wheel and drum, with horns, form the chief ornament; no steam indicator or brake are to be seen; but there is a poking handle, like an iron walking-stick, which, on every move made a rattle and clink-clank enough to frighten a statue. Yet often as it brought its load to the surface, the banksman would have to run and give the fly-wheel a "lift" with his shoulder.'[52]

Winding engines were often operated by boys, sometimes with disastrous results. For example, at one of Palmer Morewood's pits at Somercotes, a fourteen-year-old winding engineman drew two boys over the pulley, seriously injuring them, in 1840. The winding enginemen at Somercotes were said to work from 5 a.m. to 10 p.m. or later, for which the butties would only pay two shillings a day. Men were not prepared to work for this: the rate for an adult winder at this time was at least three shillings a day.[53] At Oakerthorpe, the gin was driven by a boy of ten, and at one of the Somercotes iron pits, by a boy of eight.[54] Legislation fixing the minimum age of winding enginemen at fifteen in 1842, eighteen in 1860 and at twenty-two in 1887 cured this particular abuse.[55]

Overwinds still took place, however, and various contrivances to eliminate their dangers were invented, perhaps the most important being the Patent Detaching Hook of John King, invented in 1866. King was the enginewright at Pinxton and his invention was first tried successfully at Sleights (Pinxton) No. 1 Pit. John Hill, the engineman, 'brought the cage with a load of rock up the shaft at full speed and up to the pulley frame. The device detached the cage, which it firmly held suspended, and the rope flew up and into the engine house'.[56]

Many accidents were caused in the first half of the nineteenth century by dry (i.e. unmortared) brick linings where bricks became dislodged by corves striking the sides of the shaft. John Davis was killed at one of the Eastwood pits in this way in 1840.[57] John Fisher, whilst riding the shaft at Newthorpe Common, was similarly thrown out of the chain when the side of the shaft gave way, and was severely injured.[58] To protect riders from falling objects, a 'bonnet' (shaped like a dust-bin lid) was sometimes fitted on to the rope, but in a shaft with a double rope, the bonnet on the descending rope sometimes fouled a corve attached to the ascending rope and if the men were not clinging tightly they might well be thrown off.[59]

The Children's Employment Sub-Commissioner, J. M. Fellows, also condemned the colliery owners' failure to guard pit tops. The only properly guarded pit top he had seen in the district was at Barber Walker's Willow Lane pit. At Little London pit, by contrast, a seventeen year old banksman John Clarke had slipped on ice and fallen down the shaft, but nothing had been done to prevent a recurrence.[60]

Within the following twenty years, all pits of any size in the district fitted cages held steady by guide rails in the shafts, and by 1861 there were only about seven collieries in Nottinghamshire, Derbyshire, Leicestershire and Warwickshire without them.[61] Besides making the shafts safer, they substantially increased the amount of coal wound per draw. Despite all improvements, Nottinghamshire has suffered, however, three serious shaft accidents in the twentieth century, costing fourteen lives at Rufford in 1913, fourteen at Bilsthorpe in 1927 (both during sinking operations) and ten at Bentinck in 1915.[62]

6. UNDERGROUND HAULAGE

Underground haulage presents no problems at a bell pit, but as mining developed it became increasingly costly. As a North-country writer put it in the early eighteenth century:

> '. . . the more and further a Pit is Wrought, you see the dearer she lies in the Charge of Barrow-Men or putting, for they still keep up the first Price of a Day's Work, were you to add never so many Trams; nay sometimes a Pit may happen to have a Hitch or Dipping of the Thill or Bottom of the way, by which such Setling or Descent, you are sensible to pull a full Corfe, up such a sort of a rise requires more Strength. . . .'[63]

Here, the system of mining is bord and pillar, where each hewer works in a separate bord ('room' or 'stall') which he drives forward in the coal. The workings therefore form a series of roadways separated by thick pillars of coal. The system of haulage is described thus:

> 'Besides these Miners, called Hewers, there is another sort of Labourers which are called Barrow-Men, or Coal-Putters, these Persons take the hewed Coals from the Hewers, as they work them, or as fast as they can,

and filling the Corves with these Wrought Coals, put or pull away the full Corves of Coals, which are set, when empty, upon a Sledge of Wood, and so halled all along the Barrow-way to the Pit-Shaft by two or three Persons, one before and the other behind the Corfe, where they hook it by the Corfe-Bow to the Cable, which, with the Horses is drawn up to the top, *or to Day*, as it is their Phrase, where the Banck's-Man, or he that guides the Sledge-Horse, has an empty Sledge to set the Loaden Corfe on, as he takes it out of the Hook on the Pit-Rope, and then immediately hooking on an empty Corfe, he leads his Stead-Horse away with the Loaden Corfe, to what Place of the Coal heap he pleases."[64]

During the course of the eighteenth century, rails and horses were introduced on the underground haulage ways in the North of England; and early in the nineteenth century these were being supplemented— and in some cases largely replaced—by self-acting inclines and stationary haulage engines like the one used by George Stephenson to haul trams up an inclined plane at Killingworth Colliery in 1812.[65] In Nottinghamshire and Derbyshire, however, little progress was made until after 1840. This was due partly to the fact that the seams being worked here were fairly level, facilitating manual haulage; partly because the pits here remained comparatively small and the workings compact; and partly because local colliery owners preferred to drive roadways in the coal only, so as to reduce the cost; and the height of the seams would not permit the use of horses and limited the use of rails.

There were no pits in Nottinghamshire as bad as that of Mr. Barnes of Brampton, near Chesterfield, where the boys had to drag the trams 60 yards in a height of two feet,[66] but there were plenty where the headways were little more than three feet high. At almost all collieries in the district, the coal was conveyed from the face in corves which held perhaps a half a ton or even a ton. These were dragged through the mud for a distance of anything up to 250 yards by three asses driven by two boys. One boy, the 'between driver', usually about seven years of age, walked, or crawled, behind the second ass driving the two first. The 'hind driver', usually about twelve years of age, drove the third ass, walking backwards. He wore a dog belt to draw with as necessary, and to prevent the corve from running into the sides of the bank. The dog belt was worn round the hips and attached to the corve by a length of chain: it caused soreness to the hips, among other injuries.

When the corve reached the main wagon way, it was placed on wheels (a 'tram') and drawn along rails to the pit bottom by two boys the elder of whom wore the dog belt to pull the tram where the gradient was insufficient.[67] Where the headways were driven in a seam three feet or so high, both boys and asses suffered constant injury. Of one boy 'driving between' for Mr. Kirkby Fenton at Bagthorpe in a height of 3' 2", the Children's Employment Sub-Commissioner remarked:

'This boy had lost so much blood owing to striking his head against the roof of the bank, that he appeared quite bewildered.'[68] Similarly, there was only three feet of headroom at Robinette Colliery, Strelley (Barber Walker) and at Thomas North's Flying Nancy pit.[69]

One witness, 52-year-old Joshua Gibson, who was employed by Barber Walker, said that haulage had become more difficult in his lifetime. When he started work, ponies were sometimes used, but these had been replaced by asses which were much more difficult animals to manage, because the thinner seams then being worked would not take ponies.[70] On the other hand, J. Knighton, aged 70, said that work on the wagon-ways had been eased by the substitution of iron rails for wood.[71]

Only one local colliery appears to have used mechanical means of haulage: probably a self-acting incline. This was at Swanwick where Palmer Morewood's Bailiff explained that they had drawn coal out of a 2' 7" seam by means of a rope wound round a wheel mounted at the corner of the gateway at the side of the workings. He thought that it would be inhuman to use boys for such work.[72]

Not until the second half of the century did mechanical haulage become common in Nottinghamshire. The new collieries of the Leen Valley, of which we shall have more to say in a later chapter, led the way in this as in so many other things, and the older pits of the Erewash Valley had to mechanize in order to compete with them. For example, a steam haulage engine with three boilers was erected underground at Pinxton in 1856. According to Fred Smith: 'The smoke from the boilers came up No. 10 shaft and then up the cupola behind No. 1 winding engine house. This hot air provided the means of ventilating the pit.'[73]

At Bulwell Colliery, the smallest of the Leen Valley mines, which was sunk in 1869, one of Thomas North's old locomotive engines was put to use for underground haulage. This monster, usually known as the 'Shonky' engine, was mounted upside down, its flanged wheels facing the ceiling, in an engine house a few yards from the pit top. A steel wire rope ran from the engine over a pulley and down the shaft. When the underground haulage was working at full speed, the 'Shonky' engine danced up and down on its housing and visitors expected to see it fly out of the window and down the shaft.[74]

However, compressed air haulage engines, introduced from France in 1850 (the first being erected at Govan Colliery, near Glasgow) were quickly recognized as being superior to steam engines for underground haulage because of their safety. Even where neither steam nor compressed air was introduced in this period, haulage roads of reasonable height facilitated the use of ponies instead of donkeys and these were supplemented by self-acting inclines.[75] In the twentieth century electricity was eventually to oust the remaining steam engines, compressed air and ponies.

7. CONCLUSION

The coal mines of Nottinghamshire, in common with the rest of the East Midlands coalfield, were technologically backward in 1840. The twenty years which followed, however, saw rapid technological change. Cages held steady in the shaft by guide rods replaced corves swinging freely; furnace ventilation became almost universal; and underground haulage systems improved beyond recognition. Several collieries equipped with the latest plant came into operation starting with the new Babbington Colliery of Thomas North at Cinderhill in 1843 and Langton Colliery, Pinxton, in 1844. The older mines of substantial size like Portland Colliery, Selston (opened in 1821) were modernized so as to be able to compete with these new collieries whilst many of the smaller mines had closed, or were on the point of closing, by 1860.

The District Mines Inspector for Yorkshire, Derbyshire, Nottinghamshire, Leicestershire and Warwickshire in his first report (1851) was in no doubt as to the reason for the improvement which was then taking place in many parts of his district:

'Happily, the requirements of humanity and of sound economy are to a certain extent identical as regards improved ventilation and mechanical contrivances in mining, for the latter are conducive, not only to the safety and health of the workpeople, but also to cheapness of production.'[76]

Warwickshire and Staffordshire still lagged behind, however. The Inspector reported that many mines in those counties still relied entirely on natural ventilation (especially where there was little firedamp but plenty of black-damp) and that shaft guide ropes were 'not yet universal in my district, and in Warwickshire and Staffordshire they are rare.'[77] These two counties were backward also in the field of labour relations.

To sum up, in the region as a whole, significant technological advances which must have resulted in a greatly improved productivity, took place in the twenty or twenty-five years following 1840,[78] and Nottinghamshire advanced more quickly than some other parts of the region.[79] This short-term improvement in productivity, however, should not obscure the long-term tendency towards diminishing returns to effort. Bell-pit production, as practised during disputes in

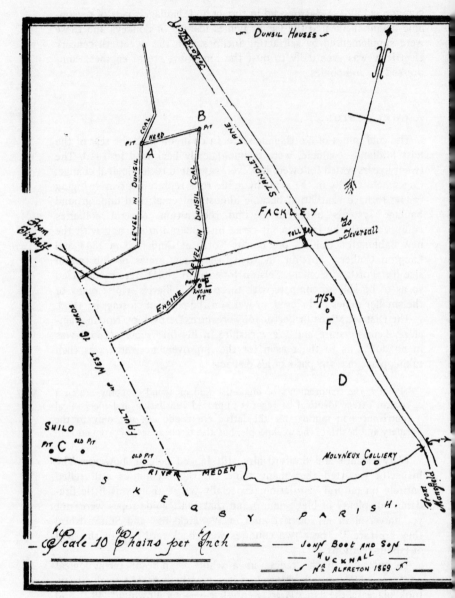

PLAN OF TEVERSAL ANCIENT WORKING, 1869

1921 and 1926, was at the rate of about a ton per man per day, there being little labour employed on non-productive operations. As pits become deeper, and as their workings advance away from the pit bottom, the proportion of 'non-productive' to productive labour increases and the output per man per day falls. Nef quotes two examples (at Beaudesert, Staffordshire, in 1589 and at Kincardine in 1679) when the output per man per day was about twelve hundred-weight.[80] This compares favourably with nineteenth and early twentieth century results. At Cinderhill in 1920, for example, productivity averaged about 14 cwts. per man shift overall when on day-work and about 18 cwts. when on piecework.[81] There are pits in South Wales even today where productivity is still running at about this rate.

It follows that, in periods when there were no significant technological changes, productivity (that is, the amount produced on average by one employee in a given unit of time) tended to fall continuously. A surge in demand could only be met, therefore, either by increasing the number of pits in production (or the number of shifts worked per day) with concomitant increases in the labour force, or by lengthening the working day. There is little doubt that the colliery owner of the eighteenth century, faced with a fall in the amount of coal produced in an hour, tried to compensate by increasing the hours worked.

REFERENCES

1 I. A. Richmond, *Roman Britain*.

2 R. S. Smith, *The Willoughbys of Wollaton, 1500–1643* (Unpublished Ph. D. Thesis), Nottm., 1964 pp. 78–80.
Victoria History of the County of Nottinghamshire, Vol. II, p. 325.

3 J. U. Nef, *The Rise of the British Coal Industry*, 2 vols., London, 1932, reprinted by Frank Cass and Co. 1966, Vol. I, p. 59.

4 F. A. Henson & R. S. Smith, 'Detecting Early Coal Workings from the Air', *Colliery Engineering*, June 1955, p. 256, but see R. S. Smith, *The Willoughbys of Wollaton*, pp. 131–4.

5 R. S. Smith, 'Huntingdon Beaumont; Adventurer in Coal Mines', *Renaissance and Modern Studies*, Vol. I, Nottm., 1957, pp. 132–134. Subsequently cited as ('Huntingdon Beaumont').

6 R. S. Smith, 'Britain's First Rails: A Reconsideration', *Renaissance and Modern Studies*, Vol. IV, 1960, p. 122.

7 W. Gray, *Chorographia: or a Survey of Newcastle upon Tyne*, 1649, Reprinted 1883, p. 20, cited R. S. Smith, 'Huntingdon Beaumont'.

8 R. S. Smith, 'Huntingdon Beaumont', p. 124. For a description of horse gins see E. O. Forster-Brown, 'History of Winding', *Historical Review of Coal Mining*, London, 1924, pp. 170–1 and Appendix (subsequently cited as *Historical Review*)

9 R. S. Smith, 'Huntingdon Beaumont', passim.

C

10 Henson and Smith, art. cit.
    I. C. F. Statham, *Winning and Working*, London, 1929, pp. 167–8.
11 ibid, pp. 167–8. See also *Historical Review*, pp. 48–57.
12 N.C.B. Survey Dept.
13 Harpur Hill Mine Plans.
14 *Historical Review*, pp. 44–46 and Appendices pp. 10–11.
15 *Teversal Parish Register*. (I am indebted to Mr. W. Clay Dove for this reference.)
16 *Nottingham Review*, 8th March 1870.
17 Matthew Wheeler, *Life of Matthew Hayes*, Nottm., 1899, p. 124.
    See also *Report of H.M.I.M.(Midlands) for 1869*, p. 50.
18 Nef op. cit., I, illustration facing p. 59
19 G. G. Hopkinson, 'Inland Navigations of the Derbyshire & Nottinghamshire Coalfield 1777–1856', *Journal of the Derbyshire Archaelogical Society*, 1959, p. 37.
20 ibid, p. 22.
21 The sough mouth is between 'A' Winning Colliery and Westhouses Station, and the sough drains the Blackwell Main (Top Hard) coal then runs past the old Hucknall Colliery of Mellors Bros. and on to Diminsdale, connecting with the New Inn level which drains into the Great Lake at Hardwick Park (see Chatsworth Estate Plans, EM 378, 381 (Added) and 1052, and Report by John Boot on the Dunsil Ancient Workings in the Parish of Teversal dated 14th December 1869).
22 Corruption of 'Wallower'. (See *Children's Employment Comm. (Mines) 1842, first Report, App. Part II*, p. 257.
23 Hopkinson, art. cit., p. 22.
24 R. S. Smith, *Huntingdon Beaumont*, passim.
25 *Nottingham Review* 7th and 28th May 1869.
    H.M.I.M. Report for Midlands Inspection District for 1869 (Mr. Evans's Report), pp. 56–7. The Mines Inspector gave instructions for the underviewer, Millership, to be prosecuted, but held the lessees to be blameless because 'they placed full confidence in their agent.'
26 *Historical Review*, p. 110. The anecdote is Roger North's.
27 ibid, p. 126.
28 H.M.C. *Report on the MSS. of Lord Middleton*, 1911 (Comnd. 5567) pp. 192–3. Lime will absorb a small quantity of blackdamp, but not enough to be effective.
29 *Historical Review*, p. 107.
30 ibid., pp. 131–132.
31 *Children's Employment Commission (Mines) First Report, 1842, App. Pt. II*, pp. 266–307.
32 Wheeler, op. cit., p. 49.
33 ibid., p. 86.
34 Henry Walker, *Pinxton Old and New* (articles published in the Alfreton & Belper Journal and mounted in a Press Cutting Book) p. 11.
    Fred. Smith, *History of Pinxton* (typescript, n.d.), p. 7.
35 Walker, op. cit., p. 9.
36 *Children's Employment Commission (Mines) 1842, First Report, App. Pt. II*, pp. 284, 295 and 310.
37 ibid, p. 329.
38 H.M. *Inspector of Mines' Report for the Midlands Inspection District*, (Report of Mr. Evans) 1864, pp. 63–4.
39 Report of Mr. Evans for 1877 and *Nottm. Daily Express*, 26th June 1877.
40 *Historical Review*, pp. 122–3.

41 e.g. W. Purdy, *Colliery Explosions and their Prevention—A Miner's Letter to H.M. King George V, etc.*, Eastwood, 1911, p. 18.

42 The last ventilation furnace—at Walsall Wood—was in use from 1879 to 1950. High Park was one of the first Notts. Collieries to have a fan (installed 1868) followed by Sleights No. 2 (Pinxton) in 1872.

43 Wemyss Reid, *Memoirs and Correspondence of Lyon Playfair*, London, 1899, pp. 37–8, 42 and 102–3.

44 *Nottm. Daily Journal*, 5th January 1880 and *Blackwell Notice Book* (Ms.) Notice dated 31st July 1880. Lamps with naked flames crept back into use at many pits, despite the Inspector's warning.

45 George Parkinson, *True Stories of Durham Pit Life*, London, 1912, pp. 17–18. Descriptions of riding the shaft at Pinxton are given by Henry Walker, op. cit., p. 2, and M. Wheeler, op. cit., p. 53. Parkinson's description relates to winding by steam engine. No doubt the numbers wound per draw would be smaller with a whim-gin.

46 The contrary view (put by Prof. T. S. Ashton and Dr. J. E. Williams among others) that Newcomen engines were used for pumping only and not for winding, is not borne out by the evidence. For example:
    (1) Newcomen winders are described and illustrated in the *Proceedings of the Institution of Mechanical Engineers*. October-December 1903.
    (2) An atmospheric engine winding coal from two shafts of unequal depth is illustrated in an oil painting in the Walker Art Gallery, Liverpool called *A Coal Mine in the Midlands, circa 1790*. There are thousands of copies of this.
    (3) Two Newcomen winders which were in use until the early years of the Twentieth Century at Farme Colliery, Rutherglen, are now stored at the Glasgow Art Gallery and Museum. For a list of engines—both Watt and Newcomen types—in Derbyshire see F. Nixon, 'The Early Steam Engine in Derbyshire', *Transactions of Newcomen Society, Vol. XXXI*, 1957–8 and 1958–9, pp. 17–22.

47 G. C. H. Whitelock, *250 Years in Coal*, Eastwood, 1957, p. 40.

48 F. Nixon, *Notes on the Engineering History of Derbyshire*, Derby, 1956. The term whimsey was originally synonymous with whim-gin, but was later used to denote a steam winding engine. (See Ashton & Sykes, *The Coal Industry in the Eighteenth Century*, 1964 edn., p. 5.)

49 *Children's Employment Commission, (Mines) 1842, First Report, Appendix*, Pt. II, pp. 316 and 330.

50 *Skegby Colliery Account Book.*

51 There was also a Butterley horse capstan at the Green shaft which was used for lowering pump-rods.

52 H. Walker, op. cit., p. 2. These very primitive engines had one advantage over the improved models which replaced them: they could not be handled by young boys.

53 *Children's Employment Commission, (Mines), 1842, First Report, Appendix*, Pt. II, p. 336.

54 ibid., pp. 323 and 316.

55 *Historical Review*, pp. 308–316.

56 F. Smith, op. cit., p. 11.

57 *Children's Employment Commission (Mines) 1842, First Report, Appendix*, Pt. II, p. 286.

58 ibid., pp. 304–5.

59 ibid., passim.

60 ibid., pp. 304–5.

61 *Reports of the Inspectors of Mines (Mr. Hedley's Report)* London, (H.M.S.O.) 1862, p. 52.

62 *Colliery Year Book and Coal Trades Directory*, 1951 edn., p. 593.

63 J. C., *The Compleat Collier: Or, the whole Art of Sinking, Getting and Working, Coal-Mines, &c. As Is now used in the Northern Parts*, London, 1708, reprinted 1968, pp. 39–40.

64 ibid., pp. 36–7.

65 *Historical Review*, p. 95.

66 *Children's Employment Commission (Mines) 1842.*
    First Report, App. Pt. II, p. 254, cited J. E. Williams, *The Derbyshire Miners*, London, 1962, p. 65.

67 ibid., p. 253.

68 ibid., pp. 283–4.

69 ibid., pp. 294 and 307.

70 ibid., p. 288.

71 ibid., p. 288.

72 ibid., App. Pt. I, p. 117. (Evidence of Joseph Tomlinson.)

73 F. Smith, op. cit., p. 15. A Waddle fan was installed at Pinxton No. 2 pit in 1872,

74 This is as the author remembers the engine in the early 1940's. The colliery closed in 1945.

75 *Historical Review*, pp. 94–100.

76 *Report of Charles Morton Esq. Inspector of Coal Mines*, 1851, p. 11.

77 ibid., p. 6.

78 See *Mines Inspectors' Annual Reports, 1851–69.*

79 Even Derbyshire, which had no growth area like the concealed coalfield of the Leen Valley, now being tapped for the first time.

80 Nef, op. cit., II, p. 136.

81 A. R. Griffin, *The Miners of Nottinghamshire*, (2 vols. 1956 and 1962,) London, Vol. II, p. 63. (Subsequently cited as *Notts. Miners, II*.) The calculation is a generous one based on the assumption that the coal-getters referred to by E. C. Fowler averaged 40 per cent of the labour force. They may well have averaged little more than 30 per cent.

   Further evidence of the tendency for productivity to fall in the long run may be found in more recent statistics. Thus output per man per year fell from 333 tons in 1883 to 293 tons in 1950—*Colliery Year Book and Coal Trades Directory*, 1951 edn., p. 492.

CHAPTER II

The Coal Owners

1. INTRODUCTION

Before the mines were nationalized in 1947, employers in the mining industry were usually referred to as 'coal owners', although many of them owned little or no coal: rather, they leased the coal which they worked from others. The colloquial name was a survival from the period when coal was usually worked by the person who owned it: the landlord, generally the owner of the soil.

2. LANDOWNERS AND ENTREPRENEURS

From the sixteenth to the eighteenth century, the most important colliery owners in Nottinghamshire were the Willoughbys of Wollaton, who took the name Middleton on entering the nobility. The Willoughbys themselves adventured money on mining operations as did many other landlords. There were some, however, like the Byrons of Newstead in the early seventeenth century, who leased out mines, preferring to let others take the risk whilst they enjoyed fixed rents.[1]

The capital invested in one of the small mines in the North of the County cannot have been very great. Sinking shafts of six to seven fathoms in Kingswood Chase and Warwickshire in the seventeenth century cost some six shillings a fathom.[2] In the late eighteenth century, shafts between seven and sixty-seven yards deep in Derbyshire cost in labour, tools and powder, from five to sixty-seven shillings a yard.[3] To this must be added the cost of driving airways (and possibly soughs), together with gins or windlasses for winding and drainage; and minor items of equipment. A whim-gin could still be bought in the nineteenth century for less than £20, so we may suppose the total fixed capital invested in a pit twenty or forty feet deep to have been no more than fifty or a hundred pounds unless long soughs were necessary. To this must be added something for working capital, for example, to finance the stocking of coal in the summer: very often, pits were idle for weeks on end through flooding following January's snows.

Extensive works like those of the Willoughbys absorbed an infinitely greater amount of capital. Deeper shafts cost much more to sink per fathom than shallow ones. Shafts in the North of England of thirty to sixty fathoms cost about fifty or sixty shillings a fathom in 1708, and much more than this where the ground was hard or where there was an exceptional amount of water.[4] A shaft sunk at Ashover to a depth of 266 yards between 1790 and 1795 is said to have cost £4,000, but this was altogether exceptional for the district.[5]

'Sinking' costs at Wollaton included almost all expenditure on capital account—drainage works for example. We have noted the £20,000 said to have been spent on a long sough in 1552. It is clear that 'sinking costs' increased steeply as the field was developed. In 1498, 'sinking' costs at £31 16s. were about one-seventh of the surplus on revenue account (i.e. receipts less hewers' wages). Between 1499 and 1549, 'sinking' costs varied between £27 and £81 (being, in the latter case, about one-fifth of the revenue account surplus). These costs then rose gradually from £106 in 1550 to £288 in 1565 then jumped sharply to £565 in 1578 representing about half the revenue account surplus. This jump was undoubtedly due to the increased cost of drainage as horse-driven, windmill, and water mill driven pumps were brought into use.[6]

The heavy cost of drainage at Wollaton may again be illustrated by reference to the £2,043 spent on sinking pits and driving a sough drained by a Newcomen engine in 1761 and 1766. Profits from Wollaton were correspondingly high, totalling £24,024 in the years 1769 to 1777. Another Middleton mine, at Trowell field, sold coal worth £3,347 in 1722 and made a profit of £14,717 in the years 1758 to 1763. A Newcomen engine was installed there in 1733 and flooding from old workings necessitated a second one three years later.[7] The cost of a large pumping engine in the early nineteenth century was about £2,000 and it consumed twenty to twenty-four tons of coal a week.[8] They can hardly have been much cheaper to buy or run eighty years or so earlier.

Sir John Molyneux's sough running from West of Blackwell to Teversal has also been mentioned. Whilst this reached a total length of about five miles it was driven gradually between 1703 and 1774 and at least two other coal owners shared the cost so that it was probably not too great a burden on the small mines of the district.[9]

In 1739 most of the collieries in Nottinghamshire and district were still owned by landowners. Selston was in the possession of Sir Wolstan Dixey and Sir Robert Sutton; Wansley was owned by Dixey and Mr. Savile. Savile and the Duke of Newcastle owned Brinsley. Mr. Plumtre and others owned Eastwood whilst Nuthall was owned by Sir John Sidley. All these pits were apparently idle at the time, possibly because the poor state of trade and the high cost of drainage rendered them temporarily unprofitable. Lord Middleton's collieries at Wollaton and Cossall were working. So, too, were the Kimberley and Bilborough collieries of Barber and Fletcher who claimed to have spent £20,000 on soughs in Derbyshire and Nottinghamshire.[10]

This was almost certainly a gross exaggeration. The partnership's pits at this date were small. For example, from their pits at Denby, they sold coal worth £274 in 1714; in 1715 they took a lease of the old Zouch coal royalty at Codnor for £120 a year and two years later sold coal worth £488 from there. Similarly, they sold £250 worth of hard coal from Shipley in 1725 and £910 worth of coal from Smalley in 1736. Their total sales in 1750 amounted to only £2,600.[11]

As opposed to the traditional colliery proprietors, who regarded pits as merely an extension of their landed estates, and mining as a rather specialized branch of farming, Barber and Company were a nascent capitalist firm. The original partnership, between the inter-related yeomen families of Barber and Fletcher had its origin in the late seventeenth century. In 1726, John Fletcher took a 99-year lease of coal in Greasley parish of Sir Robert Sutton; whilst in 1738 Robert and John Fletcher and Francis Barber took a 99-year lease of coal and lands in Strelley and Bilborough of Ralph Edge, lord of the manor and others.[12] The partnership also had collieries at Smalley and Denby (Robey's colliery) which were apparently freehold; and leasehold workings at Kimberley (owned by Lord Stamford) and Denby (owned by Mr. Lowe). Their enterprise was therefore the most extensive in the County, although the individual units were still on a fairly small scale.

One great difference between Barber Walker and a landed proprietor like Lord Middleton is that they superintended the business themselves; indeed, it is almost certain that they began by mining coal as yeomen on their own holding: first for their own consumption and then for the market. Their 99-year leases also indicate their interest in posterity. The firm is seen as having an existence separate and apart from the lives of its members.

A surprising feature of the 1738 lease is the royalty: generally 1s. 3d. a stack load (of approximately 50 cwt.), equal to 6d. per ton, which is higher than the usual royalty paid in the district some 200 years later.[13] The lease also fixed a penalty of ten shillings a load for coal not declared to the lessors: an indication of distrust.[14]

Whilst their £20,000 was almost certainly an exaggeration, they constructed soughs and other drainage works at Kimberley, Denby, Loscoe and elsewhere and they claimed that other owners were taking advantage of their enterprise by making use of their soughs. They therefore stopped up various soughs, and were accused of drowning their neighbours' workings. One competitor, Mr. Richardson, of Smalley, had been awarded £200 damages against the partnership shortly before 1739; and the other owners in the district petitioned Parliament to bring in a Bill to make the stopping up of soughs a criminal offence.[15] The partnership's extensive leases were also cited, along with the drowning of other peoples workings, as evidence of their monopolising proclivities.

Another eighteenth-century lease illustrates the tendency for this new capitalist entrepreneurial partnership to take control of operations from the older landowning proprietors. This was at Kimberley, a mine owned by the Earl of Stamford which Barbers first worked in the middle of the century at a substantial annual rent. In 1790, this was replaced by a lease which specified a rent of £5 per year for the use of the Earl's sough at Awsworth, and an annual rent of £100 for 889 loads (equal to 3,143 tons) plus 2s. 6d. for each additional load.[16]

The Barber Walker Company expanded quickly with the construction of canals which widened the market area. Much of the readily accessible coal in the Strelley-Bilborough area was worked out by the early nineteenth century, and when the Company's leases in these parishes expired in 1811, 1837, and 1838, they concentrated their operations on areas to the North. In 1841, Barber Walker had only one mine—Robinette, which was quite new—in the Strelley area. In place of the old, small pits on the outcrop, new, deeper ones were sunk to work the Top Hard seam at Underwood and Watnall. Those old pits which remained, at Eastwood, Brinsley, Cotmanhay and so on were deepened and modernized. Additional capital was brought into the firm by new members.[17]

Like the Barber Walker partnership, the Butterley Company was a bustling capitalist enterprise, but it had an entirely different genesis. Whereas the former grew naturally from its original partners' domestic production of coal, carried on as an adjunct to farming, the Butterley enterprise was founded at a particular moment in time like a modern joint stock company. Founded in 1792 under the style of Benjamin Outram and Company, its purpose was to exploit intensively the iron ore and coal measures on the Butterley Hall estate. Two of the founders William Jessop and Benjamin Outram, were engineers; another, Beresford, belonged to the landed gentry; and the other, John Wright (who was Beresford's son-in-law) belonged to a family of iron-masters and country bankers.[18]

Each partner was supposed to have contributed £6,000 to the firm's equity, but Outram appears not to have paid in cash. Wright bought out the Beresford interest for £10,000 in 1806; whilst Outram's death in 1813 established Wright as the undisputed leader of the concern.[19] In 1815, a new partnership deed was signed. John Wright contributed two-thirds and William Jessop Junior (whose father had died the previous year) one-third of the capital of £30,000. By 1858 the capital had so far appreciated as to be worth £436,000.[20] This had been achieved by ploughing profits back into the company.

The company's rapid expansion was made possible by the cutting of canals, followed by the building of railways, which enabled its ironworks to compete in the world's markets. The company's iron works, lime quarries, and pits were also connected by a network of wagonways and canals which reduced internal transport costs.

The Butterley ironworks and lime kilns gave its coal mines a regularity in demand not shared by competitors. Between April 1791 (when the firm was established) and June 1793, the output of coal totalled 3,910 tons. By 1795–6 the average annual output was over 6,000 tons. After a fall to under 3,000 tons in 1801, output rose to 7,768 tons in the year ending March 1802. By mid-century, output had grown phenomenally, reaching 438,000 tons in 1858, 631,000 tons in 1863 and 935,000 tons (of which 233,000 was from Nottinghamshire pits) in 1869.[21]

If Barber Walker and Butterley are two capitalist enterprises which succeeded, the firm of North, Wakefield and Morley may be cited as one which failed after a promising start. In 1841, North was working nine small pits in Babbington village, Greasley, Newthorpe and Awsworth. Awsworth was one of the largest mines in the district judging by the number of boys employed. There were 90 at one pit and 40 at the other under 18 years of age. In 1841–3 North sank Nos. 1 and 2 shafts at Cinderhill down to the Top Hard seam which was 8′ 3″ thick at that point.[22] This was the first large colliery on the concealed coalfield,[23] and upwards of 200 men worked underground in the mine's early years.[24] North also sank Newcastle Colliery, (Whitemoor,) in 1853; followed by Broxtowe and Bulwell (completed in 1869 by Wright and Company following North's death) besides additional shafts at Cinderhill, houses for many of his workpeople, and a railway to the Wollaton canal, linking up with an earlier network, traces of which can still be seen between Babbington village and Broxtowe. All this material investment overstrained his resources and those of the men who came into partnership with him. In consequence, he worked for immediate profit: he could not afford to take the long view on anything.

North had difficulty in getting leases. For example, he tried to lease coal from Lady Palmerston and Mr. Rolleston, two of Barber Walker's landlords, but Barber Walker intervened to prevent this. They were also advised by Robert Harrison, their General Manager, to increase their landsale at Watnall 'to upset Mr. North's attempted monopoly of land-sale in Nottingham.'[25] North was also accused of stealing coal in the 'take' of Barber Walker's Cossall Colliery.[26]

Because his 'take' was hemmed in by old workings and other firm's leaseholds, North's layout underground became widespread at an early date and his costs of production were thereby vastly increased. At the outset, however, whilst he was still producing coal from around the pit bottom, he was able to undersell his rivals. His advantage on the Nottingham market was accentuated by the completion of his railway in May 1844, in which year he was Mayor of Nottingham.[27]

In contrast with the large scale mining of North, the pits in the North of the county were still very small. At Teversal, coal was mined by the lords of the manor (first the Molyneux family and then the Carnarvons to whom the estate passed through marriage), from the seventeenth century. The main seam, the Top Hard, was virtually exhausted by 1806 and work was then concentrated in the Dunsil seam, so called because it was first worked in 1780 near the Dunsil houses. At first, the water drained away up a Top Hard shaft and into the New Inn level which discharged into the Great Lake at Hardwick Park, but in 1814 it was necessary to use a pumping engine to raise the water to the New Inn level. In 1820 the coal (a house coal, not much used for industrial purposes) could not find a market at a price high enough to cover the costs of production. As with most collieries worked by landowners, Teversal was regarded as an adjunct to the landed estate, and its profits were regarded as part of the current income of the estate. Consequently, when the income proved insufficient to meet the wages bill the 'owners of the Estate would not supply the Colliery Agents with money to pay wages with consequently the Engines and Machinery were all sold and the Workings terminated in the Parish until about the Year 1856.'[28] In 1855, Lady Carnarvon leased her Molyneux Colliery to John and German Buxton, tradesmen of Sutton-in-Ashfield. If, in fact, this had been standing since 1820 there is little wonder that it was antiquated.

German Buxton left the partnership after a short time and his place was taken by James Eastwood, a Derby ironmaster whose firm, Eastwood and Swingler, provided the working capital while John Buxton had oversight of the works. Following a quarrel with Eastwood, John Buxton left the partnership in 1865. Supervision was then left entirely to an underviewer, Joseph Millership, and deputy underviewer, George Churchill with results described in our first chapter. It appears that Molyneux relied on natural ventilation, was badly drained and had antiquated man riding facilities.[29]

Competing with Molyneux for the limited local trade was the Skegby Colliery of John Dodsley, whose Skegby Colliery Account Book would horrify a modern accountant. No distinction is made between capital items and revenue items at all; and there is no statement of liabilities and assets. Four-weekly accounting periods are used (presumably, his 'butties' were paid every four weeks). On the left hand side of the account there is first a statement showing the opening stock of coal, coal produced, coal sold, and closing stock. Below this is a list of cash receipts—almost all are payments for coal, many of them old accounts. On the right hand side of the account all items of expenditure are recorded. These include capital items (a new 'whimsey' for example) money paid on account of capital items already supplied like the £20 paid to Molas on account of 'Tubbing Bills' in October 1848[30] and repayments of loans, not to mention 'A bag of flower (*sic*) for the Hall.' Any balance left on the right hand side was apparently regarded as John Dodsley's profit, being entered as 'Balance due to John Dodsley Esq.' The credit balances for 1847 are as follows:

	£	s.	d.
28th January 1847	117	10	11
25th February	294	6	0
25th March	299	16	0
22nd April	337	13	11½
20th May	296	9	2½
17th June	264	16	3½
15th July	207	9	1

Then in period ending 12th August a mysterious item:
'Thirteen Instalments paid for Mr. Dodsley to 15 June last and £3 6s. 1d.—£482 6s. 0d.' resulted in a debit balance entered as: 'Balance due to Jno. Boot cfd. £258 17s. 6d.' John Boot was Dodsley's agent and surveyor. For the remainder of 1847 and the whole of the succeeding year Dodsley was apparently paying off debts, mainly to a Miss Cox, with the result that, for each period, there is a debit entry carried forward. At the end of 1848 the entry reads 'Balance due to J. B. £979 6s. 2d.' It is unlikely that Boot really was financing Dodsley in this period. It is much more likely that the running debit balance was merely a book-keeping entry to balance the two sides of the account.

Dodsley was lord of the manor of Skegby. The coal which his pits worked was his, and so was most of the land in the vicinity. He therefore had neither royalties nor way-leaves to pay for. His pits were shallow, the workings were not particularly extensive; and whilst the output was small, the quantity of coal demanded varied little from month to month and the scale of production was therefore constant throughout the year so far as natural conditions allowed. Under these circumstances, it was possible to purchase capital goods from current revenue, and even to charge against revenue labour cost expended on capital projects, such as sinking a new pit. Such loans as were negotiated would be personal loans made to tide Dodsley over a bad patch when the income from the pits, the farms, the lime-kilns and the brick and pottery works which he owned were insufficient to meet his business and private expenditure.[31] John Dodsley's colliery was a small one by the standards of the mid-nineteenth century, having an output of about 200 tons a week in 1847–48.

By contrast, Edward Thomas Coke, lord of the manor of Pinxton, was producing on a fairly large scale. Old Pinxton Colliery commenced working in 1780. Like all collieries of the time, it had multiple shafts—nine eventually—because of ventilation difficulties and the heavy costs of underground transport where workings were extensive. This colliery closed in 1844 (it was waterlogged during the long strike) and was replaced by Langton. There were two other collieries in production in the early nineteenth century: Sleights (later called Pinxton) and Carnfield, which lay between Pinxton and Alfreton.

Until 1847 this was purely a family concern, but in that year, Coke entered into partnership with James Salmond and George Robinson to form the Pinxton Coal Company. Coke retained twelve shares to Salmond's nine and Robinson's seven. Coke's need for fresh capital was due, no doubt, to the expense of developing Langton Colliery and modernizing Sleights. The level of demand had been immeasurably increased by the Cromford canal branch with its wharf at Pinxton, and the Pinxton to Mansfield Railway; but the Butterley Company's developing mine at Selston (Portland Colliery) intensified competition. Portland's No. 1 pit (usually called 'Isaiah's pit' after its manager Isaiah Rigley) opened in 1821 and three years later produced no less than 54,342 tons. Portland won the contract for the Mansfield Gas Works which also opened in 1821.[32]

The traditional method of financing development out of current revenue was out of the question for a development of the size of Langton, particularly having regard to the expense of the 1844 dispute and to the very low prices (6s. 6d. to 7s. a ton) ruling in 1847 in the locality.[33]

At the other end of the coalfield, Lord Middleton was still producing coal as a sole proprietor. However, in 1805, he leased his Cossall Colliery to Barber Walker, and by mid-century the time was not far off when he would prefer to rely on the certain income from royalties and way-leaves, leaving others to take the risks. This transition had already been made by most other landowning families in the district.

3. MANAGEMENT

The landed proprietors of coalmines usually left the general oversight of the mines to servants variously styled steward, bailiff and agent. The mines were, as we have said, regarded as extensions of their agricultural interests.

In the first half of the nineteenth century, and earlier, the day-to-day running of the pits was left to butties. It may be, as some have supposed, that the butty was originally no more than the chosen leader of a group of equals who contracted to work a pit. Thus Adam, son of Nicholas, with eight other men of Cossall, took a lease of Richard de Willoughby to work a pit in a field called 'le Vytestobbe' in 1316. They were to pay 12d. a week for each 'pickaxe' but were excused payment when floods or 'le dampe' stopped them from working. They were to keep the sough repaired.[34]

In the sixteenth century, the Willoughby's sub-let their pits to partners called butties and stevers: the butty being in charge underground, and the stever on the surface. The stever had to account for the coal he sold to Willoughby's pit-reeve. In 1841 stevers and butties working in partnership also ran pits under Thomas North at Babbington and at some of the Barber Walker pits.

Elsewhere, it was the usual practice to let a pit to one, or a pair, of butties. (Indeed, where stevers [stovers or stavers] are found, they can best be regarded as butties having a special responsibility for the surface. The stever is, in fact, the senior butty in the partnership.) A witness at Portland Colliery told the Children's Employment Sub-Commissioner in 1841 that the company would sink a shaft, then invite tenders from the butties. The butty who quoted the lowest price per ton for getting and raising the coal was given the contract. The butty would then engage his men, underletting to loaders and banksmen by the ton, paying the holers so much per stint, and the hammerers, woodmen, corporals, hangers-on and children by the day. The company did 'not consider they have anything to do with any of these parties but the butties.'[35]

Similarly, at Pinxton, when Mr. Coke began a new pit, he sank the shafts and prepared the headings. The agent (at that time Mr. Machin) then fixed the tonnage price and offered the pit to butties already employed at Pinxton. The butties (usually two in partnership) engaged holers by the stint, hammerers, loaders and banksmen by the ton and children by the day.[36] The butties engaged, supervized and paid the men, and provided the working capital. Sometimes they were responsible only for work directly connected with production, but in some cases they were responsible also for development work, drainage and ventilation.

Charles Morton, Inspector of Mines, considered the butty system as a bar to 'the advance of mining improvement'. He said:

'The butties are contractors with very limited capital, to whom pits are sublet, and who undertake to raise the minerals at a fixed price per ton. 'They are generally uneducated and unskilful persons, raised a step above the rank of an ordinary miner, and to whom a remuneration derivable from the proprietors on the one hand and from the labourers on the other is the chief object, regardless often of the permanent welfare of both.

'Under this system, supervision by the coalmaster or his "bailiff" is lax and irregular, and by degrees the "butty" becomes almost the sole controller of the colliery and of those who work therein.

'He is unwilling to incur any outlay in building ventilating furnaces, in making or enlarging airways, or in erecting the needful doors and stoppings; and, consequently, the pits . . . are indifferently aired.

'He allows the shafts and tramroads to get out of repair; he thinks iron "guide rods" and wooden "conductors" in pits are quite superfluous; tools, timber and other materials are by him grudgingly supplied; suggested ameliorations are objected to; his contract being terminable at short notice, he has no abiding interest in the mine; he feels no intense anxiety or definite responsibility concerning the safety and comfort of the workpeople; and his excuse is, that it is the duty of each man and boy to take care of himself.

'Butties are often directly or indirectly connected with taverns and shops, where the miners' earnings are spent in the purchase of bad and dear ale and provisions; and large quantities of intoxicating liquor are daily taken into the pits, and given to old and young in lieu of money wages.'[37]

The Inspector says that this system was unknown in Yorkshire. In the rest of his district the system varied in severity. Thus, in Nottinghamshire and the Erewash Valley butties were not normally responsible for shafts and ventilating furnaces. This no doubt was applicable to some pits in Staffordshire, Warwickshire and South Derbyshire. The same is true regarding drink taken underground, but we shall have more to say about that in our next chapter.

By the time this report was written in 1851, changes were clearly taking place in Nottinghamshire. The large new collieries, like Thomas North's Cinderhill and Babbington collieries, were much too extensive to be left to one butty to run. Further, the owner had far too much capital at risk to trust it to an uneducated butty. Legislation also had its effect, requiring, from 1850, the keeping of accurate plans; and the enforcement of increasingly elaborate safety rules as the Century progressed.

In these circumstances, the few skilful mining engineers found their services in great demand. The Boot family, for example, prospered greatly for a time. Their original home was Blackwell, and they appear to have been connected with coalmining since the eighteenth century. They had accumulated old plans and records, and when new collieries were to be sunk in the North of the county, they were usually engaged to do preliminary surveys.

The first member of the family about whom anything definite is known was Eleazer Boot (c. 1780–1861) who was living at Meden Bank, Skegby in 1897.[38] He was variously described as a 'mining agent', 'coal agent' and 'colliery manager'. His son, John Boot (1801–1893) was the agent in charge of Skegby Colliery in 1847–8, although Eleazer was also on the pay-roll. They were both paid a guinea a week, which compares unfavourably with the same amount paid to the engineer and the 3s. to 3s. 6d. a day paid to miners.[39]

Boot did the surveys, prepared the plans and had general oversight, selling the coal, keeping the books, and so on; but the day-to-day running of the pit was in the hands of two butties: one for each seam. Shortly after this, John Boot moved to Huthwaite, where the family already had some connections, and set up in practice as a land and minerals agent, his place at Skegby being taken by George Hardstaff.

John Boot's son, J. T. Boot (1835–1914), was taken into the practice, and so, too, was his son-in-law W. G. Treadwell, though this may have been after Eleazer's death. The Boots acted as agents for many local estates connected with mining (including Lady Carnarvon's) and advised on the sinking of the Stanton Company's mines at Teversal and on New Hucknall among others. J. T. Boot, who earned a reputation as an engineer and geologist, planned and supervized the sinking of Clifton Colliery too. He was proposed for membership of the Geological Society in 1872 and 1873 by Edward Hull, G. L. Greenwell and W. H. Bailey who described him as 'practically acquainted with the Geology of Midland Counties'.

With the larger companies, full-time mining engineers were employed. Two of the best known were Robert Harrison, General Manager of Barber Walker, from 1854–1892, and his contemporary William Bean who was the chief agent of the Butterley Company. Under men like these, subordinate officials were appointed in increasing numbers. About the middle of the century, the term 'viewer' came into general use, a 'viewer' being a colliery manager, taking direct charge of the works.

The terms viewer and agent were at one time synonymous but by the mid-nineteenth century, an agent was generally a man drawn from the class of land agents: a bailiff, whilst the viewer was a mining engineer. A good example of the old-style agent is C. Chouler, agent to Lord Middleton from 1790 to the 1840's. His responsibilities covered the whole of the Wollaton estate and not just the pits, and during the long illness of the Steward, Mr. Martin, he took sole charge, being responsible, for example, for overseeing the extensive renovation of Wollaton Hall in 1830. He had subordinate agents to assist him as did the agents of other large estates. No doubt many viewers had the same sort of background, but as a class they came to specialize in mining. J. T. Boot, for example, was more the mining engineer than his father although he still did some general and estate agency work.[40]

Under-viewers (i.e. under-managers) were also appointed in many

cases. Sometimes the agent or viewer was a consultant who superintended several collieries, and here the under-viewer would be in
charge of the day-to-day operations. Under-officials, i.e. overmen and
deputies, were also appointed to take charge of part of the works.
For example, whilst Joseph Machin and his successor John Chadbourne,
agents at Pinxton, had left the running of the pits to the butties until
the 1840's, they subsequently had a hierarchy of salaried officials.
Matthew Hayes was thus appointed 'night deputy and main road
repairer' about 1849, and under-manager a year later.[41]

The butty system as we have so far described it is usually referred
to as the big butty system to distinguish it from the modified system
which replaced it. At Cinderhill (sunk 1841–3), each 'stall' (i.e. a
section of a long wall face) was let to a pair of butties who were
paid a tonnage price for getting coal from their stall. They paid their
day-wage assistants, of whom there were usually only two or three,
and they provided their own light, powder and hand tools. Everything
else was provided by the company. At some collieries, a butty had
charge of a complete district, but even here he was subject to the
control of a deputy. Generally speaking, 'stalls' were larger in Staffordshire, Warwickshire and parts of Derbyshire than in Nottinghamshire,
and indeed the big butty system lingered on in South Staffordshire
and East Worcestershire until after 1907.[42]

Progressive companies like Butterley abolished the big butty system
even at their old pits in this period; and by 1851, the Butterley 'con-
tractor' (i.e. little butty) rarely had charge of more than ten people,
although a few had charge of twenty.[43] In some cases, a butty (called
a 'getter out by contract') contracted to haul the coal from the face
to the pit bottom at a tonnage price but more usually this work was
done by day-wage labour employed directly by the firm.[44]

4. CONCLUSION

Until the end of the eighteenth century, the typical colliery proprietor was a member of the landed gentry who both owned and
worked the coal, and who regarded the current surplus revenue of his
mines as personal income. By the turn of the century, this type of
owner was giving way to an *entrepreneur* intent on building a firm,
ploughing money back into the business and negotiating long leases.

The increasing size and complexity of the average colliery, together
with the need to comply with safety requirements, necessitated a
change in the pattern of management. Day-to-day control was assumed
by salaried officials, and the butty system was drastically modified.
Instead of having one butty in charge of a whole pit as with the big
butty system, it became usual from around the middle of the century

for one or a pair of butties to contract for a small stall employing six or eight men.

The increasing size and capital cost of the average colliery and the requirements of the state stimulated the growth of mining engineering as a profession. Whilst some mining engineers went into practice as consultants, others were employed by companies large enough to provide scope for their ability. At the same time, an increasing number of subordinate officials were engaged to take charge of operations underground.

REFERENCES

1 Nef, op. cit., II, p. 13.
2 ibid., I, p. 366.
3 J. Farey, *General View of the Agriculture and Minerals of Derbyshire*, London, 3 vols., 1811–17, I, p. 326.
4 J. C., op. cit., pp. 12–13.
5 Farey, loc. cit.
6 R. S. Smith, *The Willoughbys of Wollaton*, pp. 98–9.
7 G. G. Hopkinson, art. cit., p. 22.
8 J. Farey, op. cit., I, p. 338.
9 Chatsworth Estate Plans EM378, 381, and 1952.
It seems likely that colliery proprietors at Blackwell and Huthwaite also contributed towards the cost.
10 Nef, op. cit., I, map facing p. 59 (copy in Notts. County Archives.)
11 G. G. Hopkinson, art. cit., p. 23.
12 Abstract of lease in Nottingham County Records Office DDE/46/69 & 70 (Edge MSS).
13 For example, a Linby lease of 1927 specified a royalty of $4\frac{1}{2}$d. a ton, or $3\frac{1}{2}$d. if only the High Main Seam proved workable (but subject to a minimum rent.)
14 Accusations were sometimes to be made that Barber Walker took more coal in a stack load than they should. The official volume was 6 ft. high × $4\frac{1}{2}$ ft. wide (presumably square) which could be made to hold $3\frac{1}{2}$ tons or more if tightly packed.
15 Nef, op. cit., I, facing p. 59.
16 Whitelock, op. cit., p. 14. The basic royalty is equal to $11\frac{1}{4}$d. a ton, and the royalty for additional coal $7\frac{1}{2}$d. a ton.
17 Thus, Thomas Barber, James Davidson, William Herrick Dyott, Edmund Percy and Hugh Bruce Campbell financed the sinking of High Park Colliery in the 1850's—ibid., p. 30.
18 R. H. Mottram & Colin Coote, *Through Five Generations: The History of the Butterley Company*, London, 1950, p. 45.
19 ibid., pp. 45 & 47.
20 ibid., p. 77.
21 *Butterley Sales & Output Book*.
22 *The Concealed Coalfield of Yorkshire and Nottinghamshire*, London (H.M.S.O.) 1951 edn., pp. 153–4. (Subsequently cited as *Concealed Coalfield*).
23 Nef appears to suggest (op. cit., I, map facing p. 57) that coal was being

worked on the concealed coalfield at Mansfield and Newstead circa 1610. This is quite inconceivable. It is doubtful whether such deep pits could have been sunk with the primitive techniques then available, and they would have had difficulty in getting a large output to market. Nef is undoubtedly referring to Teversal (about 5 miles from Mansfield) and Annesley (the Western side of the parish a mile or more from Newstead) both on the edge of the exposed coafield. The first colliery to work the concealed coal measures, Kimberley, was sunk about 1828. It is not listed among Thos. North's mines in the Children's Employment Commission evidence, unless it was the fairly large Awsworth Colliery mentioned in the text. See *Children's Employment Commission (Mines) 1842, First Report., App. Pt. II*, p. 306.

24   White's Gazetteer of Notts., 1853 edn., p. 386.

25   Whitelock, op. cit., p. 31.

26   ibid., pp. 39–40. At his death in 1868 North owed Ichabod Wright, the Nottingham banker, £224,000.

27   Thos. Bailey, *Annals of Nottingham*, London, 1855. IV, pp. 438 & 441.

28   John Boot, *Report and Plan upon the Dunsil Ancient Workings, Parish of Teversal* (prepared for Geo. Crompton), 14th December 1869. (MSS).

29   *Nottingham Review* 7th and 28th May 1869.

30   'Tubbing' boards are used for lining shafts to hold back water. This entry (and also the Whimsey) indicate that sinking was in progress.

31   *Skegby Colliery Account Book 1847–8*, (MS.), passim.

32   J. A. Birks and P. Coxon, *An Account of Railway Development in the Nottinghamshire Coalfield*, (duplicated) Mansfield, 1949, p. 8.
      Butterley Sales and Output Book.
      Sleights & Langton Colliery Plan.
      Major-Gen. John Talbot Coke & others to the Pinxton Coal Co., Ltd., Conveyances and Assignments of Freehold and Leasehold Properties in the Counties of Nottingham and Derby.

33   *Skegby Colly. Account Book.* James Oakes (Riddings) were selling coal at from 4s. 6d. to 7s. a ton in 1841—*Children's Employment Commission, App. Pt. I*, p. 118.

34   R. S. Smith, *Willoughbys of Wollaton*, pp. 78–80.

35   *Children's Employment Commission (Mines) 1842*, First Report, App. Pt. II, p. 309 (Evidence of Bradley Mart.) For stevers see ibid., pp. 291, 302.

36   ibid., p. 329 (Evidence of James Wild).

37   Charles Morton, H.M.I.M. *Annual Report*, 1851, p. 12.

38   J. R. Raynes, *History of Wesleyan Methodism, Mansfield Circuit 1807–1907*, Mansfield, 1907, p. 34.

39   *Skegby Colliery Account Book.* (It may be that Eleazer held a sinecure. A colliery producing 200 tons of coal a week hardly had need for two agents.)

40   Statement by W. Burton, Wollaton estate wheelwright, dated Sept. 8th 1830 and found in the rafters of Wollaton Great Hall on 6th May 1954.

41   Wheeler, op. cit., p. 86–7 and 94; Walker, op. cit., p. 12.

42   J. W. F. Rowe, *Wages in the Coal Industry*, London, 1922, p. 63.
      Royal Comm. on Coal Mines First Report, Cmnd. 3548 (1907) pp. 69–71 and Appendix XIV (Report of W. M. Atkinson on 'The Charter Master System in South Staffordshire and East Worcestershire').

43   Mottram and Coote, op. cit., p. 79.

44   ibid., p. 65. This system was not, as Rowe says, peculiar to Notts. It applied to some pits in South Derbyshire, for example.

CHAPTER III

The Miners

1. INTRODUCTION

Mining was, for long, a part-time occupation, but this is, of course, a comparative term. It was not unusual even in the nineteenth century for a landowning colliery owner to use men sometimes for pit work, and sometimes for work on the land, as John Dodsley did during the 1847 harvest.[1] There is little doubt however that, by the sixteenth century, there were men in developed mining districts whose regular occupation was that of miner, even though most of them may have retained some secondary occupation to be practised when the pits were idle through flooding, inaccessibility or slack trade. In the nineteenth and early twentieth centuries, the seasonal pattern of employment was reversed: the pits working full-time in winter and short-time in summer. Many colliery owners supplied their men with cottages having large gardens to keep them busy in the summer, as did Thomas North at Cinderhill in the early 1840's.

The numbers employed in the Nottinghamshire region were quite small before the eighteenth century. Assuming Nef's figures to be of the right order of magnitude, the Trent Valley collieries which were much the most important, absorbed between 150 and 330 men at the beginning of the seventeenth century; and between 500 and 1,000 men a century later.[2] Expansion at this low rate would not entail any great search for labour: the natural process of procreation in the mining community would suffice.

To retain labour in mining, a rather less pleasant occupation than agriculture, it would be necessary to maintain a wage differential. The rate paid to miners on day rate at Wollaton was 4d. a day in 1549, and 6d. in 1551, remaining at this figure (with occasional payments of 7d.) until 1580.[3] The differential here cannot have been very great. By the beginning of the eighteenth century, the wages of colliers apparently averaged between one shilling and one shilling and sixpence per day.[4] The rates in Nottinghamshire would no doubt be at the lower end of the range. This compares favourably with the rates fixed by the Nottinghamshire magistrates for male farm labourers in 1723 of 6d. per day in winter, 8d. in summer and 1s. at harvest time.[5]

Eden towards the close of the eighteenth century, and Colquhoun early in the nineteenth, suggest a similar differential in favour of mining.[6] Despite the differential, a sudden spurt in the demand for coal, as at Wollaton in April 1602,[7] could create a temporary shortage of men, just as times of slack trade, as in the Erewash Valley in 1739, could cause a surplus.

It seems likely that the sustained increase in the demand for coal from the middle of the eighteenth century led to an improvement in the wage levels of miners, both in absolute terms and in relation to workers in competing industries, until about 1790. Unfortunately, the evidence is patchy.

At the Butterley pits, sinkers were paid 1s. 6d. to 2s. 3d. a day in 1790–7 when the average wages of miners in Derbyshire were, according to Mottram and Coote, 2s. 6d. a day.[8] A holer employed at Trowell about 1805–6 was paid 3s. 6d. a day, plus a quart of ale. These rates compare favourably with those of farm labourers (2s. a day in the Pinxton district in 1812, for example)[9] but are at about the same level as the wages paid at the Pinxton pottery. In 1796, kiln men were paid 3s. a night for work which was admittedly arduous and unpleasant, whilst skilled pottery workers were paid 3s. 6d. to 4s. 2d. a day and labourers 2s. to 2s. 8d. a day.[10]

In comparing mining wages with those of a farm labourer, regard must be had to the greater regularity of work in agriculture. Farm labourers rarely suffered accidents. It may well be that miners' wages advanced from about 1750 to 1790 or so, but there seems no evidence that the advance was sustained throughout the following half century. In real terms, miners' wages in Nottinghamshire and elsewhere in the Midlands almost certainly fell in this period; and there are cases where actual wage-rates were lower in the 1840's than in the 1790's although there may well have been fluctuations in between.[11]

For example, Joseph Chambers, the holer from Trowell would still receive his 1805 wage of 3s. 6d. a day in 1841, but without a beer allowance. (From the evidence of one of Lord Middleton's agents it can be inferred that beer allowances had been withdrawn from all Lord Middleton's mines.)[12] In the well-documented case of the stoppage of beer allowances in South Derbyshire in 1842, no extra money was paid in lieu of it, and a strike ensued in consequence.[13]

William Wardle of Eastwood had been paid 1s. a day at nine years of age in 1810; but his 9-year-old son earned only 8d. a day in 1841. Some other boys of that age earned 9d. or 10d.[14]

Joshua Gibson had been paid 1s. a day at seven years of age in about 1796 and 1s. 6d. at nine. Further back still, Sam Kirk had been paid 1s. 2d. a day at the age of ten and J. Knighton had been paid 1s. a day at the age of eleven in about 1782, which compares favourably with the rates paid in 1841: Benjamin Brown (twelve years old), for example, received only 8d. a day and Joseph Smalley, the same age, 1s. 2d. A shilling to 1s. 2d. was a fairly general payment.[15]

The general adult rate for colliers in the district in 1841 was around 3s. 6d. a day.[16] This fell in 1842 or 1843 to 3s. a day,[17] then rose temporarily at some places to 4s. following the dispute of 1844, and settled down at around 3s. 6d. during the later years of the decade, although there were still men, as some of those at Skegby, earning 3s. or less a day in 1847.[18] The earnings of miners at Butterley Park in 1851 averaged 15s. a week over the year—no more than in the 1790's Despite the deterioration in real wages, mining was still a better-paid occupation than either agriculture or framework knitting. There is no evidence of large numbers of men leaving these occupations for mining in the 1840's, but boys were undoubtedly attracted to mining who might otherwise have gone into one of these other occupations.[19]

There is little evidence regarding hours of work before the Industrial Revolution, but such as there is suggests that in this respect also, the exploitation of labour had been intensified, probably when the demand for coal rose so substantially in the mid-eighteenth century.

In the early seventeenth century, Wollaton worked twelve-hour shifts,[20] and even in 1844, this was still the standard shift length at Lord Middleton's Radford Colliery for face men (but not for others).[21] By 1782, a thirteen-hour shift, in this case 7 a.m. to 8 p.m. was being worked by Joseph Knighton of Eastwood, then an eleven-year-old haulier. At the turn of the century John Hayes worked from 6.30 a.m. to 8 p.m. at Pinxton.[22]

The Children's Employment Sub-Commissioner for Nottingham-shire and Derbyshire found most collieries working a fourteen-hour day or more in 1841. At Lord Middleton's mines, boys usually worked from 7 a.m. to 8.30 p.m. which was, with one exception, the shortest normal working day recorded. At Bagthorpe (owned by Kirkby Fenton) the boys' hours were 6 a.m. to 8 p.m.[23] At Barber Walkers' mines they were supposed to work from 5 a.m. for 'almost' twelve hours,[24] but here we see the lengthening of hours to meet the exigencies of the work in process. At Beggarlee Colliery, the butties forced the boys to work from 5 a.m. to 6 p.m. or later with only twenty minutes allowed for 'snap',[25] whilst the 'staver' at Underwood said that boys worked from 5 a.m. to 6 p.m. but the boys themselves said they worked till 7 or 8 p.m. with no break for 'snap'.[26] The road repairer on night shift at Trough Lane, another Barber Walker mine, had power to retain boys, who had been at work all day, to help him through-out the night for which they received pocket money and a day off.[27]

Six-year-old Samuel Davis had to leave home at 4 a.m. to get to Brinsley for 5 a.m. and did not reach home until 9 o'clock at night. He said
he was 'quite knocked up when he gets home.'[28]

Boys at one of Thomas North's collieries also worked from 6 a.m.
to 8 or 9 p.m. for a full day, but the butties had discovered a way to
save expense: they worked the boys twelve hours for which they
expected full output in return for three-quarters of a day's pay.[29]
At Portland, similarly, the official hours of 6 a.m. to 8 p.m. with two
hours for meals were 'stretched' by the butties. The boys were only
given an hour for meals at the most, were usually kept until 9 p.m. for
a full day, and were sometimes held back until 10 or 11 at night.
It was not unknown for a boy to be forced to stay over for a double
shift.[30]

At Pinxton also, the hours laid down by Mr. Coke were being
exceeded. According to the Agent, the boys were supposed to work
from 7 a.m. to 8 p.m., whilst according to John Hayes, a 47-year-old
collier (and father of Matthew) the official hours had been 6.30 a.m.
to 8 p.m. ever since he started work as a boy (about 1801) but in fact
the boys were now kept down until the work was done, usually 9 p.m.
but sometimes as late as 11 p.m. In addition, they rarely had more than
five minutes for 'snap', but had to eat as they worked.[31] On the other
hand, at Palmer Morewood's pits some boys only worked for twelve
or twelve-and-a-half hours a day.[32] Lord Middleton and Palmer Morewood were the only owners in the district who forbad butties to ill-
treat the boys; and they disapproved of boys under ten being allowed
down the pit.[33]

2. TOMMY SHOPS, BEER, AND BONDS

Miners in Northumberland and Durham were bound by annual hiring agreements until the 1844 dispute; but yearly bonds were uncommon in the Midlands, although there were some. The colliers at Moira
(South Derbyshire), were bound in this way in the 1840's and earlier.[34]
Two boys named Hawkins in Nottinghamshire were bound to butties
for a year in 1841.[35]

A surviving bond dated 1848 provides further evidence that this
mode of hiring was sometimes used in the Strelley-Ilkeston district.
It reads:

'An agreement made and entered into this 15th day of April 1848 between
Paul Leadbetter and John Simpson Coal Miners [butties] and William
Bennett miner all of the parish of Ilkeston. The aforesaid William Bennett
agrees to work in the pit belonging to Mr. North & Co. situated in the
parish of Strelley in the County of Nottingham from the Date above
mentioned till the 2 of October next receiving at the same time of hire-

ing one sovereign hence if The aforesaid William Bennett neglects his work through drunkenness or idleness to forfit for every such offence on shilling.'

This was probably a late survival of a practice common at an earlier period in that locality.[36] It cannot have been of any great significance by the early 1840's when, generally, the Erewash Valley masters (by decision of their combination) released men on serving a month's notice.[37] The Butterley Company, it is true, sought to bind skilled craftsmen employed in their workshops, but there is no evidence that this was done at their collieries.[38]

Of one undesirable practice, the payment of wages in truck, there is plenty of evidence. T. S. Ashton's view, that truck arose, not from the 'cupidity or ill-will' of the employers, but from 'defects of the monetary system for which the Government itself was responsible'[39] will hardly bear examination. Truck was common before the shortage of coin developed[40] and remained so after the shortage was corrected. At Pinxton, the shortage of coin was met by the production of china tokens at Coke's pottery and these circulated freely in the village, but the butties still paid in truck.[41]

The Children's Employment Sub-Commissioner was in no doubt as to the reason for truck. The butties were the owners of, or had a financial interest in, the 'tommy-shops' and beer houses: 'and a child whose parents do not expend the greater part of the wages earned in one or another of these nuisances stands very little chance of permanent employment.'[42] The District Mines Inspector similarly noted in 1851 that:

' "Butties" are often directly or indirectly connected with taverns or shops, where the miners' earnings are spent in the purchase of bad and dear ale and provisions;'[43]

Some beer houses were tommy-shops also. At Portland Row, Selston (a row of forty-seven houses built in 1823 for men working at Portland Colliery), No. 1 filled both functions. Nos. 25 and 26 were also occupied as one property used as an ale-house in 1851.[44]

In 1841, it was the common practice in Nottinghamshire and the adjoining part of Derbyshire to pay wages in public houses on Saturday nights at fortnightly or monthly intervals. The money was not handed over until a sufficient quantity of ale had been consumed. The Vicar of Greasley said that Barber Walker paid wages on Friday nights, but those at other pits had 'their change to procure and accounts to arrange at a public-house on the Sunday'.[45]

Truck was common also in the framework knitting trade, and at a meeting of the Basford Poor Law Union in 1844 it was stated that three-quarters of the workpeople in Basford, Bulwell and Arnold were then paid in truck,[46] in contravention of the Truck Act of 1831.[47] One coalowner, at Hucknall Huthwaite, was taken to petty sessions for trucking in 1844, but the case (heard before one magistrate, himself a coalowner) was 'blown over'. The man 'informed of' made 'no secret of his truck shop', according to a local newspaper.[48]

Truck was one of the chief grievances of miners in the Midlands during the dispute of 1844. A representative meeting of the men, held at Brimmington in February, insisted on the abolition of truck. Long pays (the payment of wages at fortnightly or monthly intervals which forced men to seek credit) were also attacked.[49] Some Leicestershire miners, who had written proof of truck payments, declared their intention of suing their employers.[50]

Most subsequent Coal Mines Acts contained injunctions against truck. It is likely, however, that the publicity which the Miners' Association was given in 1844 did more than legislation to bring the practice to an end. Also important was the change from the big butty system to the little butty system which took place in Nottinghamshire and the Erewash Valley in the middle years of the century. Even at Butterley Park, where the pits were small, the change had been made by 1851. By the 1860's the truck system in this County was dead, despite the odd contradictory example.[51] In South Derbyshire and Staffordshire, where the big butty system lingered on, so, too, did truck and the payment of wages in public houses.[52]

Beer payments have been mentioned earlier. These were of several kinds. One was a fairly widespread practice of allowing beer (and other refreshments) to men doing particularly difficult jobs in sumps, wind roads, and so on.[53] This has led Hilton to suppose that beer was usually supplied to men doing building work and that it is because of this that beer payments were called 'buildases'.[54] Frank Hodges suggested a more likely derivation from Buildwas Abbey, Shropshire, where 'the monks demanded unpaid service from their tenants'.[55] A second, and more important, practice, to which colliers referred when they spoke of the buildas system, was to provide beer as part of the normal daily wage. The existence of the system at the Wollaton pits may be inferred from the evidence previously cited of Joseph Chambers and Charles Chouler.

More important evidence, which indicates that the system was customary in the Wollaton-Strelley district in the eighteenth century, is provided by the 99-year lease between Edge and others and the Barber Walker partnership dated 1738. This provided that 2¼ per cent of the royalty payments should be deducted for the colliers' drink. It was, apparently, the owner of the coal, and not the lessee, whose duty it was to pay for the ale.[56] Although 'the takings off for colliers' drink' were still being made from the royalty payments in 1837, there is no evidence that the men were still receiving their beer. It seems likely that the allowance was withdrawn at Strelley at the same time as at Wollaton, that is in the early nineteenth century.

It is true that 'An old Member' of the Nottinghamshire Miners' Association writing in 1891 said:

'. . . we are reminded of an old veteran miner, who has worked in the mines over half a century and, of course, was working in the pits when the great strike occurred in 1844, which had for its object the abolition of the Bilders and Truck System. The Bilders system allowed men and boys to work from 6 o'clock a.m. to eleven a.m. for the allowance of a sup of small beer or second-hand ale, and in many cases nothing, not even thank you.'

However, this man may well have been working in a part of Stafford-shire where we know that beer was still supplied in 1836–42, or in South Derbyshire.[57] He may, indeed, have been reminiscing not about the 1844 dispute at all, but the South Derbyshire beer strike of 1842. That the buildas system still existed in some parts of the Midlands in 1851 is attested by the district Mines Inspector; but there is no evidence that it did so in Nottinghamshire.

3. DISCIPLINE

We have already indicated that the butties provided the working capital used in mines, and engaged the labour. It has been argued by some that the recruitment of labour presented problems which the butty was able to solve; and that it was this function which justified the existence of the butty system. This argument cannot be sustained. The big butty system existed at a time when the labour force grew steadily and naturally; and it was replaced by a new style of management in the middle years of the nineteenth century when the labour force expanded rapidly. Accurate figures are not available, but rough estimates can be deduced. We have seen that the labour force of the Trent Valley mines was of the order of 500 to 1,000 at the beginning of the eighteenth century. There was little, if any expansion between 1700 and, say 1760. From 1760 the growth in demand and the improvement in transport enabled the Nottinghamshire-Derbyshire coalfield to grow substantially.

This growth should not, however, be exaggerated. The twenty pits working in and around Nottinghamshire listed by Farey in 1808 were unlikely to have employed more than 1,000 to 1,500 people between them, and if we include the remainder of the Erewash Valley pits, the order of magnitude is still only around 2,000. We may also deduce the approximate size of the labour force from output figures for the

Erewash Valley. In the first decade of the nineteenth century these totalled around 375,000 tons. Assuming an output per man-year of 200 tons, this gives a total labour force of 1875.[58] A similar calculation for 1840 produces a manpower figure of 2,625. These figures can do no more than indicate orders of magnitude, but they are near enough to show that the labour force was still small, and its growth rate quite modest. From then, and particularly after 1850, the expansion was more rapid. The 1851 Census suggests a population of 4,592 miners in Nottinghamshire alone.[59] This figure is, however, an exaggeration.[60] The enumerators included some miners' wives and impossibly young children in the statistics and were careless in other respects, too. For example, William Turner of 16 Portland Row, Selston, was credited with three wives, all of whom were described as miners though one was a girl aged five and another a boy aged two.[61] The females included in the county's total of coalminers are fictional. There is no evidence that females were ever employed underground in Nottinghamshire, let alone in 1851. It is true, however, that there were a few female surface workers just beyond the county boundaries in 1841.[62]

Prior to 1850, mining communities, largely housed by the colliery owners, produced their own increase. True, there must have been an influx into Pinxton about 1780 when Old Pinxton Colliery was opened, and into Selston in 1821-3 when Portland was opened, just as there was into Cinderhill in the early 1840's. It is evident that the opening of a new field (or the substantial expansion of an old one) attracted a nucleus of men from older and less prosperous coalfields. In the nineteenth century, there was a general movement of men from Staffordshire,[63] Derbyshire (and, after 1850 Leicestershire) into Nottinghamshire, for example. But most migrations prior to 1840 were short-distance ones; as, for example, when the Hayes family moved from Pinxton to Selston about 1829 to work at the new Portland Colliery.[64]

The provision of colliery houses guaranteed a steadily expanding labour force once the community was established. Thus, of the 119 tenants of the Cokes at Pinxton in 1839, there were eight families of Elliotts and seven of Cotterills, among other shared surnames; and most families had, beside the husband, one or more boys who almost invariably worked in the pit from the age of six or eight.[65] The Cokes also drew some labour from South Normanton, an old coal-mining district of fluctuating prosperity.[66]

In 1841, at the time of J. M. Fellows's investigation, there was considerable short time working indicating a surplus of labour rather than a shortage. It may be concluded, then, that the butty was not employed to find labour. His task was to discipline the labourer.

John Dodsley's motive in employing butties may be deduced from his Skegby Colliery Account Book for 1847–8. The Top Hard butty, William Cheetham, was paid prices varying between 2s. 2d. and 2s. 10d. a ton; and the Dunsil butty, Richard Wardle, was paid 3s. to 3s. 4d. a ton, this seam being more difficult to work. By contrast, the cost of getting Top Hard coal by day work in December 1848 was 4s. 4d. per ton taking into account direct labour, candles and powder alone whilst the selling price was only 6s. 6d.[67] At Riddings in 1841, James Oakes and Company usually paid their butties 3s. 6d. to 4s. 6d. a ton when the selling price was commonly 4s. 6d. to 5s., but occasionally as much as 7s. This evidence indicates that the butties, with their bullying, forced a profit out of pits which were incredibly primitive.

Henry Walker, writing of his early days in the pits at Pinxton (the 1830's and 40's) said:

'A few of the Butties in these pits were humane and kind, but others were most cruel and brutish. So much were the men made to submit that I have seen a pit company who have had a grievance and "capped" (ceased work) beaten all round with a stick. Once I saw the same villain spin a handful of men and lads round the pit top as they hung in chains; then he ordered them to be lowered to the bottom and march off to their work like good lads!'

Walker goes on to describe the style of some of the corporals appointed by butties to supervize the boys on the haulage roads:

'These slave-drivers would arm themselves with a stick or thong, fix themselves in some convenient spot, and as a lad (about naked) came by with his wagon, which he had to push, would strike him on the back. . . . Added to his sixteen hours a day, the writer carried the marks of such ill-usage often.'[68]

A casual examination of the report of J. M. Fellows, the Children's Employment Sub-Commissioner, might lead one to suppose that cruelty of this kind was exceptional,[69] but the evidence he cites is at variance with this conclusion. Brutal treatment was common except at the pits of Lord Middleton and Palmer Morewood.[70]

The new collieries sunk from 1841 onwards substituted improved equipment and methods, supervized by salaried officials, for the brutalities of the big butty system. And those old collieries which remained in production had to modernize in order to compete. The shortening of hours, the improved equipment and techniques and the abolition of the big butty system went hand in hand. Modernization was, in any case, forced on the owners by the removal of boys under ten years of age from the labour market under the terms of the Mines Act of 1842.

4. RELIGION, RECREATION AND ENTERTAINMENT

The traditional mining village offered little entertainment outside the public house. Miners in general drank a great deal. The hot, dusty mines predisposed men to drink, and as we have seen, at many places the men were expected to drink by butties who owned, or had a financial interest in, a public house.[71]

The public house also provided some modest comfort in comparison with miners' houses of the period. Ten houses and gardens in a row at Pinxton, built in the late eighteenth century, covered an area of thirty-eight perches or just under 1150 square yards a considerable proportion of which was reserved for the garden. There were two small rooms downstairs, scullery and kitchen, and two bedrooms perched in the slope of the roof.[72] Many houses in Pinxton had no ready access to water even in the early twentieth century, but had to purchase it by the bucketful from the owner of a nearby well. Even the solidly-built houses in Portland Row, erected in 1823 and recently demolished, were very small having regard to the sizes of most of the families living in them. They had a scullery, a kitchen and a pantry downstairs and two bedrooms measuring about 14 ft. by 10 ft. and 10 ft. square respectively, upstairs. No. 25 had an additional room which was used as a chapel. The one real comfort enjoyed by miners' families was an abundance of coal.[73] If the houses were small, at least they were warm.

The public house was a place where a man could stretch out a little and hear the news. The Pinxton miner of the 1830's and 40s. kept in touch with the outside world by hearing the 'news' read on Saturday night at a public house where the radical *Nottingham Review* was taken.[74] Despite stern injunctions to the contrary from the magistrates,[75] a great deal of gambling took place at the public house. Bets were laid 'on which collier could lift the greatest weight, or fight the longest battle', on dog fights, cock-fights, prize-fights, skittle-matches and so on.[76]

Some men were merely light drinkers. John Hayes, for example, 'only got a glass or two of beer now and then, and was so good humoured with it that his children all felt sure of special favour when he had a sup of, what he called, "reet good ale".' Many men, however, drank more than was good for them and fighting and quarrelling resulted.[77]

The Methodist revival provided the public house with a competitor: the chapel. Whatever spiritual and psychological contortions resulted from 'conversion', it was the universal opinion of contemporary observers that Methodism improved the behaviour and standards of the mining community.[78] Methodists drank lightly, if at all, and did not gamble. They dressed neatly to go to chapel, and kept their houses clean and tidy. Money formerly spent on drink and gambling paid for soap, curtains and the like.

Further, whilst Methodists formed a minority of the mining population, their standards of behaviour and appearance resulted in a general improvement.[79] An extreme example is presented by William Stocks, one of the early Methodists of Pinxton, who used to distribute tracts every Sunday. As he moved from house to house 'he on many occasions had to reprove people for the sin of Sabbath breaking, for it was the loose habit of many to clean boots, get vegetables out of the garden, shave their beard, visit public houses, stroll about untidily, or read newspapers, but at his appearing the sinners about Zion were afraid and hid themselves and some were persuaded to lead a better life and induced to go and hear the word of the Lord read and preached in the chapel.'[80]

A survey of the Butterley Company's employees in the parishes of Aldercar, Langley, Loscoe, Codnor and Heanor taken in September 1856 established that, in a population of 1647, there were only five couples living together without being married, and only ten illegitimate children. The Church of England had forty-four adherents, only one of whom was a communicant, whilst dissenting chapels had 301 adherents, both figures excluding children who attended Sunday School only. Of the children, only twenty-six had not been baptized. One woman, Mrs. Pool, said: 'I shall take all my children to the church and have them baptized. They have been baptized by the Ranters but I don't think it's right.' This traditional view regarding the superiority of Church christenings (which applied equally to marriages and burials) was held by many even of those who attended chapel.

Methodism came fairly late to the villages of the North Nottinghamshire coalfield. For example, Methodist services are said to have been held in a house at Skegby from about 1804, but this seems unlikely, the first Wesleyan chapel only being built in 1844. The Wesleyan cause at Kirkby-in-Ashfield probably dates from about 1815, and Pinxton (evangelized by Henry Davenport or Devenport of Kirkby) from 1817. The cause at Huthwaite dates from 1807, but the first chapel was not built until 1815. It cost £262 1s. 2d.[81] Even at South Normanton, where the Wesleyans had a cause from the beginning of the century, their following grew but slowly until the 1820's, and their first chapel was not acquired until 1827.

Chapels were encouraged by colliery owners. The original Wharf Methodist Chapel at Pinxton was built by John Coke in 1832, for example,[82] whilst at the new housing developments at Cinderhill and Meden Bank (Stanton Hill) mission rooms were built by Thomas

North and the Stanton Company respectively. It was the rule, rather than the exception, for colliery owners to give financial support to the chapels.

Many of the colliery agents were Methodists themselves. At Pinxton Joseph Machin and his successor John Chadbourne belonged to the Wharf Wesleyan (later U.M.F.) Methodist Chapel.[83] Eleazer Boot, a prominent mining agent, founded the Huthwaite Wesleyan Methodist Chapel and was the trustee there from 1807 to 1859, when he was succeeded by his son John Boot, who held the office until 1889.[84] Lady Carnarvon, for whom John Boot acted as agent, was a generous supporter of the chapel.[85]

John Smith, an agent of the Butterley Company at Butterley Park in 1851, was a Primitive Methodist local preacher.[86]

Parkinson indicates why the colliery owners and their officials gave help to the Methodist cause:

'Many were being saved and the colliery viewer, Tom Smith, had the good sense to see that the converted men were punctually at the pit on Monday morning instead of lounging at the public house. He offered to alter Jacob Speed's cottage at the end of the row, so that it could be used as a chapel.'[87]

As the need for colliery officials grew, Methodists stood a good chance of promotion because of their sobriety. It was an added advantage to attend the same chapel as the colliery agent. Thus Matthew Hayes from the Wharf chapel at Pinxton became first a deputy and then an under-manager; but attendance at the same chapel did not help Matthew's friend Henry Walker when he was refused both a job and a house by the company because of his radicalism.[88]

In the course of his masterly study *The Making of the English Working Class*, E. P. Thompson has argued that Methodism was conservative politically; that it sustained the power of the employers by teaching its followers to discipline themselves into complete submission to authority; and that even the Sunday schools taught little more than obedience and an elementary ability to read (but not to write).[89]

But the Wesleyan societies of the mining villages were distant, both in space and in outlook, from the Methodist Conference. A Methodist mining official, guided by whatever inner compulsions may have been born in him at his conversion, was likely to be a far less harsh taskmaster than the butty and his corporals. Further, the collier or holer working on piece-work rates had no need of a spiritual spur.

These Wesleyan societies took no part in the political controversies which troubled their brethren in large urban areas.[90] The Methodists of Pinxton, at any rate, were radicals (taking an active part, for example, in the great dispute of 1844) despite the connection of the colliery owner and agent with the chapel. The Primitives were the most radical of the Methodist denominations, but they were not so different from the others as is traditionally assumed. Predominantly working-class congregations, like those in mining villages, tended to be radical, irrespective of whether they belonged to one connexion or another. The traditional view is supported by a great deal of very doubtful evidence as, for example, when Dr. Morris describes William Brown (of the New Connexion), George Spencer (of the Wesleyans), and John Spiers (of the United Methodist Free Churches) as Primitives. An even stranger case is that of Arthur Horner, described by Dr. Williams as a Primitive Methodist although he was, in fact, a Baptist.[91]

As to the treatment of children at Sunday School, whatever physical correction John Wesley may have advocated, Sunday School teachers are usually described as 'kind'.[92] It is hardly to be supposed that the parents of boys who suffered harsh treatment at the hands of butties all the week would send them for more of the same on Sunday. Further, it appears to have been the almost universal practice in the coalfield to teach writing until 1870, although admittedly there were few, if any, Methodist Sunday Schools in the district before about 1818.[93]

Indeed, the local Wesleyan societies had little support until after the Primitive Methodist revival of 1817. It appears that the Wesleyans were just as much beneficiaries of the revival as the Primitives themselves. This may be illustrated by reference to South Normanton where the Primitive Methodist cause was established in 1817 as a consequence of 'the intense spirit and sincere utterances of Primitive Methodism's foremost woman pioneer, Sarah Kirkland'.[94] The Primitives had a chapel (a converted farm building) at once; in contrast with the Wesleyans who had been able to manage without one and continued to do so until 1827 when the Primitives moved to a larger, purpose-built chapel because the original one had become too small for them. The Wesleyans then took over the old chapel from the 'Prims'. Soon, they also found the room too small for them because of their 'rapidly increasing numbers', and they enlarged it so as to hold a congregation of 110. In 1845, they required even larger premises and they built a new chapel. The old one was then taken over by the Original Methodists.

The earliest Original Methodist societies seceded from the Primitive Methodists' Belper Circuit in 1839, because of their total opposition to a paid ministry. Their local preachers normally paid their own travelling expenses even, and also contributed to collections.[95] The Originals became extremely strong locally, establishing causes in most mining villages of the Erewash Valley. Like the 'Prims' they were enthusiastic. Thus, in 1850:

'North Wingfield Camp Meeting was held on Sunday, the 20th June. It commenced by perambulating the neighbourhood, singing, praying and exhorting at intervals; followed by preaching services in the open-air, both before and after dinner; the word was listened to with attention by the congregation. In the evening was a Lovefeast, the people got more into faith, and a divine influence rested upon the assembly.'[96]

In considering the character of Methodism in the mining villages we need to appreciate then that the impetus came from the most radical section, and that even the Wesleyans conducted their affairs with far more fervour than their brethren in the large urban centres. Before long, the Wesleyan Societies themselves were riven by the controversies of 1849–51, and new denominations were formed. The Wharf Chapel at Pinxton became part of the new United Methodist Free connexion (established 1857) as did several others. Where the trust deeds placed ownership firmly in the hands of the Wesleyan establishment, the secessionists, who were often in the majority, then built their own chapels.[97]

For converts, the chapel became a place apart. Parkinson, speaking of the chapel converted from a cottage in his Durham mining village, puts it this way:

'The chapel thus created was the centre of almost all extra-domestic life. Its only competitor was the public-house; and gradually, all that made for good living, high character, and even the elements of education, found its home and sphere in the little sanctuary. The work was maintained at the cost of many sacrifices and much self-denial by the poorly paid pit men, who found in the Methodist services their consolation amidst hardships and their inspiration and hope for better things to come.'[98]

Sunday became a day apart, something more than a day of rest. This may again be illustrated by reference to Parkinson:

'Thus some of the happiest memories of my early days centre round the Sunday. Saturday night, for instance was a time of preparation. All the week's work was done, and everything connected with it put out of sight. The whole night's rest lasting till day-light on Sunday morning, the one family dinner of the week, the Sunday School and the public services, all combined to create an oasis in the wilderness, filling the atmosphere with welcome fragrance as it drew near. It was literally the day of days, a veritable Elim of wells and palm trees, with a desert on either side as barren and desolate as Shur or Sinai to the Israelites of old.'[99]

Miners at the primitive Nottinghamshire collieries of the early nineteenth century lived brutish lives. For months at a stretch, they saw daylight only on Sunday (except when trade was poor.) Many of them, especially the boys, did work which tired them physically but which made no demands on the intellect. Indeed, even the skill which the coal face man brought to his work was acquired without much mental effort and thereafter was a knack applied almost instinctively. Life was one long, dull round of work, bed, and Sunday for the boys; and the same, relieved by beer-drinking and gambling, for the men.

The value of Methodism to the miners of our period is not dependent on the truth or falsity of its doctrines. Any Messiah, of almost any creed, might have done almost as much social good in providing a focus of interest outside the weary round of everyday life. Many miners, thought to be oafs, proved to be men of intelligence and sensibility when once their imaginations had been stirred by this outside influence. Methodism was a catalyst which brought unsuspected talents to the surface.

Further, men who learnt to read in order that they might trace for themselves the wanderings of the children of Israel went on to read other things: radical newspapers and pamphlets, for example. Men who learnt to take an active part in chapel affairs went on to lead in other spheres too. Methodism brought home to many the need for improvement; and improvement came to be related to the needs of the mining community. It is significant that the period of ascendancy of the Original Methodist connexion in the Erewash Valley, with its struggle against 'hireling' ministers set in authority over, and extracting money from, the lay members, coincides both in time and in purpose with the struggle against the butties.

Unlike the parish church, the chapel was a place where a miner could feel at home; a place where he could give expression to his emotions. When Matthew Hayes attended a service at Pinxton parish church, he was reproved by the rector for interjecting 'Praise the Lord', 'Hallelujah' and 'Amen' at what he considered appropriate points in the service. 'He left the church feeling that he had been at a service where a muzzling order was in force . . . he much preferred the Methodist meetings at which he could worship God and express his inward joy without being afraid of the minister asking him not to make the responses in the wrong places.'[100]

Matthew also sampled a Roman Catholic service where 'Their singing and music were well rendered but Matthew understood very little of what was said or sung and on leaving the place he humbly confessed that although his curiosity had been gratified, his soul had not experienced the blessedness of sincerely worshipping God.'[101] Only in the Methodist chapel, with its extempore prayers, its hell-fire oratory and its rousing hymns could a man like Hayes obtain the release of emotional tension which was so necessary to his well being.

It has become fashionable to condemn Methodist Sunday schools, and one acknowledges that they were of limited usefulness. The average collier boy was too tired to be able to assimilate useful knowledge: at the Radford Church Sunday School in 1841, for example, the collier boys, were duller than the rest on account of their tiredness.[102] Further, many of the teachers themselves knew little more than their pupils: those who knew a little taught those who knew nothing. Some of the best teachers were children who had spent a few years at day school George Parkinson took charge of the writing class at Sherburn in 1844, when he was sixteen. This is how he described his work:

> 'On Saturday nights, after my six days' work was done, I put on my second-best suit and, with a tin candlestick and some candle-ends provided by my mother and my Aunt Bessy, I went up to the chapel. There I spent my whole evening ruling copy books and writing headings for the writing lessons in the Sunday School on the following day.'[103]

The Sunday school at Pinxton produced some notable scholars like Joseph Hancock (who became a prominent trade union leader). Matthew Hayes (a colliery official and an outstanding local preacher) his brother William, (who became an American Episcopal Methodist Minister,) Peter, John and Henry Walker and Henry's son Frank, who became a Methodist minister and who began his 'serious study of classics by nailing pages of a Greek grammar on to a coal prop, and glancing at it, looking up my lamp every time I passed it'.[104] Peter Walker, junior, became a fine amateur musician, much in demand for conducting oratorios. Again, one of the Butterley Company's senior Agents, John Smith, 'a man of untiring industry, acknowledged talent and real respectability' was 'raised . . . out of the first Sabbath-School ever commenced in this locality, taught in a small room about eleven feet square, by one teacher only'.[105]

However, John Smith himself acknowledged the superiority of day schools over Sunday schools. Speaking in 1851 of the day schools established about ten years earlier at Codnor Park, Ironville, Riddings and Ripley he said 'Since then there has been a rapid improvement in our young men in their intelligence and morals. . . . Thirty years ago this neighbourhood was as ignorant as any part of South Staffordshire that I have known. It began to be visibly better about twenty years ago, but it was not till after the good day schools were set on foot that the great advance has taken place. There are a deal of colliers now who are very fairly instructed, and who cultivate their minds, and amuse themselves also by learning music. . . . Before the day-schools there were only Sunday-schools. They were first established here about thirty-three years since; they did good, but the great good has been done since the day-schools were begun.'[106]

There were some day schools in mining districts before 1841, of course, but few miners' sons attended them. The Pinxton day school in 1841 had 56 boys and 20 girls on the register and they paid 1d. per week for reading and 2d. for writing. Collier boys employed by the Pinxton Colliery Company were allowed to attend on days when they were unemployed. Similarly, at the Trowell free school, in addition to the thirty full-time scholars, collier boys employed by Lord Middleton were allowed to attend on days when they were off work.[107] The Coal Mines Act of 1842 made it illegal for boys under ten to be employed underground and many younger boys were then sent to school. The Mines Act of 1872 made part-time attendance at school compulsory for pit boys.[108] Of the 676 adults included in the Butterley survey of 1856, only 216—less than a third—could not read. This is some measure of the effectiveness of the elementary schooling in the locality referred to by John Smith.

Mechanics Institutes also date from this period: one was established at Mansfield in 1831 and another at Sutton-in-Ashfield in 1842.[109] Reading rooms and libraries were also founded by the more far-sighted colliery owners like the Butterley and Pinxton companies, and many colliery officials and contractors were learning elementary surveying techniques like dialling. The shortening of working hours and the development of the provision of facilities for technical study sponsored by the Science and Art Department (established by the Board of Trade in the 1850's) made possible the growth of a body of working-class mining engineers.

Life for the mid-nineteenth century collier was earnest. But there were still the great annual festivals to break the monotony a little. In 1841, the recognized holidays were Christmas Day, Good Friday and a day or two at Whitsuntide;[110] but in addition every village had its Feast or Wakes. The Wakes week was the one time in the year, apart from Christmas when 'tables were spread with the best provisions their means would allow.'[111] In 1778, the magistrates complained that at these 'Wakes or feasts which are annually holden in the several Parishes, Towns, Villages and Hamlets within the County of Nottingham Diverse Riots and Disorderly doings frequently arise by Persons Assembling and Meeting together to be guilty of Excessive Drinking Tippling Gaming or other unlawful exercises'.[112]

Most miners in this period had gardens. During the summer months when trade was slack they were able to spend at least one, and often two or three, days a week gardening. Some kept pigs, others bred dogs or pigeons or kept poultry. Flower shows were popular in the 1860's[113] and probably earlier, and they still attract a great deal of support in mining villages. The annual Sunday School treat was another of the year's great occasions, even though it might be held only a mile or two away. The Wharf Methodist treat, for example, was often held at Brookhill Hall, home of the Coke family, who largely owned the Pinxton pits. The scholars also regarded it as a privilege to be allowed to go up to the Hall to sing Carols on Christmas Eve, when 'nature's requirements were met with hearty good will from the old squire'.[114]

Certainly, Christmas was a great time for all the family. Some colliery owners gave their men a Feast—as John Dodsley did in 1846 when trade was good.[115] Robert Watchorn's mother always saved up enough money to buy her boys new clothes at Christmas.[116] Other parents, not so fortunate, managed at least to provide some kind of Christmas gift. By the second half of the century, football and cricket were becoming popular among miners. At many collieries, brass bands were organized. To be 'in the band' at Babbington, for instance, became synonymous with having a good job.[117] At other places, cricketers or footballers or St. John's Ambulance Brigaders were similarly favoured.

Marches and demonstrations, whether on account of the marriage of The Prince of Wales (later Edward VII) when, says Robert Watchorn, who was five years old at the time, 'after parading what seemed like many miles for many hours, I was thankful when we arrived at the tent in the market place and were given tea and cake as a welcome diversion', or organized by the Miners' Union, were memorable occasions. At the 1875 Demonstration of the Derbyshire and Nottinghamshire Miners' Association, for example, there were '6,000 men wearing white gloves and rosettes . . . carrying colourful banners' with twenty brass bands.[118]

Circuses, too, were popular. As Watchorn tells us: 'Then there was the coming of the circus, that annual event of the one-ring show, with its multi-coloured animals and their skilful riders, the rollicking clowns, the feasts of peanuts and the grotesque features of the side shows with their unforgettable personalities.'[119]

In the latter part of the nineteenth century, people with quieter tastes were increasingly catered for. The Mechanics Institutes, to which reference has already been made, were social as well as educational establishments. At Pinxton in 1883, the old wharf Chapel was converted into a 'commodious restaurant with billiards, coffee and smoke rooms and a library of 610 vols'.[120] Similar institutes were established in other villages.[121] Drab though such places may seem nowadays, their value was immense.

There were, of course, other diversions but since these are peculiar neither to mining villages nor to the nineteenth century, there is no point in dwelling on the subject at length. No doubt the housewives of the time did just that, so much so that the doings of D'Ewes Coke and 'Brookhill Bess' still provide vicarious pleasure to the women of Pinxton a hundred years or more after the event.

APPENDIX A

1842 CHILDREN'S EMPLOYMENT COMMISSION: LIST OF COLLIERIES IN
NOTTINGHAMSHIRE AND DISTRICT REPORTED ON BY J. M. FELLOWS
Showing Safety Features

Owner	Pit	Whether having: Bon-net	Mortared Bricks	Davy lamp	Winding apparatus	Depth yds.	Headways ft. in.
Lord Middleton	Radford	Yes		No	9 h.p. engine	63	4 6
Lord Middleton	Trowell	Yes		Yes, but }	6 h.p. engine	112	3 6
Lord Middleton	Wollaton	Yes		never wanted	8 h.p. engine	100	3 6
K. Fenton	Williamson's (Bagthorpe)	No	Yes	Yes	15 h.p. engine	126	3 4
K. Fenton	Creswell's (Bagthorpe)	No	Yes	Yes	10 h.p. engine	78	3 2
Barber-Walker	Eastwood		No				3
Barber-Walker	Beggarlee (2)	No	No	No	10 h.p. engine	104	
Barber-Walker	Watnall-Trough Lane	No	Yes	No		142	4
Barber-Walker	Watnall-Middle	No	Yes	No		134	4
Barber-Walker	Watnall-Wharf					134	4
Barber-Walker	Underwood	No*	No	No	18 h.p. engine	140	3
Barber-Walker	Cossall	No		No		64	3 2
Barber-Walker	Strelley (Robinette)						
Barber-Walker	Greasley or Moor Green (Willow Lane)	No	Yes	No	20 h.p. engine	190	
Barber-Walker	Brinsley (2)	Yes (1 Shaft only)	No (Shaft very bad)	No	14 h.p. engine	158½	4
Barber-Walker	Newthorpe No. 2.	No	Yes }	Yes, but }		91	4
Barber-Walker	Newthorpe No. 3	No	Yes	seldom		100	3 6
Barber-Walker	Newthorpe No. 3. (Lord Melbournes)	No	Yes	wanted	Engine	23	3 8

APPENDIX A—*continued*

1842 CHILDREN'S EMPLOYMENT COMMISSION: LIST OF COLLIERIES IN
NOTTINGHAMSHIRE AND DISTRICT REPORTED ON BY J. M. FELLOWS

Owner	Pit	Whether having: Bon-net	Mortared Bricks	Davy lamp	Winding apparatus	Depth yds.	Headways ft.	in.
T. North & Co.	Babbington: Roughs	No	No	No		50-60	3	3†
T. North & Co.	Williamson's Soft	No	No	No		70	3	3
T. North & Co.	Williamson's Hard	No	No	No		158	4	
T. North & Co.	Henry Hunt's Hard	No	Yes	No		101	4	4
T. North & Co.	New London (Greasley)	No	No	No		70	4	4
T. North & Co.	Newthorpe Common (New Pit)	No	Yes	No	16 h.p. engine	70	3	8
T. North & Co.	Newthorpe Common (Cottage Pit)	No	No	No	Engine winds both shafts	40	3	4
T. North & Co.	Nuttall or Awsworth: Hutchby's	No	No	No		50	3	6
T. North & Co.	Nuttall or Awsworth: Twiggers‡	No	No	No		50	3	
Butterley	Kirkby Portland No. 1.		Worked out					
Butterley	Kirkby Portland No. 2.	No	Yes	Available	25 h.p. engine	180	4	6
Butterley	Kirkby Portland No. 3.		Worked out					
Butterley	Kirkby Portland No. 4.	No	Yes	Available	20 h.p. engine	180	4 to 4	6
Butterley	Kirkby Portland No. 5.	No	Yes	Available	works both shafts	180	4	6
Butterley	Kirkby Portland No. 6 & 7.	Not yet	worked					
Butterley	Summercotes (Upper Pit)†				Whim-gin	38	4	
Butterley	Summercotes (Lower Pit)†				Whim-gin	27	4	
Butterley	Summercotes Coal Pit		Yes	Being headed out				

APPENDIX A—*continued*

John Coke	Pinxton No. 1.	No		No	14 h.p. engine	60	4	3
John Coke	Pinxton No. 9.	No	Yes		8 h.p. engine	70	3	9
John Coke	Sleights No. 2.	No	Partly	No	Engine	130	3	6
John Coke	Sleights No. 3.	No	Yes	No	20 h.p. engine	114	4	
John Coke	Carnfield No. 1.	No	Yes	Available	30 h.p. engine	112	3	9
John Coke	Carnfield No. 2.	No		Available	works both	100	3	2
W. Palmer Morewood	Swanwick: Landsale Pit				1 horse gin	20	5	
W. Palmer Morewood	Crabtree Pit	No		No	2 horse gin	35	5	
	Summercotes				8 h.p. engine	42		
Saml. Woolley	Old Birchwood: Old Hard	Yes	Partly	Available	12 h.p. engine	130	4	5
Saml. Woolley	Soft	Yes	Partly	Available	works both	95	4	5
Saml. Woolley	New Hard	No		Available	10 h.p. engine	115	3	6
Humphrey Goodwin	New Birchwood: Balguy	No	No	Used in heading only	Engine works both	80	4	
Humphrey	Shady	No	No			60		
Goodwin	Landsale	No	No		Whim-gin (1 horse)	60	4	

* Bonnet used 'when it rains'   ‡ Sometimes known as the 'Flying Nancy' Pit   † Iron pits

APPENDIX B

FATAL ACCIDENTS IN COAL MINES (AND IRONSTONE MINES WORKED IN CONNECTION WITH COAL) IN DERBYSHIRE, NOTTINGHAMSHIRE, LEICESTERSHIRE AND WARWICKSHIRE

	Explosions	Inundation of water	Falls of Coal and roof	In shafts	Crushed by trams	Total deaths	Tons of coal raised	Tons raised for each death
1856	3	—	21	16	6	46	4,500.000	97,000
1857	15	—	14	6	20	55	4,750,000	86,000
1858	—	—	16	16	10	42	5,060,000	121,000
1859	2	—	18	13	7	40	5,560,000	134,000
1860	3	—	21	13	13	50	6,215,000	124,000
1861	3	23*	21	15	7	69	6,503,000	94,000
1862	2	—	25	4	12	43	6,647,000	154,000
1863	4	5	26	9	8	52	7,000,000	134,000
1864	11	—	30	9	16	66	7,300,000	110,606

* This inundation was at Clay Cross, Derbyshire. It was by far the worst disaster in the district in this period.

Source: Report of the Inspector for Mines for 1864 (Report of Mr. Evans) London, H.M.S.O., 1865, p. 61.

REFERENCES

1 Skegby Colliery Account Book.
2 A. R. Griffin. *The Nottinghamshire Coalfield, 1550–1947.* (Unpublished typescript in Nottinghamshire County Library) I, pp. 13–14 (Subsequently cited as *Notts. Coalfield.*
3 R. S. Smith, *Willoughbys of Wollaton*, pp. 121–2.
4 T. S. Ashton, 'The Coalminers of the Eighteenth Century', *Economic History*, I, (1928), p. 314.
   The Compleat Collier (1708) suggests wages of 12d. or 14d. a day for sinkers, 14d. a day for banksmen and 10d. or 11d. a day for barrow-men underground—J. C., op. cit., pp. 14 and 39.
5 K. Tweedale Meaby, *Extracts from County Records of the Eighteenth Century*, Nottingham, 1947, p. 232.
6 Dorothy George, *England In Transition*, London, 1953, pp. 25 and 153. Cole and Postage, *The Common People*, 1746–1938, London, 1938, pp. 79 and 84.
7 R. S. Smith, art. cit., p. 137.
8 Mottram and Coote, op. cit., pp. 54 and 59. T. S. Ashton, art. cit., p. 314. The contradicting evidence of Farey (op. cit., I, p. 341) relating to wages at Tibshelf in 1808 is clearly wrong.
9 Walker, op. cit.
10 *Pinxton Pottery Account Book* (typewritten abstract).
11 T. S. Ashton argues that wages probably kept pace with prices during the

French wars. He takes 1s. 8d. (paid at Barlow, in rural North Derbyshire) as the normal wage in 1780, and 3s. 4d. (paid in Durham) as the normal wage in 1813. This cavalier treatment of the evidence will not stand close examination. C. P. Griffin's researches in Leicestershire and South Derbyshire support the view that miners' real wages fell substantially between 1790 and 1840.

12 *Children's Employment Commission, (Mines) 1842*, First Report, App. Pt. II, p. 263 (Evidence of C. Chouler).

13 C. P. Griffin, *The Economic Development of the Leicestershire and South Derbyshire Coalfield*, (Unpublished Ph. D. Thesis) Nottm., 1969. The strike affected the Swadlincote, but not the Moira, collieries. See also J. E. Williams, *The Derbyshire Miners*, London, 1962, p. 89.

14 *Children's Employment Commission, (Mines) 1842*, First Report, Pt. II, p. 287.

15 ibid., pp. 288–9 and 301.
Kirk's wages were:

Age	Year	Job	Rate	
			s.	d.
6	1778	Gin Driver		8
10	1782	Haulier(UG)	1	2
13	1785	Haulier	1	8
17	1786	Holer	1	8

Another witness, John Wilson (Swanwick) was paid 4d. a day in 1778 as a 7-year-old gin driver and about 1s. on going underground in 1781.

16 ibid., p. 261 et seq. Wm. Wardle a Barber Walker employee, gave the average normal weekly wage for adults as 14s. to 15s. with some men earning over 20s. At that time, pits were on short time, and earnings averaged 9s. per week. James Davis (employed by Lord Middleton) earned 3s. 6d. a day as a holer. Similarly, at Pinxton, colliers on piece-work normally earned about 3s. 6d. a day in the 1840's, but if they encountered bad geological conditions they could earn next to nothing.

At Riddings (J. Oakes & Co.) the adult day rate was 3s. 6d., but piece-workers could make 4s. to 5s.—*Children's Employment Commission App. Pt. I*, p. 118 (Evidence of E. Fletcher.)

17 *Nottingham Review*, 5th April 1844.

18 Skegby Colliery Account Book, H. Walker, op. cit., p. 22. M. Wheeler, op. cit., p. 88. Mottram and Coote, op. cit., p. 79 C. P. Griffin's evidence for Leicestershire and South Derbyshire supports the view expressed in the text.

19 Agricultural labourers earned about 2s. a day except for harvest time. Framework knitters could earn as little as 5s. a week.

Joseph Reeve, age 16, told the Children's Employment Sub-Commissioner that he was a stockinger from nine to twelve years of age, but left for mining because the pay was better, though the work was harder. (App. Pt. II, p. 300) Joseph Wilson (aged 12) said that he would rather draw a plough than work in pit (ibid., p. 284) Patrick Pollard (aged 11) was the son of an Ilkeston shoemaker. (ibid. pp. 295–6).

20 R. S. Smith, *The Willoughbys of Wollaton*, p. 116.

21 Some men (presumably holers) worked from 12 midnight or 1 a.m. to 10 or 11 a.m. *Children's Employment Commission, (Mines) 1842*, First Report, App. Pt. II, pp. 266–7 (Evidence of James Davis, a holer).

22 ibid., pp. 288, 331–2.

23 ibid., p. 283.

24 ibid., p. 286 (Evidence of R. Harrison, General Manager).

25 ibid., pp. 289–90.

26 ibid., pp. 292–3.

27 ibid., p. 291.

28 ibid., p. 295.

29 ibid., pp. 304–5.

30 ibid., pp. 309–10.

31 ibid., pp. 329–332.

32 ibid., pp. 338–339. They appear to have worked 6.30 a.m. to 8 p.m. at one pit, however—ibid., pp. 336–7.

33 ibid., pp. 330, 338, and 263, op. cit., App. Pt. I, p. 117.

34 C. P. Griffin, op. cit.

35 *Children's Employment Commission (Mines) 1842 First Report, App. Part II*, pp. 289 and 293.

36 See, for example, the case of John Dennis of Awsworth, an absconding collier from Lord Middleton's coalmines, heard by Nottingham magistrates on 13th January 1717—K. Tweedale Meaby, op. cit., p. 234.

37 E.g. *Children's Employment Commission (Mines) 1842 First Report, App. Pt. II*, p. 327 (Evidence of Wm. Bettison, Agent for Marehay and Old Birchwood.)

38 See Twelve-month hiring agreement of William Baggaley, 'Fitter of Engines and Machinery' dated 28th February 1823.

39 T. S. Ashton, *The Industrial Revolution 1760–1830*, London 1948, p. 100.

40 See, e.g. J. Burnley, *History of Wool and Woolcombing*, 1883, pp. 161–3. See also G. W. Hilton, *The Truck System*, Cambridge, 1960, for a general, but disappointing discussion.

41 H. Walker, op. cit., pp. 7 and 22, J. Haslem, *The Old Derby China Factory: The Workmen and Their Production*, London, 1876, p. 243.

42 *Children's Employment Commission (Mines) 1842 First Report, App. Pt. II*, p. 252.

43 *Report of Mr. Morton*, p. 12.
   Silberling's Index is not very useful as an indicator in these circumstances. (T. S. Ashton, art. cit., and J. E. Williams, op. cit., appear to attach a lot of importance to it.)

44 *Census Enumerator's Return, 1851* (Kirkby parish, not Selston.)

45 *Children's Employment Commission (Mines) 1842 First Report App. Pt. II*, p. 306. See also p. 255 (Report of J. M. Fellows.)

46 *Nottingham Review*, 9th February 1844.

47 1 and 2 Wm. IV. cap. 37.

48 *Nottingham Review*, 5th July 1844.

49 ibid., 15th March 1844.

50 ibid., 31st May 1844.

51 Mottram and Coote, op. cit., p. 79.
   J. E. Williams, op. cit., p. 62.

52 See, e.g., *Nottingham Review*, 26th April 1867 and *Royal Commission on Mines, First Report. Cmnd. 3458 (1907)*, p. 5.

53 *Skegby Colliery Account Book*, J. E. Williams, op. cit., p. 29.

54 G. W. Hilton, op. cit., pp. 33 and 35.

55 *Historical Review*, p. 342.

56 *Edge MSS* (Notts. County Record Office) DDE 30/6 and 46/69.

57 *Hucknall Illustrated Labour Journal*, December 1891.

58 J. Farey, op. cit., I, pp. 188–215 and 328–331; *Royal Comm. on Coal, (1871)* Vol. III, App. No. 26, p. 16. This gives canal sales only. I have added 25 per cent for land sale.

59 *The 1851 Census, Ages, Civil Conditions and Occupations, Vol. II*, pp. 531–609.

60 Census totals generally exceed the actual figures substantially because they include retired and unemployed miners. In 1891, for example, the Census overstates the number of miners in Nottinghamshire by over 8,000 (29,854 to 21,512).

61 The Census Enumerator for Portland Row distributed 'ditto' marks with fine abandon. He was not alone in this.

62 *Children's Employment Commission (Mines) 1842 First Report, App. Pt. II*, p. 251.

63 One of Skegby's shafts, sunk by Staffordshire men, was called Brierley Hill. This is still the colloquial name of Sutton Colliery. See also places of birth on Census Returns.

64 Wheeler, op. cit., p. 12.

65 *Tithe Apportionment Register*, 1839 Wheeler, op. cit., p. 20.

66 *Children's Employment Commission (Mines) 1842 First Report, App. Pt. II*, p. 332.

67 *Skegby Colliery Account Book*, cited A. R. Griffin, *The Notts. Coalfield*, I, 61.

68 Walker, op. cit., p. 1.

69 *Children's Employment Commission (Mines) 1842, First Report, App. Pt. II*, p.252.

70 ibid., pp. 263–339 (and Pt. I, pp. 117–8—Evidence collected by Dr. Mitchell) Many owners had no idea as to the actual conditions under which their men were employed—see A. Wilson and H. Levy, *Workmens' Compensation* 2 vols., Oxford, 1939, I, p. 16.

71 See, e.g. J. E. Williams, op. cit., p. 59 et seq.

72 *Tithe Apportionment Register, 1839*. Mrs. Walvin thinks the floors were of bare earth, as were some others in the village.

73 Even in Huntingdon Beaumont's day, Wollaton colliers were allowed to take soft coal home—R. S. Smith, art. cit., p. 130.

74 Walker, op. cit., p. 6.

75 Tweedale Meaby, op. cit., p. 247.

76 ibid., p. 6. For a Durham parallel see G. Parkinson, *True Stories of Durham Pit-Life*, London, 1912, p. 10.

77 Wheeler, op. cit., p. 10.
Robert Watchorn, *Autobiography* (edited H. F. West), Oklahoma, 1948, p. 10.

78 E.g. J. M. Fellows' Report: *Children's Employment Commission (Mines) 1842, First Report, App. Pt. II*, p. 257.

79 'Keeping up with the Jones's' is no new phenomenon.

80 Wheeler, op. cit., p. 70.

81 J. R. Raynes, op. cit., pp. 26–7, 34–5 and 39–40.
Walker, op. cit., p. 8.

82 ibid., pp. 9–10.

83 Wheeler, op. cit., pp. 64 and 94.

84 Raynes, op. cit., p. 34.

85 John Boot's *Trustee Account* (held by his descendant, Mr. G. C. Oakley, to whom I am indebted for the reference.)

86 Mottram and Coote, op. cit., p. 79.

87 Parkinson, op. cit., p. 13.

88 Rev. F. Walker in a letter to Miss Walvin dated 15th January 1955.
The Wharf Methodist Chapel was Wesleyan until 1849 after which it joined the United Methodist Free connexion.

89 E. P. Thompson, *The Making of the English Working Class* (Pelican edn.) Harmondsworth, 1968, pp. 385–440.

Mr. Thompson's argument is subject to a number of major qualifications, but the space allotted to these forms so small a proportion of the whole as to give an entirely inadequate impression of their importance. I recognize, however, that the summary of Mr. Thompson's main argument given in the text is an over-simplification forced upon me by a lack of space.

90 See, e.g. D. A. Gowland, 'Political Opinion in Manchester Wesleyanism 1832–57', *Proceedings of the Wesley Historical Society Vol. XXXVI*, February 1968, pp. 93–104.

91 Wheeler, op. cit., passim, G. M. Morris, op. cit., pp. 300 and 305, J. E. Williams, op. cit., p. 78, Walker, op. cit., passim.

92 E.g. Wheeler, op. cit., p. 56. Nottingham Primitive Methodists were advised by Hugh Bourne in 1835 that '. . . the children must be encouraged; and there must not be the least harsh treatment'—cited G. M. Morris, op. cit., p. 207.

93 J. R. Raynes, op. cit., passim. Mottram and Coote, op. cit., p. 79. Dr. Thompson accepts that the proscription of writing was only temporary.

94 D. M. Grundy, 'A History of the Original Methodists, VII,' *Proceedings of the Wesley Historical Society, Vol. XXXVI*, p. 143.

95 ibid., p. 144.

96 cited ibid., p. 148.

97 At Somercotes, the trustees sold the chapel to the Church of England so as to prevent it falling into the hands of the radical congregation. The latter then appealed to Marsden Smedley of Matlock for help and he built a new (U.M.F.) chapel for them on Birchwood Lane.

At Annesley Woodhouse, the reformers who formed the majority wanted to take over the chapel (built in 1815) but were prevented by the wording of the trust deeds. The reformers then built a new chapel. Raynes, op. cit., p. 29.

98 Parkinson, op. cit., p. 13.

99 ibid., p. 8.

100 Wheeler, op. cit., p. 60.

101 ibid., p. 75.

102 *Children's Employment Commission (Mines) 1842, First Report, App. Pt. II*, p. 264.

103 Parkinson, op. cit., p. 65.

104 Rev. Frank V. Walker in a letter to the writer dated 27th February 1955. This would be in the late 1860's or early 1870's.

105 John Tomlinson, Secretary of the Original Methodist Connexion, in a letter dated 1852, cited D. M. Grundy, art. cit., p. 118.

106 Mottram and Coote, op. cit., pp. 78–9.

107 *Children's Employment Commission (Mines) 1842, First Report, App. Pt. II*, p. 257.

Day schools were very heavily subsidized by the colliery owners.

108 35 and 36 Vict., cap. 76. The hours of boys were restricted to ten a day (sec. 6) and they were to attend school for twenty hours a fortnight. (sec. 8).

109 Bailey, op. cit., IV, pp. 371 and 429.

110 *Children's Employment Commission (Mines) 1842 First Report, App. Pt. II*, p. 255.

111 Wheeler, op. cit., p. 10, Mottram and Coote, op. cit., p. 98.

112 Tweedale Meaby, op. cit., p. 147.

113 Watchorn, op. cit., p. 14. Mottram and Coote, op. cit., pp. 97–8.

114 Walker, op. cit., p. 21.

115 He does not appear to have repeated this in other years.

116 Watchorn, op. cit., p. 24.

117   Cf. Mottram and Coote, pp. 96–7.
118   A. R. Griffin, *The Miners of Nottinghamshire 1881–1914*, Nottm. 1956, p. 19. (Subsequently cited as *Notts. Miners I*).
119   Watchorn, op. cit., p. 14.
120   Walker, op. cit., p. 23.
121   E.g. The Underwood Institute founded in 1892 by Thomas Barber, Whitelock, op. cit., p. 42.

CHAPTER IV

Transport and Marketing

1. INTRODUCTION

S ince coal is a bulky commodity, transport costs form a major part of the delivered price. In the sixteenth to eighteenth centuries, the small 'land-sale' pits to the North of Nottingham, like Selston, Skegby, Teversal and Heath served a purely local market. Insofar as they expanded at all, they expanded slowly in response to the general increase in population in small towns like Mansfield, Sutton-in-Ashfield, Alfreton and Hucknall Torkard. The Morrisons of Selston, it is true, operated iron mills in the sixteenth century and these consumed some locally produced coal as did the lime-kilns of Teversal. But industrial demand was small,[1] and the pits often stood idle in winter when the roads were muddy.

The Trent Valley pits were more fortunately placed, being close to Nottingham and to a navigable waterway. Even so, in winter the miry state of the roads made transport difficult and raised costs. In the Cossall-Trowell Moor area there were, until recently, traces of paved ways used by the pack-horses to convey coal when the roads were impassable to carts. In 1604 Huntingdon Beaumont laid down his wooden rails from Strelley to Wollaton lane end, and these brought down his transport costs. However, he was still unable to compete on the London market with sea-borne Newcastle coal, which sold at a delivered price of 10s. 3d. to 12s. a ton in 1608 compared with Beaumont's projected 18s. a ton.[2] The Erewash Valley coalowners were similarly unable to break into the London market at the end of the eighteenth century for much the same reasons. Farey considered that coal produced inland for the London market should pay a smaller duty than coal produced on the coast, to offset the higher transport costs, but this was not done.[3] The inland coalfields were not able to penetrate the London market to any extent until the building of the railways.

2. ROADS, CANALS AND RAILWAYS

Contemporary observers had mixed views as to the benefits of turnpike roads, but there need be no doubt that they facilitated the transport of coal in winter. The owners of coal mines around Ashby-de-la-Zouch, for example, were so well served by turnpike roads that they gave the Thringstone to Nanpanton Canal (the Charnwood Forest branch) little support.[4]

The Nottinghamshire and Derbyshire collieries benefited greatly from canals, however, particularly the Erewash Canal, begun in 1777, and, linking with it, the Cromford Canal begun in 1790. These were followed by the Leicester Navigation, completed in 1794, which connected Leicester and Loughborough with the Trent, thereby enabling the Erewash Valley coalowners to transport their coal by water to those towns. Previously, if Celia Fiennes is to be believed, Leicester people burnt either Warwickshire coal or cow-dung.[5] Low transport costs gave Nottinghamshire and Derbyshire colliery owners a virtual monopoly in Leicester for a third of a century.

The building of canals, in widening the market area and thereby increasing demand whilst the productive capacity of the industry lagged behind, raised pit head prices. Low observed in 1798 that, whilst the prices of coal at places a long way from the collieries (e.g. Newark and Retford) had fallen with the opening of canals, prices at places nearer to the mines had risen.[6] The existence of canals which provided cheap, water-borne transport to distant markets caused many owners of land-locked collieries to construct railways from their pits to the nearest canal. Such a railway is described in the *Repertory of Arts and Manufactures* for 1800[7] thus:

'. . . at Brinsley in Nottinghamshire, one horse drew, on a rail road where the declivity was one third of an inch at a yard, 21 waggons, of 5 cwt. each, which with their loading of coals, amounted to 43 tons 8 cwt., the same horse drew seven tons up the cart road. It must be observed, that in both the foregoing statements, the cwt. is 120 lb. On this road the rails are three feet long, 33 lbs. weight and calculated to carry two tons on each wagon, laid four feet two inches wide, on stone or wood sleepers, placed on a bed of slack, so as to fix it solid and firm. The expense of completing one mile of such a road, where materials of all descriptions lie convenient, and where the land lies tolerably favourable for the descent, will be about 900 L. or 1,000 L. per mile, single road, fenced, etc. exclusive of bridges, culverts or any extra expense in deep cutting or high embankments. Rails are made from 20 lb. to 40. lb. per yard, agreeable to the weight they have to bear.'

The most striking network of wagonways in the district was, perhaps, that which converged on the Cromford Canal branch at Pinxton. Some of the rails used here were apparently wooden ones; wooden rails were, indeed, in use at the Pinxton lower pit as late as 1808. On these wooden railways, the flanges were on the wheels whereas the iron railways of the time usually had the flanges on the rails.[8] Rail connections were established for all the pits in the vicinity: Winter-bank Pit at South Normanton, all the Pinxton pits, Carnfield, the Mellors' pits at Huthwaite (Old Hucknall Colliery), and Blackwell among others. A very much longer railroad was built from Mansfield to Pinxton. A private bill was mooted in connection with this project in 1811, but the work was not completed until 1819 owing, so it is said, to a controversy between Jessop and Outram (the railway's principal promotors) as to which type of rails should be used. Jessop favoured edge rails (where the flange is on the wheel) whilst Outram preferred flanged plates.[9] Judging by a section of rails recovered in 1939, Jessop appears to have won. The rails, which were cast at the Butterley Company's works, were affixed to stone sleepers by means of spikes driven into wooden plugs.[10] The Act for the formation of 'The Mansfield and Pinxton Railway Company' dated 16th June 1817 gave the Company an authorized capital of £22,800. The work took almost two years to complete, and when the first train of coal was drawn into the Company's wharf at Mansfield at 9 o'clock on the morning of Tuesday, 13th April 1819, the whole town joined in celebrating the event.[11]

This railway was worked partly by horses and partly by gravity. It is said to have reduced the price of coal in Mansfield to about 8s. or 8s. 6d. from between 10s. and 13s.

In the year ending Lady Day 1834, the railway carried the following goods:

Coal and Coke	50,000 tons
Sand	2,161 tons
Stone and Brick	1,496 tons
Lime	687 tons
Timber and Slate	258 tons
Metals (chiefly Iron)	170 tons
Manure	565 tons
Corn and Malt	383 tons
General Merchandise	1,435 tons

The Company's income for the year totalled £1,966 3s. 9d. against expenditure on repairs and salaries of £485 13s. 2d. A dividend of £4 10s. per £50 share was declared[12] but this was unusually high. In the late 1820's four per cent was the usual dividend.[13] In 1840, the Company considered going over to steam locomotives, but did not do so; and in 1847 the Midland Railway Company obtained an Act of Parliament enabling it to purchase the line. The purchase price was £21,066 13s. 4d.[14]

The Midland Railway is said to have been founded at a meeting of local colliery owners held in the Sun Inn, Eastwood, on 16th August 1832 for the purpose of deciding measures to combat the competition of the developing Leicestershire coalfield. A railway, engineered by Robert Stephenson and completed in July 1832, connected Swannington (the centre of the Leicestershire coalfield) with Leicester thereby breaking the virtual monopoly formerly held by the canal-borne coal of Nottinghamshire and Derbyshire. The traditional story is that the Nottinghamshire-Derbyshire colliery owners requested the canal companies to reduce their carriage charges by 3s. 6d. a ton, but they refused to reduce them by more than 1s. 6d. a ton. The Sun Inn meeting therefore resolved that:

'there remains no other plan for their adoption than to attempt to lay a railway from these collieries to the town of Leicester.'

In fact, the canal companies offered a reduction of one-third (i.e. about 2s. 4d. since the average cost of transport was about 7s. 0d.). One suspects that the railway promoters were merely trying to find an excuse for the action which they intended to take in any case.

The subscribers to this new projected railway were: Barber Walker (who subscribed £10,000) E. M. Munday, John Wright, Francis Wright, the Duke of Portland, Palmer Morewood and John Coke (£5,000 each) James Oakes (£2,500) Mr. Brittain, Coupland and Goodwin and Messrs. Haslam (£1,500 each). Because of Parliamentary opposition, their proposed Erewash Valley line was not constructed until 1846-7, by which time the Midland Counties Railway (as their enterprise came to be called) had amalgamated with the North Midland to form the Midland Railway Company.[15]

In the meantime, despite the development of the Leicestershire coalfield, the canal-borne coal of Nottinghamshire and Derbyshire continued to supply a large share of the growing Leicestershire market.[16] By the middle of the nineteenth century, most of the Erewash Valley mines were well served by canals and railways, but there were still a few landsale collieries like Skegby. One of the most frequently recurring charges in the Skegby Account Book from 1847-8 was 'turnpike charges'.[17] Collieries like this were unable to expand in the same way as their competitors, but Skegby was now the exceptional, and, not, as a few decades earlier, the modal case.

3. MONOPOLY AND COMPETITION

We have already noted Huntingdon Beaumont's attempt to create a monopoly by leasing, and restricting the output of, the collieries of his competitors. We have noted also the accusation made in 1739 that Barber and Company were trying to monopolize the market by drowning the workings of their rivals.

In the early nineteenth century, a combination of colliery owners regulated the trade. This body most probably had its origin in attempts made by the canal companies in 1798 to eradicate fraudulent practices connected with the measurement of coal. Rates were based on the ton; but the amount of coal reckoned to be equal to a ton varied from one wharf to the next.

The committees of the Cromford, Derby, Erewash, Grantham, Leicester, Melton Mowbray, Nottingham, Nutbrook, and Trent canal companies had meetings with the principal colliery owners.

'. . . and after some discussion it was agreed to put an end to all diversities of weights carried on these canals, by the erection of a sufficient number of Weighing-Houses upon them, and of so modifying their several sets of Bye-Laws relating to Tonnage, that every Boat used on them, should previously be numbered, described, and gauged in the most minute and accurate manner at their joint expense. . . .'[18]

The association of colliery owners appointed general clerks to ascertain the weight of the coals in each boat, calculate the value at the tonnage price 'fixed by each individual Coal-Master on his coals at the . . . Meeting of the Coal-masters', and collect the cash for the particular owner concerned. The cash was paid over to the owners 'at short stated periods'. Thus, all the associated colliery owners knew both the prices charged and the quantities sold by their fellows.

The building of the weigh houses and the gauging of the vessels were entrusted to Thomas Walker of the Barber Walker Company. The only large coal owners using the Cromford, Erewash and Nottingham canals who refused to join the arrangement were Lord Middleton and William Drury Lowe according to information given to Farey in 1808. It is not clear whether the tonnages of coals carried on the three canals which Farey gives for year ending June 1808 include those from Lord Middleton's and Mr. Drury Lowe's pits. Farey's figures are:

Hard coals	205,006	tons
Soft coals	37,289	tons
Cobbles	27,161	tons
Cokes	24,384	quarters

According to a Royal Commission Report the total quantity of Erewash Valley coal sold by canal in 1808 amounted to 303,837 tons[19] and we may be tempted to regard the difference between the two totals (34,381 tons) as the sale of Middleton and Drury Lowe. This is, indeed, a possibility. However, it is impossible to be sure that the two figures cover exactly the same geographical area.

Another interesting set of figures points fairly clearly to the existence of a system of regulation of trade. Here, the total sales of 'sundry

Collieries in the Counties of Nottingham and Derby' (presumably the Erewash Valley Association mines) are tabulated for the years 1808 to 1818. The total figures are compared with the 'real' sales of Barber Walker and a small producer, S. Daykin and Co., and the 'real' sales are compared with what appear to be the quotas allotted to the two companies of 24·3 per cent and 4·8 per cent respectively of the market. Over the eleven years, Barber Walker sold 759,675 tons against a 'quota' of 743,712; whilst S. Daykin and Co. (in the nine years 1810 to 1818—they appear to have commenced operations in 1810) sold 142,742 tons against a 'quota' of 121,599. The document appears to be an argument for a readjustment of the quotas in favour of the two companies. The highest annual figure for the Associated collieries was 310,892 tons in 1815, and the lowest 241,491 tons in 1818.[20] In 1834, a local coalowner alleged that prices were being depressed artificially by the Coalowners' Association so as to force non-members to accept regulation of the trade or face bankruptcy.

At about the same time, Barber Walker were reputed to be buying collieries (e.g. at Eastwood from Dr Manson in 1838 and Hill Top from Fullard and Richardson in 1857) in order to restrict their output and so reduce competition. Further, the Agent of Lord Melbourne, F. F. Fox wrote to Melbourne in 1848 advising him not to renew Barber Walker's coal lease unless they agreed to take more enterprising men into association with them. Their policy was to restrict output so as to maintain the price thereby depressing the royalty owner's income.[21]

Two substantial coalowners, Lord Middleton and Thomas North remained outside the association in the 1840's.[22] Also the owners of the Leen Valley pits sunk in the third quarter of the century were generally opposed to restriction on philosophical grounds, besides being conscious of the superior productivity of their mines. It became increasingly difficult, therefore, for the association to control the 'apportionment of the Vend' although they were apparently still trying to do so in 1858.[23]

The colliery owners of the inland coalfields found when they entered the London market that trade in the metropolis was regulated by a merchants' 'ring'. In order to overcome this, some of the larger companies appointed their own London agents. Butterley, for example, appointed the Clay Cross Company to act for them together with Mr. N. Pegg from 1852 to 1855. Subsequently, a Mr. Parry and Pegg were the company's London agents. In the year ended April 1856, they sold 73,287 tons between them, and the rapidity with which the London sales grew is an indication of aggressive salesmanship.[24] Again, Bulmer's *Directory* of 1895 said that the Pinxton Company had 'broken through the trammells of the Coal Ring and supply coals direct from their depots without the intervention of middlemen, and their necessarily increased prices'.[25]

The railway companies, who placed annual contracts for monthly deliveries of coal at fixed prices complained in 1900 that a coal owners' 'ring' was responsible for the high price of coal. This was denied by Emerson Muschamp Bainbridge at the time, but in 1903 A. B. Markham admitted the existence of an understanding between certain large companies, including his own, 'to charge certain prices and to sell only to certain agents'.[26] Several colliery owners' associations were operating at this time, but with the exception of the Leen Valley association, they acted in unison in the matter of pricing policy.

Thus a meeting was held at the Midland Hotel, Derby on Wednesday 15th March 1899 'to consider the question of prices and contracts for the ensuing year' having regard to wage settlements arrived at in the Federated District a short time previously. Those invited originally were: Eckington, Birley, Sheepbridge, Staveley, Grassmoor, Holmewood, Clay Cross, Pilsley, Rothervale, Stanton, Shirebrook, Bolsover and Shireoaks.[27] In fact three further companies were represented at the meeting: Nunnery, Blackwell and Alma. It was resolved that current prices should be maintained, that a minimum advance of 1s. per ton should be demanded on all future contracts and that 'a deputation from this meeting wait upon the Erewash Valley C. Owner's Ass'n and other bodies with a view to discussing the advisability of demanding an increase in list prices of 6d. and an increase on contract prices of 1s. 6d. per ton for the ensuing year'.[28]

In the same file as this correspondence is a pencilled note of another meeting held also in the Midland Hotel Derby on 15th March 1899 which appears to have been a committee of the Derbyshire, Nottinghamshire and Leicestershire Colliery Owners' Association. Some people were present at both meetings. It is clear, indeed, that membership of the various associations overlapped.

A further meeting of North Derbyshire and South Yorkshire owners held at Derby under the Chairmanship of Mr. E. Barnes of Grassmoor on 25th July 1899 resolved:

'That if the London Merchants advance prices 1s. to the public on August 1st, price lists be issued at 6d. advance on last list price.

'That in the event of London Merchants not advancing on August 1st., it is agreed to advance present current prices 6d. per ton subject to the Erewash Valley Coal Owners doing likewise.'[29]

Another meeting of the same sort held on 28th March 1900, which decided on an increase of 5s. per ton on contract prices, included several Erewash Valley owners including Butterley, Blackwell, Shipley and New Hucknall.[30]

REFERENCES

1 A. C. Wood, *A History of Nottinghamshire*, Nottm., 1947, p. 150.
   C. H. Wood (ed.), *Hardwick Hall*, Derby, n.d., p. 9.
2 R. S. Smith, 'Huntingdon Beaumont', p. 121. Nef, op. cit., II, pp. 400–1.
3 Farey, op. cit., I, p. 186. The duty on coal 'imported' into London was unique. No such dues were levied elsewhere in the country. These dues were not abolished until 1890.
4 C. P. Griffin, op. cit.
5 C. Morris (ed.) *The Journeys of Celia Fiennes*, London, 1947, p. 162. They also burnt wood from Charnwood Forest and coal from Leicestershire mines.
6 R. Low, *General View of the Agriculture of Nottinghamshire*, 1798, cited C. P. Griffin, *Robert Harrison: The Development of the Managerial Function in a Coal Mining Partnership* (unpublished B.A. dissertation,) at Nottm., 1965, cap. 5.
7 Quoted J. A. Birks and C. P. Coxon, op. cit., p. 2.
8 ibid., p. 2 H. Walker, op. cit., p. 7. Farey, op. cit., III, p. 288. There was another wooden railway at Greasley.
9 Birks and Coxon, op. cit., p. 3.
10 ibid., p. 4.
11 *Nottm. Daily Journal*, 17th April, 1819, cited Birks and Coxon, op. cit.
12 Birks and Coxon, op. cit., pp. 8–9.
13 G. G. Hopkinson, art. cit., p. 36.
14 Birks & Coxon, op. cit., p. 13.
15 F. S. Williams, *The Midland Railway, Its Rise and Progress*, London, 1878, pp. 6 et seq. See also Birks and Coxon, op. cit., G. G. Hopkinson, art. cit., Leicester Navigation Minute Book 16th July 1832 and Leicester Journal 31st Aug. 1832.
16 G. G. Hopkinson, art. cit., p. 37.
17 *Skegby Colliery Account Book.*
18 J. Farey, op. cit., I, pp. 182–187.
19 *Royal Commission on Coal*, 1871, Vol. III, App. No. 26, p. 16.
20 C. P. Griffin, *Robert Harrison*. Chapter 5.
21 D. Spring, *English Landed Estates in the Nineteenth Century*, London, 1963, pp. 126–7.
   (I am indebted to C. P. Griffin for this reference.)
22 It is probable that Palmer Morewood and Drury Lowe also remained outside.
23 C. P. Griffin, loc. cit.
24 *Butterley Sales and Output Book.*
25 T. Bulmer & Co., *History, Topography and Directory of Derbyshire*, Preston, 1895, pp. 675–6.
26 J. E. Williams, op. cit., p. 179.
27 Letter signed A. G. Barnes (Grassmoor Collieries) addressed to the Holmewood Company and dated 27th February 1899. The Federated District (or Area) included all the major inland coalfields, but excluded Durham, Northumberland and South Wales.
28 Letter signed E. Edmund Barnes (Grassmoor Collieries) addressed as above, dated 16th March 1899 and headed 'London Prices, House Coal'.
29 Letter signed E. Edmund Barnes addressed to the Hardwick Co. dated 26th July 1899.
30 Letter signed A. G. Barnes to the Hardwick Co. dated 30th March 1900.

CHAPTER V

The Emergence of a County Miners' Union

1. INTRODUCTION

Generally speaking, trade unions flourish when trade is good. An improvement in the state of trade reduces the competition between workers for employment. The desire to make a profit whilst demand conditions are favourable disposes employers to settle trade disputes peacefully. Faced with a strike, employers, middlemen and the community at large are inclined to say 'Here we are losing our time; we are losing our harvest. . . . For God's sake, settle, and pay anything.'[1] A trade union which obtains an improvement in the wages and conditions of its members is likely to attract support. Further, as its membership and income increase, it will be able to afford to spend money on its organization, and its bargaining position will be improved. On the other hand, a deterioration in the state of trade increases the competition between workers for employment. Employers are able to enforce reductions in wage-rates, and where these are resisted by organized workers, lock-outs result. These are, almost inevitably settled on the employers' terms. Under these circumstances, trade unions lose members, their incomes dwindle and their capital is eaten into, even where it is not entirely dissipated in lockout pay and out-of-work benefit. The first half of the nineteenth century saw many unions in various trades founded and prospering during the upswing of a trade cycle only to collapse on the downswing of the same cycle.[2]

Political agitation, on the other hand, is intensified during a slump. Thus, the Chartist movement reached its apogee in 1842, which coincided with a major trough in the trade indices.[3] The sting was taken out of the movement by the improvement in trade which followed during the succeeding four years. As political agitation declined, trade union agitation increased under the stimulus of economic recovery, but many of the unionists were themselves associated with Chartism.[4]

2. THE FIRST UNION IN THE NOTTINGHAMSHIRE COALFIELD (1844)

The Miners' Association of Great Britain and Ireland, formed at Wakefield in 1841 under the leadership of Martin Jude, spread throughout the northern coalfields but did not reach the Midlands until 1844. Its membership was then said to be at least 100,000 and it employed no fewer than fifty-three agents, aptly described by the Webbs as 'missionary organizers', who visited every colliery in the country.[5]

The first lodge to be formed in Nottinghamshire was Kimberley, which had 101 members by the third week of January 1844.[6] Soon, lodges were flourishing at most collieries in Nottinghamshire and Derbyshire. The aims of the union in these two counties were: to support men who might be victimized because of their adherence to a trade union; to abolish the truck system, to secure weekly, instead of fortnightly or monthly pays, and to secure a reduction in working hours to eight per day.[7]

At some collieries, the men came out on strike in support of their demands, but at others the owners acted first, locking-out all trade union members. At a meeting of coal owners of the two counties held on 11th March 1844 at Derby, it was resolved that employment should be refused to union members and that 'the masters present should not employ any miner after the first of April without producing a certificate from his master, of having given due notice and behaved himself properly'.[8]

To the Owners' Association the union was 'uncalled for and unjust'.[9] They were prepared to concede some of the men's economic demands, but few of them would tolerate organization among their men. Two owners, who were not members of the Owners' Association, however, conceded the men's immediate demands fairly quickly and their pits re-started work whilst coal was selling at high prices.[10] Thus, Lord Middleton's Radford colliers went back on 3rd April, and Thomas North's colliers at Cinderhill went back on 23rd April at 4s. per day of eight hours.[11] North's Kimberley Colliery remained idle, apparently, until half-way through June, when the men re-commenced paying into the Union's fund.[12] The most probable explanation for this is that North was anxious to re-start production at Cinderhill and Babbington quickly so as to improve his competitive position in the Nottingham market. In the second week of May, North's private railway line from Cinderhill to his new wharf on the Wollaton Canal side at Radford opened and he was able to reduce his prices at Nottingham from 15s. 6d. to 10s. a ton.[13] Barber, Walker and Company were very concerned about the strength of North's competition.[14] His top hard workings, still only a matter of yards out of the pit bottom, had a seam section of eight feet.[15] Everything was in North's favour—geographical location, transport facilities, geological conditions. He could not afford to allow his dislike of trade unionism to keep his new pits idle. His Kimberley Colliery was not nearly so important to him.

The Barber Walker Company were said to 'have become odious to the poor miners . . . by the conduct of themselves and one of their agents'. Certainly, their men remained on strike for some time.[16] The Butterley Company induced their Portland (Selston) Colliery employees to return to work on 17th May 1844 by paying increased wages. However, they were re-employed only on condition that they signed the 'document' abjuring trade unionism. This became a favourite device with the owners.[17]

Many Derbyshire pits were out for thirteen or fourteen weeks, Pinxton included. When, at the end of this period, the Pinxton men returned to work on the owners' terms, their leaders were refused employment. The Hayes family, for example, had to leave Pinxton for Staveley, where they were unknown.[18] During the dispute, the Pinxton old Colliery became waterlogged and was abandoned, but by this time the new Langton Colliery was ready to start work.

The 1844 dispute was an underdogs' revolt. The Pinxton men, for example, made it clear that they were striking against their 'butties' as well as against the owners. They declared 'That we will not work any more at any price for William Harvey and W. Pepper.' They considered '. . . The Buttie sistem a very great evil amongst colliers'. In the potteries, some pits where the men were on strike, were kept in production by butties.[19] This division between butties and colliers was a feature of the big butty system, but at the new Cinderhill and Babbington Collieries, this division was absent because here there were many butties—almost as many, perhaps, as day-men at the face. Lord Middleton's pits were worked by Steavers (variously spelt) and butties—but they were closely supervised by the agents of Lord Middleton, a model employer who would not, for example, allow boys under ten to work underground, who forbade corporal punishment, and who insisted that the dog-belt should not be worn by boys under sixteen or eighteen years of age.[20] At the pits in the Northern part of the county the big butty system with its concomitant, the payment of wages in truck, was at its worst, and it was against the 'butties' at such a pit—Skegby—that the men struck for higher wages in August 1844 as the first great mining dispute flickered out.[21] Elsewhere, the union had virtually collapsed, its leaders victimized and its members cajoled or forced into withdrawing their support.

During this dispute, the miners had enjoyed considerable popular support. Shopkeepers and market traders at places like Nottingham,

Mansfield, Bulwell and Kimberley gave money and foodstuffs to the Miners' Association Committee. At Nottingham, a public committee with headquarters at the *Derby Arms* was elected to raise funds and to protect the public from impostors.[22] Miners demonstrating in Bulwell were given 'eight large clothes-baskets full of bread, cheese and bacon, with ale, which was served out to them by the inhabitants'.[23] Regular collections were taken at workshops and factories in Nottingham, and the framework knitters of Bulwell and other places made regular contributions of 1d. per week.[24] This raised an average of about £2 a week from Bulwell, and, for a particular week, the following sums from other places: Kimberley, 12s. 6d.; Calverton, 16s.; Arnold, 14s. 3d.; and Basford 11s. 8d.[25] James Sweet, a barber by trade, and secretary of the Nottingham Chartists was an active organizer of collections,[26] and it seems likely that the organization which sprang so quickly into life to raise funds for the miners was provided by the Chartists. The work involved in raising money from people who could only afford to contribute a copper or two at a time, points to the existence of an organization far superior to anything the Nottinghamshire miners possessed at that time. Consider this list of collections held so early in the dispute as the first week in April for instance:[27]

	£	s.	d.
Mr. Burton's factory, Carrington	1	6	4
Mr. Harvey's shop		3	3
Mr. Butler's glass shop		2	0
Mr. Fawcett's shop		5	9
Mr. Robertson's factory, New Basford		11	4
Messrs. Riddle and Birkins factory, Sherwood		12	4
Mr. Burton's factory, Sherwood		12	4½
Carrington Brewery		1	8
Mr. Bates' shop		4	2
Mr. Bunting's shop		4	0
Mr. Thackeray's factory		3	0
Mr. Berry's factory		1	8

A connection with the Chartists is also suggested by the meeting held in support of the miners at the Chartists' Nottingham headquarters, the Democratic Chapel, Barker Gate, on 12th March 1844.[28] One of the speakers was Thomas Vernon, a local leader of the Miners' Association who, at another meeting, had said: 'the masters were afraid that if the men got their object now, they would next strike for the Charter, but this was ridiculous'.[29]

The White Cow Inn at Radford was recognized as the organizing centre for the Miners' Association in Nottinghamshire. James Gould, the treasurer, had his headquarters there.[30] Radford was a Radical hot-bed, and of the organizers of the 1844 union, Samuel Smith of Radford was the only one known to play a part in the formation of the Nottinghamshire Miners' Association some four decades later.[31]

The union had a connection with Methodism, too, even if not a particularly strong one. The leaders were described by a Derbyshire paper as 'mostly ranter preachers',[32] but there was little truth in this. Some Primitive Methodists undoubtedly joined the union, but radical action was frowned on by the connexion at this date. Further, miners' meetings in 1844 were not marked by the quasi-religious ceremonial which was to become common two decades later. The Pinxton lodge, it is true, had Wesleyan Methodists—the Hayes family and others—actively engaged in the dispute. John Hayes was a member of the Lodge Committee;[33] whilst his sons, Matthew and William, were members of one of the teams of 'beggars' who at Matthew's suggestion, visited non-mining districts on money-raising expeditions:

> 'They all felt they were striving for what was right and just, and believed that their fellow working men in other parts of the country, who were in employment, would sympathise and render them assistance. They began with music and singing in the streets, and long journeys were made by companies of ten or twelve, who were sent in different directions, two of each company being selected to officiate as beggars.'

The team which included the Hayes Brothers, went to Mansfield, Blidworth, Epperstone, Edingley, Oxton, Calverton, Bennington, Hoveringham, Newark and Grantham. At Grantham, they had just commenced the singing of 'Would Jesus have the sinner die', when they were interrupted by a constable who threatened to prosecute them as vagrants.[34]

One team of 'beggars' were 'taken up at Sutton-in-Ashfield . . . and committed to Southwell'. They were released on Saturday, 20th April, when they 'were met on the road by four or five of their comrades who had brought with them their musical instruments, and headed them, playing some popular airs as they passed through Mansfield on their way home'.[35]

The idea of begging in this way was derived from the method of raising funds for Wesleyan foreign missions suggested by Dr. Coke.[36] It is probable that other branches had Methodist members too. However, the Methodist connection with mining trade unionism was to be far more important in future agitations.

The dispute in Nottinghamshire was part of a wider struggle. In Northumberland and Durham, the men struck work on 5th April 1844, for payment by weight instead of measure, higher wages, and the abolition of the yearly bond.[37] Their experiences in 1832, when they were defeated by blacklegs brought in from other coalfields, had taught them the need for national organization. It would not, on this occasion, be possible for a family of colliers like the Hayes family to be tricked into going North by coalowners because Union agents had visited every colliery in the land, and they remained to organize the resistance of the men when their employers started to lock them out. The Nottinghamshire and Derbyshire agent, Mycroft, was remarkably energetic,[38] and the speed with which other areas were organized, indicates that the rest of the fifty-three agents must have been equally so. At the Glasgow National Conference held in March 1844, at which Nottingham and other Midland counties were represented, it was resolved that '. . . we, the delegates from the different parts of the Kingdom, do hereby pledge ourselves to do all in our power to assist them [i.e. the Durham and Northumberland miners] in their struggle, and also to prevent men from coming amongst them; and, if possible, still further to restrict our labour'.[39]

The strike in Durham which lasted for five months succeeded in giving 'the death-blow to the Yearly Bond, which henceforth began to give place to fortnightly contracts'.[40] The Miners' Association in the Northern counties managed to continue in existence until the economic crisis of 1847–8.[41] In Nottinghamshire, however, nothing was heard of it after early August 1844 when the Skegby strike was its last manifestation.

This early collapse was due in part to the inexperience of the Nottinghamshire miner. The employers' use of 'the document' and the 'blacklisting' of leading unionists must also have played its part. It is significant that of the principal leaders of the 1844 union, Clarke, Duroe, Walker, Thomas Vaughan, Thomas Vernon, James Smith, Samuel Smith and William Porter (who acted as district secretary) only one, Samuel Smith of Radford[42] is known to have played an active part in the later unions. It was said[43] that the others were forced to leave the industry.

The harmful effect on the unity of the men of the big butty system, however, cannot be overestimated.

It is doubtful whether the union disappeared quite as quickly as its lack of publicity in the local press suggests. The Cinderhill Lodge for example paid £7 9s. into the strike fund as late as 21st June, when nearly all the collieries were back at work.[44] It seems likely that trade union membership continued there, and at Radford, for a while, since at both places the men had returned to work without undertaking to leave the union. This is speculation. That the Miners' Association of Great Britain and Ireland languished in the economic crisis of 1847-8 is a fact. There was a recrudescence in 1850-1 when the officials for Notts. and Derbyshire were John Morley (President) Thomas Watson (Agent) and George Goulder (Secretary) but despite the goodwill of one coal-owner, Charles Binns of Clay Cross it did not last long.[45]

3. THE DERBYSHIRE AND NOTTINGHAMSHIRE MINERS'
ASSOCIATION (1863)

Following the collapse of the Miners' Association, there was, it
seems, a complete absence of trade union activity in the coalfield.
According to Dr. Williams:

'This is probably explained by the fact that the men were not subjected
during this period to any serious economic pressure. Following the depression of the years 1847 and 1848, there were reductions in miners' wages
generally, resulting in a fall of just over three per cent between 1840 and
1850. The cost-of-living, however, had fallen more than that during the
same period. Thereafter, during the prosperous 'fifties, miners' wages began to rise. . . . It is generally agreed that whilst wholesale prices rose
fairly sharply the increase in the cost-of-living was not very great. Thus,
comparatively modest wage increases were sufficient to secure a rise in
the standard of living.'[46]

This analysis is of doubtful validity. Other trades, which were
affected by the same market forces as the miners, show a considerable
development of trade union organization and activity in this period.[47]
The argument which Dr. Williams appears to be using, that the miners
failed to organize in this period because they benefited from the
steadily improving economic climate, is a *non sequitur*. It is precisely
under these sorts of conditions that trade unionism has made its
greatest advances.

Even among miners there was some organization in the 1850's.
Alexander McDonald started his work among the English miners in
1856.[48] The South Yorkshire Miners' Association which came into
being on 10th April 1858 'following upon bitter struggles in the coalfield', owed much to McDonald's leadership.[49] In the same year, a
national conference of sorts was organized by McDonald at Ashton-
under-Lyne.[50]

In Nottinghamshire, however, there was no unionism among the
men until 1863. That is not to say there were no unionists until then.
Clearly, there were men like Henry Walker of Pinxton and Samuel
Smith of Radford, who had played an active part in the earlier union
and who remained loyal to the Trade Union idea. The 1844 Union had,
after all, achieved something.

Its permanent achievement was a reduction in the hours of work.
It is doubtful whether it had any long-term effect on the level of
wages, however. We know that the usual pay for a collier immediately prior to the 1844 dispute was around 3s. a day, and we saw that
at Radford, Cinderhill and Babbington, the union secured an advance
of 1s. a day. Wages were increased at some other collieries, too:

Skegby and the Portland pits among them. However, it seems probable that even without a union the men could have expected some increases in wages with improvement in trade between 1842 and 1847 just as there were decreases in 1841–2.[51] Further it is certain that some of the increase which they did receive was soon lost. Some Leicestershire miners who were induced to return to work on improved terms complained within a matter of weeks that their employers were already altering those terms to the men's detriment.[52] Even if this did not happen in Nottinghamshire, wages would certainly have been forced down during the crisis of 1847–8. In the case of Butterley, the average earnings of miners were around 15s. per week in 1851, whilst the contractors averaged about £1 and the overmen were paid a fixed wage of £1 per week.[53]

From a survey taken among Butterley men in 1856, it would seem that there were still many colliers even then who earned no more than the pre-1844 average. Quite a number give their wages as 3s. or 3s. 6d. per day, and some even less, though these may have been the very young and the very old rather than mature, active colliers. A very few colliers earned 5s. per day, but it is probable that a similar survey taken in 1841, would have revealed a few men earning as much on piece-work. The majority of colliers in the survey earned 3s. to 3s. 9d. a day; but to balance those whose earnings were higher than this there were a few earning quite a bit less—for example John Moore of New Main pit who had a wife and five young children to keep on 2s. a day and Samuel Grainger of 40 Horse pit who had a wife (but no children) to keep on an almost unbelievable 1s. a shift.[54]

The 1844 Union may not have had any lasting effect on wages but, by focusing attention on the evils of the Truck System, it probably went a long way towards securing its abolition; it achieved a permanent reduction in the hours of work. Further, for a time, unity had meant something to the men. Men in work had paid into the strike fund to support those still out and there had been public demonstrations of solidarity. The 1844 Union had meant something. It could not have been altogether forgotten by any of its former members. Their next experience of trade unionism would owe something to the memory of the first great struggle.

The union which started in 1863[55] had a look of permanence about it which its predecessor had never had. Instead of being faced with an immediate stoppage, it apparently organized quietly, until 23rd December 1865, when it was formally inaugurated at a meeting at Eckington.[56] Further, the unity of the men was not weakened to anything like the old extent by the butty system. Indeed, at pits like Cinderhill and Babbington, still owned by North, and the new Hucknall pits owned by J. E. Ellis, butties played a leading part in the agitation. At these collieries, there were not many more day wage men at the face than there were butties. It was only at the backward pits that the big butty system still existed. The Brierley Hill pit of John Dodsley at Skegby, soon to close and to be replaced by the larger Sutton Colliery to which for a time it gave its name, was one of these: and it is significant that a delegate who worked at the colliery, William Breakwell, called for the abolition of the butty system at a National Conference which opened at Nottingham on Tuesday, 13th November 1866. This may have been a major issue at Skegby, but at most places, it went unremarked.[57]

Another factor making for permanence was the Act of 1860, which allowed the colliers to appoint a fellow employee to act as checkweighman. This legislation was defective in that the colliery owner had the right to discharge a troublesome checkweighman. It therefore required courage of a very high order on the part of an honest checkweighman. Such men did, as it happens, come forward to provide miners' lodges with good leadership. Victimization was common until, in the 1887 Act, the checkweigher's position was made more secure.[58]

The first outburst of militancy in this period was at Cinderhill in November 1865. Here, Topley, Sills and Company, butties, had failed to pay their daywage men and the latter had applied, unsuccessfully, for payment to North. All the men came out in sympathy with those involved.[59]

The union was recognized by some ten coal-owners in the two counties, Thomas North being among them.[60] The Staveley and Clay Cross Companies and J. E. Ellis of Hucknall were, however, bitterly opposed to it. The disputes of 1866–7 were therefore of two types. Some were disputes involving demands for better conditions of service—more pay for less hours as one speaker put it—whilst the others were recognition disputes.

The Derbyshire and Nottinghamshire Miners' Association was affiliated to the Miners' National Union (M.N.U.), a body established in 1863 with Alexander McDonald as its President.[61] The M.N.U. sent organizers like Philip Casey of Yorkshire into the district and provided funds for strike pay. The chief organizer of the D. and N.M.A. was William Brown, who had been induced to assist with the work by Joseph Edwards, the Union's first agent. Brown left his home in Hunslet to become a full-time agent of the D. and N.M.A. on 22nd October 1866.[62] He was paid 5s. 6d. a day.[63] Like many of the leaders of the Association, Brown was a Methodist local preacher, a powerful speaker who could also sing well.

Under his leadership the work of organizing the Union resembled a religious revival. At meetings, prayers were said and hymns from the 'Miners' Hymn Book' were sung. One of Brown's earliest visits to Nottinghamshire was at Hucknall Torkard on Sunday, 1st July:

'. . . There was also an open-air service held in the afternoon in connection with the "Miners' Association" which was devotionally and religiously conducted. And the same parties held an interesting meeting at night upon the Green which was very numerously attended, and at which Mr. Brown, from Hunslet, delivered a very humorous and interesting address.'

A meeting of locked-out miners at Hucknall in January 1867 similarly opened with a hymn from the 'Miners' Hymn Book' and closed with the Doxology.[64]

The men at the Cinderhill, Babbington and Newcastle pits of Thomas North, secured an eight-hour day in the late summer of 1866. For four months they produced, according to William Brown, more coal in eight hours than they had previously produced in twelve hours.[65] Then, early in January 1867 by which time North was in a precarious financial position, his agent offered a revised agreement to give a tonnage rate of 1s. 8¾d. for coal and 11d. for slack, and a ten-hour day. The Union branch resisted this attempt to increase their hours and reduce their rate of pay but when North gave notice of the change, it was accepted without a struggle.[66] Next, North was said to want to increase the hours still further to twelve a day and to reduce wages to 15 per cent below the level of eight years previously, during which time the price of Cinderhill coal had risen by 4s. a ton to 12s. 6d.[67] The men rejected this and were therefore locked out in February 1867. William Brown said that now that they were out, they should insist upon all their grievances being corrected. They should refuse to produce any more than 21 cwt per ton instead of 28 cwt, and they should insist on an end to the practice of making arbitrary stoppages from their pay.[68]

The practice of requiring more than 20 cwts. to the ton was widespread, and it was probably derived from a conversion of capacity measure into equivalent weights. The common capacity measure in South Nottinghamshire and parts of Derbyshire was the 'Rook'. Nef has estimated the weight of a Wollaton 'Rook' of 1610 at between 1 ton and 1 ton-and-a-half.[69] In the mid-nineteenth century and earlier, most colliery owners in the district required their workmen to produce 27 to 28 cwt. to the ton.

The arbitrary stoppages complained of by the Cinderhill men were deductions made for mixing coal and slack, or for sending dirt up in the coal. At the end of February 1867, the Cinderhill men's representatives met North and his agent Barber when a settlement was arranged largely on terms submitted by the Union. During the meeting, however, Barber inserted into the proposed new contract drawn up by the Union a clause which said: 'If slack is sent up in the coals, or dirt or coal is sent up in the slack, the said trams shall be wholly forfeited.'[70] The men went back to work not realizing what a hostage to fortune their deputation had given. Contrary to a promise which he had given to the deputation, North took out all the 'allowance' payments to contractors which normally amounted to between fifteen shillings and five pounds a stall, depending on conditions, and some butties found themselves as much as two pounds in debt to their day-wagemen in consequence. The men accused North of acting dishonourably. He had specifically undertaken to continue allowance payments to two members of the deputation who were butties—John Green and Thomas Lucas (of 5d. and 1¾d. per ton respectively), but had not done so. The seven-hundred odd miners involved therefore came out on strike again on Monday, 11th March 1867.[71] They soon returned, but the deductions for slack continued until the union took North to the County Court in July 1867. A witness at this hearing, William Green, checkweigher, alleged that some trams had been confiscated when they contained only ½ cwt. of slack in 12 cwt. of coal. The judge suggested that the two sides should agree on what was a reasonable amount of slack, and if necessary refer points of dispute to an Umpire.[72]

Thereafter, labour relations at the Cinderhill pits improved. The men were fortunate in having their own checkweighmen, William (Peg-leg) Bolstridge, George Case and William Green.[73] North may have been a difficult employer, but at least he recognized the Union: whilst he could not afford to pay high wages, he could not afford strikes either. The other disputes in this period were at collieries where the owners refused to recognize the Union.

The Hucknall pits (Nos. 1 and 2) were sunk in 1861–3 by Mr. J. E. Ellis, a Leicestershire Quaker, to exploit the Top hard seam. They were the first pits to be sunk in the Leen Valley proper. Hucknall is on the concealed coalfield, and to sink pits there would have taken a considerable amount of capital. Mr. Ellis was a paternalistic Liberal, who believed that trade unions drove capital out of an industry or locality, thereby reducing the fund available for the payment of wages and thus causing more damage to the men than to the owners. He and his partner Walker believed that there was an identity of interest between master and man.[74]

In 1866, Ellis attacked the Union leaders vigorously. He locked the unionists out at the beginning of September and he held meetings of non-unionist colliers. Saxton, one of the leaders of the Hucknall Branch, pointed out that while Ellis and Walker attacked the men's Union, they approved of the masters' 'union'; whilst Joseph Stevenson believed that the men who had been induced to return to work were 'by nature treacherous'.[75]

The men at Hucknall were trying to bring down the hours of work which were, at twelve a day, plus winding times, the longest in the county. It seemed as though Ellis, having sunk so much capital into his colliery, was determined to recoup his expenditure in the shortest possible time.

By 19th January 1867, when the lock-out was almost five months old, many of the Hucknall men had found work elsewhere, thereby easing the drain on the Union's funds,[76] and nothing is heard of the dispute by the end of February. It seems certain that the men obtained some reduction—probably to ten hours—in the length of the working day, as miners at Clay Cross did in very similar circumstances. The owner of Clay Cross, Charles Binns, conceded a ten-hour day, subject to the breaking-up of the Association.[77] Besides Hucknall, there were relatively minor disturbances at Kimberley, Butterley; and at Eastwood, where the Barber Walker Company were said to be willing to pay higher wages if the men would desert the Union.[78]

The most serious disputes in which the Association was involved, however, were in North and South Derbyshire. In North Derbyshire, the Staveley and Clay Cross Companies locked out all Union members and turned them out of their houses.[79] Both companies reduced the hours of work once the Union was scotched, however. The miners of South Derbyshire were in a far more backward state than those of North Derbyshire and Nottinghamshire. Their wages were said to average 15s. a week, and they worked a twelve-hour day, but in addition, truck and the payment of wages in public-houses was still common among them.[80] As soon as they joined the Association, they were locked out.

Both in North and South Derbyshire, the owners organized anti-union societies. Charles Markham of the Staveley Company was particularly active in this direction. A 'Free Labour Association' was formed to rescue the men from the 'tyranny of trade unionism'. Besides meetings, this body also organized feasts to seduce the lockouts from their allegiance to the Association.[81] A professional organizer of strike-breaking teams, Tidd Pratt, was employed by the owners in North Derbyshire.[82] In South Derbyshire, besides their Free Labour Associations, the owners had a printed 'black list' of active unionists issued over the signature of F. Peel, secretary of the Masters' Association.[83]

Anti-union activities were also fostered in the Erewash Valley. In November 1867 for example, some seven-hundred people, mainly employees of James Oakes, and Company, sat down to dinner at a demonstration held at Selston for the purpose of making a presentation to Thomas Naylor 'a gentleman who has done much in opposing its [i.e. trade unionism's] introduction into . . . the Erewash Valley'.[84]

Charles Markham of Staveley, like J. E. Ellis of Hucknall, was a

Liberal. So, too, was J. G. Jackson, M.P., of the Clay Cross Company.[85] All three were opposed to trade unionism; all three supported non-unionist societies.[86] Ellis and Markham were, however, to change their attitudes completely once their employees were given votes. The miners of Nottinghamshire and Derbyshire have cause to be grateful to the sponsors of the 1867 and 1884 Reform Bills.

The lock-outs at Staveley, Clay Cross, Hucknall, South Derbyshire and elsewhere,[87] and the strike at the Babbington collieries, all but broke the Association. In January, 1867, lock-out pay amounted to £750 per week for the men then involved.[88]

The members who were in work paid substantial levies—at one stage as much as 2s. a week.[89] In addition, the South Yorkshire Miners' Association, who were anxious to secure a successful outcome of the struggle in Derbyshire, sent considerable sums. In the five months to the end of February, 1867, they had sent some £870. In October, 1867, the South Derbyshire lock-outs were costing £280 a week, of which South Yorkshire were paying £200.[90]

Appeals for funds were also made to bodies outside the mining industry. The Organized Trades Council at Nottingham agreed to raise money for the Association in February 1867 [91] whilst the United Kingdom Alliance of Organised Trades[92] raised a levy of 2d. a week for the miners of Derbyshire and Nottinghamshire. The London Trades Council also helped.[93]

The constant drain on the Association's funds was too great, however, to be met by the help available. William Brown reported to the M.N.U. conference in late November 1867 that some nine-hundred men in Nottinghamshire and Derbyshire were out, most of them having been locked out for over eight months. The total membership of the Association had fallen from its maximum of 7,500 to between 1,300 and 1,400, almost all of whom were in Nottinghamshire and South Derbyshire, the North Derbyshire branches having by now collapsed. Between £4,000 and £5,000 had been distributed in lock-out pay. The Conference agreed to collect a weekly levy of 3d. per week from all its members to support the Association's lockout fund. The same Conference also decided that it would not pay strike pay in the future, nor would it pay agents to organize the districts.[94] From this point the M.N.U. was to degenerate into a consultative body concerning itself with legislative matters and very little else.[95]

By this time, the centre of the conflict was South Derbyshire, but by the beginning of April 1868 this fourteen-months-old dispute also was at an end. The men had been defeated by the depressed state of trade and by strike-breakers recruited in Staffordshire. Consequently, when they tried to obtain employment, they were unable to do so since their places had been filled by 'blacklegs';[96] and there was no work available in other trades. The *Nottingham Review* reported on 3rd April 1868 that few of the late lock-outs had been able to find work, and that the associated coal owners of Nottinghamshire, Derbyshire, Leicestershire and Staffordshire would not give them employment unless they produced 'clearance' certificates from their last employers.

This was a difficult time for the Association. The Derbyshire branches had gone out of existence, and the state of trade rendered an early recovery impossible. Indeed, in April 1868 the North Derbyshire coalowners reduced wages by ten per cent because of the fall in coal prices.[97] The depression deepened during 1869 and there was little real improvement until late 1871. From then onwards, recovery was rapid. The declared value of coal exported provides an indication of the movement of trade in this period:

TABLE 1 AVERAGE DECLARED VALUE (F.O.B.)
OF COAL EXPORTED[98]

Year	Value (per ton)		Year	Value (per ton)	
	s.	d.		s.	d.
1863	8	10	1868	9	9
1864	9	4	1869	9	5
1865	9	6	1870	9	6
1866	10	1	1871	9	8
1867	10	2	1872	15	6

The Derbyshire and Nottinghamshire Miners' Association was resuscitated in 1871. Brown had by now moved to Hanley to organize the Staffordshire miners. After the collapse of the Derbyshire branches there was little to keep him in the district, although it seems unlikely that the Association completely disappeared as Dr. Williams implies.[99] Some lodges with checkweighmen almost certainly survived. Thus, Case, William Green (who was the Nottingham District Chairman of the D. and N.M.A.)[100] and William Bolstridge retained their positions as checkweighmen at Cinderhill for some years, and Bolstridge was still acting both as checkweighman and lodge chairman in 1889.[101] The re-formed Derbyshire and Nottinghamshire Miners' Association had William Peach, a Primitive Methodist of Selston, as its Secretary.[102]

The improvement in trade in the winter of 1871–1872 led to improvements in wages at many collieries. The Babbington pits (Cinderhill, Babbington, Newcastle, Broxtowe, Kimberley and Bulwell) had been bought by the Seely Family in 1872.[103] The Seelys unlike their predecessor, North, were liberal employers, and from this time disputes at the Babbington pits were rare. Many employees enjoyed cottages with gardens, pig-sties, coals, water and gas for a weekly rent of 2s. 6d. They also had medical attention, and an entitlement to sick pay in return for a small weekly payment into the Babbington Collieries Field Club.[104]

Agitation amongst the Butterley men started towards the close of 1871, and on December 23rd 1871 the general manager of the company, Sir John Alleyne, had notices posted which conceded the workmen's right to appoint and pay checkweighmen and which specified the conditions on which they were to be allowed to carry out their duties. Coal was still to be weighed at 25 cwt. (of 120 lb.) to the ton for the purpose of wage calculations, however. The men strongly objected to producing 3,000 lbs. of coal for 1 ton's pay, and the agitation intensified.

In a second notice posted three days later, Sir John referred to three demands made by members of a deputation which had met him on the checkweigh issue. These were: that all mineral sent to bank should be paid for; that the number of lbs. to the ton should be reduced; and that Mr. John Smith, Manager of Butterley Park Colliery, should be dismissed. Sir John rejected these demands, and announced that in future he would deal with the men direct, and not with deputations. He concluded:

'I cannot believe that the old respectable and steady Workmen intend to leave their employment on such grounds as these. I shall be willing to meet the Workmen individually or collectively either at this or the Colliery Offices. More deputations I must politely decline. But as I have stated above, I will meet the Workmen employed at each pit individually at their respective pay offices.'

On the following day, 27th December, a letter was sent to the Company by the men's Committee announcing that a general meeting had agreed to accept terms offered to their deputation, namely that the ton should be reckoned as 25 cwt. of 112 lb. (i.e. 2,800 lb. against the previous 3,000 lb.) and that the wages should be calculated by reference to the pit bank weigh machines.

The management, at the same time, awarded an increase of 4d. per ton, but because of the alteration in the calculation of the cwt. (i.e. a reduction from 120 lb. to 112 lb.) 2d. of this was taken back. The men then demanded the same pay for the new weight as for the old, and came out on strike when the management refused to concede this.[105] On 22nd January Sir John issued another poster in reply to a resolution submitted by the workmen and signed by Charles Clark. He deplored the men's action in striking without notice, and said that the demand for the same money for 112 lb. as for 120 lb. was neither reasonable nor just. He again appealed to the 'old and respectable workmen' not to tolerate a prolonged strike.

On the following day, Sir John went into print once more with the following 'Notice to Workmen':

'Any workman being stopped, questioned, or in any way interfered with, in going to or from his work, is particularly requested to immediately inform the foreman under whom he is employed.'

Then on 24th January, despite his recent announcement, he met another deputation of workmen, when it was agreed that the 2d. a ton in dispute should be split. The rate to be paid for the new ton of 2,800 lb. was to be 3d. more than the rate applying in December, and not 4d. more. Sir John also agreed to permit checkweigh committees to operate, but reserved the right to object to up to half the members of each committee.[106]

Then the Butterley men in August 1872 demanded 'to have their coal weighed at 21 cwt. to the ton in the presence of checkweighmen and an advance of 6d. a ton together with fifteen per cent on all day work'.[107] The battle of weights was finally won early in 1873, (following the enactment of the Coal Mines Act of 1872) when wages were calculated on a ton of 2,240 lbs. for the first time. This remained unchanged thereafter.[108]

The loaders at the new Clifton Colliery came out on strike in August 1872 for shorter hours and an increase in pay.[109] Men at the Pinxton Company's pits and at South Normanton, also struck for the right to employ checkweighmen, and for increased tonnage rates and shorter hours. In January 1873 a bitter strike developed at the Eastwood and Moor Green Collieries of Barber Walker and Company in connection with a reorganization of hours occasioned by the fixing of a statutory ten-hour day for boys. The men demanded an eight-hour day.[110]

By 1873 wages had advanced by over fifty per cent since 1871.[111] The newspapers were full of talk about a 'coal famine', and prices were unprecedentedly high. During the first fortnight of July 1872 for example, the price of best coal in Melton Mowbray advanced from 16s. 6d. or 17s. 6d. to 21s. or 22s. Normally, coal prices fall at this time of year.[112] Under these circumstances, the Union prospered. At the Butterley pits, a Conciliation Board was formed in September 1873 at the suggestion of Sir John Alleyne, and for a short time it worked well,[113] but it collapsed as soon as the economic climate worsened.

This was in April 1874 by which time the down-turn in prices and the level of business activity was marked. The Company took off a premium payment of 2d. per ton of coal got; introduced a wider screen at Britain Colliery, which 'robbed' the men of at least 1 cwt.

per ton; stopped making payments for heading and gate ripping in addition to contract prices, and annulled the payment of 1s. 3d. per ton for slack which was no longer saleable. Finally, trucks from South Wales and Cannock Chase where miners were on strike were introduced on 3rd April and the Butterley men refused to load them although the Company maintained that they were not from the firm on strike, but from regular customers. The secretary of the Union Committee for the Butterley pits wrote to Sir John Alleyne about the introduction of these trucks, but Sir John is reported to have replied that 'he would not on any account countermand the loading of any trucks and that as the Board had so grosely (sic) interfeard with the private arrangements of the B. Co. in making the demand he would now see the Board no more, it having broken faith as a *Conciliatory Board*'.[114] The men at Butterley Park, Ripley, Marehay and Hartshay collieries thereupon withdrew their labour on 13th April 1874. Other collieries joined in subsequently. A week later, some 2,000 people assembled on Ripley market place were told that the Union would support them whilst they were out. The D. and N.M.A. now had forty-six lodges, and it was affiliated both to the Miners' National Union and to the rival, more militant, Amalgamated Association of Miners.[115]

However, the South Yorkshire Miners' Association had no intention of pouring thousands of pounds down the Derbyshire drain as it had done in 1868.[116] The D. and N.M.A. could not afford disputes of this magnitude.

Early in May, the Company's General Manager was asked to receive a deputation, but he refused. A mass meeting of strikers to which this news was communicated decided, after a long discussion, 'That the men return to work on Tuesday, and that if any man is ordered to return home after he has gone to work, that no one take his place.'[117]

The men returned, but eleven of their leaders were refused employment. In September 1874 some 1,100 employees of the Butterley Company signed a petition to their employers pleading that these men should be allowed to return to work: '. . . and that the men may be dealt with in harmony with the golden rule "As ye would that men should do unto you, do ye even so unto them" and your petitioners will ever pray.' The Company were unmoved, however, and the men concerned were said to be unable to find colliery employment for the rest of their lives.[118] This is, however, unlikely.

The month of May 1874 saw a series of disputes at the Pinxton pits. For example, there was a stoppage at the No. 8 pit, Top Hard, which started on 1st May and lasted for five or six weeks. The men had to return on the owners' terms.[119] The recession of 1874 deepened into depression. The average declared values of coal exported fell from

20s. 6d. in 1873 to 17s. in 1874, 13s. 1d. in 1875 and 10s. 10d. in 1876.[120]

The Association was faced with a series of wage reductions which it could not do much to resist. The Association had itself become a colliery proprietor in 1874, when it formed the Derbyshire Co-operative Mining Society at Ripley. The Society mined coal on the Stanley Lodge Estate, Ilkeston, where it had purchased the freehold of approximately 104 acres of land. Many of the 3,000 shares of the Society were taken up by colliers. The collapse of the Society in 1878 was said (by James Haslam of the Derbyshire Miners' Association) to be due to its inability to obtain wayleaves over the land of a neighbouring landowner which separated them from the railway line to Derby; but the depressed state of trade must have had something to do with it.[121]

The crisis in the Association's affairs came in midsummer 1875 when the seasonal decline in trade accentuated the effect of the depression. By 17th August, when the Annual Demonstration took place at Ripley, some 7,000 men were out resisting reductions in wage-rates. Dispute pay during the year had cost the Association £1,047 out of a total expenditure of £5,302. The total worth of the Union was £4,953, but this represented little more than a week's strike pay. Edward Smith of Pinxton, an old friend of the Walker family and a trade unionist of long standing, moved a resolution urging that all disputes should be settled by arbitration, and other speakers made it clear that they would prefer disputes to be settled peacefully.[122]

The men who were out belonged to the Butterley, Swanwick and Annesley pits. In each case, notices for reductions had been posted as decided by the owners' association, and since the men refused to accept them, they were locked out. The Butterley men had sent a deputation to see Mr. Strick, the Agent, on 6th August to ask that the notice of a wage reduction should be withdrawn. Mr. Strick received them courteously but said that the reductions were necessitated by the state of trade and the notices could not therefore be withdrawn.[123]

The Morewood's (Swanwick) Colliery, lock-out began in mid-July. The men held firm until late September, when those who lived in colliery houses were given notice to quit.[124] On 29th September, the men agreed to resume work at a ten per cent reduction in rates provided that their leaders were not victimized.[125] This was a vain hope. The eight leaders were dismissed for good. The men therefore came out again, but soon drifted back.[126]

Some of the Butterley men managed to find work at other collieries.[127] The men were also helped by gifts from market traders and other sympathizers,[128] and for spiritual sustenance, they looked to the

Methodists who organized camp meetings and services for them.[129] In mid-September, the M.N.U. sent a deputation to try to arbitrate between the Company and the men, but Sir John Alleyne refused to meet them.[130] In October, the D. and N.M.A. appealed for financial aid to the South Yorkshire Association but the latter refused to help, since their own members had been forced to accept the ten per cent cut which the Butterley men were resisting.[131]

Left without funds to meet the men's essential needs, the Association was unable to continue the struggle. Before long, all the men were back at work on the Company's terms.

At Annesley, the men were forced back for the same reason. Here, they were led by Aaron Stewart, who had come from Leicestershire in 1871, and who was to play an important part in building a strong trade union movement in the coalfield.[132] However, under the circumstances which existed in 1875, no amount of strong leadership could prevent defeat. If the experience of the Clay Cross and other North Derbyshire men is typical, almost all the increases won during the boom were lost during the succeeding four years.

The Association's membership fell steeply from the 6,000 of May 1875.[133] The organization was still in existence in 1878 when Edward Smith, speaking at South Normanton, told the men that the owners had taken advantage of their disunity.[134] The Association was, however, completely moribund by this time, and it was destined to remain so, pending an improvement in the state of trade.

Such an improvement came in 1880. During the cold weather of early January, house coal prices in the Nottingham area rose, and an agitation started among the men for increased wages. This agitation was centred on the Leen Valley, where the new, relatively efficient collieries were situated.[135] Aaron Stewart, who was elected check-weighman at Annesley in this year, had much to do with organizing the agitation;[136] and so had Joseph Hopkin, of Cinderhill. Hopkin, who was a native of Bulwell, had worked at several collieries, including Rotherham, Stavely, and Clowne before settling down at Cinderhill in 1879. He had been dismissed from every pit at which he had worked, on account of his trade union activities.[137]

Apart from Annesley, the Leen Valley pits had been quiet during the struggles of 1874–5. The stoppages at the Erewash Valley pits, which felt the effects of trade recession more than their more efficient competitors, had cost the Leen Valley men a good deal of money without any tangible benefits. It is from this period that the isolationist attitude of the Nottingham district stems. The strength of this feeling in the 1880's can be gauged from the voting for the Nottinghamshire Miners' Association's first agent in 1884. Joseph Hopkin secured 25 votes against only one vote for Edward Smith of Pinxton, who had been one of the leading men in the old D. and N.M.A. The other two candidates polled fifteen votes between them.[138]

Further, when the Nottinghamshire Miners' Federation was formally inaugurated in July 1881, all the lodges represented were from the Leen Valley.[139] Some pits in the Northern part of the County: Silverhill, Hucknall Huthwaite, and South Normanton, had been organized by the South Yorkshire Association until a few years earlier;[140] and for some years, the areas covered by the Derbyshire and Nottinghamshire Associations were to overlap at places like Stanton Hill, South Normanton, Pinxton, Stapleford and, later, Mansfield, so that there were divided loyalties in these districts. Eventually, clear demarcation lines were drawn but even then, the rivalry between the Leen Valley and the Erewash Valley continued within the Nottinghamshire Association.

4. CONCLUSION

The trade unions (of 1844 and 1863) were formed as parts of national organizations, and they owed much to the agents sent into the district by the respective national bodies. They prospered whilst the state of trade was good, but flagged on the downswing of the trade cycle. The 1844 Union, was, to some extent, under the influence of Chartists. The 1863 Union, on the other hand, owed much to the Methodist denominations, which provided it with its leaders.[141]

The Derbyshire and Nottinghamshire Miners' Association, formed in 1863, lasted a good deal longer than the earlier body, whose active life, indeed, was of less than a year's duration. Conditions had changed a great deal since 1844. The big butty system had been replaced at most places by the little butty system, so that the division between butties and others was not nearly so marked. Indeed, whereas the earlier Union had seen the butties as enemies, the later one was largely led by butties and by checkweighmen who were employed by them.

The Unions were successful in securing progressive reductions in the length of the working day. Few men or boys were working more than ten hours a day (plus winding times) in 1875 against the fourteen to sixteen hours which had been common in the early 1840's. Wage-rates were also higher, but to what extent, if at all, this was due to trade union activity, it would be difficult to say. Union agitation certainly precipitated wage increases, but these may have been given in any case. Where the Unions tried to maintain relatively high wage rates on the downswing, they invariably lost.

Perhaps the most important gains made by the men in the 1860's and 1870's were to do with the weighing of coal. The 1860 Act authorized the appointment of checkweighmen, but only where the

Owners were agreeable to such appointments. Agreement was reached on this issue at many collieries (e.g. Cinderhill) in the period 1866–7; but there were other cases where the privilege was not gained until the great coal famine of the early 1870's. This issue was closely bound up with the calculation of the ton for payment purposes. Generally, the colliers had to produce from 25 to 27 cwt. to the ton; and the cwt. itself was sometimes reckoned as 120 lb. One of the aims of 'Billy Brown's' Union was to have wages calculated on the basis of a ton of 2,240 lb.; but generally speaking it was not until the boom of the 1870's that this was conceded.

Despite the appointment of checkweighmen, complaints about the weighing of coal persisted. Allegations that weighing machines were inaccurate, that checkweighmen were either suborned or, if they proved incorruptible, that they were prevented from doing their duty or even refused entry to the premises; allegations regarding excessive deductions for dirt and slack; these were frequent not only in the 1870's but throughout the years. Malpractices were common even in the first half of the twentieth century but there is little doubt that the position was a vast improvement on the period prior to the introduction of checkweighmen.

REFERENCES

1   Lloyd George addressing representatives of the Mining Association and the Miners' Federation of Great Britain, 27th May 1921.
2   Cf. E. H. Phelps Brown, op. cit., p. 219.
3   E.g. H. A. Shannon, 'Bricks—a trade index', *Economica*, New Series, No. 1., 1934, pp. 300–18.
    W. W. Rostow, *British Economy of the Nineteenth Century*, Oxford, 1947, pp. 33–4.
4   S. and B. Webb, *History of Trade Unionism, 1666–1920*, London, 1920, (T.U.) Edn., p. 175.
5   ibid., pp. 181–2.
6   *Nottingham Review*, 26th January 1844.
7   ibid., 15th March 1844.
8   ibid., 29th March 1844.
9   Loc. cit.
10 Loc. cit and 5th April 1844.
11 ibid., 5th April, 26th April and 3rd May 1844. John Dodsley of Skegby was the first owner to concede an increase, on 29th March.
12 ibid., 21st June 1844.
13 ibid., 10th May 1844, 29th March 1844 and 17th May 1844.
14 Whitelock, op. cit., p. 31.
15 *Nottingham Review*, 17th May 1844.
16 ibid., 3rd May 1844.
17 ibid., 24th May 1844.

The wording of the Document used by the colliery owners is given in a letter to the *Nottingham Review* of 12th April 1844
It is as follows:

'. . . That they will not, during their employment at . . . colliery, nor while working under the same master, countenance, join, or in any wise be attached or belong to any lodge, order or association, which is a combination to enable the men to stick out against their employers for any cause, advance of wages or otherwise howsoever.'

18 Wheeler, op. cit., pp. 76–7.
19 *Derbyshire Courier*, 27th April and 4th May 1844 cited J. E. Williams, op. cit., pp. 122–3 and *Nottingham Review*, 29th March 1844.
20 *Children's Employment Commission (Mines) 1842, First Report*, App. Pt. II, p. 263 et seq.
21 *Nottingham Review*, 9th August 1844.
22 ibid., 15th, 22nd and 29th March; 5th, 12th, 19th, 26th April et seq.
23 ibid., 5th April 1844.
24 ibid., 5th April and 17th May 1844.
25 ibid., 19th April and 3rd May 1844.
26 ibid., 29th March and 3rd May 1844. See also F. W. Leeman, *Co-operation in Nottingham*, Nottm. 1963, pp. 13–14.
27 *Nottingham Review*, 12th April 1844.
28 ibid., 15th March 1844.
29 *Derbyshire Courier*, 6th April 1844, cited J. E. Williams, op. cit., p. 92.
30 *Nottingham Review*, 26th July 1844.
31 ibid., 29th March 1844, et seq., Griffin op. cit., I, pp. 7, 8, 14, 24, 180.
32 *Derbyshire Courier*, 6th April 1844, cited J. E. Williams, op. cit., p. 90. For examples of official Primitive Methodist opposition to Chartism in this period, see G. M. Morris, *Primitive Methodism in Nottingham 1815–1932* (Unpublished Ph.D. Thesis) Nottm., 1967, pp. 246–8.
33 *Derbyshire Courier*, 4th May 1844, cited J. E. Williams, op. cit., p. 123.
34 Wheeler, op. cit., pp. 73–5.
35 *Nottingham Review*, 26th April 1844.
36 Wheeler, op. cit., p. 73. Dr. Morris sees this as evidence of Primitive Methodist activity, but there is no evidence that any 'Prims.' were involved at all. See Morris, op. cit., p. 299.
37 R. P. Arnot, *The Miners*, I, London, pp. 41–3, Webb, op. cit., pp. 181–6.
38 His name appears in most issues of the *Nottingham Review* in the period February to May 1844.
39 Arnot, op. cit., I, p. 42.
40 ibid., p. 43.
41 Loc. cit. Rostow gives the trough as 1848—op. cit., p. 33.
42 He signed the first set of Registered Rules of the N.M.A.—see Griffin, op. cit., p. 180. The Clarke of 1844 may have been the same man as the Herbert Clarke who was active in the 1866 Union, and the Walker may have been Henry Walker of Pinxton, who was certainly an active member of both unions.
43 By an old miner in 1894.
44 *Nottingham Review*, 21st June 1844.
45 *Northern Star*, 28th Sept. 1850, 11th and 18th Jan. 1851. (I am indebted to Mr. J. B. Smethurst for these references.
46 J. E. Williams, op. cit., p. 98. Williams relies on indices which mean very little to an industry where truck was widespread, and which in any case have a fairly wide margin of error.
47 Webb, op. cit., pp. 180–232.

48   Arnot, op. cit., p. 44.
49   ibid., pp. 49–50.
50   Webb, op. cit., p. 302. This was the first national conference since 1850, when Jude had tried to re-start the Miners Association of Great Britain and Ireland, ibid., pp. 299–300.
51   Rostow, op. cit., p. 33. As we saw earlier, 3s. 6d. seems to have been the average wage in 1841.
52   *Nottingham Review*, 31st May 1844.
53   Mottram and Coote, op. cit., p. 79. A few contractors, who had as many as 20 men made 'rather more than £1 a week'.
54   *Butterley Statistical Survey, 1856*. Grainger was probably an old man. Neither he nor his wife could read. It was not uncommon for companies to allow aged miners to continue at work for a pittance doing light labouring jobs.
55   *Nottingham Review*, 9th November 1866 reports William Ball as saying that the Union was started three years earlier by himself and another man who had 'died in the work'. On 18th January 1867 the *Review* further reports that Thos. Hill and Charles Barber, a deputation from the D. and N.M.A. to the London Trades Council, stated that their Association had been formed three years earlier and that in September 1866 meetings had been called to get more men to join and 900 did so, whereupon certain companies locked out all Unionists. A similar report is in the *Colliery Guardian*, 19th January 1867.
56   *Royal Commission on Trade Unions, 1867–9*, Eighth Report, Evidence of Brown, Q, 16402, cited J. E. Williams, op. cit., p. 103. The meeting described by Brown cannot have been, as he claimed, the first meeting of the new union.
57   *Nottingham Review*, 16th November 1866. Although Brown, at a meeting at Ilkeston, urged the holers and loaders to join the Union, whatever the butties did—see ibid 11th January 1867.
58   50 and 51 Vict., cap. 58. This provided that an employer could only secure the dismissal of a check weigher on the ground that he had impeded or obstructed the working of the mine; and he had to prove his case before a court of summary jurisdiction.
59   *Nottingham Review*, 23rd March 1866. A 'blackleg', George Barratt, was assaulted by William McWilliams, one of the strikers, on 21st January.
60   *Nottingham Review*, 9th November 1866.
61   Arnot, op. cit., p. 44.
62   *Royal Commission on Trade Unions 1867–9*, Eighth Report, Evidence of Brown, Q, 16417, cited J. E. Williams, op. cit., 103.
63   *Nottingham Review*, 19th October 1866.
     Brown was said to be building houses out of the money which the miners paid him. He hotly denied the story.
64   *Nottingham Review*, 6th July 1866, and 4th January 1867. See also A. R. Griffin, 'Methodism and Unionism in the Nottinghamshire-Derbyshire Coalfield 1844–1890', *Proceedings of the Wesley Historical Society*, Vol. XXXVII, Spring 1969.
65   ibid., 8th February 1867.
66   ibid., 11th January and 8th February 1867.
67   ibid., 8th February 1867.
68   ibid., 22nd February 1867. The lock-out therefore became a strike.
69   Nef. op. cit., II, p. 377. At South Nottinghamshire pits stacking coal at the pit top is still called 'Rooking'.
70   *Nottingham Review*, 12th July 1867.

71 ibid., 15th March 1867.
72 ibid., 17th January 1868 and 12th July 1867. According to Wm. Brown, North agreed to pay for the whole of the tonnage that had been stopped plus half the men's legal costs. *Royal Commission on Trade Unions, etc. Eighth Report.* Q, 16418.
73 ibid., 28th December 1866.
74 ibid., 16th November, 21st and 28th December 1866 and 11th January 1867.
75 ibid., 4th January 1867 and ibid., 18th January 1867. William Brown claimed to have advised the Hucknall men against coming out: he thought they could have obtained a reduction in hours peacefully. If Brown's account is right the dispute was a strike, not a lock-out, but this does not affect the issues involved. Brown's account obscures the fact that this was primarily a dispute about union recognition. He was also trying to gloss over his own militancy, and his evidence needs to be treated with caution. *Royal Commission on Trade Unions, etc. 1867–9 Eighth Report.* Q, 16421–61424.
76 ibid., 25th January 1867.
77 ibid., 16th November 1866. Strangely, Binns had supported the earlier Union in 1850.
78 ibid., 16th November 1866 and 1st February 1867.
79 ibid., 16th November 1866 et seq. See also J. E. Williams, op. cit., pp. 105–115 and Griffin, *Notts. Miners, I*, pp. 12–17.
80 *Nottingham Review*, 26th April 1867.
81 ibid., 4th January 1867.
82 ibid., 16th August 1867. He presumably belonged to the Tidd Pratt family of Newark.
83 ibid., 13th December 1867.
84 ibid., 8th November 1867.
85 J. E. Williams, op. cit., p. 111.
86 Markham, indeed, gave £2,000 to start an anti-Unionist Sick and Accident Fund—See *Nottingham Review*, 6th September 1867.
87 E.g. Pinxton, where the unionists were accused of causing a fire in one pit. See J. E. Williams, op. cit., p. 115.
88 *Nottingham Review*, 18th January 1867.
89 ibid., 11th January 1867.
90 ibid., 25th October 1867.
91 ibid., 8th February 1867 and 31st May 1867.
92 Webb, op. cit., 258–9.
93 *Nottingham Review*, 1st March, 27th September and 6th December 1867.
94 ibid., 22nd November 1867.
95 Cf. T. Ashton, op. cit., p. 9, whose inaccurate implication that the M.N.U. had never concerned itself with wages questions was repeated by Arnot with some slight qualification, op. cit., I, p. 55.
96 *Nottingham Review*, 27th March 1868.
97 ibid., 3rd April 1868.
98 *Colly. Year Book and Coal Trades Directory, 1951 edn.* p. 559, and F. A. Gibson, *The Coal Mining Industry of Great Britain*, etc., Cardiff, 1922, p. 158.
99 J. E. Williams, op. cit., p. 118.
100 ibid., 16th November 1866.
101 *Nottingham and Midland Counties Daily Express*, March 23rd 1889.
102 *Nottingham Daily Journal*, 21st August 1875.
103 *Nottingham Review*, 26th August 1870. Wright & Co. held the collieries for a short time between North's death and Seely's acquisition of the business.

104 *Derbyshire Times*, 17th August 1872, quoted J. E. Williams, op. cit., p. 132, and *Rules of the Babbington Collieries Field Club*.

105 Letter to Workmen dated 20th January 1872 signed J. G. N. Alleyne.

106 Letter to Workmen of 25th January 1872 and poster bearing same date.

107 J. E. Williams, op. cit. p. 132.

108 *Butterley Sales and Output Book*. See A. R. Griffin, 'Checkweighing Arrangements at the Butterley Company's Collieries, 1871–3', *Bulletin of the Society for the Study of Labour History*, Spring, 1969.

109 *Nottingham Daily Journal*, 24th August 1872.

110 J. E. Williams, op. cit., p. 132.

111 ibid., p. 133, and J. Haslam and Others, op. cit.

112 *Nottingham Daily Journal*, 20th July 1872.

113 *Nottingham Daily Journal*, 27th April 1874.

114 Letter to Fitz-Herbert Wright (unsigned) in Butterley Company's archives. Each side was apparently equally sincere in considering that the other had broken faith on conciliation.

115 ibid., 25th April 1874.

116 ibid., 18th and 21st May 1874.

117 ibid., 7th May 1874.

118 Griffin, op. cit., I, p. 18, J. E. Williams, op. cit., pp. 165–167. *Nottingham Evening News*, 12th August 1937.

119 Griffin, op. cit., I, p. 19. This is based on Mr. Job Smith's notebook.

120 Sources *Colly. Year Book and Coal Trades Directory*, 1951 edn., p. 559 and Gibson, op. cit., p. 158.

121 J. E. Williams, op. cit., p. 149.

122 *Nottingham Daily Journal*, 21st August 1875.

123 *Nottingham and Midland Counties Daily Express*, 9th August 1875 and 16th August 1875.

124 ibid., 20th September 1875.

125 ibid., 2nd October 1875.

126 *Nottingham Daily Journal*, 16th October 1875.

127 *Nottingham and Midland Counties Daily Express*, 1st September 1875.

128 *Nottingham Daily Journal*, 16th September 1875.

129 *Nottingham and Midland Counties Daily Express*, 11th September 1875.

130 ibid., 18th September 1875—report of W. Pickard, a member of the deputation.

131 J. E. Williams, op. cit., p. 165.

132 W. Hallam, op. cit., pp. 65–7.

133 *Nottingham Daily Journal*, 29th May 1875.

134 *Ilkeston Pioneer*, 10th January 1878, cited J. E. Williams, op. cit., p. 165. South Normanton had been organized both by the D. and N.M.A. and the South Yorkshire Miners' Association. It withdrew from the latter in July 1876—see Williams, op. cit., p. 168.

135 *Nottingham Daily Journal*, 5th January 1880.

136 Hallam, op. cit., p. 30.

137 Griffin, op. cit., I, pp. 54–5.

138 *N.M.A. Minute Book*, January 19th 1884.

139 *Nottingham Daily Journal*, 30th July 1881.

140 J. E. Williams, op. cit., p. 168.

141 I do not suggest that these two classes were mutually exclusive.

PART II

CHAPTER I

The Exploitation of the Concealed Coalfield 1850—1900

1. INTRODUCTION

The exposed coalfield of Nottinghamshire and Derbyshire lies roughly to the West of a line drawn from Nottingham to Chesterfield. This is the area where the coal seams basset out on to the surface. Wollaton, Bilborough, Nuthall, Kimberley, Selston, Pinxton and Teversal mark the edge of the outcrop, which extends in the North as far West as the Pennines. All the early coalmines were located on this exposed coalfield. Since the coalfield was worked piece-meal, the average pit tended to be small having a 'take' circumscribed by faults, old workings, and competing pits. In 1945, there were still sixty-six collieries with an average labour force of 603 on this exposed coalfield.[1]

In the first half of the nineteenth century, as we have seen, a few collieries just to the East of the exposed coalfield were sunk, mainly by Thomas North and his partners. These collieries were able to use the same means of transport as the Erewash Valley pits of the exposed coalfield: gang-lines, turnpike roads and canals. In the second half of the century, the growth of the railway system encouraged the large-scale exploitation of the top hard seam, well to the East of the outcrop. The phasing of the series of sinkings was largely determined by the demand situation.

The new collieries were mainly centred around the Leen Valley: Newcastle, (Whitemoor) sunk in 1853, Hucknall 1 and 2 sunk in 1861–2, Bulwell in 1867, Annesley in 1865, Bestwood in 1871–2, Linby and Watnall No. 1 in 1873 and Newstead in 1875. Two new mines—Clifton sunk in 1868–9, and Wollaton in 1874, which were outside the Leen Valley, belong to the same complex and are loosely regarded, as are the Babbington pits, as Leen Valley pits.[2] There were other new sinkings on the edge of the concealed coalfield in the Sutton-in-Ashfield area, too: New Hucknall (sunk 1876–9), Teversal (1868), Silverhill (1875) and Sutton (1873).

2. TRANSPORT AND MARKETING

As we have seen, the Erewash Valley pits were served by the Cromford and Erewash Canals, their branches and connections and connecting 'gang-lines'. The Mansfield to Pinxton railway, although horse-drawn, served a useful purpose whilst one proprietor, Thomas North, had built a substantial private branch line intended to be worked by steam-driven locomotives in 1844.

As early as 1832, the colliery owners of the Erewash Valley had determined to promote a railway line to link their pits with Leicester. However, owing to the rivalry between North Midland and Midland Counties railway companies, this line was not built until 1846–7, following the amalgamation of the two companies.[3] It linked the Erewash Valley with London and thus contributed to the more intensive exploitation of the coalfield as the pull of the London market grew. By 1855–6 the Butterley Company's sales in London had reached 73,287 tons, as against the 45,000 tons sold during the twelve months to April 1853, the first year for which any such sales are recorded.[4]

The Midland Railway Company embarked on the construction of a line linking Nottingham to Mansfield in 1847, and this was completed as far as Kirkby by October 1848. It ran through Lenton, Radford, Basford, Bulwell, and Linby. The Company also purchased the old Mansfield to Pinxton Railway, and commenced relaying the line to take steam locomotives. Finished in October 1849, this completed the main line from Nottingham to Mansfield. Subsequently, the line was extended to Worksop. Various branches between the Erewash Valley Extension and the Mansfield to Nottingham line were subsequently built. One of these, opened in August 1869 and linking Basford with Bennerley Junction, served pits in the Hucknall and Watnall area, and, later, Beauvale and High Park Collieries.[5]

The Mansfield line came to serve the Kirkby (Summit and Lowmoor) Newstead, Linby, Annesley, Hucknall and Bestwood collieries.[6] A branch line connecting with the Chesterfield main line at Westhouses and the Mansfield to Worksop line at Pleasley was constructed piece meal between 1861 and 1874 to serve the new Silverhill, Teversal, Sutton and Pleasley collieries as well as the older collieries, like Tibshelf.[7]

The Great Northern Railway opened an Erewash Valley line in August 1875, and a Leen Valley line in 1881.[8] Although the Midland and Great Northern Railways had entered into a Coal Traffic Agreement which provided that 'the rates from the Yorkshire, Derbyshire and Nottinghamshire collieries, carried by either or both companies to London should be equitably adjusted to each other so that, as far as possible, the through charge from the various collieries should be made fair one with the other', competition between the Companies for traffic was beneficial to the colliery owners.[9] Railway rates may not have fallen so low as they would have done in the absence of such an Agreement; but neither did they rise so high as a monopoly might have forced them.

The rapidity with which railway sales expanded may be illustrated by the example of the Butterley Company. In 1849, Rail sales amounted to 62,786 tons. This figure increased gradually year by year until 1852 (109,669 tons) then leapt to 170,588 tons in 1853; 285,063 tons in 1856 and 491,369 tons in 1860. Individual years apart, this total was not greatly exceeded until the 1880's. Rail sales totalled 645,951 tons in 1890 and 961,343 tons in 1900.

Canal sales, on the other hand dropped almost continuously: 30,444 tons in 1856; 29,531 tons in 1860; 19,369 tons in 1870; 31,611 tons in 1880; 16,981 tons in 1890 and 16,733 tons in 1900. Landsales rose from 26,249 tons in 1856 to 92,116 in 1860 and 176,754 tons in 1870, then fell to 91,754 tons in 1880, 55,202 in 1890 and 52,547 in 1900.[10]

In 1856, the Midland Railway carried 867,288 tons of coal from Erewash Valley collieries, of which 240,205 tons were received at London Stations and a further 105,717 tons at Kew Junction for the South Eastern and South Western Railway. Some 145,405 tons came from Pinxton, 133,929 from Pye Bridge and 115,718 from Heanor. Next highest were Cotes Park with 98,829 tons and Langley Mill with 95,162. Sutton, on the other hand, supplied only 76 tons.

Pinxton seems to have been particularly successful in the London market at this early date. In 1852, for example, of the 33,800 tons of coal conveyed to London on the Grand Junction Canal, Pinxton supplied 10,499, although this figure probably includes all coal shipped from Pinxton Wharf. The next highest tonnages are Stoneyford 5,857, Moira 3,859, Loscoe 2,376 and Butterley 2,259. On the other hand, Eastwood's total was only 29½ tons. Strangely enough, in 1867, 337½ tons of coal from Eastwood were conveyed to London by canal despite the development of the railways in the intervening period.

The stimulus which railways gave to the development of the Nottinghamshire-Derbyshire coalfield is indicated in these comparisons:

TABLE 2 COAL OUTPUTS FOR NOTTINGHAMSHIRE AND DERBYSHIRE

	Notts	Derbys		Notts	Derbys
1854	813,474	2,406,696	1874	3,125,176	7,152,944
1864	796,700	4,470,750	1884	5,091,603	8,581,001
1865	1,095,500	4,595,750	1894	6,821,830	11,472,579
1866	1,600,560	4,750,520	1904	8,918,170	15,078,680
1869	1,575,450	5,460,000	1914	11,510,230	16,939,286

(Sources: Royal Commission on Coal, 1871, Vol. III, p. 98 and App. pp. 63, 82 and 92. F. A. Gibson, op. cit., pp. 23 and 24).

3. CAPITAL AND ENTERPRISE

From the middle years of the Century, the demand for coal rose continually. During the period 1853–1862, annual output for Great Britain and Ireland averaged 70,385,000 tons. The average then increased in the following decade (1863–72) to 104,521,000.[11] The pressure of increasing demand caused a general upward tendency in the price-level. In these circumstances, much new capital was sunk into mining enterprises. As we have seen, five new collieries were opened in the Leen Valley alone, between 1867 and 1872.

The period 1871–3, sometimes called the coal famine, saw the declared average value of coal exported rise from 9s. 8d. to 20s. 6d.— a level it was not to reach again until 1916.[12] The prices of coal from the new Clifton Colliery sold by a Nottingham coal merchant, indicate the trend in 1872. Best house coal, for example, rose in price as follows:

TABLE 3. BEST HOUSE COAL PRICES IN NOTTINGHAM[13]
1872

	s.	d.		s.	d.
6th January	14	6	29th June	15	0
2nd March	13	6	10th July	16	0
11th May	14	0	20th July	17	0
22nd June	14	6	27th July	17	6

In March 1873 E. G. Loverseed, a local philanthropist, inaugurated a 'Coal Help Fund' to supply industrious working men, earning not more than 23s. a week, with coal at 10d. a hundredweight. The people of Nottingham, traditionally vociferous on the subject of famine prices, attended mass meetings called to protest at the high price of coal.[14]

Barber Walker and Company had its most profitable year to date in 1873. The capital value of the assets in that year was £187,600, an increase of £138,365 since the valuation of 1856. This capital appreciation is described by Whitelock as 'a tribute to the restraint exercised by the Partners in their withdrawals from earnings over the interim seventeen years'.[15] It is also an indication of the profitability of mining enterprises during the period.

The Butterley Company provides another example of the 'ploughing back' of profits. The partners' capital had appreciated from £30,000 in 1830 to £400,000 in 1860 and £500,000 in 1883. Five years later, the firm became a private limited company with a capital presumably realistically valued, of about £740,000.[16] By the time that the Leen Valley pits became fully productive the 'coal famine' was over, and prices were falling steeply. The average declared value of exported coal fell from 20s. 6d. in 1873 to 13s. 1d. in 1875 and reached its lowest point of 8s. 8d. in 1879.[17]

The number of collieries in production in Great Britain increased from 2,782 in 1869 to 4,933 in 1875, and whilst the demand for coal continued to rise, it did not, in the short run, keep pace with the increase in productive capacity. In 1878, the High Park, Moor Green, Brinsley and New Watnall collieries of Barber Walker made a small profit of £9,000, but this was partly offset by losses on Cotmanhay and Eastwood amounting to £2,550. Barber Walker's sales dropped from 652,007 tons in 1886 to 648,584 tons in 1887 whilst the average selling price dropped from 5s. 5¼d. per ton to 5s. 3d. per ton. The General Manager reported on 1st February 1887:

'Some years ago, we could always command a good price for the produce of our Top Hard Seam of coal, but since the opening of the Leen Valley Collieries the price obtained has been gradually falling, and during the past year the average price has been reduced to the lowest point I have ever known during the whole of my long experience.'[18]

The Leen Valley pits had the advantage of a thick seam of virgin top hard coal, relatively free from faulting. They were new and technologically up to date, and their workings were close to their respective pit bottoms. They tended to expand output as prices fell in order to maintain their revenue and this tendency depressed prices still further. Older pits, whose costs of production were higher, could only rely upon the profits of good years to offset the losses of bad ones. If a boom were too long delayed, such a colliery might have to close.

It is not sufficiently understood that a colliery is quite unlike a factory, which can, without difficulty, be closed temporarily when revenue is insufficient to cover variable cost. If a colliery's revenue is insufficient to cover variable cost, the proprietor may have to decide whether to keep his pit open or to close it for good. This is due to the fact that conditions underground deteriorate quickly when a pit stands: water builds up, roadways settle, and so on. Where a colliery does close temporarily, the cost of maintaining it in good condition is very much higher than with a factory, and may well become prohibitive within a matter of months.

The catalogue of abandonment plans show that quite a number of old collieries in the North of the County closed in this period to be replaced by larger collieries using more efficient equipment. The Skegby pits of John Dodsley for example, were replaced by Sutton Colliery (originally called 'New Skegby') worked by the Skegby Colliery Company in 1873.[19] Dodsley retained the ownership of the land and minerals however. The nearby Molyneux pit, flooded out in 1869, was re-opened after a while, but closed in 1878. The Teversal and Silverhill Collieries of the Stanton Company were sunk a few hundred yards away in 1868 and 1875 respectively.[20]

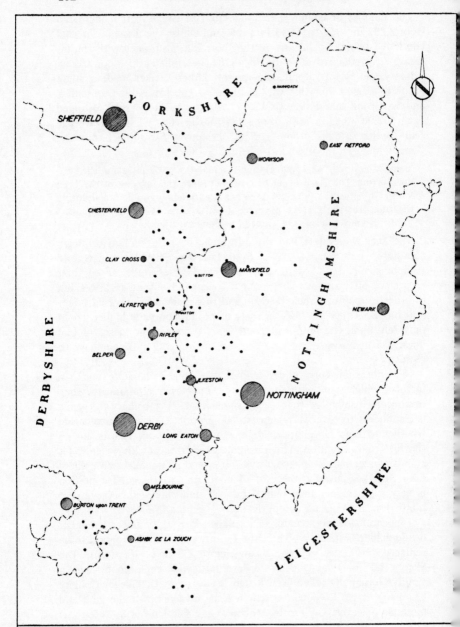

EAST MIDLANDS COALFIELD.

DECEMBER 1960.

Similarly, the Hucknall Huthwaite pits of John, William and Nathan Mellors were replaced by the New Hucknall Colliery the first shafts of which, Nos. 1 and 2, were sunk in 1876–9. William Muschamp was the Company's founder, although he died before it came into legal existence on 1st January 1877. Muschamp had purchased mineral rights from Nathan Mellors for £1,450, from Mrs. Miller, for £1,500, and from the Society of Friends for £120. From J. T. Boot, farmer, surveyor and mining engineer, Muschamp bought surface and mineral rights for £1,400. Other initial expenses, including coal rents, interest, professional charges, the purchase of surveying instruments and Muschamp's expenses over ten years totalled £3,897, plus a premium to the vendor of £6,632 making a total of £15,000. Muschamp's expenses during 1876, which were also reimbursed by the Company, totalled £5,402. The largest item was the £1,169 spent on labour including the manager's salary of £150. In addition, John T. Boot and Co. had received £61 3s. 6d. for professional services.[21] The Company also had royalty rents to pay to the total of £1,190 1s. This included two years' arrears owing to the Duke of Portland at £371 a year; and six years' arrears to various other freeholders at £1 per acre per year.[22]

The old Hucknall (Huthwaite) Colliery apparently closed in 1868 when the Dunsil Seam was abandoned. It would appear, therefore, that there was a gap of about eight years between the closure of the old colliery and the commencement of the New Hucknall sinking, during which time William Muschamp took over the engagements of the Mellors family, for example by paying royalty rents.

The evidence is, however, conflicting. The colliery plans show that working ceased in the Top Hard Seam in 1859 and in the Dunsil Seam in 1868 and yet in plans submitted to Parliament in November 1873, the Midland Railway Company proposed to extend a railway from B. Winning Colliery to Old Hucknall and some work was actually done on the proposed extension shortly afterwards. Again, there was a Hucknall Huthwaite Branch of the South Yorkshire Miners' Association having 67 members in November 1874 and 45 members in April 1876.[23]

During 1877, the sinking of the two shafts was pushed forward quickly. By 30th June 1878 the partners had answered calls to the tune of £47,515 15s. made up as follows:

	£	s.	d.
William Muschamp (Executors)	16,265	16	2
Emerson Muschamp Bainbridge[24]	8,250	0	0
Cuthbert Bainbridge	7,000	0	0
Thomas E. Fenwick	5,999	18	10
J. M. Vickers	5,000	0	0
Robert Robson	5,000	0	0

By the end of the year, it had been necessary to make further calls bringing the total to £52,270. Emerson Bainbridge purchased part of the Muschamp Executors' stock, and he became the Chairman of the New Hucknall Colliery Company Ltd., upon its incorporation in 1879. There were three classes of shares created called respectively 'Fully paid', 'A Ordinary' and 'B Ordinary'. The original share capital of £64,981 was made up as follows: [25]

> 600 'Fully Paid' Shares at £100–£60,000
> 22 'A Ordinary' Shares at £70–£1,540
> 254 'B Ordinary' Shares at £18 10s.–£3,441

The shareholders were the old six partners, plus G. B. Bainbridge with one share valued £18 10s. By 31st December 1884 the number of 'A' Ordinary Shares had increased to 31, and the number of 'B' Ordinaries to 266, bringing the par value of the Company's issued share capital up to £67,091.

The Company's property was valued at £69,881 at 31st December 1879. This included the £4,470 paid for minerals by Muschamp, further minerals bought by the Company for £2,789; and £58,450 paid for plant.[26] This new colliery was, then, a considerable investment. The cost of plant should be compared with the cost of a whim-gin, all the plant necessary at one of the small shallow pits still being sunk on the exposed coalfield. A very efficient type of gin still cost less than £20.[27]

The tendency for the older type of colliery owner operating as a sole proprietor and sharing the capital costs of the enterprise with butties to give way to joint stock companies was a feature of the Leen Valley and district development, too.

With the abandonment of Old Radford Top Hard in 1861 and Catstone Hill, Strelley and the Old Engine pit, Trowell, a few years later, the Middletons severed their connection with the management of colliery enterprises.[28] The Wollaton Colliery Company formed in April 1875—with a capital of £105,000 in £100 Shares—to exploit the newly sunk colliery at the side of the Wollaton Canal, leased the major part of its coal from Lord Middleton.[29] It also took over Radford, where new pits were sunk.

The new colliery at Clifton, sunk by Sir Robert Clifton, also absorbed a lot of capital. Coal was proved in 1867, and the first sod was cut on 19th June 1868.[30] The mining engineer was J. T. Boot. The *Nottingham Review*, referring to the seam struck by the borers at Clifton, said that its 'value and extent hold out most hopeful promises of remuneration to its promoter'. The remuneration did not come quickly enough to be of any use to Sir Robert however, since he died shortly after the pit was opened. In May 1870, Saul Isaacs took a lease of the colliery[31] and in June, he announced that he would meet all accounts which had accrued prior to his taking possession.[32] Fortunately for Mr. Isaacs, the boom of 1871–5 coincided with his pit's period of maximum productivity. The works were completed by June 1871 when Isaacs announced that 'a good supply of coal can always be had at the pit bank'. He described one grade as being 'equal to best Swanwick' and another as 'equal to Pinxton'.[33] Since his transport costs to Nottingham and the towns in the Trent Valley were lower than anyone else's, and much lower, despite the railway, than those of Swanwick or Pinxton, he was placed in a very strong competitive position.

Coal may be regarded, with reservations, as a homogeneous commodity. The quality of coal from a particular seam does not generally vary much, and consumers will usually buy their coal from the cheapest market. There are, nevertheless, differences in coal qualities which colliery proprietors did their best to exaggerate. For example, coal produced from the 'Plymouth' pits at Pinxton sold at higher prices than similar coal from neighbouring pits owned by the same company because it was thought to be of a better quality. Coal from the other pits was therefore often given the Plymouth label in order to attract the higher price.[34] It was because of the effectiveness, albeit over narrow price differentials only, of this artificial product differentiation that Isaacs attached the 'equal to best Swanwick' and 'Pinxton' tags to two of his grades.

The immediate success of Isaacs's enterprise made owners of adjoining property 'anxious to discover whether the same beds exist under their estates'. New pits and ironworks were under contemplation, but did not materialize.[35] Probably it was just as well that they did not. Clifton was not, in the long run, a profitable undertaking. Major W. E. Walker, speaking for the Nottingham and Clifton Colliery Company in 1912 said that in its 44 years, the Colliery had 'never yet paid the shareholders a copper in dividends, and I do not think it likely that it ever will'.[36]

In June 1872 the Sheepbridge and Staveley Coal and Iron Companies jointly leased for eighty years the top hard coal under Col. Webb's Newstead Abbey Estate. The capital required by the Newstead Colliery Company Ltd., a joint subsidiary, was estimated at £120,000.[37]

After 1875, few new collieries were sunk for some years. The depression which affected the coal trade severely, lasted despite a temporary improvement in the early 1880's, until 1888. For the marginal producers, these were difficult years. Thus, the firm of T. H. and G. Small, lessees of an old colliery at South Normanton (called Winterbank or Wincobank) and of Kilburn (or Stanley) Colliery, Derbyshire, went bankrupt in 1885 with liabilities of between £20,000 and £30,000. Winterbank Colliery finally closed in 1889, to be replaced in 1892 by the South Normanton Colliery, owned by a limited company whose principal shareholders were Durham men. The original directors were: A. Mein (chairman), S. Fielden, I. W. Laverick, and T. Young, and its Share capital was £7,000.[38] The neighbouring New Hucknall Colliery Company, which was a much larger undertaking, continued to make profits even in the worst years as the following table indicates:[39]

TABLE 4. SHOWING PROFIT, ETC., OF NEW HUCKNALL COLLIERY CO., LTD. 1881–1889

| Year (or half Year) | Profit | | Wages cost per ton (to nearest 1d.) | Output (Tons) |
	Total	Per ton s. d.	s. d.	
1881 (1st half)	1,973	6·4	3 3 ⎫	
1881 (2nd half)	3,285	5·4	3 3 ⎬	145,923
1882	5,717	8·7	3 0	157,350
1883 (1st half)	7,149	1 9·4	3 0 ⎫	
1883 (2nd half)	3,198	10·7	3 2 ⎬	151,836
1884 (1st half)	2,983	10·5	3 3 ⎫	
1884 (2nd half)	1,358	5·2	3 5 ⎬	130,761
1885	3,318	6·7	3 3	118,225
1886	3,558			
1887	3,079	3·7	2 11	199,719
1888	6,433	5·2	2 10	297,285
1889	13,895	10·1	3 1	330,084

There is no reason to doubt that the new top hard collieries of the Leen Valley were equally successful, with the possible exception of Annesley. The *Nottingham Journal* reported on 22nd March 1884 that the Leen Valley collieries were doing much better than their competitors.

Even the Butterley Company, despite its old pits, continued to produce profits. As we have seen, the partnership's stock was valued at £500,000 in 1883, and £740,000 in 1888, when it was transformed into a limited company.[40] This apparent increase may have been due in part to a more realistic valuation in 1888, but it at least indicates that the Company cannot have been badly hit by the depression in iron and coal. In 1887, the Company acquired land and minerals at Kirkby. The colliery sunk there, which was Butterley's first venture into the concealed coalfield, was to be one of the biggest in the country, generating its own electricity.[41] A brickworks was also constructed next to the colliery.

The New Hucknall Company also acquired land at Kirkby and, in 1894, sank a new colliery—Bentinck—largely out of the profits made at New Hucknall.[42] The Company placed £10,000 in reserve for the 'Kirkby New Winning' in 1892 and a further £5,000 in 1893. In addition, New Hucknall's revenue covered the cost of Bentinck's winding engine (£1,845) and locomotive (£991) both purchased during 1893. The cost of sinking during 1894—£26,943—was similarly covered. During 1895, when sinking costs totalled £35,988, the Company's paid up share capital was increased from £73,240 to £87,120.[43] The estimated value of the Company's property and minerals at the same date was £164,207.

Bentinck started to produce coal (from the Deep Soft Seam) in March 1896 and by the end of the year it had produced 18,827 tons. The total cost of sinking the pit and installing the heavy capital equipment was in excess of £80,000. In addition, coke ovens had been built there. At the end of 1896, the £10,517 spent on coke ovens at New Hucknall some years previously was written off completely, so strong was the Company's financial position.[44]

The bulk of the share capital of the New Hucknall Company was still in the hands of the original partners and their families. Of the capital subscribed at the end of 1896 totalling £111,720, E. M. Bainbridge held £22,125 plus a share in several joint holdings. Of the 53 entries in the list of shareholders, eight relate to Bainbridges, seventeen to Fenwicks, four to Robsons, two to Dawsons, six to members of the Vickers' family, and four to Muschamps.[45]

This resembles the spread of holdings in the Pinxton Company which was converted from a partnership into a Limited Company in 1901. All the original shareholders were descendants of the three partners of 1847, Edward Thomas Coke, James Salmond and George Robinson, although in the meantime, the twenty-eighth shares into which the partnership's capital had been divided in 1847 had been subdivided into 1,120th shares. The value of the properties conveyed in 1901 was £84,000.[46] The most probable reason for the decision to form a limited company was the need to raise fresh capital to reduce the expense of underground haulage. Electric generating equipment which provided lighting on the surface, as well as power for haulage underground was erected in 1901. In 1904 the Pinxton Company formed a joint subsidiary with the Coppée Company of Brussels to erect and operate a by-product plant with fifty-two coke ovens. This undertaking, called the Pinxton Tar Distilleries, provided, as did the smaller plant at New Hucknall, a market for large quantities of slack, which would otherwise have been virtually unsaleable.[47]

The Barber Walker partnership had its Colliery Works and Stock valued at £49,235 in 1856. The depression of the late 1850's resulted in the closing of several of the older collieries. The profit for 1858, at £3,113, was considered low by the general manager although it is in fact over 6 per cent on the capital of roughly £50,000. The new High Park Colliery near Moor Green, sunk to the Top Hard seam in 1860 after delays occasioned by flooding, strengthened the Partnership's competitive position. The pit was a large one, and the 6 feet thick seam only 195 yards deep. This was the first colliery in Nottinghamshire to produce 1,000 tons a day, although it was some time before this was achieved.[48] In 1872, the general manager of the Company contrasted his policy of financing new works from profits accrued in the good years with that of other companies which, according to him, raised new capital for each new pit.[49]

In 1872 the Moor Green Colliery, having two 13 ft. diameter shafts some 286 yards deep, went into production. Its winding engines and sidings cost over £10,000, and the cost of sinking, set against current revenue, had produced 'losses' in the balance sheets for the previous two years. In the Spring of the year, sinking commenced at the New Watnall Colliery, which was to be the Company's largest colliery to date.[50] Despite the expense of sinking Watnall and of opening up the Deep Soft and Deep Hard Seams at Brinsley and Underwood, 1873 was the most profitable year Barber Walker had experienced.[51] As we have seen, the capital assets in that year were valued at £187,600, an increase of £138,365 since 1856, an average annual increase of £8,139.

The depression which developed in 1876 caused a drop in the Company's vend of 70,000 tons. The collieries went on to half-time working and 429 fewer men were employed. Two brickyards were closed, and work was stopped on the erection of workmen's cottages.[52] The profit for 1878 was down to £6,450 representing a return of about 3½ per cent on the capital then employed. By Barber Walker standards, this was disastrous.[53]

By 1890, which was the best trading year since 1873, the Company employed 3,041 persons. During the year, the pits, working full time, produced 995,990 tons, half as much again as in 1887, when output was 648,584 tons. In 1899 it topped the million mark for the first time.[54]

By contrast, the Annesley Colliery would appear to have been undercapitalized. This colliery was sunk in 1865 by the Worswick family who came from Leicestershire.[55] (The Worswicks worked Coleorton and Swannington Collieries in Leicestershire until about 1879, by which time the pits were about worked out. Besides sinking Annesley, they also put money into the nearby Linby Colliery.) It seems likely that the earnings of the good years had been distributed to the partners, insufficient funds having been put to reserve. The colliery was ventilated by furnace and its plant was described by a consulting mining engineer in 1901—when the colliery was little more than thirty-five years old—as antiquated. The lease of the top hard seam, which was due to run out in 1904, was offered to Barber Walker but they decided not to take it.[56] It may be, of course, that the Annesley Company's financial policy was the result of the short lease they held. There would be little incentive to sink a great deal of capital into the project with such a short tenure. The lease was taken over by a new syndicate in the autumn of 1904. This new company, which was headed by Mr. Chambers of the Hardwick Colliery Co., also bought the plant belonging to the Worswicks.[57] Again, when Annesley was bought out by the New Hucknall Company in 1924 the new owners had to spend considerable sums on new plant, equipment and development. The top hard seam was, by then, worked out, and the colliery had suffered from a period of mis-management which took the New Hucknall Company some years to put right.

The second half of the nineteenth century saw the growth of a body of mining engineers. As we have noted, the only salaried official employed by the average colliery owner in the early nineteenth century was the agent (called the bailiff or ground bailiff in some districts). The actual day-to-day management of most pits was in the hands of butties. The agent's primary duties were to bargain with butties on getting prices, to negotiate leases, to make surveys and draw plans, and to sell the coal. He had little interest in safe systems of working. The increasing amounts of capital tied up in colliery enterprises as the scale of operations grew made colliery owners conscious of the need to employ salaried staff to protect the works. This tendency was reinforced by legislation providing for safety rules to be made and enforced.

The 1850 Act (13 and 14 Vict., cap. 100), which made it compulsory for plans to be kept and to be made available for inspection by an Inspector of Mines, had much to do with the creation of a profession of mining engineering. John Boot was the agent for John Dodsley earning a guinea a week in the late 1840's. After the passing of the 1850 Act, however, he left Skegby to practice as a consultant mining engineer and surveyor, though he did other work, too. He farmed the Windmill estate at Hucknall Huthwaite and he acted as an estate agent besides his purely mining work. He produced plans for all kinds of purposes. His son, J. T. Boot, was brought up to the business, and other people were employed too.[58] G. H. Bond and R. G. Coke were, like the Boots, kept busy with mining surveying work of one kind and another, chiefly for valuation and royalty assessment purposes.[59]

People like Boot acted for the smaller proprietors, who could not afford full-time professional staff. This kind of arrangement could be unsatisfactory as in the case of Molyneux Colliery where Boot considered that his only duty of care was to the landlord, the Countess Carnarvon, and not to Eastwood, who worked the colliery. Eastwood and his partner Swingler were in business as iron-masters at Derby where they had two works with twenty-five puddling furnaces and three rolling mills. They left the running of the colliery to unlettered and irresponsible officials and the 1869 inundation was a natural consequence of this unsatisfactory position. The larger concerns employed engineers of their own like W. Bean, the Butterley Company's Agent at Portland Colliery in the mid-nineteenth century, who was called upon to act as a consultant engineer in connection with litigation between Barber Walker and Co., and the Nottingham and Grantham Railway Company in 1861.[60]

However, even some of the larger proprietors were advised by viewers with extensive practices. For example, J. T. Woodhouse, who acted as viewer for North and others in the 1860's, told the Select Committee of 1873 that he had worked in Leicestershire, Warwickshire, Derbyshire and Nottinghamshire. Men like this took articled pupils, who became viewers or managers themselves when they had served their time. Usually, by the 1860's, where a peripatetic viewer superintended a fair-sized colliery, the proprietor would employ an underviewer—usually a practical collier with elementary technical knowledge—to exercise daily supervision and to report as necessary to the viewer.

The 1872 Act[61] which specified that each mine must be under the care of a certificated manager, gave impetus to the development of mining engineering as a separate profession. Further, it gave emphasis to a process which was already apparent—the tendency towards specialization. Surveying became increasingly a separate function for which, eventually, a Home Office examination was devised. The larger companies employed commercial managers to take over the buying and selling functions; whilst the introduction of modern machinery in the twentieth century made necessary the employment of mechanical and electrical engineers.[62]

The colliery manager had, however, two duties which were, to some extent, mutually incompatible. He owed a duty to the State to see that all the operations of the mine were carried out with safety and that all the equipment conformed to the statutory requirements. He also owed a duty to his employers to see that production costs were kept down and that revenue was maximized.

In contrast to people like Bean of Butterley and Harrison of Barber Walker who spent the whole of their working lives in the district, there were other colliery managers who moved around. For example, Henry Lewis who managed first Annesley and then Linby (from about 1894) came from Leicestershire with the Worswicks.

Despite the growth of joint stock companies, individuals still assumed entrepreneurial functions in the coalmining industry. We have already seen what a very substantial stake Emerson Bainbridge had in the New Hucknall Company. Besides being the major shareholder and chairman, Bainbridge was also the consulting engineer. The legal business of the Company at the turn of the century was in the hands of Featherstone Fenwick, one of the directors who practised as a solicitor in Newcastle-on-Tyne. Thomas Day, the company secretary, ran the office from day to day just as the colliery manager ran the pit from day to day; but effective management was still exercised. by Bainbridge and Fenwick.[63]

Similarly, the Barber family exercised a considerable degree of personal control of the Barber Walker Company after its incorporation. Some members of the family were mining engineers, whilst others were solicitors.[64]

The Wright family occupied much the same position in the Butterley Company.[65] Of the smaller companies, the Seelys retained control of Babbington, the Ellis family of the Sherwood Company, and the Bayleys of the Digby Company; whilst James Oakes and Company remained a private family concern. So, too, did Denby (Drury-Lowe family) and Swanwick (Palmer Morewood). Effective control of the Pinxton Company, on the other hand, went out of the hands of the Coke family after the Company's incorporation in 1901. Thereafter, salaried officials exercised effective control, although there were still two members of the family (Gen. E. S. D'Ewes Coke and Col. Basil E. Coke) on the board of directors in 1936.[66]

In all this, there was no room for the butty. He remained, but only as a superior workman in charge of producing coal from one stall. His span of control would not normally exceed two or three; although there were exceptional cases, as at Bestwood in the 1880's where each butty had several stalls. Increasingly, the deputy was taking responsibility for maximising production from his district. The unions deplored this, and attempted to have a deputy's duties restricted to securing the safety of the men.[67] The need to have a deputy on each district was dictated by the provisions of mining legislation which made it illegal, for example, for ordinary workmen to fire shots.[68] However, the types of duties exercised by a foreman in a factory were superimposed on the deputy's safety functions. As the butty's importance as an organizer of production declined, so that of the deputy grew. With the development of conveyor mining in the twentieth century, it was to grow still further. Curiously enough, however, the new collieries around Mansfield, sunk between 1890 and 1925, reintroduced butties who remained powerful until face conveyors rendered the system completely anachronistic.

4. LABOUR

Throughout the second half of the nineteenth century, the demand for coal mining labour grew, reaching its peak in 1920. During the period 1872–83, the number of wage-earners employed above and below ground averaged 482,000; the average for the next decade was

552,000; for the period 1893–1902 it was 713,000; for the following decade 936,000; and for 1913 to 1922 1,068,000.[69]

Between 1874 and 1920 the number of men employed underground in Nottinghamshire increased from 9,099 to 41,979; and the number employed both above and below ground increased from 12,228 to 52,883—a four-fold increase.[70] The increased numbers were no doubt supplied in part by the natural increase in the mining population. It was certainly true of this period that miners' sons were expected to follow their fathers into the pit. In the more isolated parts of the county—Pinxton and Selston, for example, there was little opportunity for employment outside the industry anyway. Children played at pits before they went down, and for the average boy in a mining village the thought of going anywhere else but to the colliery did not enter his head.

Even for boys living in places like Basford, where other work was available, underground pay, coupled with what was expected of them, took them to the pit. Boys aged thirteen were paid a basic 1s. 6d. per day at Pinxton in 1902, and 1s. 8d. per day at Eastwood in 1908. The actual wages paid were higher than these basic rates, an average rate of 2s. a day being a conservative estimate.[71] A boy of thirteen would be lucky to earn more than 5s. a week in any other job.[72]

At the Babbington (Cinderhill) Collieries, it was customary for the manager to interview men whose sons were known to be about to leave school. He would say: 'Tell your Johnny to start ganging at No. 4 Pit on Monday morning,' or words to that effect.[73] This happened invariably with those living in Company houses, and they formed a substantial proportion of the labour force. Men who lived away from the pit enjoyed a greater degree of independence.

The provision of housing attracted adults to a particular pit, too. Whilst a pit was being sunk, temporary accommodation would have to be found for the sinkers, many of whom moved, like the Irish navvies of the canal and railway building era, from place to place. When New Hucknall was sunk, six wooden huts were bought from Blackwell to house the sinkers. Presumably, they had filled the same function at Blackwell. As work proceeded with the pit, houses would be built too so that a substantial nucleus of the future labour force would be housed in proximity to the colliery. At New Hucknall, £14,235 was spent on workmen's cottages; and similar provision was made at Bentinck.[74] At Annesley, Bestwood, Newstead and Stanton Hill, new villages were built by the companies concerned.

Some men were attracted into Nottinghamshire from other districts, like the Leicestershire people who came to work at Hucknall, Annesley and Linby. Between 1874 and 1884, when Nottinghamshire's labour force grew from 12,228 to 15,333, Leicestershire's fell from 4,878 to

4,618.[75] This movement of men cannot, however, have been so significant after 1890, when all districts were expanding: the Midland districts more than most. Warwickshire expanded its labour force from 5,572 to 19,068 between 1890 and 1914; similarly, Leicestershire expanded its labour force from 5,358 to 10,339. Nottinghamshire continued to recruit from Leicestershire but the reverse process also took place although on balance Nottinghamshire no doubt gained. Derbyshire, whose labour force roughly doubled between 1874 and 1920; and Staffordshire, which also expanded much less rapidly than Nottinghamshire, undoubtedly suffered net losses of men to Nottinghamshire throughout the period, too.[76]

Further, we know that men came into mining from other employments. That they were prepared to do so is due partly to the high wages paid in mining in comparison with wages paid in agriculture and manufacturing industry; partly to the fact that houses with low rentals were available at most pits and that coal was supplied at concessionary rates;[77] and partly to the greatly improved conditions in the more up-to-date mines. The conditions under which miners worked in the first half of the century: long hours in ill-ventilated workings with uncomfortable, if not dangerous, shaft-riding facilities, were a positive bar to the entry of many people into the industry. Each improvement in working conditions would have the effect of increasing the potential labour force at each level of earnings. The Leen Valley pits became particularly attractive to work in. They were all fairly new; they were profitable pits paying higher than average wages; from 1892 or earlier they did not work on Saturdays;[78] and from 1895 the Hucknall men enjoyed an eight-hour day.[79]

The miner of the Leen Valley in the last quarter of the nineteenth century earned an average wage in excess of 5s. a day, (by 1900, indeed, a faceworker could expect 7s. 10d. a day)[80] compared with £1 a week at the most for a farm labourer working much longer hours. Agricultural wages in the south of England, where farmers did not have to compete for labour with industrial employers, were no more than 13s. or 14s. a week.[81] Consequently, even a few southern farm labourers found their way into the Nottinghamshire coalfield. Again, let us compare the wages of colliers with those of industrial workers. In 1900, a skilled fitter could earn something like 36s. a week in a large town in the provinces.[82]

Similarly, colliery craftsmen (e.g. fitters, blacksmiths or joiners) working in the Erewash Valley were paid 5s. 11d. a shift in June 1914: which reflects the level of earnings of craftsmen in the engineering and building industries. The average rate for piece-work coal getters in the same district was 9s. 10¼d., and for day paid coal getters, 6s. 10¼d. In the Leen Valley, the disparity was even greater. The rate for a

I

craftsman was 5s. 6¼d., for a piecework coal getter, 9s. 8¼d. and for a day paid coal getter, 8s. 2¼d. Even the unskilled labourer working underground in the Leen Valley received 8d. a day more than a skilled surface craftsman.[83] An unskilled labourer going underground could therefore expect to increase his income considerably.

It would appear that the wage position of colliers had improved relative to that of other workers during the second half of the nineteenth century. In the Butterley survey of 1856, farm labourers are shown as earning 13s. or 14s. a week, surface labourers about the same; 'engineers' (i.e. winding enginemen) between 15s. and 18s., joiners and carpenters 20s., wheelwrights 21s. or 22s. and banksmen 18s. to 20s. Colliers' wages varied widely, but 5s. per day was about the maximum, and 15s. to 20s. a week the norm. There were, by this time, little butties (stall men or stall's men as they were called in the Survey) who made what they were able to earn, which would no doubt be considerably more than a pound a week in many cases. By and large the collier was better paid than the farm labourer or surface labourer, little if any better paid than enginemen and banksmen, and slightly worse paid than skilled surface craftsmen. Furthermore, even the farm labourer had the advantage of a regular 13s. or 14s. a week, whereas the collier's earnings varied widely with the state of trade. However, by the early years of the twentieth century, as we have seen, colliers were considerably better paid even than skilled craftsmen.

The influx of men from other occupations was accentuated during the boom years. Thus, the numbers employed in the mines went up from 510,284 in 1887 to 606,509 in 1890 nationally, and from 17,018 to 20,390 in Nottinghamshire.[84] The leaders of the Miners' Federation expressed their concern at this increase. Frank Hall of Yorkshire, speaking at a Conference in 1890, said:

'Since the coal trade had improved, their pit banks had presented a similar spectacle to what they did in 1872, and they were again being visited by farm labourers. He did not say that out of any disrespect to their agricultural friends, but, he did say "Every man to his trade". Let agriculturalists therefore stick to the land and they as miners would stick to their trade in the coal pits.'

Nottinghamshire's William Bailey said frankly:

'At a time like the present, when they were striving to get better wages, it was very important that they should try to prevent anyone who chose to apply from being allowed to go down the mine. The object aimed at in employing them was not so much that they might get coal as that men should be so plentiful as to make it easy to run down wages.'

The Miners' Federation therefore proposed that it should be illegal to employ at the coal face any man who had not entered the industry before the age of 16.[85] They were not able to obtain the legislation they sought, however, and the influx continued.

Bailey's statement as to the owners' motives in accepting so many employees is not without justification. Colliery owners tended to engage sufficient labour to cover their needs at times of maximum demand. Now, the demand for coal is seasonal, and since a pit had sufficient labour to satisfy the maximum winter demand, it follows that in summer time, it had a surplus of labour. Short-time working in the summer months was therefore the rule. Further, a substantial number of men were 'market men', that is, men with no regular jobs to go to. Each day, they had to report to an official either on the pit top or, more likely, underground, who would either allocate them to a particular job or send them home. A large 'market' was used to depress wage-rates; and it reinforced the disciplinary powers of the butties, who would quickly return a man to the market if he failed to exert himself to their satisfaction.

The influx of men from other occupations, mainly frame-work knitting and agriculture, created difficulties for colliery owners, however. A witness before the *Select Committee on the Causes of the Present Dearness and Scarcity of Coal, 1873*, estimated that it took three years to make an agricultural labourer into a collier, because they tried to use tools in restricted spaces in the same way as they would above ground. More adaptable in some ways (probably because they were quicker-witted) were the framework knitters. The Worswicks in the Leen Valley employed a large proportion of ex-framework knitters successfully. Thomas North, on the other hand, had endless trouble with them. They started work poorly clad and undernourished with their hands soft; and they brought with them their undisciplined habits. The Babbington ex-framework knitters were notorious for the celebration of 'Saint Monday', and absenteeism was also bad on Tuesdays. Why North's experience should have been different from that of Worswick is difficult to say. The fact that Linby and Annesley had such a strong nucleus of men who had followed their employers from Leicestershire may have had something to do with it.[86]

5. CONCLUSION

Throughout the second half of the nineteenth century, the tendency was for the price of coal to move upwards, although this long-term trend was obscured by short term fluctuations. Peaks occurred in 1854, 1861, 1867, 1873, 1884, 1890 and 1900. Troughs occurred in 1851, 1860, 1863, 1869, 1879, 1887 and 1896. The average declared value of coal exported at successive peaks in this period rose as follows: [87]

TABLE 5 SHOWING TREND OF COAL PRICES FROM 1848 TO 1900
(To nearest 1d.)

Year	Value (F.O.B) s. d.	Average pit head price s. d.
1848	7 8	
1854	9 7	
1861	9 0	Not available
1867	10 2	
1873	20 6	
1884	19 2	5 5
1890	12 5	8 3
1900	16 6	10 10

During the upswing of a trade cycle, new collieries were sunk in large numbers. The period of greatest material investment was during the upswing which culminated in 1873. Material investment in the coal industry, particularly when it takes the form of new sinkings, is 'lumpy'. One or two new collieries may well double the output in a particular district. Because the capacity of the industry cannot readily be expanded the short-term effect of an increase in the demand for coal when the industry is already working to capacity is to send prices up sharply, as happened in the early 1870's. This induces *entrepreneurs* to invest in new collieries which usually come into production when the trade cycle is already past its peak, thus pushing prices down. This accounts in part for the violence of the short-term fluctuations in the price of coal in our period. These fluctuations must not be allowed to obscure the secular movement of prices. The average pit head price of coal in 1900 was double the 1884 price; and the average value of exported coal in 1900 was 120 per cent higher than in 1850.[88]

The size of the industry increased too. The average annual output in the decade 1893–1902 at 203,323,000 tons was almost treble the average annual output (70,385,000) of the decade 1853–1862.[89]

In Nottinghamshire, the 1860's and 1870's saw the opening up of the Leen Valley, whose prosperity was founded upon the profitability of the top hard seam. Towards the end of our period, pits were also coming into production in the Mansfield district. These developments were facilitated by the growth of an integrated railway system. The new pits were large, in comparison with the old pits of the Erewash Valley. The very considerable amounts of capital required to open them out were provided in the main by limited liability companies. The old private owners still retained a substantial degree of control in many cases, however. This is true of the Barber, Ellis, Seely, Bayley and Oakes families. On the other hand, landowners like Lord Middleton and the Cokes of Pinxton allowed the management of coal-mines to pass out of their grasp. In future, their connection with the mining industry was to be restricted in the main to the receipt of royalty rents. The day-to-day management of the pits, which had, in earlier times, been in the hands of butties (in some cases steavers and butties) loosely supervised by Agents now required a hierarchy of salaried officials to comply with the regulations as to safety contained in the Coal Mines Acts of 1850 and later, and to safeguard the owners' capital equipment. Deputies, who were responsible primarily for the safety of the men on their respective districts, concerned themselves increasingly with ensuring the maximum output of good quality coal. They were, as yet, however, more concerned with quality than quantity. The butties, who were now as a rule small men having charge of no more than a stall each, ensured the maximization of output.

The rapidity with which the new techniques of production and systems of management replaced the old has perhaps been underestimated in the past. In 1841, all the pits in Nottinghamshire relied largely, and in most cases entirely, on natural ventilation; all pits used hazel corves for winding coal (the men having to ride the shaft clinging to the rope or chains), the headroom in all mines was the height of the seam or an inch or two more; underground haulage was by exertion on the part of boys and donkeys; and all pits were run by big butties.

The next quarter of a century saw a complete change. Many old mines went out of existence in the 1840's and 1850's, and many new, modern mines were sunk. All these new mines had furnace ventilation (soon to be replaced in most cases by fans) cages and guides; decent roadways and, after a time if not at once, underground haulages. Further, they were run on the little butty system with salaried officials taking charge of operations.

Further, the few collieries which had been established on the old system of working and which continued in production, were improved in all these various ways (with one or two exceptions). Portland Colliery may be taken as an example. The No. 1 Shaft was sunk in 1821, and in 1841 this colliery was being operated much like any other in the county. However, by the 1850's, it had been converted into a modern colliery. The improved equipment made possible a big increase in output. As against the 54,342 tons of 1824, Portland produced 94,923 tons in 1859, indicating a capacity of 500 tons a day or more.

So far as organization is concerned, the Butterley Statistical Survey of 1856 makes no mention of butties but does include a number of *stall's men* (i.e. little butties having charge of one stall or maybe a few stalls on one face). By 1869, the Molyneux mine, which still relied on natural ventilation and primitive winding facilities, was regarded as altogether out of the ordinary and the nearby Skegby Colliery was probably the only one in Nottinghamshire still run by big butties. Within a few years, both were closed.

It would not be an exaggeration to say that the coming of the railway in the late 1840's transformed the Nottinghamshire coalfield within little more than a decade. A large number of small pits gave way to a much smaller number of relatively large collieries. Further, whereas the small pits of the 1840's were not substantially different from those of the eighteenth, or even the seventeenth century—the only real improvement being the introduction of steam power in winding and pumping—the new collieries were modern ones which changed little in organization or equipment until the twentieth century. For Nottinghamshire at least it is misleading to say that mining did not undergo an industrial revolution. The changes which we have here summarized were revolutionary both in scope and in tempo, being completed in a quarter of a century or less.

These changes resulted in a considerable improvement in productivity in the short term; but, as we saw earlier, all such improvements in productivity are gradually eroded away as the working faces move further and further out from the pit bottom; and as deeper and less easily worked seams replace the shallower and more easily worked ones. Further, when one seam has been won from an area, workings in other seams in the same area will face problems of roof control which again will reduce productivity. Thus, when Pilsley Colliery, Derbyshire, was thirty years old (in 1895) its 1,000 men produced 1,200 tons a day from three seams, giving a productivity little better than a bell pit.[90]

The introduction of the little butty system was accompanied by an anachronistic relaxation in the division of labour. In 1841 the Children's Employment Sub-Commissioner noted (at, e.g., the Portland pits) that the butty employed specialists, separately paid, for holing, loading, hammering (i.e. breaking down the coal) and setting supports ('woodmen'). The little butty and his assistants, on the other hand, carried out all the coal-face operations (except holing as a rule) working as a team. It seems, therefore, that there was a greater degree of specialization in the first half of the nineteenth century than in the second half.

The expansion of the industry in the second half of the century, accompanied by higher prices and wages, brought many people from other occupations, particularly farming, into the industry. This inflow of 'green' labour was greater when trade was booming than during periods of depression, and was one of the factors responsible for the fall in productivity which was so marked a feature of the mining industry from the 1880's. A substantial proportion of new entrants into the industry were still drawn from mining villages, however. Miners' sons followed their fathers into the pits partly because of the lack of opportunities outside, partly because mining wages, particularly for juveniles, were higher than wages in competing occupations anyway, and partly because it was the done thing. Generally speaking, the collier's son was destined for the pit from birth.

Despite temporary setbacks, the mining community of the second half of the nineteenth century exuded Victorian optimism. Miners and mine-owners were becoming increasingly prosperous in an increasingly prosperous world. There seemed no reason to doubt that this trend would continue indefinitely in the twentieth century.

APPENDIX A

OUTPUT, NUMBER OF PERSONS EMPLOYED, AND OUTPUT PER PERSON
EMPLOYED, IN NOTTINGHAMSHIRE 1874–1920

Year	Output tons	Persons employed Underground	Surface	Total	Output per person employed Underground	Overall
1874	3,125,176	9,099	3,129	12,228	343	255
5	3,265,368	9,618	3,095	12,713	339	256
6	3,582,995	10,294	3,311	13,605	348	263
7	3,877,322	10,182	3,210	13,392	380	289
8	4,106,392	10,633	3,278	13,911	386	295
9	4,316,954	10,772	3,459	14,231	400	303
1880	4,432,393	10,357	3,235	13,592	427	326
1	4,758,060	10,670	3,374	14,044	445	338
2	4,957,725	11,056	3,279	14,335	448	345
3	5,315,880	11,795	3,491	15,286	450	347
4	5,091,603	11,963	3,370	15,333	425	332
5	5,285,178	12,454	3,520	15,974	424	330
6	5,361,718	12,593	3,554	16,147	425	332
7	5,596,075	13,291	3,727	17,018	421	328
8	5,929,666	13,803	3,577	17,380	429	341
9	6,582,582	14,917	3,936	18,857	441	349
1890	6,861,976	16,540	3,850	20,390	414	336
1	7,221,047	17,342	4,170	21,512	416	335
2	7,159,750	18,093	4,202	22,295	395	321
3	5,328,838	18,676	4,445	23,121	285	230
4	6,821,830	18,769	4,502	23,271	363	293
5	6,564,859	18,707	4,827	23,534	350	278
6	6,623,529	18,051	4,708	22,759	366	291
7	6,970,424	18,337	4,687	23,024	380	302
8	7,770,047	19,590	4,909	24,499	396	317
9	8,224,441	20,159	5,117	25,276	407	325
1900	8,626,177	21,507	5,475	26,981	401	319
1	8,198,267	22,159	5,624	27,783	369	295
2	8,656,570	23,538	5,972	29,510	367	293
3	8,703,025	23,869	6,300	30,169	364	288
4	8,918,170	24,811	6,264	31,075	359	286
5	9,309,360	25,346	6,341	31,687	367	293

APPENDIX A—*continued*

Year	Output tons	Persons employed Underground	Surface	Total	Output per person employed Underground	Overall
1906	10,414,859	26,434	6,730	33,164	393	314
7	11,728,886	28,494	6,921	35,415	411	331
8	11,028,639	29,295	7,278	36,573	376	301
9	11,106,702	30,500	7,351	37,851	364	293
1910	11,180,353	30,657	7,206	37,863	364	295
1	11,623,250	31,586	7,761	39,347	368	295
2	11,122,832	31,791	7,665	39,456	349	281
3	12,394,491	32,461	7,921	40,482	380	306
4	11,510,230	32,684	8,336	41,020	352	280
5	11,800,572	30,300	8,176	38,485	389	306
6	12,347,150	32,216	8,559	40,775	383	302
7	12,914,619	34,154	8,682	42,836	378	301
8	11,823,493	33,459	8,757	42,216	353	277
9	11,347,311	39,442	10,035	49,477	287	229
1920	12,119,398	41,979	10,904	52,883	288	229

Source: F. A. Gibson, op. cit., p. 24.

APPENDIX B

COALS TRANSPORTED TO LONDON
BY RAIL IN 1870 (TONS)
FROM NOTTINGHAMSHIRE COLLIERIES

	By L.N.W.R.	By G.W.R.	By G.N.R.	By M.R.
Annesley	2,297	529	5,341	24,202
Babbington*	2,245	1,179	13,617	25,251
Cotmanhay	2,442		2,606	6,506
Eastwood	2,455		6,464	8,564
Hucknall	1,077	56	3,297	28,183
Mexboro'	95	4,538		
Plumtree	991		61	3,658
Portland	545			2,713
Radford	30			
Retford	747	10		
Skegby	144		14	2,232
Teversall	159	24	389	3,031
Hill Top	21			
New Birchwood	15,698	11,718	17,609	22,156
Pinxton	11,528	8,064	30,668	20,524
Pye Bridge	5	178		4,542
Upper Birchwood	836		961	319
Cotes Park		156		7,888
Digby			109	2,339
Shireoaks			587	1,752
Sutton			69	

*Includes coal shipped from Basford (presumably Newcastle Colliery).
Source: Royal Commission on Coal, 1871, Vol. III, Appendix 124, pp. 106–111.

APPENDIX C

SALES OF COAL FROM EREWASH VALLEY COLLIERIES 1803–1869

	Tons		Tons		Tons
1803	254,268	1819	262,722	1834	295,473
1804	234,474	1820	313,877	1835	343,154
1805	235,004	1821	331,840	1836	377,103
1806	267,204	1822	279,441	1837	402,675
1807	285,069	1823	319,873	1838	350,146
1808	303,837	1824	318,624	1839	377,606
1809	321,056	1825	370,078	1840	420,418
1810	265,151	1826	294,747	1841	416,034
1811	287,200	1827	288,676	1842	410,945
1812	279,280	1828	276,552	1843	330,869
1813	301,345	1829	256,732	1844	334,159
1814	305,157	1830	253,498	1845	412,405
1815	298,482	1831	255,759	1846	385,605
1816	280,592	1832	299,079	1847	475,779
1817	241,570	1833	316,187	1848	427,670
1818	236,372				

Source: Report on the Royal Commission on Coal, Vol. III, 1871, Appendix No. 26, p. 16.

SALES OF COAL FROM EREWASH VALLEY
COLLIERIES 1803–1869
CONTD.

	Canal sale tons	Railway sale tons	Total tons
1849	386,955	43,820	430,775
1859	208,905	968,026	1,176,931
1869	192,902	1,709,061	1,901,963

Note: The figures for 1803 to 1848 show sales by canal only. The first Erewash Valley railway line was opened in 1849.

Source: Royal Commission on Coal, 1871, Vol. III, p. 95 and Appendix 90, p. 91.

In both periods, tonnages sold by landsale as well as coals consumed by the colliery companies themselves are additional to the figures shown.

For the second period, sales from collieries not belonging to the Erewash Valley Association (which are additional to the above) are estimated at 78 tons a year.

LIST OF COAL MINES IN NOTTINGHAMSHIRE IN 1869

No.	Name of colliery	Where situated	Owner's Name
1	Annesley	Mansfield	W. Worswick
2	Awsworth	Mansfield	E. C. Gillatt
3	Beau Vale	East Wood	Barber, Walker, and Company
4	Beggar Lee	East Wood	Barber, Walker, and Company
5	Brinsley	East Wood	Barber, Walker, and Company
6	Cinder Hill	Nottingham	J. Wright
7	Cotmanhay	East Wood	Barber, Walker, and Company
8	Digby	East Wood	Hall and Company
9	East Wood	East Wood	Barber, Walker, and Company
10	Giltbrook	Nottingham	Hicks and Company
11	High Park	Nottingham	Barber, Walker, and Company
12	Hill Top	Nottingham	Barber, Walker, and Company
13	Hucknall Torkard, No. 1.	Nottingham	Ellis and Company
14	Hucknall Torkard, No. 2	Nottingham	Ellis and Company
15	Kimberley	Nottingham	J. Wright
16	Mexbro'	Mansfield	Butterley Company
17	Molineux	Mansfield	Eastwood and Swingler
18	Newcastle	Nottingham	J. Wright
19	Plumtree	East Wood	Butterley Company
20	Portland	Mansfield	Butterley Company
21	Shire Oaks	Worksop	Shire Oaks Colliery Company
22	Skegby	Mansfield	Skegby Colliery Lime and Brick Company
23	Teversall, No. 1.	Mansfield	
24	Teversall, No. 2.	Mansfield	Stanton Iron Company
25	Underwood	East Wood	Barber, Walker, and Company
26	Watnall	East Wood	Barber, Walker, and Company

Source: Report on the Royal Commission on Coal, Vol. III, 1871, Appendix No. 27, p. 27.

LIST OF COAL MINES IN THE ALFRETON, RIPLEY AND ILKESTON AREAS OF DERBYSHIRE IN 1869

No.	Name of colliery	Where situated	Owner's name
68	Berrister Lane	Alfreton	C. Seely and Company
69	Brand's Hard Coal	Alfreton	Butterley Company
70	Brand's Soft Coal	Alfreton	Butterley Company
71	Butterley Park	Alfreton	Butterley Company
72	Carnfield, Hard Coal	Alfreton	Coke and Company
73	Carnfield, Soft Coal	Alfreton	Coke and Company
74	Coates Park	Alfreton	C. Seely and Company
75	Coates Park	Alfreton	J. Oakes and Company

APPENDIX E—*continued*

No.	Name of colliery	Where situated	Owner's name
76	Codnor Park	Alfreton	Butterley Company
77	Forty Horse	Alfreton	Butterley Company
78	Highfield	Alfreton	Oakerthorpe Iron Company Limited
79	Hartshay	Alfreton	Butterley Company
80	Langley	Alfreton	Butterley Company
81	Langton	Alfreton	Coke and Company
82	Loscoe	Alfreton	Butterley Company
83	Newlands	Alfreton	Butterley Company
84	New Main	Alfreton	Butterley Company
85	Oakerthorpe	Alfreton	Oakerthorpe Iron Company Limited
86	Pinxton	Alfreton	Coke and Company
87	Pye Bridge	Alfreton	James Oakes and Company
88	Riddings	Alfreton	James Oakes and Company
89	Ripley	Alfreton	Butterley Company
90	Shirland	Alfreton	Shirland Colliery Company
91	South Normanton	Alfreton	Joseph Swann
92	Sleights	Alfreton	Coke and Company
93	Swanwick	Alfreton	C. R. P. Morewood
94	Tibshelf, Old	Alfreton	Edward Chambers
95	Tibshelf, New	Alfreton	Edward Chambers
96	Tibshelf	Alfreton	J. Moseley
97	Tibshelf Blackshale	Alfreton	C. Seely and Company
98	Upper Birchwood	Alfreton	Butterley Company
99	Denby, Old	Ripley	W. D. Lowe
100	Denby, New	Ripley	W. D. Lowe
101	Denby Iron Works	Ripley	G. and W. Hope Dawes
102	Kilburn	Ripley	Executors of J. Ray
103	Marehay	Ripley	Butterley Company
104	Morley Park	Ripley	Disney
105	Pentrich	Ripley	Wm. C. Haslam
106	Whiteley	Ripley	Butterley Company
107	Waingroves	Ripley	Butterley Company
108	Awsworth	Ilkeston	Digby Coal Company
109	Bennerley	Ilkeston	F. C. Gillatt
110	Cotmanhay	Ilkeston	Barber, Walker and Company
111	Granby	Ilkeston	Butterley Company
112	Heanor	Ilkeston	J. Eley
113	Heanor	Ilkeston	Bircumshaw and Company
114	Heanor	Ilkeston	J. Argyle
115	Heanor	Ilkeston	J. Prince
116	Rutland	Ilkeston	Executors of Potter
117	Shipley, Soft Coal	Ilkeston	Alfred M. Mundy
118	Shipley, Hard Coal	Ilkeston	Alfred M. Mundy
119	Stoneyford, Old	Ilkeston	J. Wooley
120	West Hallam	Ilkeston	H. B. Whitehouse and Son
121	West Hallam	Ilkeston	Lieut.-Col. Newdegate

Source: Report on the Royal Commission on Coal, Vol. III, 1871, Appendix No. 27, pp. 26 and 27.

REFERENCES

1 *North Midland Coalfield—Regional Survey Report*, London, H.M.S.O., 1945, pp. 21–22.

2 *The Concealed Coalfield of Yorkshire and Nottinghamshire*, London, (H.M.S.O.) 1951, pp. 119, 130, 154, 187, 199, 212 and 256 and Colliery Sinking Plans.

3 Birks and Coxon, op. cit., pp. 19–20.

4 *Butterley Sales and Output Book.*

5 Birks and Coxon, op. cit., pp. 22–27.

6 ibid., p. 27.

7 ibid., p. 43.

8 ibid., pp. 55–6.

9 ibid., p. 53.

10 *Butterley Sales and Output Book.*

11 Ministry of Fuel and Power, *Statistical Digest*, 1951, London, 1952, p. 20.

12 Gibson, op. cit., p. 158.

13 From advertisements in the *Nottingham Daily Journal* on the dates given.

14 *Nottingham Daily Journal*, 1st March 1873.

15 Whitelock, op. cit., p. 35.

16 Mottram and Coote, op. cit., p. 91.

17 Gibson, op. cit., p. 158.

18 C. P. Griffin, *Robert Harrison*, chap. IV, also *Royal Commission on Coal, 1871*, Vol. III App. 27, pp. 17–53 and A. M. Neuman, *Economic Organization of the British Coal Industry*, 1934, p. 145.

19 In 1885, the Agent of New Skegby was John Hobson, and the Manager, Joseph Harvey.

20 *Catalogues of Plans of Abandoned Mines*, London, (H.M.S.O.), various dates, N.C.B., Survey Department Records. The founder of the Stanton Company was George Crompton, a Derbyshire banker.

21 *New Hucknall Colliery Company's Journal No. 1.* The New Hucknall Colliery may be taken as typical of the new mines being opened out in this period—especially those working the Top Hard Seam. The Company was also typical of the new type of colliery enterprise, and a detailed examination of its capital structure and operational results should therefore be interesting.

22 Some of these rents were clearly fixed minimum rents where coal was not being worked.

23 The closure dates for Old Hucknall are taken from the abandonment plans. The information concerning railway developments is supplied by Mr. P. Stevenson of the Railway and Canal Historical Society. For the Hucknall Huthwaite Branch of the South Yorkshire Miners Association see J. E. Williams, op. cit., p. 168.

    In addition to the Old Hucknall Colliery, the Mellors family had workings usually referred to as 'Blackwell Colliery' situated roughly mid-way between the present New Hucknall and 'B' Winning Collieries. These appear to have been abandoned finally in 1851 according to the plans.

24 Emerson Muschamp Bainbridge, mining engineer of Sheffield, was a founder of the more important Bolsover Company—see J. E. Williams, op. cit., p. 176.

25 This was the share capital at the end of 1879—*New Hucknall Colly. Co. Ltd., Balance Sheets, Vol. I.*

26 Loc. cit.

27 J. H. Collins, F.G.S., *Principles of Coal Mining*, London, 1876, pp. 70 and 91. A colliery worked by whim-gin was still in operation at Oakerthorpe in 1893.

28 The Old Radford Colliery was still working, apparently, in 1875 since a Lodge of that name was represented at the 1875 Demonstration of the D. and N.M.A.

29 *Nottingham Daily Journal,* 3rd April 1875.

30 *Nottingham Review,* 12th June 1968. Morris's *Nottinghamshire Directory, 1869,* p. 325.

31 ibid., 15th April and 27th May 1870.

32 ibid., 7th June 1870.

33 *Nottingham Daily Journal,* 24th June 1871.

34 I have this information from the Pinxton Company's last secretary, Mr. J. Eyre. For much the same reason London merchants attached the 'Derby Brights' label to coal from other districts.

35 *Nottingham Daily Journal,* 6th April 1872.

36 Griffin, op. cit., I. p. 199. The seams are heavily faulted in the South of the coalfield.

37 *Nottingham Daily Journal,* 8th June 1872.

38 J. E. Williams, op. cit., pp. 177 and 204; Derby (Drury-Lowe) Correspondence Book; Abandonment Plans for Winterbank, and *Annual Report* of the South Normanton Colliery Co. Ltd. for 1892–3. A Durham family, the Meins, ran the South Normanton Company. In its earlier years it employed the following Officials:

Secretary—Henry Johnson Mein (of Houden-le-Wear, Durham);
Manager—James Mein;
Cashier—Andrew Mein;
Clerk—William Hartford Mein.

(Source: T. Bulmer, op. cit., p. 685).

39 *New Hucknall Colliery Company, Balance Sheets, Vol. 2.*

40 Mottram and Coote, op. cit., p. 91.

41 ibid., p. 95. There were two pits, called 'Summit' and 'Low Moor', comprising Kirkby Colliery.

42 The New Hucknall pits were called 'Portland' and 'Carnarvon' after the Company's chief freeholders. These names were rarely used, however, which is as well for the avoidance of confusion since the Butterley Company had a Portland Colliery at Selston. Bentinck was also named after a local coal-owner. It is sometimes called 'Kirkby Bentinck'.

43 Prepaid calls excluded in both cases—*New Hucknall Colly. Company Ltd.'s Balance Sheets, Vol. 2.* Bainbridge's statement to the *R.C. on Coal Supplies* quoted by Taylor, art. cit., p. 64, that 'In the concerns I have to do with we never put aside any redemption sum' was misleading to say the least.

44 Loc. cit.

45 Loc. cit. There are not 53 separate names: some people owned shares jointly with others and their names, therefore, appear more than once. For example, E. M. Bainbridge's name appears four times.

46 *Major-General John Talbot Coke and Others to the Pinxton Coal Co. Ltd.,— Conveyances and Assignments of Freehold and Leasehold Hereditaments in the Counties of Nottingham and Derby,* Wigan, 1901, pp. 11 et seq.

47 F. Smith, op. cit., p. 17.

48 Whitelock, op. cit., pp. 28–29.

49 ibid., p. 32. Many other companies did, in fact, pursue the same policy as Barber Walker—e.g. New Hucknall & J. E. Ellis & Co.

50 ibid., p. 33.

51 Whitelock, op. cit., p. 34.

52 ibid., p. 35.

53 ibid., p. 36.

54 ibid., pp. 40 and 41.
55 *Reports of H.M. Inspectors of Mines* for 1856–1864.
56 Whitelock, op. cit., p. 43.
57 *Nottingham Guardian*, 7th October 1904.
58 E.g. John Boot's son-in-law W. G. Treadwell, who later practised as a mining engineer at Alfreton.
59 E.g. Whitelock, op. cit., p. 28. The firm of Coke, Turner & Co. are still in practice as mining engineers.
60 *Royal Commission on Coal, 1871, Vol. III*, Appendix 142, p. 153 and Whitelock, op. cit., pp. 29–30.
61 *35 and 36 Vict. cap. 76.*
62 See, e.g., Whitelock, op. cit., p. 43 (re appointment of Mr. A. G. McTurk, mechanical engineer,) and pp. 203 et seq.
63 See letters from Fenwick to Day in Balance Sheet Book, Vol. 2.
64 Whitelock, op. cit., pp. 203 et seq.
65 Mottram and Coote, op. cit., passim.
66 F. Smith, op. cit., p. 7 and *Pinxton Company's Annual Return* 1936.
67 Agreement between the N.M.A., Derbyshire Miners' Association and National Association of Colliery Deputies of 1918.
68 *S.R. and O, 1913, No. 953*, Clause 6.
69 Ministry of Fuel and Power, *Statistical Digest, 1951*, London, 1952, p. 20.
70 F. A. Gibson, *The Coal Mining Industry of the United Kingdom*, Cardiff, 1922, p. 24, and Mines Inspectors' Reports.
71 Griffin, I, op. cit., pp. 139–142 and Vol. II, p. 37.
72 So late as 1938, 10s. a week was the most a boy aged 14 could expect to earn in the Nottingham district except in the mining industry. The writer's father-in-law, who left school in 1910 worked for a few months in a textile factory for 4s. 6d. a week, and was then engaged at Gedling Colliery on the recommendation of his brother at a wage more than double his factory wage.
73 I have this from the late Mr. W. Bolstridge, among others.
74 *New Hucknall Colly. Co. Ltd., Balance Sheets Vols. 1 and 2.* A further £1,000 was spent on a Workmen's Institute.
75 *Mines Inspectors' Reports.* (Many Leicestershire men left the district because Snibston Colliery was closed for a considerable time by reason of a law case.)
76 ibid.
77 Concessionary coal was not as cheap then in real terms as it is today. At New Hucknall, for instance, Concessionary Coal produced a revenue of 2s. 5d. a ton in 1893 when the average pit head price of coal sold commercially was 6s. 9d. a ton. Concessionary coal prices, which once represented a third or a half of normal prices, now represent less than a twentieth of the normal prices in many cases since they have remained unchanged whilst retail coal prices have advanced greatly.
78 Griffin, op. cit., I, pp. 79, 193; Rowe, op. cit., p. 25.
79 Griffin, op. cit., I, pp. 108–9.
80 ibid., Vol. I, p. 44; II, p. 37, J. W. F. Rowe, op. cit., p. 72. The 7s. 10d. for a faceworker is derived from the 1886 rate of 5s. 3d. plus 50 per cent awarded by the Federated Area Conciliation Board.
81 E. H. Phelps-Brown, op. cit., p. 175.
82 G. D. H. Cole and R. Postgate, *The Common People, 1746–1938*, London, 1938, p. 430.
83 Griffin, op. cit., II, p. 34.
84 Gibson, op. cit., pp. 11 and 24. The decennial census returns for Nottinghamshire show a run-down in the numbers employed in agriculture and

framework-knitting concomitant with the increase in the mining labour force. Unfortunately, however, the Census figures for coalminers are improbably high. In 1891, for example, there were 29,854 men shown as coalminers in Nottinghamshire, whilst the actual labour force at this date was 21,512 according to Gibson (op. cit., p. 24). The explanation probably is that the Census figures included ex-miners who were retired or unemployed. A comparison of occupational groups in the 1851 and 1891 Censuses may be in-interesting:

Numbers shown as employed in certain occupations in
1851 and 1891 respectively

Occupation	1851	1891
Coal Miners	4,592	29,854
Hosiery	23,294	15,377
Agricultural Labourers and Farmers	32,643	15,884

Sources: *The 1851 Census, Ages, Civil Condition and Occupations*, Vol. II, pp. 531–609, London, 1854.
The 1891 Census, Area, Houses and Population, Vol. II, pp. 690–698, London, 1893.

85 Arnot, op. cit., I, p. 113. T. Ashton, *Three Big Strikes in the Coal Industry*, Manchester, n.d. p. 84.

86 *Select Committee on the Causes of the Present Scarcity and Dearness of Coal, 1873*, Evidence of J. T. Woodhouse, Q, 3734–3964.

87 *Colly. Year Book and Coal Trades Directory, 1951 edn., p. 559* and Gibson, op. cit., p. 158. The 1863 trough was a very minor one with no real significance. There was a further peak in the value of exported coal in 1894.

88 Loc. cit. See also tables in Gibson, op. cit., passim.

89 Ministry of Fuel and Power, *Statistical Digest, 1951*, London, 1952, p. 20.

90 Bulmer, op. cit., pp. 215 and 674. The Bolsover productivity was exceptional, made possible by a combination of: (a) new plant; (b) thick, fault-free top hard coal which is easily worked; (c) proximity of working faces to the pit bottom; (d) a concentrated lay-out which is possible with a new pit; (e) a young, hand-picked labour force.

CHAPTER II

The Nottinghamshire Miners' Association—Formation and Consolidation 1881—1892

1. INTRODUCTION

We have argued earlier that trade union membership fluctuates with the trade cycle. In this chapter, we shall see that fluctuations in the membership of the Nottinghamshire Miners' Association followed this general rule. To postulate a strict mathematical relationship between variations in the state of trade and variations in trade union membership would be to ignore the humanity of human kind, however. All kinds of factors influence the actions of men besides fluctuations in the state of trade.

The improvement in demand which ushered in the Nottinghamshire Miners' Association in July 1881 was a minor one. Indeed, when the trade cycle reached its peak in 1884, the average national pit head price of coal was only 5s. 5d. per ton: that is, 5d. below the lowest point in the succeeding trade cycle in which the price fell from its 1890 peak of 8s. 3d. to its 1896 trough of 5s. 10d. to reach a major peak, 10s. 10d, in 1900.[1] Further, the slump of the middle 1880's was so severe that the collapse of mining trade unions could have been expected. The national average pit head price of coal fell to 5s. 2d. in 1885 and 4s. 10d. in the two succeeding years. Similarly, the average declared value of coal exported fell to 8s. 2d. in 1887 as against the previous troughs of 8s. 8d. in 1879; 9s. 5d. in 1869; 8s. 10d. in 1863 and 8s. 11d. in 1860 and 1862. Not since 1853 had the price fallen so low, and it was never to fall so low again.[2] Nevertheless, the miners' trade unions did not collapse, although some of them came very close to it.

The mining community seems, in this period, to have been conscious of the long-term trend: the slump of the middle 1880's was, one feels, seen by many as a temporary break in the inevitable progress of the industry. The loss of confidence in the industry's future, which was to be so marked a feature of the 1920's, was absent in the

128

1880's. For the miners, the fall in the cost-of-living cushioned the effect of the fall in earnings. In working-class budgets of the late nineteenth century, food was the major constituent. The table below, produced by the Co-operative Wholesale Society, shows how marked was the fall in the cost of the average working-class family's grocery bill in this period:

TABLE 6 SHOWING THE COST OF AN AVERAGE WEEKLY FAMILY
ORDER OF 21½ LB. OF GROCERIES[3]

Date	Cost (d.)	Purchasing power of £1 Sterling expressed in groceries in same proportions (lb.)	Cost of Food Index 1914 = 100
1882	90·32	57·13	117·83
1883	86·54	59·62	112·90
1884	79·20	65·15	103·32
1885	72·16	71·51	94·14
1886	67·25	76·73	87·73
1887	67·77	76·14	88·41
1888	70·81	72·87	92·38
1889	72·01	71·66	93·94
1890	66·75	77·75	86·59
1891	69·26	74·65	90·36
1892	69·61	74·13	90·81
1893	68·69	75·12	89·61
1894	60·63	85·11	79·10
1895	58·38	88·39	76·16

It is true that the coal trade suffered in the recession of the middle 1880's. However, the demand for coal fell by a very small margin, and for a short time, as this table shows:

TABLE 7 SHOWING OUTPUT OF SALEABLE COAL FROM NOTTINGHAMSHIRE
1879–1895[4]

Year	Output	Year	Output
1879	4,316,954	1887	5,596,075
1880	4,432,393	1888	5,929,666
1881	4,758,060	1889	6,582,582
1882	4,957,725	1890	6,861,976
1883	5,315,880	1891	7,221,047
1884	5,091,603	1892	7,159,750
1885	5,285,178	1893	5,328,838*
1886	5,361,718	1894	6,821,830
		1895	6,564,854

* Great lockout occurred here

Clearly, the demand for coal, regarded long-term, was expanding greatly. At the same time, because new collieries often came into production when demand was falling temporarily, the short-term drop

K

in the price of coal which would have occurred anyway tended to be accentuated. Thus, the *Nottingham Daily Journal* complained in June, 1881, that new pits coming into operation, like Trowell Moor, caused added depression through over-production.[5] The increased capacity, in other words, temporarily outstripped the increasing demand.

In this kind of situation, there will have been some under-employment of resources, including labour. There was not, however, much actual unemployment. Productivity fell steadily throughout this period, whilst the numbers employed steadily increased.[6] There were sound economic reasons, then, for the survival of trade unions like the Nottinghamshire Miners' Association in this period—the absence of any great degree of unemployment, the fall in the cost-of-living, which ameliorated temporary reductions in earnings, and the general tendency for the demand for coal to increase.

There were, in addition, non-economic factors of some importance. By the 1880's, trade unions had become respectable and Liberal trade union leaders were being accepted into the Party's 'Establishment'. Liberal politicians recognized the importance of the trade union vote. Thus, we find Col. C. Seely of the Babbington Coal Company during his 1880 Parliamentary Election campaign addressing railway servants in Nottingham and advocating '. . . a fair pension to the widow of the man killed on the railway or in the coalmine'.[7] Similarly, J. E. Ellis, Quaker proprietor of the Hucknall Collieries, who also had Parliamentary ambitions, addressed a meeting of the Amalgamated Society of Engineers on Saturday 26th January 1884 when he appeared to be claiming credit for the reduction in the hours of work of his colliers from the twelve or thirteen hours a day, which was in vogue at Hucknall twenty years before, to a much lower number of hours.[8] In June of the same year, Mr. Ellis took the chair at the first annual demonstration organized by the Nottinghamshire Miners' Association, and his agent, Mr. F. N. Ellis, was on the platform with him.[9] At the 1887 Demonstration, the chair was taken by Alderman Cropper of Nottingham[10] whilst in 1888, Thomas Bayley, a proprietor of the Digby Colliery Company, who was also a Liberal Parliamentary candidate, presided. With him on the platform were Henry Broadhurst, a Liberal M.P. and trade union leader, and an Irish Party M.P.[11] Ellis, Seely and Bayley assisted the Association tremendously. They were almost certainly the 'influential colliery proprietors' who opposed the idea of reducing miners' wage-rates in May 1884 and who persuaded the Coalowners' Association to seek a reduction in freight charges as an alternative way of alleviating their economic difficulties.[12] With support of this kind, there was little fear that the Association would collapse completely.

Further, miners were becoming better educated and less shortsighted. The average man who works very long hours has little time or energy for any but selfish pursuits during the restricted amount of spare-time available to him, but the reduction in the hours of work from anything up to sixteen, to round about ten hours a day gave colliers time to think. Further, Methodists were concerning themselves more and more with social reform and less with the arid theological arguments current in the first half of the century. The trade unions were the chief beneficiaries of this development. All these factors help to account for the survival of the Nottinghamshire Miners' Association in the slump of the mid-1880's.

2. THE CONSTITUTION OF THE ASSOCIATION

When the union was founded in 1881, it was called the Nottinghamshire Miners' Federation. The original branches were at Arnold, Annesley, Clifton, Wollaton, Whitemoor, Bestwood, Newstead and Cinderhill.[13] All these places are near Nottingham, are on the concealed coalfield, and are in or near the Leen Valley. There is no colliery at Arnold, but many Bestwood miners lived there. It was to be a feature of the Union's organization during its early years that some men were organized in branches based on the places where they lived, although the majority were organized in branches (often called lodges) based upon individual collieries. A certain amount of friction developed between pit lodges and competing branches. Unfortunately, the terms 'lodge' and 'branch' were sometimes used synonymously.

The Union was originally a federation of semi-autonomous lodges, In the Rules registered on 17th September 1884, provision is made for them to be allowed to dissolve: the final sentence of Clause 1 reads:

'No lodge shall be allowed to dissolve except by a majority of three-fourths of its members.'[14]

Further, Rules 45 and 46 provided that lodges should retain two-thirds of the subscriptions, and that each lodge should have three trustees 'to invest their money to the best use'.[15]

The Federation's supreme government was vested in a Council consisting of a president, agent, financial secretary, treasurer, and 'one experienced member duly elected' by each lodge. Each lodge was free to determine the length of time its delegate should serve on the Council, and delegates had to present their credentials afresh at each meeting.[16] A district committee of not less than five members was to act between Council meetings. Whilst the president was to be elected by Council every six months, the financial secretary, and the treasurer were subject to yearly elections although paradoxically the rule relating to the treasurer also provided that 'He shall serve during the pleasure of the Association'.[17] The first treasurer appointed in 1884 was not a miner at all, but a sympathetic milkman from Bulwell named John Jackson. Originally, the Federation's monies had been in the hands of a cashier, Charles Blinco, but this post was abolished on 27th October 1883.[18]

The entrance fee was fixed at 1s. 6d. for full members and 9d. for half-members, whilst the normal weekly contributions were 3d. and 1½d. per week respectively. Council had power after consulting lodges to call for levies in order to keep the accounts in balance.[19] It is clear from the Minute Book for 1883–1885 that levies were being raised regularly in that period.

The objects of the Federation were to secure improved safety legislation; to see that bargains were honoured by employers; to prevent illegal deductions from wages; to protect members who were unjustly treated by colliery owners or officials; to try to obtain compensation for personal injuries due to the negligence of employers or their agents; to ensure the proper weighing of minerals sent to bank; to provide lock-out and strike pay; to give aid to other trade unions; and 'To shorten the hours of labour in mines; and to improve the moral and social position of the mining population.'[20] Rule 44 provided:

'That at any colliery where the workmen in the association are in a minority, the council or district committee shall not be at liberty to authorize a strike; nor shall the members of the lodge or lodge officials injudiciously imperil their position whilst the majority are apathetic and indifferent; but should the majority (non-members) decide to strike, the association shall, after investigating the case, support its members until such dispute is settled, or they have obtained work elsewhere.'[21]

It is very doubtful whether the members of the Committee appointed to draft these rules did so without outside help. The wording of Rule 44 quoted above, for instance, was hardly the work of Joseph Hopkin, (President), William Kay (Secretary), George Lane, Aaron Stewart or Charles West, the five committee members.[22] It is at least possible that they were assisted by someone like J. E. Ellis.

Be that as it may, the federal structure of the Association proved a source of weakness. The Bestwood Lodge disappeared in 1883, the Hill Top Lodge formally seceded in 1885 as a protest against the new (registered) rules;[23] and Wollaton threatened to secede following an unsuccessful strike in the summer of 1884.[24]

Again, it appears that some lodges were sending incorrect statements of accounts to Council, and in July 1884 the agent and secretary were empowered to investigate the matter. The secretary, William Kay, was asked to retire at the same meeting,[25] his place being taken by Aaron Stewart, the Annesley checkweighman, who was then 39 years of age. He started work in the mines (at Coleorton, Leicester-shire) at the age of eight, but had managed to acquire a reasonable education, and he was also energetic.[26]

William Mellors of Linby Colliery persuaded Council to set up a Rules Revision Committee with a view to strengthening the central control of the Union.[27] This Committee was appointed on 14th July 1885 and the revised rules were registered on 3rd December 1885.[28]

The name of the Union was changed to the Nottinghamshire Miners' Association, and this change of title correctly represents the change of emphasis in the rules. The powers of the lodges to secede and to hold separate funds were removed. Rule 20 reads:

> 'There shall be for this association one general fund, which shall be applied for the relief of those members and families who may have been thrown out of employment by strikes, lock-outs, or victimized, and for management. This fund shall be under the guidance and control of the association's council, and shall be supported and disbursed as provided in these rules.'[29]

In order further to prevent branch committees from spending union money on refreshment (liquid or otherwise), as they were alleged to have done previously, Rule 31 provided that:

> 'Any branch appropriating the funds of the association to any purpose whatever not specified in these rules, shall be dealt with by the council, or as the law directs.'[30]

In other respects, the rules were much the same as before. In particular, the procedure for calling strikes was still aimed at preventing them except as a last resort. Strikes were not to be called at collieries where unionists were in a minority. Where the union had most of the men in membership, the lodge had first to ensure that a majority of members of the union working at that colliery was in favour of striking. Members were to 'register their votes for or against such strikes individually in the lodge books'. Then, the issue had to be explained to Council, who would, if they thought fit, submit the question to branches . . . 'after which, if the dispute cannot be arranged, and the majority of the members are in favour of such lodge coming out on strike, each lodge shall pay a proper and fair share, sufficient to pay the full members of the lodge 8s. per week, and 1s. per head for each child under thirteen years of age not at work, and 4s. per week for each half member'.[31]

Something like three months could be expected to elapse under this procedure between the dispute arising, and the strike commencing. Members guilty of precipitate action could not claim strike pay.

Both rule books also contain a list of fines to be levied on officials and members of the Union who were guilty of breaches of rules. Most

of them were to do with failure to attend, or arriving late at, or misconduct whilst attending, meetings of various kinds. They ranged
from 6d. for delegates being late at Council meetings to 2s. 6d. for
members 'attending meetings of any kind when drunk and disturbing
business'. Fines could also be levied on members for finding fault with
other members or officials, or for swearing at meetings. A fine of
2s. 6d. was to be levied on any member 'boasting of his independence
towards his employers or managers on account of being a member
of this association'.[32]

3. DISPUTES

Between August and the middle of October, 1881 there were three
advances in the selling price of coal in Nottingham.[33] The top hard
collieries in particular benefited from the demand for steam coal for
the lace factories which were reported to be working from 4 a.m. to
12 midnight.[34] At a conference organized by the M.N.U. in December
1881 it was decided to press for a general advance of ten per cent
in wage-rates. Agitation followed in all districts, including Nottinghamshire, but without success. The coal-owners associations refused
to meet the M.N.U. deputation.[35]

However, the pits made good time throughout the winter; and
earnings were therefore higher than for some time past. The seasonal
drop in demand was not so marked as in the previous few years,[36]
but the unions waited until the Autumn before renewing their demand
for higher wage-rates. A national conference held at Manchester
with representatives from almost all the non-sliding scale areas opened
on 13th October 1882. It was decided that notices should be tendered
for a 15 per cent increase in wage-rates on 16th October. Most colliery owners offered a ten per cent advance as a compromise, and the
reconvened national conference agreed that such offers should be
accepted.[37]

The owners could well afford to pay the increase. The general
trend is shown by the profit per ton at New Hucknall which rose
from 5·4d. in the second half of 1881 to 8·7d. in 1882, and 1s. 9·4d.
in the first half of 1883. Wages costs, despite the ten per cent increase,
fell from 3s. 3d. a ton in 1881 to 3s. a ton in 1882 and the first half
of 1883.[38] One colliery company owned by Seely, the Liberal family
(the Babbington Company) gave increases of 11 to 12½ per cent to its
workmen in Nottinghamshire and Derbyshire without waiting for the
formal demand for 15 per cent.[39]

The Bestwood Coal and Iron Company, operating a large, new,
profitable colliery in the Leen Valley, refused to concede an increase
at all and it was the only company in Nottinghamshire to do so. A

strike which lasted for three months ended in failure. The men were supported from Union funds supplemented by collections in other trades. At the conclusion of the strike, some of the active unionists at Bestwood were refused employment and the lodge left the Federation.[40] In the autumn of 1883, the previous year's tactics were repeated. At some collieries, notices for an advance in wage-rates were put in, but they had to be withdrawn. A circular asking the owners of Nottinghamshire to meet representatives of the men was ignored. The only companies in the county to concede increases were Digby, Butterley and Manners.[41] If New Hucknall's results are typical, trading conditions were by no means as difficult as they had been a few years before, or as they were to become a year later. The profit per ton fell from 1s. 9·4d. in the first half of 1883 to 10·7d. in the second half-year; whilst wages costs rose from 3s. to 3s. 2d. Output for the year was down to 151,836 tons (compared with 157,350 in 1882) and it was to fall still further, to 130,761 tons in 1884 and 118,225 tons in 1885.[42]

During 1883 the miners' unions nationally sought the co-operation of colliery owners in restricting output by adopting an eight-hour day and a five-day week, but the owners refused to co-operate.[43] In Lancashire, the union tried, unsuccessfully, to enforce an eight-hour day against the opposition of the owners but they were defeated.

During the early part of 1884 there were disputes at the Trowell Moor pit of Dunn Bros. (which had been working for only one day a week during February, and which was notoriously inefficient), where the owners demanded that 21 cwts. of coal should be produced for one ton's pay;[44] at Wollaton, where the Company confiscated 'gathered coals' (i.e. coal dropped from the trams on to the haulage roads), reduced wages, stopped supplying home coal and finally victimized the checkweighmen and other active union members;[45] and at Silverhill and Teversal where the owners increased the rents of company houses by 3d. a week, and imposed a charge of 3s. a ton for home coal for which the workmen already paid the equivalent of 4s. 5d. a ton by way of reduced piece-work prices. The Stanton Company subsequently closed both Teversal and Silverhill for a time because the state of trade made production unprofitable.[46] The Wollaton Company attempted to crush the union branch. They proceeded by giving notice of reduced wages to eleven stalls only. The Union District Committee resolved '. . . that if the men are permitted to submit to any reduction whatever, another section of the colliery will be attacked till the whole pit is reduced . . . if a battle is to be fought it will be better for the entire colliery to be engaged in it than allow it to be took in sections in the manner attempted by the company'.[47] Council agreed to 'give their hearty support to both Union members and non-union miners as well if they will but all come out.'[48] Some of the butties were, however, refusing to pay their share of the checkweighman's wages, and this was almost certainly connived at by the owners, who hindered the checkweighman, John Hopkinson 'from doing his duty, he being a staunch society man'.[49] A sycophantic butty, John Hatton, alleged that Hopkinson had tried to coerce him into membership of the union.[50] Hopkinson, along with other active unionists, was excluded from the Company's employ.[51] An attempt to induce the Wollaton lodge to secede from the Union was defeated, and new branch officials were appointed.[52] The Silverhill and Teversal men who struck were non-unionists. However, the Union considered that their action was justified, and they were therefore given financial support.[53]

The mild winter of 1884–5 intensified the depression in the mining industry, and in March 1885, the Coal-owners' Associations decided to reduce wages.[54] In Yorkshire, the owners gave notice of a 10 per cent reduction which brought the men out on strike for two months. They were defeated.[55] The Yorkshire strike, by reducing the supply of coal coming on to the market, helped Nottinghamshire a little. For all that, most companies reduced wage-rates generally by the 10 per cent gained in 1882.[56] The owners of Cossall, Oakwell, Manners and Stapleford Collieries, near Ilkeston, imposed a reduction of 3d. a ton equivalent to $12\frac{1}{2}$ per cent, however, and a seven weeks' strike, accompanied by rioting, resulted. Eventually, a reduction of $1\frac{1}{2}$d. a ton was accepted as a compromise, but the alleged leaders of the rioting were refused employment thereafter.[57]

A national conference held in Nottingham in September 1885 decided to campaign for a 15 per cent increase in wages but the campaign was a complete failure. Only 200 men in Nottinghamshire obeyed the Union's instructions to hand in strike notices, and they quickly withdrew them.[58] Similarly, a national conference held in November, 1886, decided to agitate for a seven-hour day and increased wage rates. Reports given at this Conference indicated that Nottinghamshire miners, who were earning between 4s. 9d. and 5s. 3d. a day, were among the best paid in the country.[59] However, the total membership of miners' unions—about 106,700—comprised no more than a fifth of the labour force, [60] and some districts, including Nottinghamshire, were too weak to be effective. A recalled conference held in January 1887 decided that '. . . seeing, as we do, that the weakness of our position is the want of organization amongst the men, we call on the mining population to organize together as a condition of success'.[61]

Meantime, some one hundred colliery owners of Derbyshire, South Yorkshire and Nottinghamshire had decided at a meeting held on Friday 27th August 1886 to ask all owners to increase the prices of best house coal by 6d. a ton and nuts for the London market by 3d.[62]

Whether this resolution had anything more than a momentary effect it is difficult to say. The national average pit head price of coal, which fell from 5s. 2d. in 1885 to 4s. 10·5d. in 1886, fell still further, to 4s. 9·87d. in 1887.[63] It would appear, however, that Nottinghamshire enjoyed rather better trading conditions. Output for Nottinghamshire, rose from 5,361,718 in 1886 to 5,596,075 in 1887.[64] The demand for coal was stimulated by a cold spell in January, by an increased demand for pig iron (iron and steel works consumed some 42 million tons of coal during the year, compared with 46 million tons in 1903 and 18·74 million tons in 1938);[65] and by a demand for slack for making briquettes, now coming on the market for the first time.[66] The top hard pits were relatively busy producing steam coal for industry. The New Hucknall Colliery Company sold 199,719 tons of coal in 1887 compared with 118,225 tons two years earlier. Profits per ton were much lower—3·7d. as against 6·7d.—but total profits—at £3,079—compared favourably with the £3,318 of 1885. The older pits of the Erewash Valley, which supplied mainly household coal were working short time for low prices, however.[67]

Towards the close of 1887, signs of a recovery became more apparent. The Lancashire coal-owners, who felt in June that they had no option but to reduce wage-rates by 10 per cent because they were working at a loss, agreed in July to 'adjourn the wages question until further notice'.[68] The average price of coal at London Docks rose from 13s. a ton on 8th July to 13s. 6d. on 18th August, 15s. on 14th September and 15s. 8d. a week later.[69]

A national conference held on 11th October 1887 at Edinburgh recommended that a policy of output restriction should be adopted 'to clear off surplus stocks and secure a ten per cent advance'. Output was to be restricted by introducing an eight-hour day and a five-day week, and surplus stocks were to be reduced by a general one-week's holiday.[70] The weakness of the miners' organization was demonstrated, however, when the question of seeking a legally enforced eight-hour day was discussed. The proposal was opposed strongly by Northumberland and Durham, and the majority in its favour—53,000 in a vote of 373,000—was small. Subsequently, Durham and South Wales withdrew from the agitation.[71]

Northumberland, Durham and South Wales, where 'the price of the product rose and fell greatly in the trade cycle, and was largely fixed by international competition, so that there was little possibility of reducing the falls, albeit at the cost of unemployment, by restricting output',[72] were tied to sliding-scales. The South Wales sliding-scale at the turn of the century provided, for example, 'that for each change of 1¼d. from the basic seaport price of 7s. 8d. a ton there should be a change of 1¼ per cent in the rate of wages being paid in each place in

December 1879'.[73] In addition, in Northumberland and Durham, the hours of work of colliers were already well below eight per day, whilst the hours of boys over 16 years of age were longer than anywhere else in the country: two shifts of colliers being served by only one shift of haulage hands.[74] Any reduction in the hours of boys would, the men felt, lead to an increase in on-cost labour at the expense of their wages.[75]

Meantime, the campaign for a ten per cent increase in wages and a restriction of output met with little success. At some pits[76] in Nottinghamshire the men refused to work more than eight hours a day early in January. The Bestwood men were locked out in consequence. The failure of other districts to implement the eight-hour day led to the formal abandonment of the policy by Nottinghamshire on 21st January when the men were advised 'to hold back the notices until the men of Derbyshire and Yorkshire gave in theirs'.[77] The only company in the county to concede a wage increase was Wollaton, whose employees obtained increases of 2d. a ton in the soft coal seam and 1d. a ton in the hard coal seam after a three-day strike in November 1887. In May 1888 the Company gave notice to reduce wages to the old level; and sixty-odd active trade unionists who would not accept the reduction were dismissed. The remainder of the colliers came out on 'sympathy' strike on 30th May 1888. The Company repeated their tactics of 1884 in refusing to deal with the union Agent, William Bailey and the checkweighman, J. Saxton. They could not dismiss Saxton as they had done his predecessor, however, since the checkweighman's position had been made more secure by the Act of 1887. It was alleged that 'black-lists' of Wollaton men had been issued to Leen Valley colliery owners. Dawson, the manager, denied this, but it is more than likely that the information came from Bayley, Ellis or Seely, all of whom were on terms of friendship with William Bailey.

For a month, the 700 men involved received strike pay of 8s. a week, plus 1s. a week for each child under twelve, but by the beginning of July there was only enough money left in the strike fund to pay 2s. a man. Some non-unionists were already back at work, despite vigorous picketing, and on 2nd July the dispute was settled on the Company's terms. Active unionists were victimized as in 1884, but the branch remained strong, nevertheless.[78]

In the late summer of 1888 the agitation for a 10 per cent advance in wage-rates was resumed. However, at a national conference held in Manchester on 25th September, it was reported that colliery proprietors were not very encouraging in their replies to applications for an advance. Accordingly, it was decided that notices for a 10 per cent advance should be handed in to expire in all (Midland) districts on 27th October. This move, coming as it did at a time when all districts were making good time and prices were moving upwards, was immediately successful. In Lancashire, Cheshire, Nottinghamshire, Staffordshire, Leicestershire, Shropshire and North Wales the advance was conceded within a fortnight. In Yorkshire and Derbyshire, however, some 40,000 men had to strike for the advance, most of them for one week but a few for as long as three weeks.[79]

The 1888 campaign was a display of sound trade union strategy. The campaign was launched at a time when the seasonal demand for household coal was superimposed upon the cyclical increase in demand for industrial coal. The New Hucknall Company for example, sold 297,285 tons of coal at a profit of 5·2d. per ton in 1888 against 199,719 tons at a profit of 3·7 per ton in 1887.[80] Further, all the Midland districts submitted their notices at the same time. Those companies who were most anxious to take advantage of the rapidly improving state of trade paid for peace with alacrity: they did not even haggle about the figure. The laggards, like Barber Walker, Bestwood and Annesley in Nottinghamshire, came into line when they saw that their men were determined. The unions also established a joint strike fund into which the men back at work would pay to support those whose employers refused to give way.

In the spring of 1889, a campaign for a second ten per cent increase in gross earnings was launched, supported once more by the threat of strike notices. A strike fund to be fed by a levy of 6d. a week in respect of each man at work was to support those whose employers proved recalcitrant.

In Nottinghamshire, Yorkshire and some other areas, most owners offered in May an immediate increase of 5 per cent with a further 5 per cent to follow on 1st October. Where such offers were made, they were accepted by authority of a national conference. Altogether, only 6,000 men had to come out on strike, and of these, only the 3,000 men of Somerset—an unprofitable coalfield—were out for any length of time.[81]

In Nottinghamshire, there was some little friction in connection with this campaign at Silverhill and Teversal, Barber Walker's pits, Clifton, Trowell Moor, and New Hucknall.[82] The New Hucknall Company did not extend the increase to its low-paid day wage workers. Their balance sheet shows how little justification there was for this. The profit for 1889 at £13,895 was more than double the record profit of £6,433 earned in 1888. Profit per ton was 10·1d. against 5·2d. and output was up from 297,285 to 330,084.[83]

In the autumn, the unions decided to press for a third increase. A conference held in Newport at the end of November to 'consider the state of trade and the advisability of asking for another advance in wages' decided that all non-sliding scale districts should apply for a ten per cent advance. This was conceded without a struggle in less than a fortnight.[84] The real significance of the Newport Conference, however, was the decision taken there to form a Miners' Federation of Great Britain. The old Miners' National Union was dominated by Northumberland, Durham and South Wales, whose wages were regulated by sliding-scales; and who were opposed to the Eight Hours Bill advocated by the Midland districts. The Midland leaders felt that a new national federation should be formed with 'a policy of joint action when necessary on general and national questions affecting wages and restriction of labour'. They recalled that the 1882 wage increase had been lost because the counties were attacked one by one, and they felt that if they were to keep the 30 per cent advance they had now won, it was necessary to have a permanent central organization to co-ordinate their activities.[85]

The founder-members of the Miners' Federation of Great Britain were: Yorkshire, Lancashire, Midland Federation (Staffordshire, Worcestershire, Cannock Chase, and Shropshire), Nottinghamshire, Forest of Dean, Bristol, Radstock, Warwickshire, North Wales, Stirlingshire and Monmouth. The other Midland counties (Derbyshire, South Derbyshire and Leicestershire) joined shortly afterwards.[86]

The colliery owners of the Midland counties formed a corresponding Federation, and the two organizations met for the first time on 4th March 1890 to consider an application for a further 10 per cent advance in wages. The owners' side 'disputed that prices had risen to such an extent as to justify the advance, or any advance whatever'.[87] In fact, the industry could afford the advance very well. The average pit head price of coal rose from 4s. 10d. in 1887 to 6s. 4d. in 1889 and 8s. 3d. in 1890.[88] The quantity sold also increased: from 162,119,812 tons in 1887 to 176,916,724 tons in 1889 and 181,614,288 tons in 1890. It was to rise by a further 3·8 million tons in 1891.[89] The New Hucknall Company produced 334,349 tons (some 4,300 more than the record year 1889) at a profit per ton two-and-a-half times that of the previous year: 2s. 1·4d. against 10·1d. Net profits were almost £23,000 higher at £36,247.[90]

In Nottinghamshire, some 5,000 men came out on strike on 12th March 1890. Others were working out their notices. Some owners, mainly in the Leen Valley, offered an immediate 5 per cent advance with another to follow on 1st July. These offers were accepted. The national settlement, when it came, was that at collieries where a local offer had not already been made and accepted, a 5 per cent advance should be given at once with another to follow on 1st August.[91]

The wages agitation was now over. In little more than two years, the miners' unions of the Midland coalfields (the 'Federated Area' or 'District') had secured a 40 per cent increase on basis rates. Now they concentrated on the legal limitation of the hours of work. For a period of two years, the agitation for an eight-hour day took precedence over other business. Mass meetings, conferences, leaflet campaigns at election time, even a strike ballot in which an overwhelming majority of those voting were 'in favour of a national or international strike' to obtain the eight-hour day,[92] all these activities occupied the time and the energy of the union's leaders. In the event, the only country to strike on this issue was Belgium. The Miners' Federation of Great Britain concentrated instead on canvassing support for an Eight Hours Bill. As its Secretary, Thomas Ashton, said:

'The eight hours question is a big one; there is work in it for every member of every miners' union. The opponents against the bill are strong and powerful: The Government; the most influential members on both sides of the House of Commons; the House of Lords; the coal-owners; but the most formidable opponents are in our own ranks—the miners of Northumberland and Durham.'[93]

The opposition proved too powerful, and the agitation had no immediate or early success.

In Nottinghamshire, there was a 26 weeks' strike at the new Kirby Summit Pit in 1891 over the refusal of the Butterley Company to pay rates equivalent to those being paid in the Leen Valley. The men received 8s. a week strike pay, plus 1s. for each child under 12 years of age. In addition, voluntary collections taken at collieries throughout Nottinghamshire and parts of Derbyshire averaged 3s. to 5s. a man. The men were remarkably successful in keeping blacklegs away from the colliery, and eventually, the company had no option but to come to terms.[94]

The national average pit head price of coal fell from 8s. 3d. in 1890 to 8s. in 1891 and 7s. 3d. in 1892.[95] Output in 1891 was, however, almost four million tons up on the previous year and even in 1892, despite the gloomy stories of the colliery owners, output at 181,786,871 tons was higher than the 181,614,288 tons of 1890.[96] The New Hucknall Company's profit in 1891 at £40,370 was over £4,000 more than in 1890; and the 1892 profit of £37,097 was still up on the 1890 profit of £36,247. The Company's profit per ton rose from 2s. 2·4d. in 1890 to 2s. 2·7d. in 1891 and then fell slightly to 1s. 11·5d. in 1892. Output rose from 334,349 tons in 1890 to 363,256 in 1891 and 373,133 in 1892.[97] If this Company's results were typical, a substantial further general advance in wage-rates was certainly justified.

However, such an advance was not sought. The union leaders apparently felt that greater leisure was to be preferred to higher wages. They also appear to have regarded the 1888 wage plus 40 per

cent as a 'fair' wage, and to have deliberately refrained from extracting the maximum economic advantage from the situation. The owners
were to show no such moderation when the market situation deteriorated.

4. ORGANIZATION AND LEADERSHIP

We have already discussed the organizational forms of the Union
in our section on its Constitution. The following table shows fluctuations in membership and, for comparison, the annual average pit head
price of coal, which is an indicator of the state of trade.

TABLE 8 SHOWING FLUCTUATIONS IN MEMBERSHIP AND THE STATE
OF TRADE 1881–92[98]

Year	Membership	National avg. pit head price of coal (per ton)		Price of coal from Midland pits	
		s.	d.	s.	d.
1881	Union Formed	5	0 (1882)	6	11·88 (1882)
1883	2,167	5	8	5	11·88
1884	1,041	5	5	6	0·24
1885	1,067	5	2	5	9·00
1886	350	4	10·50	5	6·36
1887	1,633	4	9·87	5	7·80
1888	1,959	5	0·60	5	5·64
1889	7,549	6	4·20	6	6·72
1890	10,888	8	3	7	6·36
1891	18,341	8	0	7	5·16
1892	17,011	7	3	7	3·84

It will be seen that the first peak in membership of the Union was
reached in 1883. On the downswing of the trade cycle, membership
fell away to reach bottom in 1886. In the following year, under the
stimulus of new and energetic leadership, coupled with signs of an
impending improvement in the state of trade, membership grew at
a satisfactory rate.

William Bailey was brought into the County to address open-air
meetings in the closing months of 1886.[99] Previously, the leadership of
the Union had been in the hands of Joseph Hopkin, who was the full-
time agent from January 1884 to the autumn of 1886, when he was
induced to relinquish the post. Subsequently, he was unemployed until
after the 1892 Parliamentary Election, when he was given employment
at the Babbington Collieries as a reward for helping Col. C. Seely
during the election campaign.

Hopkin and Bailey were both local preachers and they were both
members of the Liberal Party. However, Bailey was much more forceful
than Hopkin. He had been the checkweighman at Norwood Colliery,

Killamarsh, from 1875 until 1884, when, after an eighteen weeks' strike, the management would not allow him on the premises. He was invited to address meetings in Nottinghamshire on the advice of James Haslam of the Derbyshire Miners' Association, for whom he had acted as Election Agent in 1885.[100] His ability as a speaker and organizer commended him to the N.M.A. Council, who appointed him agent from 1st January 1887. He was fortunate in coming into office at a time when trade was showing signs of improvement. By June 1887 membership had increased to 771,[101] and it increased still further— to about 1,500 by November,[102] by which time the Hill Top and Best-wood Lodges had been re-admitted.

Several new branches were formed during 1887: notably, Sutton, Old Basford, Selston, Kimberley, Clifton and Underwood. By April 1888 there were 25 branches: an increase of 14 since November 1886 when Bailey opened his campaign.[103] The geographical spread had also widened. At the earlier date, all but two of the branches were in or near the Leen Valley and the two exceptions, Stanton Hill and Huthwaite, were insignificant in size. At the later date, the Leen Valley and the Erewash Valley were equally well represented.

Membership at the end of 1888 was only 326 higher than at the end of 1887, but thereafter it mounted rapidly. This upward movement maintained its momentum until 1892, when the worsening trade conditions caused it to fall off slightly.

5. CONCLUSION

We have seen that the Nottinghamshire Miners' Federation came into existence in 1881 during the mild improvement in trade. It stemmed from the meetings of Leen Valley checkweighmen and a few other people, who had been members of the earlier Derbyshire and Nottinghamshire Miners' Association or, as in Joseph Hopkin's case, of other unions.

William Hardy of Codnor, Edward Smith, Joseph Hancock and his son J. G. Hancock of Pinxton, William Bolstridge of Cinderhill and the veteran Samuel Smith of Radford had all been active in the earlier union. So, in all probability, had Aaron Stewart of Annesley. Joseph Hopkin had been an active member of the militant South Yorkshire Miners' Association. These men provided links with the past. However, whereas the old union had been dominated by the old mining areas of the exposed coalfield, the new Union was based upon the Leen Valley, where butties formed something like one half of the coal-face labour force.

Until the end of 1885, the Union remained, in fact as well as in name, a Federation of semi-autonomous lodges, some of which were almost certainly in existence before the Federation itself. These lodges retained two-thirds of the subscriptions, besides having additional separate funds of their own in some cases.[104] The revised rules of 1885 converted the Federation into an Association where far more power was exercised by the central body.

In this period, the Union flourished when trade was good and languished when trade was slack. Membership reached its perigee in 1886, when there were no more than 350 men on the books. With the improvement of trade from 1887 on, however, the number of members rose rapidly. This was due partly to the improvement in trading conditions leading to greatly increased earnings, and partly to energetic leadership and sound organization.

The Association joined with other county unions to form the Miners' Federation of Great Britain in 1889. The exporting areas, Northumberland, Durham and South Wales, being tied to sliding scales, remained outside the Federation. From this date, the M.N.U. represented these three districts only.

The colliery owners of the inland coalfields formed an organization complementary to the M.F.G.B., and the area which the two organizations covered was called the 'Federated Area'. Whilst this area contained a high proportion of low-cost producers, it also contained some high-cost producers, particularly in the older mining districts like the Erewash Valley. The wage policy of the Federated Coal-Owners was dictated by what the marginal producers were able to afford.[105] The differential in efficiency between high-cost and low-cost producers was, however, so great that the Coal-Owners' Federation had a tendency towards instability which was shortly to become apparent.

REFERENCES

1 Gibson, op. cit., p. 157 (figures to nearest penny).
2 ibid., pp. 157–8 and *Colly. Year Book and Coal Trades Directory*, 1951 edn., p. 559. (Figures to nearest penny).
3 Source: *The People's Year Book*, (The Annual of the English and Scottish Co-operative Wholesale Societies) Manchester, 1926 edn. pp. 194 and 5. The prices are wholesale prices and the Groceries are made up as follows: 1 lb. bacon; 2 lb. butter; ½ lb. cheese; 12 lb. flour; ½ lb. lard; 1 lb. oatmeal; 4 lb. sugar; and ½ lb. tea.
   Cf. Phelps-Brown, op. cit., p. 273.
4 Gibson, op. cit., p. 24.
5 *Nottingham Daily Journal*, 11th June 1881.
6 *Mines Inspectors' Reports*.
7 *Nottingham Daily Journal*, 15th March 1880. Col. Seely was elected— see ibid., 2nd April 1880.
8 ibid., 28th January 1884.

9 ibid., 9th June 1884.
10 ibid., 9th April 1887.
11 *Hucknall Star and Advertiser*, 6th April 1888.
12 *Nottingham Journal*, 15th May 1884. The freight charge to London by rail was 8s. to 8s. 6d. a ton for Nottingham coal, compared with 4s. a ton for sea-borne coal from Newcastle—see ibid., 17th April 1884.
13 *Colliery Guardian*, 28th July 1881, cited Griffin, op. cit., I, p. 23.
14 *Rules, 1884 set*, p. 3. The words 'branch' and 'lodge' are often used synonymously, but the word 'branch' is used also to distinguish a residential area branch from a pit lodge.
15 ibid., p. 15.
16 ibid., pp. 4–5.
17 ibid., pp. 5–7.
18 *N.M.F. Minute Book*, 27th October 1883.
19 *Rules, 1884 set*, pp. 10–11.
20 ibid., pp. 3–4.
21 ibid., p. 15.
22 *N.M.F. Minute Book*, 24th November 1883.
23 ibid., 17th January 1885, 2nd February 1885 and 14th March 1885.
24 ibid., 2nd August 1884 and 27th September 1885.
25 ibid., 5th July 1884.
26 ibid., 27th September 1884.
27 I have this from the late Mr. E. Mellors. The Rules Revision Committee comprised: W. Mellors, J. Hollyhead, and J. Tomlinson—*N.M.F. Minute Book*, 14th July 1885.
28 *Rules, 1885 set*, p. 24.
29 ibid., p. 9.
30 ibid., p. 11.
31 *Rules, 1884 set*, p. 12 and 1885 set, p. 12.
32 *Rules, 1884 set*, p. 26,, and 1885 set, pp. 22–3.
33 *Nottingham Daily Journal*, 15th October 1881.
34 ibid., 22nd October 1881.
35 T. Ashton, *Three Big Strikes in the Coal Industry*, Manchester n.d., pp. 8–11.
36 The *Colliery Guardian's* trade reports, reproduced in the *Nottingham Daily Journal* throughout this period, are useful guides to the state of trade although they rarely give statistical evidence.
37 T. Ashton, op. cit., pp. 13–15.
38 *New Hucknall Colly. Co., Balance Sheets Book No. 1*.
39 *Nottingham Daily Journal*, 5th and 7th October 1882.
40 *N.M.F. Minute Book*, 29th September and 27th October 1883, *Hucknall Illustrated Labour Journal*, November 1891.
41 *Hucknall Illustrated Labour Journal*, January 1892, N.M.F. Minute Book, 8th September 1883 and 8th October 1883 and *Nottingham Daily Journal*, 2nd January 1884. In each case the increase was of 7½ per cent.
42 *New Hucknall Colly. Co., Balance Sheets, Book 1*.
43 T. Ashton, op. cit., pp. 15–21.
44 *N.M.F. Minute Book*, 8th March 1884; *Nottingham Daily Journal*, 5th April 1884.
45 *Nottingham Daily Journal*, 24th May and 13th June 1884; *Nottingham Trades Council Minute Book*, 29th August, 1884; *N.M.F. Minute Book*, 28th April, 10th May, 13th May, 14th June and 5th July 1884.
46 *Nottingham Daily Journal*, 17th May, 10th, 12th and 14th June 1884. People would, of course, have been employed on pumping and other duties concerning the safety of the workings.

L

47 *N.M.F. Minute Book,* 28th April 1884.
48 ibid., 13th May 1884.
49 *Nottingham Trades Council Minutes,* 29th August 1884.
50 *Nottingham Daily Journal,* 24th May and 13th June 1884
51 *N.M.F. Minute Book,* 5th July and 27th September 1884.
52 ibid., 2nd August and 27th September 1884.
53 ibid., 24th May and 5th July 1884.
54 *Nottingham Daily Journal,* 28th March 1885.
55 T. Ashton, op. cit., pp. 35–37.
56 Griffin, op. cit., I, pp. 40–41.
57 *Nottingham Daily Journal,* 25th July, 8th and 22nd August and 19th September 1885.
58 T. Ashton, op. cit., pp. 37–38.
59 ibid., pp. 48–49 cited Griffin, op. cit., I, p. 44.
60 Gibson, op. cit., p. 11.
61 T. Ashton, op. cit., pp. 50–1.
62 *Nottingham Daily Journal,* 28th August 1886.
63 Gibson, op. cit., p. 157.
64 ibid., p. 24.
65 ibid., pp. 578–9.
66 See *Colliery Guardian* trade reports in *Nottingham Daily Journal.*
67 *Nottingham Daily Journal,* 2nd April 1887.
68 T. Ashton, op. cit., pp. 55–60.
69 Report by W. Bailey, Agent of the N.M.A. cited Griffin, op. cit., I, p. 47.
70 T. Ashton, op. cit., pp. 60–1.
71 ibid., pp. 62–3.
72 Phelps-Brown, op. cit., p. 133.
73 ibid., p. 132.
74 T. Ashton, op. cit., p. 48.
75 Cf. S. and B. Webb, op. cit., pp. 391–2.
76 Notably Wollaton, Bestwood and Babbington.
77 Griffin, op. cit., Vol. I, pp. 50–1.
78 *Nottingham Daily Express,* 21st and 31st May; 15th, 18th, 20th, 27th, 30th June and 3rd July 1888.
79 T. Ashton, op. cit., pp. 68–70. The Annesley men had to strike for a short time; and there were preliminary hesitations on the part of the Barber Walker and Bestwood Companies—*Star and Advertiser,* Hucknall, 16th November 1888.
80 *New Hucknall Colly. Co., Balance Sheet,* Book I.
81 T. Ashton, op cit., pp. 73–79. *Nottingham Daily Guardian,* 29th and 30th May; 10th and 14th June and 1st July 1889.
82 *Nottingham Daily Guardian,* 10th and 14th June, and 1st July 1889.
83 *New Hucknall Colly. Co., Balance Sheets,* Book I.
84 T. Ashton, op. cit., pp. 79–83.
85 ibid., p. 81.
86 ibid., p. 82.
87 ibid., p. 86.
88 Gibson, op. cit., p. 157.
89 ibid., p. 11.
90 *New Hucknall Colly. Company, Balance Sheets,* Book I.
91 T. Ashton, op. cit., pp. 87–89; *Nottingham Daily Guardian* 17th March to 25th March 1890.
92 The Nottinghamshire voting was: in favour of strike, 9,625; against 414; blank papers returned, 219—Griffin, op. cit., p. 74.

93 T. Ashton, op. cit., p. 111.

94 *Hucknall Star and Advertiser*, 23rd October 1891.

95 Gibson, op. cit., p. 157.

96 ibid., p. 11.

97 *New Hucknall Colly. Co., Balance Sheets, Book I.*

98 Sources: *Membership* (except for 1883 and 1887–1890) from Registrar-General of Friendly Societies Records; 1887–1890 from a printed report of W. Bailey, N.M.A. Agent; 1883 from N.M.A. Minute Book; Prices from Gibson, op. cit., p. 157. The pit head price figures, being annual averages, are not really fine enough for our purpose. As a rough indicator of the state of trade, however, they are acceptable, but it must be borne in mind that fluctuations in coal prices occur from week to week.

99 I am indebted to the late Albert Bailey for letting me have sight of material relating to his father, William Bailey and father-in-law, Joseph Hopkin. Mr. Hopkin's grandson, Mr. C. Varnam was also helpful.

100 J. E. Williams, op. cit., pp. 489–490.

101 Griffin, op. cit., I, p. 46.

102 *Star and Advertiser*, Hucknall, 4th November 1887.

103 ibid., 6th April 1888 and Griffin, op. cit., I, p. 54.

104 e.g. Linby, which lent £20 to the Association out of its 'private' fund in 1886. Linby had its own benevolent benefits—see Griffin, op. cit., I, p. 54.

105 Differences in ability to pay were taken care of, to some extent, by basis prices which varied from pit to pit.

CHAPTER III

The 1893 Lockout and its Consequences

1. INTRODUCTION

The year 1892 saw a marked deterioration in trading conditions. The national average pit head price of coal for the year, at 7s. 3d., was 9d. lower than in the previous year and 1s. lower than in 1890.[1] Output fell by almost four million tons—from 185,479,126 tons in 1891 to 181,786,871 in 1892, but this was more than accounted for by the six million tons lost in Durham because of a trade dispute. Nottinghamshire produced only slightly less coal than in the previous year— 7,159,750 tons in 1892 as against 7,221,047 tons in 1891.[2] The Durham miners were locked out for three months, during which time they received no less than £33,385 16s. from the M.F.G.B., but they were finally forced back to work at a 10 per cent drop in wage-rates.[3]

Northumberland also suffered reductions in wage-rates amounting to 6¼ per cent, justified by Thomas Burt, M.P., the leader of the Northumberland miners, by reference to the fall in price of coal. Thomas Ashton, Secretary of the M.F.G.B., in a reply to Mr. Burt, said:

'The Federation policy may be called noisy and aggressive, the National Union watchful, firm and conciliatory; but the aggressive policy is what the men require. Of what use is the firm and watchful policy of the National Union to the poor, struggling men in Durham? The men are simply being starved into submission. Oh for one month of the aggressive policy of the Federation! Had Durham been members of the Federation, a general strike would have been declared, and none would be watching, all would be fighting.'[4]

The Federation met the fall in the demand for coal by a policy of output restriction. A conference was called to consider the advisability of 'laying the whole of the pits in the nation idle for two or more weeks with a view of clearing away the surplus coal in the markets and thus maintain the miners' wages'.[5] However, the 'outside' districts (i.e. Northumberland, Durham and South Wales) refused to subscribe to this policy.

148

During the third week of March 1892 all the pits of the Federated District were at a standstill. The men were not out on strike but were 'taking their spring holiday' as William Bailey explained to the New Hucknall men.[6] Subsequently, the Federation decided that one day in each week should be a 'play' day. Every pit in Nottinghamshire stood idle on Saturdays from 16th April to 27th August; and in the Leen Valley, the five-day week was tacitly accepted by the owners as a permanent arrangement and within a few years became accepted as the custom of the district.[7]

The Miners' Federation were of the opinion that fluctuations in the price of coal were greatly exaggerated by speculators who had 'held the coal owners and colliers by the throat and governed the markets, and collieries have been worked at a loss and miners' wages below a comfortable living point; and then political economists of a certain school have said it is the inexorable law of supply and demand which cannot be altered'.[8] The Federation considered the wage-level attained in 1890 to be an irreducible minimum which should be a first charge upon the industry. Throughout 1892, they made it clear that they would not countenance any reductions in rates. Durham and Northumberland had now joined the M.F.G.B., the former following the 1892 lock-out, the latter in 1893, but their leaders behaved, as Arnot says, 'like horses in the proverb: they might be led, or driven, by their members to the waters of the Federation, but its policy they would not drink'.[9] Durham, indeed, accepted a wage cut in 1893 contrary to Federation policy. This led a Federation conference to resolve, on 5th May, 'that any county adopting such action in future cannot be retained as part of the Miners' Federation of Great Britain'.[10]

In the early months of 1893, attempts were made in several districts to reduce wages by cutting basis rates. It will be appreciated that wages in this period consisted of two elements; first the wage-rates paid in 1888 which formed the 'basis'; and second a percentage addition (at this time, forty per cent) which came to be termed the 'current percentage'. The M.F.G.B. was concerned with negotiating the percentage additions only, and these were uniform throughout the Federated Area. Basis rates, which were determined by reference to geological conditions, travelling times underground, the profitability or ease of working of particular pits or seams of coal, the bargaining ability of negotiators, and a dozen other things, were fixed locally. Contract rates were negotiated at pit level, but day-wage rates were increasingly becoming the subject of county-wide negotiations.

Basis rates, then, were under attack in the early part of 1893: in the Midland Federation, Cumberland, the Forest of Dean, Somerset and Bristol. Where men were locked out, the Federation gave them financial support.[11] Then on 30th June the Federated Coal-Owners made a formal demand for a general 25 per cent reduction consequent on a 35 per cent reduction in coal prices since 1890.[12]

William Bailey ridiculed the owners' case at pit gate meetings. He said that the increase in wages cost since 1888 was 1s. 3d. a ton, whilst pit head prices were still 2s. 6d. a ton higher than in the period immediately preceding the first application for 10 per cent.[13] These figures are of the right order of magnitude. The New Hucknall Company's wages cost per ton, for example, rose from 2s. 10d. in 1888 to 4s. in 1892.[14] The National average pit head price of coal in 1892 was 2s. 2d. per ton higher than in 1888, and 2s. 5d. higher than in 1887, whilst the average pit head price at Midland collieries in 1892 was 1s. 10d. higher than in 1888 and 1s. 8d. higher than in 1887.[15]

The miners of Nottinghamshire made it plain that they were not prepared to accept a cut in wages. Some Nottinghamshire coal-owners were equally opposed to a reduction, and one of them, Col. C. Seely, M.P., made his opposition public.[16] However, when the time came, he issued his employees with lock-out notices along with other owners in the county.[17]

2. THE LOCKOUT

The Lock-out notices expired throughout the Federated Area in the last week of July 1893. Men at those collieries where lockout notices had not been issued, themselves gave notice to terminate contracts.[18] Durham and Northumberland continued at work, and their membership of the Federation was therefore deemed to be at an end.

At the outset of the dispute, Nottinghamshire's William Bailey moved at a National Conference that all men should be allowed to 'resume work at the old rate of wages . . . where the notices are unconditionally withdrawn, or where no notice has been given for a reduction'. This motion was defeated by 120 votes to 64.[19] On 29th September, when the dispute was two months old, this decision was reversed. It was then resolved:

'That where no reduction is asked for, the men be allowed to return to work, providing that all men working for any company, or at any colliery can return at once, so far as the conditions of the pit or pits will allow.'

'That all men who may be allowed to resume work at the old rate of wages pay a levy of one shilling per day or five shillings per week during the continuance of the lock-out.[20]

In Nottinghamshire, several colliery proprietors had shown their sympathy for the men. Alderman Thomas Bayley, M.P., of the Digby Company, was the chief speaker at a Miners' Demonstration held on Bulwell Forest on 12th August, when he urged the men to stand firm behind their leaders. Low wages resulted from the excessive and un-fair competition of some colliery proprietors. He implied that he was prepared to re-open his pits at the old rates of wages.[21] On 29th September he announced that he had broken with the Coal-Owners' Federation whose demand for a 25 per cent reduction in wages was unjustified. He hoped that the miners would refuse to go back to work at any colliery where the full pre-stoppage wage was not offered.[22] Colonel Seely had been similarly sympathetic to the men throughout the dispute. He had made loans available at the colliery office through-out September; and his wife had provided meals for the children of employees at Babbington and Newcastle.[23]

F. N. Ellis, of the Hucknall Company, indicated that they also had been opposed to the demand for a 25 per cent reduction, although they considered that a smaller reduction would have been justified. Lewis of the Annesley Colliery, on the other hand, alleged that his company had not wished to give their men notice for a reduction, but they had finally done so because of the pressure brought to bear on them by other proprietors, and in particular, F. N. Ellis.[24]

The N.M.A. officials asked all colliery companies in the county to withdraw the lockout notices, and most of them had done so by 12th October. Of the Leen Valley pits, only Bestwood showed any reluct-ance to re-open at the old rate of pay, and even they held out for only a few days longer than the others.[25]

On the other hand, the New Hucknall Company offered to re-employ their men at a 15 per cent reduction in wage-rates.[26] This offer was refused. The Company's accounts show how unjustified the proposed reduction was. The net profit during the first half of 1893 was £10,729: roughly 14 per cent on share capital. The profit per ton at 1s. 3·2d. was some 8·3d. less than in 1892, but was still satis-factory.[27] Besides New Hucknall's 1,150 employees, men at Pye Hill, Selston, Kirkby, Pinxton and Pollington remained out.[28] All these pits with the exception of Kirkby, were in the Erewash Valley and they were very much less profitable than the newer Leen Valley pits working the top hard Seam. Kirkby was a developing pit owned by the Butterley Company, whose other collieries were in the Erewash Valley.

In the federated district at large, some 87,538 men were back at work at the old rate of wages by 30th October, against 228,485 still locked out. The tendency was for more and more owners to capitulate as time passed.[29] Apart from the substantial levies from the men who were back at work, the Federation's dispute fund was fed by collec-tions organized by the *Daily Chronicle* and many local newspapers, including the *Nottingham Daily Express*; by private donations, by collections taken at churches, chapels, football matches, factories, in the street, and elsewhere. By the last two weeks of the dispute, the union was able to pay 4s. and 5s. in lock-out pay, and in addition, local funds provided supplementary help.[30] Contrary to the usual tendency, the longer the dispute lasted, the stronger did the men's financial position become.[31]

Various attempts at a general settlement came to nothing because the owners insisted upon a reduction in wage-rates which the Miners' Federation refused to accept. The Federation's case was that the existing wage-levels represented 'a fair, just and reasonable rate of wages' which they would 'fight campaign after campaign if need be to keep'. They had not sought increases after the fourth advance of 10 per cent was obtained in 1890 since 'they were content for wages to remain at the rate then obtained' which was 'considered fair'.[32]

On 13th November the Prime Minister, Mr. W. E. Gladstone, wrote to Thomas Ashton, Secretary of the Federation, offering the services of the Foreign Secretary, Lord Rosebery, as a mediator in the dispute. Lord Rosebery was not to 'assume the position of an arbitrator or umpire, or himself vote in the proceedings', but was to 'confine his action to offering his good offices in order to assist the parties in arriving between themselves at a friendly settlement of the questions in dispute'.[33]

Both the Miners' and the Coal-Owners' Federations accepted the Prime Minister's suggestion and their representatives therefore met, under the Foreign Secretary's chairmanship, on Friday 17th November 1893 at the Foreign Office. At this meeting, terms of settlement were drawn up and agreed upon by both sides. These provided for the establishment of a Board of Conciliation having equal representation from the two sides and an independent chairman with a casting vote. The Board was to determine the rate of wages on and from 1st February 1894: but in the meantime the men were to return to work on the pre-stoppage conditions.[34]

This settlement was duly endorsed by a National Conference held the following morning and the pits re-opened on Monday 20th November.

3. THE FEDERATED AREA CONCILIATION BOARD

The miners regarded 1893 as a great victory.[35] A souvenir poster bearing illustrations of the miners' delegates, the Foreign Office Committee room in which the Joint Conference of 17th November was held and of Llewellyn Smith, the Secretary of the Conference, found its way into many miners' homes. For those who took part in the dispute, the Rosebery settlement brought 'Peace with honour'.[36]

However, the meetings of the Conciliation Board did not go as smoothly as had been hoped. The miners' representatives attempted to have written into the Rules of the Board a minimum percentage on basis rates below which wages could not fall: a provision requiring owners to disclose their proceeds and profits to help to determine a fair level of wages; and a further provision requiring each owner to deposit with a joint committee a list showing the standard rates of wages paid at his colliery in June 1893. The owners refused to accept these suggestions and they were supported by the independent chairman, appointed by the Speaker of the House of Commons, Lord Shand. This led William Bailey to stigmatize Shand as a 'biassed partisan' who had 'shown so little consideration for the points held to be vital by the men and their representatives on the Board as to strike them all out of the rules, while endorsing and approving every point the owners pressed for'.[37]

Despite Bailey's gloomy forecast, the Board, once its Rules were adopted, worked reasonably well. Wages remained at the old level until 1st August 1894 when they were reduced to 30 per cent above the 1888 basis. It was then agreed that, for a period of two years, 30 per cent should be regarded as the minimum and 45 per cent as the maximum percentage. Negotiations were to take place within these two limits.[38]

During the following four years the miners of the Federated District 'maintained their standard of minimum wage [of 30 per cent above 1888], while in other coalfields there were successive reductions' as Arnot says.[39] For Dr. J. E. Williams, the historian of the Derbyshire miners, this success was illusory. Dr. Williams criticises Page Arnot who 'believes that the lock-out was a victory for the miners, despite the fact that by the conciliation agreement, the principle that wages should follow the price of coal had been re-asserted'. Similarly, he criticises the historian of the Nottinghamshire miners, for subscribing to 'the traditional mythology [sic] handed down by the Secretary of the M.F.G.B., Thomas Ashton, in his *Three Big Strikes in the Coal Industry* (M.F.G.B., n.d.).'[40]

The apparent success of the M.F.G.B. in obtaining a minimum percentage above the 1888 basis wage was vitiated, according to Williams, by two factors. First, the trend of coal prices from 1887 to 1914 was upward and there was thus 'never any necessity for the coal-owners to demand a return to the 1888 level of wage-rates'. Second, 'although nominal rates were maintained, earnings in the years immediately following the lock-out actually declined because of the short-time working'.[41] The first argument is a speculation on what might have been. The hard fact is that coal prices fell considerably between 1894 and 1897, but the miners of the Federated District retained their 30 per cent advance. Further, the principle of having a minimum percentage was never again questioned, not even during the dark years of the 1920's. The second argument will not hold water. The less efficient collieries certainly experienced a great deal of unemployment in the years immediately following the great lock-out,[42] (as they did whenever trade was depressed,) but the more efficient collieries were not nearly so badly affected. During the period 1888 to 1892 the high profits attracted much additional capital into the industry and new pits were sunk. Further, the more efficient companies made vast profits some of which they invested in new developments and improved equipment. There were no startling changes, but enough to improve the competitive position of the pits concerned. As always, however, the new capacity only became productive when the boom was over. Much low cost coal therefore came on to the market at a time when demand was depressed. The high cost coal failed to find buyers and the pits which produced it worked short time. But the most efficient firms actually sold more coal during the depression and their pits made good time. Thus, the outputs of the Butterley and New Hucknall Companies increased as follows:

TABLE 9

Date	Butterley	New Hucknall
1891	710,565 tons	363,256 tons
1892	817,533 tons	373,133 tons
1894	834,540 tons	437,574 tons
1895	895,226 tons	425,164 tons
1896	901,439 tons	447,238 tons
1897	931,125 tons	545,674 tons

Nationally, there is no evidence of increased short-time working as the table below indicates:

TABLE 10 SHOWING NUMBERS EMPLOYED, OUTPUT AND PRODUCTIVITY
1892–1898

	Output United Kingdom	Nos. employed below ground	Tonnage raised per person empd. below ground
1892	181,786,871	544,797	333
1894	188,277,525	565,091	333
1895	189,652,562	559,555	338
1896	195,351,951	551,639	354
1897	202,119,196	552,700	365
1898	202,042,243	561,463	359

Source: Gibson, op. cit., p. 11.[43]

In the absence of significant technological changes, (and there were none in this period), the tonnage raised per person employed below ground will reflect fairly accurately any changes in time worked, at least in the short term. The general tendency in this period was for the average output per man per year to increase slightly: [44] the increase over five years was of the order of ten per cent. This could not have been achieved had the degree of short-time working greatly increased. Further, the table below calls into question, if it does not disprove, the notion, to which Williams gives credence,[45] that the Northern counties had captured trade from the Midlands by reducing wages and thereby cutting costs and prices. It will be seen that the output of Durham and Northumberland rose very little in this period.

TABLE 11 SHOWING OUTPUT IN NORTHUMBERLAND AND DURHAM 1891 to 1897

	Northumberland Tons	Durham Tons
1891	9,330,359	29,807,523
1892	9,528,834	23,834,027
1893	9,112,788	30,819,070
1894	9,541,199	32,556,924
1895	8,694,651	31,133,253
1896	9,027,752	32,762,539
1897	9,768,459	33,819,068

Source: *Annual Report of Secretary for Mines and H.M. Chief Inspector of Mines for 1934, pp. 122–3 (Table 9).*

(N.B. The 1892 Output for Durham was seriously affected by a lengthy trade dispute.)

The sceptical attitude of Dr. Williams to the belief that 1893 was a victory for the miners presumably arises from his acceptance of the extreme left-wing view on conciliation. This leads him to say of this period:

'Mr. Arnot says nothing of the mounting opposition to the conciliation policies of the miners' leaders which culminated in the minimum wage agitation of 1910–12.[46]

In fact, the minimum wage agitation of 1910–12 originated in South Wales which was outside the Federated Area and there was no great enthusiasm for it in the better-paid districts.[47]

The Conciliation Board did not, as Williams implies, 'peg' wages between 1897 and 1914. One of the two determinants of wage-rates—the so-called 1888 basis—was left to negotiation at colliery and district level. The district leaders therefore took for granted the overall movements of wages negotiated by the Federated Area Conciliation Board, and concentrated, with considerable success, on raising basis day-wage rates and piece-work prices.[48] Further the sharp seasonal increases and reductions in wage-rates which were so marked a feature of the industry before 1888 were smoothed out. Conciliation may have prevented the miners from pushing wages up to the limit in the boom years of 1900 and 1907, as Dr. Williams asserts,[49] but it also helped to stabilize earnings, to give miners a sense of security, and to improve labour relations in the industry. These are not inconsiderable achievements.

4. THE LEEN VALLEY

From 1893 the special character of the Leen Valley became more clearly marked. The colliery owners of the Leen Valley pits, together with the Digby, Wollaton, Clifton and Babbington Companies formed an association of their own which they called 'The Nottingham and Erewash Valley Colliery Owners' Association'. The other owners remained members of the old Colliery Owners' Association which was affiliated to the Federated Coal-Owners. William Bailey pointed out that the Leen Valley owners were not parties to the Federated Area Conciliation Board proceedings and he suggested that they should continue to pay the 40 per cent addition to the 1888 basis wage when the other owners reduced the percentage to 30.[50]

In practice, the owners of the Leen Valley applied the percentage variations of the Federated Area Conciliation Board, but they retained their separate organization, and negotiations on district questions had now to be discussed with two owners' associations. In the Leen Valley, too, the men enjoyed a five-day week from 1892. The owners made no attempt to open their pits on Saturdays even in the boom years. However, when men in other parts of the county attempted to obtain the same privilege, their employers sued them for breach of contract.[51]

William Bailey attempted to obtain an eight-hour day in the Leen Valley also, but he was successful only with the Hucknall Company. Bailey looked to Ellis, the Hucknall proprietor 'to start the movement in the Leen Valley'. Ellis did so in 1895,[52] but the other owners failed to follow his example.

Three of the principal owners in the Leen Valley Association, Bayley, Ellis and Seely, were enlightened employers and were on terms of friendship with union leaders. Partly because of this, and partly because its pits were more profitable, the Leen Valley enjoyed more satisfactory labour relations than the Erewash. Because its wages were comparatively high,[53] it was able to attract and to hold a stable and efficient labour force.

5. CONCLUSION

The 1893 Lock-out demonstrated that the Miners' Federation of Great Britain, unlike previous national associations of miners, was a permanent organization. The Federation entered the dispute determined to safeguard the principal of a minimum wage to be recognized as a first charge upon the industry. In this it was successful.

The Federation made it clear that its quarrel was with the colliery owners and not with the nation at large. Allowing men to go back to work at all collieries where the owners would agree to pay the pre-stoppage wage was a strategical master-stroke. The men at work helped to support those still out, and the profits so obviously being made by the collieries which were back at work induced other owners to re-open their pits. Further, liberal newspapers espoused the men's cause and much help, both in cash and kind, was subscribed by their readers. The Government also adopted a helpful attitude in the later stages of the dispute. The Conciliation Board, set up at the conclusion of the dispute, functioned reasonably well once the initial difficulties over the drafting of its constitution were overcome.

In Nottinghamshire, those companies whose pits were in the Leen Valley—and several others too—broke away from the Colliery Owners' Association to form an organization of their own. Nottinghamshire was therefore divided into two separate wages districts. There was to be a certain amount of rivalry between Leen Valley and Erewash Valley branches of the Nottinghamshire Miners' Association in consequence. On the whole, however, the division in the ranks of the owners was to the union's advantage. Concessions obtained in one wages district were to be used as a bargaining lever in the other.

The 1893 lock-out was the first great mining dispute in which the men could claim a victory.[54] This victory, incomplete though it may have been, nevertheless ensured the consolidation of the Miners' Federation of Great Britain and the demise of the outmoded Miners' National Union. A defeat for the miners, on the other hand, would probably have wrecked the Federation.

REFERENCES

1 Gibson, op. cit., p. 157.
2 ibid., p. 24.
3 T. Ashton, op. cit., p. 137 et seq.
4 ibid., pp. 139–40.
5 ibid., p. 131.
6 Nottingham Daily Guardian, 2nd February 1892.
7 T. Ashton, op. cit., pp. 156–7; Griffin, op. cit., I, p. 193.
8 ibid., p. 134.
9 Arnot, op. cit., Vol. I, p. 221.
10 T. Ashton, op. cit., p. 195.
11 ibid., pp. 192–195.

12　ibid., p. 196.
13　Griffin, op. cit., I, p. 89.
14　*New Hucknall Colly. Co., Balance Sheets, Book I.*
15　Gibson, op. cit., p. 157 (figures to nearest 1d.).
16　*Nottingham Daily Guardian,* 1st July 1893.
17　Griffin, op. cit., I, p. 89. At two collieries, Lodge and Sutton, the owners did not give notice.
18　T. Ashton, op. cit., p. 207. Some 16,510 men in the Midland Federation resumed work contrary to Conference decision very early in the dispute. They had not been given notice, and they continued to receive the pre-stoppage wage—Ashton, op. cit., p. 211. Some 218,328 underground men were given notice in the Federated area, whilst 42,642 were not given notice—ibid., p. 200.
19　ibid., p. 210.
20　ibid., p. 213.
21　*Nottingham Daily Guardian,* 14th August 1893.
22　Griffin, op. cit., I, p. 94.
23　ibid., pp. 89, 92 and 94.
24　*Hucknall Star and Advertiser,* 13th October 1893.
25　Loc. cit.
26　Loc. cit.
27　*New Hucknall Colly. Co., Balance Sheets, Book I.*
28　*Hucknall Star and Advertiser,* 13th October 1893.
29　T. Ashton, op. cit., p. 221.
30　ibid., pp. 214–6, Griffin, op. cit., Vol. I, pp. 95–6.
31　T. Ashton, op. cit., p. 216.
32　ibid., pp. 206–7.
33　Letter from Gladstone to Ashton, cited T. Ashton, op. cit., pp. 229–30.
34　ibid., p. 233.
35　Griffin, op. cit., I, pp. 97–8 and 101; Ashton, op. cit., p. 236. In the present writer's youth, old miners still looked back with pride on the outcome of the 1893 lock-out.
36　Arnot, op. cit., I, illustration facing p. 236.
37　*Nottingham Daily Express,* 6th April 1894, cited Griffin, op. cit., I, pp. 116–120.
38　Arnot, op. cit., I, p. 255.
39　ibid., p. 255.
40　J. E. Williams, 'Labour in the Coalfields: A Critical Bibliography', *Bulletin of the Society for the Study of Labour History,* No. 4, 1962, pp. 26–7.
41　ibid., p. 26. Imperfect evidence in support of this view will be found in J. E. Williams, *The Derbyshire Miners,* London, 1962, pp. 349–50.
42　*Nottingham Daily Guardian,* 29th April 1895.
　　Dr. Williams gives two examples of short-time working following (and according to his argument, resulting from) the 1893 settlement. He says that the following figures, based on the wage sheets of one of the largest collieries in Derbyshire, give some indication of the decline in miners' earnings in this period:

Year	Avg. No. of days worked per week	Total wage base 1892–3 = 100
1892–3	4·00	100
1893–4	2·26	64
1894–5	2·16	43

At another large colliery, the miners were working five days a week at 7s. 6d. or 8s. a day in 1892 compared with one or two days a week at 6s. 9d.

or 7s. 6d. a day in 1895. (*Society for the Study of Labour History Bulletin,* No. 5. (1962) p. 50.) Dr. Williams leaves us to infer that these cases are typical, but if they were, we should expect to find a catastrophic fall in output per man year. There was no such fall. Dr. Williams's argument is unsound for two reasons: first he argues 'post hoc ergo propter hoc' that short-time working was caused by the settlement of the lockout; and second he generalizes for the country as a whole from two untypical local examples.

43 I have used Finlay Gibson's figures out of deference to Dr. Williams, who prefers them to those given in the *Colliery Year Book and Coal Trades Directory* which are copied from Mines Inspectors' Reports. The differences between the two sets of figures are much too small to affect the argument one way or the other, as these examples show:

OUTPUT FOR GREAT BRITAIN 1892–8

according to Mines Inspectors' Reports* (reproduced in *Colly. Year Book and Coal Trades Directory*)		*According to* F. A. Gibson
1892	181,786,871	181,786,871
1893	164,325,795	164,325,795
1894	188,277,525	188,277,525
1895	189,661,362	189,652,562
1896	195,361,260	195,351,951
1897	202,129,931	202,119,196
1898	202,054,516	202,042,243

* E.g. Annual Report of Secretary for Mines and H.M. Chief Inspector of Mines for 1934, pp. 122–3. (Table 9).

44 At the present day, colliery closures, increased mechanization and the replacement of inefficient faces by efficient ones is having the effect of increasing productivity by between 5 and 10 per cent per annum. The rate of change in the 1890's was nothing like as great.

45 J. E. Williams, *The Derbyshire Miners,* London, 1962, p. 350.

46 J. E. Williams, art. cit., p. 26.

47 J. E. Williams, op. cit., p. 408 et seq; Griffin, op. cit., I. pp. 164–618.

48 Griffin, op. cit., I, pp. 104–162. J. W. F. Rowe, *Wages in the Coal Industry,* London, 1922, pp. 46–56.

49 J. E. Williams, *Society for the Study of Labour History Bulletin,* No. 4 (1962), p. 26.

50 *Nottingham Daily Express,* 6th April 1894, cited, Griffin, op. cit., I, 116–120.

51 Griffin, op. cit., I, p. 105.

52 Ellis-Bailey correspondence, cited ibid., pp. 108–9.

53 *Coal Industry Commission Reports, (1919)* Vol. III, Cmd. 361, pp. 99 and 107, cited Griffin, op. cit., I, p. 34.

54 The criteria of 'success' in negotiations here adopted involve value judgments which are unlikely to gain universal approval. Whilst the miners' victory was incomplete; that some important gains were registered seems to the present writer to be beyond argument.

CHAPTER IV

The Development of the Mansfield Area 1890—1926

1. INTRODUCTION

The Leen Valley pits were sunk in the 1860's and 1870's, most of them between 1871 and 1875 in response to the upsurge of demand which was so marked a feature of the early years of the decade. Newstead, sunk in 1875, completed this series of sinkings.[1] There were few sinkings then until the 1890's, when the first large collieries in the Mansfield area were developed: Kirkby Summit, Bentinck, Creswell and Warsop. These were completed (as was the comparatively small South Normanton Colliery) between 1890 and 1896, as a result of the profitable state of the industry between 1889 and 1892. The next series of sinkings: Gedling (1900–2) Mansfield No. 2 (1904–5) Sherwood No. 1 (1902–3) followed by the Boer War boom.

There were further projects at Kirkby in 1912–15 when the North shaft was sunk below the top hard, and the Lowmoor shaft was sunk; at Rufford (1912–13) and Welbeck (1915) which completed this series. Future sinkings, in the 1920's were to be still further to the East, well into the Concealed coalfield, and the further East the sinkings went away from the outcrop, the deeper were the seams so that at Harworth (sunk between 1920 and 1923) the top hard seam was proved at a depth of 2,787 ft.

If a mine is to be sunk to a considerable depth, it must be a large one to justify the high cost of sinking. The collieries on the Eastern side of the coalfield are therefore larger enterprises than those on the Western side. Just as the Leen Valley pits were larger than the old Erewash Valley pits, the Mansfield area pits tended to be larger still. The opening up of the Leen Valley was duplicated in this new mining district. The large new collieries were sunk to the Top Hard seam, which they were able to work efficiently, particularly whilst their workings were still near the pit bottom. They had no difficulty with transport, their coal being taken to market mainly by rail. Their capital

WHIM-GIN AT PINXTON GREEN (DISMANTLED 1965)

WHIM-GIN FROM OLD PINXTON (THE GREEN
SHAFT) RE-BUILT AT SOUTH NORMANTON IN 1966

PORTLAND No 1 COLLIERY, 1821

PINXTON NOS. 1 AND 6 HEADGEAR SHORTLY BEFORE DEMOLITION
(KINGS PATENT DETACHING HOOK WAS PROVED HERE)

An agreement made and entered into this 15 day of April 1848 between Paul Leadbetter and John Simpson Coal Miners and William Bennett miner all of the Town of H. Keston. The aforesaid William Bennett agrees to work in the pit belonging to H. & Youth &Co situated in the parish of Shelley in the County of Nottingham from the Date above mentioned till the 2 of October next receiving at the same time of hireing one sovereign hence if The aforesaid William Bennett neglects his work through drunkeness or idleness to forfit for every such offence on shilling ────William Bennett ✗ his Mark

Witness Robert Skearington

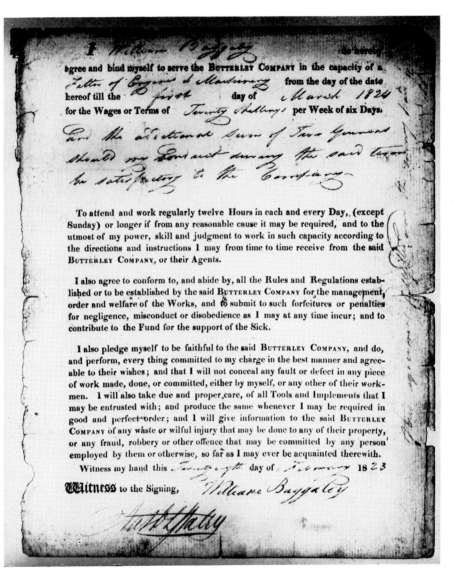

I William Baggaley do hereby
agree and bind myself to serve the BUTTERLEY COMPANY in the capacity of a
Setter of Engines & Machinery from the day of the date
hereof till the first day of March 1824
for the Wages or Terms of Twenty Shillings per Week of six Days.
and the additional Sum of Two Guineas
should my Conduct during the said term
be satisfactory to the Company —

To attend and work regularly twelve Hours in each and every Day, (except
Sunday) or longer if from any reasonable cause it may be required, and to the
utmost of my power, skill and judgment to work in such capacity according to
the directions and instructions I may from time to time receive from the said
BUTTERLEY COMPANY, or their Agents.

I also agree to conform to, and abide by, all the Rules and Regulations established or to be established by the said BUTTERLEY COMPANY for the management,
order and welfare of the Works, and to submit to such forfeitures or penalties
for negligence, misconduct or disobedience as I may at any time incur; and to
contribute to the Fund for the support of the Sick.

I also pledge myself to be faithful to the said BUTTERLEY COMPANY, and do,
and perform, every thing committed to my charge in the best manner and agreeable to their wishes; and that I will not conceal any fault or defect in any piece
of work made, done, or committed, either by myself, or any other of their workmen. I will also take due and proper care, of all Tools and Implements that I
may be entrusted with; and produce the same whenever I may be required in
good and perfect order; and I will give information to the said BUTTERLEY
COMPANY of any waste or wilful injury that may be done to any of their property,
or any fraud, robbery or other offence that may be committed by any person
employed by them or otherwise, so far as I may ever be acquainted therewith.

Witness my hand this Twenty eighth day of February 18 23

Witness to the Signing,   William Baggaley

BUTTERLEY BOND (1823)

PORTLAND ROW, SELSTON, 1823 (DEMOLISHED 1965)

MINERS' HOUSES OF THE 1930's AT EDWINSTOWE
(BUILT BY BOLSOVER CO. FOR THORESBY)

NAPOLEON SQUARE, CINDERHILL

NAPOLEON SQUARE, CINDERHILL
(THOMAS NORTH'S RAILWAY)

WINTERBANK, SOUTH NORMANTON (CLOSED 1889)

SOUTH NORMANTON COLLIERY, SUNK 1892
(HEADSTOCKS DEMOLISHED 1969)

HIGH HOLBORN PUMPING SHAFT, BABBINGTON
VILLAGE (THIS PIT CEASED WORKING ABOUT 1860)

TANDAM HEADGEAR AT BABBINGTON COLLIERY,
CINDERHILL (SUNK 1841–3)

SUTTON COLLIERY, DURING 1896 DISPUTE

was drawn in the main from older mining enterprises and so was their skilled labour force. Unskilled labour was attracted into the industry by the relatively high wages offered.

2. CAPITAL AND PROFITS

The tendency for the older type of landowning colliery proprietor to die out was almost complete by this period. The Dodsley family lost control of their pits partly, it would appear, through indebtedness. Robert Marsh Eckersley Wilkinson Dodsley, son of John, mortgaged part of his estate on 18th October 1872 in the sum of £18,285 to Lt.-Col. William Gregory Dawkins of London and Sir John William Ramsden of Ferrybridge, Yorkshire. This property appears to have included the Skegby pits. Further mortgages were negotiated in respect of the same property in the succeeding seven years totalling a further £16,923. These transactions were almost certainly connected with the sinking of Sutton Colliery in 1873 which appears to have been undertaken by a partnership dating from 1858, (the Skegby Colliery Brick and Lime Company) which came to be known as the 'Sutton Colliery Company'.[2] Dodsley sold seven acres of his estate to the Stanton Ironworks Company Ltd. in 1880 for £788, subject to the retention by Dawkins and Ramsden of 'All mines of Coal and other Minerals lying within and under the same parcel of land or any part thereof and the right to get work and carry away the same but only by subterranean operations.'[3] On the land, the Stanton Company built the village of Stanton Hill, which housed many of the workers at their Teversal and Silverhill Collieries.

The Sutton Company found physical conditions at their colliery to be unconducive to profitable operations. In June 1896 a dispute caused partly by an attempt to reduce basis wage-rates because of the colliery's serious difficulties and partly, by difficulty in fixing prices for machine-cut coal brought Sutton to a standstill, and it remained idle until April 1898 when a settlement was reached, doubtless facilitated by the improved state of trade.[4] In July 1897 the Company had negotiated a debenture loan from their bankers, the Crompton and Evans Union Bank Ltd., amounting to £30,000 at 5 per cent per annum.[5] This was not discharged until June 1902, by which time the Blackwell Colliery Co. Ltd. of Derbyshire had expressed an interest in acquiring the colliery which they did in the following year.[6]

Unlike most of the new collieries in the county, Sutton was working an area of coal where there were many old workings. It was larger and deeper than the old Skegby pits which it replaced, but not much. Its output in the period mid-April to mid-May 1896 averaged 197 tons of coal a day. Most of this came from the top hard Seam, the

M

remaining 20 tons or so a day coming from the one face in the Dunsil Seam. It will be remembered that these same two seams were the ones worked by John Dodsley in the late 1840's. The Company were now forced to sink deeper in order to find fresh coal to work, but their heavy capital equipment was suitable only for shallow seam working. In order to work seams deeper than the 198 yards of the top hard and 230 yards of the Dunsil, new winding engines, headstocks, and other equipment had to be purchased.[7] They could not be purchased from revenue account surpluses, since these were non-existent. There were losses of £1,750 in 1895, £1,942 in the first half of 1896 and £1,330 in the second half of the year, when the colliery stood idle because of the strike. These losses are equal to 7·3 per cent of the paid up capital of £24,100 in 1895 and 13·6 per cent of it in 1896.[8]

The Company's share capital was composed of 100 Founders' Shares of £1 and 6,000 Ordinary Shares of £10 of which only £4 had been called up by the end of 1896. Some equity holders, however, had paid calls in advance to the total of £4,412, presumably to help the Company over its period of financial difficulty. In addition, Crompton and Evans Union Bank Ltd. had advanced some £9,184 on overdraft up to the end of 1896. As we saw above, debentures of the value of £30,000 were taken up by the Bank some six months later.

Wages costs were very heavy at this colliery, largely because of the geological difficulties. The roof in the top hard was poor; whilst the Dunsil workings exhibited a marked dip and were subject to flooding. The wages cost per ton of coal in 1896, at 5s. 1d.,[9] compares unfavourably with New Hucknall's 3s. 6d. and South Normanton's 4s. 2d. in the same year.[10] In an attempt to reduce labour costs, an electric coal cutter was put to work in the Sutton dips section of the top hard seam on 14th May 1896, and it worked fairly satisfactorily during the few weeks prior to the complete stoppage of the pit.[11]

During the stoppage, the East shaft was deepened from 198 yards to the Low Main horizon at 467 yards. New headgear, winding gear and electric pumps were also installed, and a pair of second-hand steam engines for underground haulage were brought into use.[12] These may have improved the efficiency of the pit, but the Low Main Seam proved disappointing, having a friable roof which was difficult to control. The Blackwell Company, which absorbed Sutton in 1903, found it an unprofitable undertaking.[13]

The Stanton Ironworks Company were more fortunate with their Silverhill and Teversal Collieries. The new mining village which the Company built was called Stanton Hill. The same company owned the first colliery to be sunk on the Northern outskirts of Mansfield, Pleasley, opened in 1877. Later, in 1928, they sank Bilsthorpe Colliery over to the East.

The Bolsover Company followed Stanton's lead, sinking mines to the North and East of Mansfield. The Bolsover Colliery Company was founded in 1889 by Emerson Muschamp Bainbridge. It sank Bolsover Colliery in 1890–1; Creswell in 1896–8 and Mansfield (Crown Farm) in 1904–5.[14] By 1905, Bolsover was raising an average of 2,850 tons a day, Creswell a further 3,000 to 3,200 tons a day and Mansfield was expected to produce a million tons a year. In July 1910 an average over a five-and-a-half day period of 4,469 tons per day on single shift winding was achieved at Mansfield Colliery,[15] in which, according to Frank Varley, some £400,000 had been invested.[16] In 1912 Rufford Colliery was sunk, and in the 1920's two other very large collieries, Clipstone and Thoresby completed the Company's enterprises, making it the third largest colliery concern in the country.[17] The Bolsover Company was notorious for employing butties who had charge of large sections of the collieries, and who not only paid for their 'stalls', but had to make regular weekly payments to various officials thereafter.

Another Derbyshire firm, the Staveley Coal and Iron Company, also extended its field of operations to the Mansfield district, sinking Warsop in 1893–5. There were big butties at Warsop also.[18] Indeed one of them, who subsequently bought his way into Mansfield Colliery is said to have retired a wealthy man at about 48 years of age.

Staveley already had an interest in the county, being joint owner with the Sheepbridge Company of Newstead Colliery. The same joint subsidiary sank Blidworth Colliery in 1924. By 1942 the Staveley-Sheepbridge group was producing an average of 19,650,000 tons of coal a year—a greater output than that of any other colliery undertaking in the country.[19]

Another of the Mansfield area collieries, Sherwood, was sunk in 1902–3 by a company founded by the Ellis family, owners of the Hucknall pits, called the Sherwood Colliery Company. According to one of the Company's officials,[20] the initial capital outlay was drawn from the profits made at Hucknall.

At Kirkby, the Butterley Company deepened the North Shaft below the top hard in 1912 and sank Lowmoor pit some three years later. Its great venture in the area East of Mansfield: Ollerton, came after the War. This colliery took six years, from 1921–27, to sink and was not fully equipped for a further ten years. Its capital equipment cost £840,566 and the expenditure on building a new village to house the miners brought the total up to just under £1,500,000.[21]

The Barber Walker Company also expanded to the East. Ever since the turn of the century, they had been seriously worried about the depletion of their reserves. The total output for 1896 was 727,989 tons of which 46 per cent was top hard coal. The general manager reported that, if this rate of extraction were maintained, the Company's top hard reserves would be worked out by 1908.[22] It was therefore decided that a new pit should be sunk on virgin coal, and in 1902 exploration work was commenced at Bentley, Yorkshire. The sinking of the shafts proved to be a costly business on account of the depth of the seams, and the nature of the strata. The first 100 ft. of No. 2 shaft cost £17,673 8d. to sink.[23] Heading out from the Pit Bottom commenced in 1908.

The Company's next venture was at Harworth, North Nottinghamshire which marks the limit of the Mansfield area coalfield. Indeed, in many ways it resembles a South Yorkshire pit. Before the Great War a company in German ownership, the Northern Union Mining Company Ltd., was in the process of sinking a colliery at Harworth. Its property was impounded and its German employees interned on the outbreak of war. Subsequently, the Coal Controller invited tenders for the mining rights previously held by the Northern Union, and the Barber Walker Company's tender of £80,100 paid in full by June 1917 was accepted.[24] A subsidiary, registered as a private limited liability company and styled 'The Harworth Main Colliery Company Ltd.' was established in 1917 but by April 1922 this subsidiary had had to borrow something like £500,000 from the parent company and members of the Barber family and it was therefore wound up.[25]

Sinking at Harworth, which was by the cementation process owing to the waterlogged nature of the strata, commenced on 4th June 1919. The two shafts were 971 and 979 yards deep respectively. Sinking took four years and five months; and it was not until September 1924 that the winding engines were officially opened. Development work underground progressed very slowly owing to the unexpectedly heavy faulting of the strata, and the colliery's expected optimum output was not achieved.[26] According to Whitelock:

'By December, 1930, the surface plant was more or less complete, but the difficulties underground continued, and there appeared to be no real prospect of their abatement. Profits which had been envisaged were not forthcoming, and those which were being made by other units, were being absorbed at Harworth.'[27]

In order to offset the comparatively high costs of production it was decided to build a coke oven plant to make use of the soft small coal from the bottom three feet of the seam. The market price of small coal was very low at this time; but small coal of coking quality like that at Harworth could produce handsome profits if converted into by-products in modern coke-ovens. Harworth's battery of thirty ovens, which cost £185,000, came into production in 1934; and further ovens were added later. The plant had then an intake capacity of 600 tons of wet coal a day. The plant had, says Whitelock, 'a most satisfactory record of profits, compensating to some extent the difficult and expensive conditions at the Colliery'.[28]

The New Hucknall Colliery Company sank Welbeck Colliery in 1913–15. This was a highly profitable company, well able to finance the sinking of a new colliery out of the profits of New Hucknall and Bentinck. Its operations in the period 1893 to 1900 are summarized in the table below: [29]

TABLE 12 SHOWING CAPITAL, PROFIT, ETC. OF NEW HUCKNALL COLLY. CO., LTD. 1893–1900

Year	Share Capital Subscribed £	Tonnage	Average price per ton s. d.		Profit £	Profit per ton s. d.		Wage cost per ton s. d.	
1893	81,480	241,435	6	9·3	14,340	1	2·2	4	0·2
1834	81,480	437,574	6	2·0	32,034	1	5·5	3	7·8
1895	97,800	425,164	5	7·1	19,833		11·2	3	6·5
1896	111,660	447,238 (includes 18,827 from Bentinck)	5	2·9	12,031		6·7	3	6·0
1897	115,180	545,674	5	4·1	12,887		5·6	3	8·4
1898	115,470	315,261 (First Half-year only)	5	4·8	25,059		9·5	3	5·2
1899	119,500	374,009 (First Half-year only)	6	0·2	45,725	1	0·3	3	10·6
1900	125,000	787,794	9	11·8	157,177	3	11·9	4	8·1

N.B. Figures in Cols. 3, 4, 6 and 7 for 1898 and 1899 relate to the first half year only. The annual figures for those years are not available.

On 1st January 1901 the Company was reconstituted. The share capital was increased from £125,000 to £312,500 by the issue of 37,500 Preference Shares at £5 each.

The total share capital subscribed then remained substantially unchanged until 1913, when the total was increased to £436,700 made up as follows:

12,000	Ordinary "Fully Paid" £5 Shares	60,000
6,000	Ordinary "A" £5 Shares	£30,000
17,600	Ordinary "B" £5 Shares	£88,000
17,800	New Ordinary £5 Shares (£4 paid)	£71,200
37,500	Preference £5 Shares	£187,500

By this date, some £151,888 had been spent on capital plant for the new Welbeck Colliery. This compares with the total spent on capital plant at New Hucknall of £94,802, and at Bentinck, of £108,553 (including coke ovens and brickworks.)[30] By the time the new colliery was a fully productive unit, December 1916, some £274,534 had been spent on colliery plant and in addition a branch railway had cost £29,443 and land and houses for employees a further £68,972 making £372,950 altogether.

This expenditure was partly financed by the issue of mortgage debenture bonds to the value of £100,000 during 1915 and early 1916. These were all redeemed by 1923; a half of them for shares and the other half for cash. The total share capital issued, which stood at £454,500 in 1914, 1915 and 1916, rose to £504,500 in 1917[31] and then to £631,300 in 1918. It then remained unchanged until 1923 when it rose to £853,200.[32]

There is no doubt that Welbeck proved a profitable investment. Its effects on the Company's financial position are obscured, however, by the circumstances of war and of post-war boom and slump. The table below summarises the Company's operations from 1901 to 1916.

TABLE 13 SHOWING CAPITAL, PROFIT, ETC. OF NEW HUCKNALL COLLY. CO., LTD. 1901 TO 1916

Year	Share Capital Issued £	Tonnage	Avg. price per ton s. d.	Profit £	Profit per ton s. d.	Wages per ton s. d.
1901	312,500	701,150	9 3·2	96,451	2 8·4	5 1·6
1902	312,500	718,503	7 6·9	48,666	1 3·9	4 10·3
1903	312,500	660,012	7 2·0	28,634	0 10·2	4 10·6
1904	312,500	708,539	6 8·6	29,099	0 9·7	4 6·7
1905	312,500	782,477	6 1·9	30,553	0 9·3	4 3·9
1906	312,500	803,589	6 1·1	33,288	0 9·1	4 2·9
1907	312,500	983,678	7 2·3	70,447	1 4·9	4 8·8
1908	312,500	947,263	7 7·0	53,086	1 1·2	5 0·6
1909	312,500	865,640	6 7·1	26,745	0 7·3	4 11·1
1910	312,500	926,789	6 7·3	32,476	0 8·2	4 10·2
1911	312,500	933,094	6 6·5	19,663	0 5·0	4 11·7
1912	314,289	964,729	7 4·1	53,154	1 0·9	5 1·6
1913	436,700	1,110,009	8 8·4	99,744	1 9·2	5 7·6
1914	454,500	1,096,224	8 7·7	75,081	1 4·4	5 10·2
1915	454,500	1,177,495	10 5·2	103,076	1 9·0	6 11·7
	+98,875 Debs. +11,077 From Welbeck					
1916	454,500	1,442,811	13 5·5	197,994*	2 8·8	8 4·8
	+100,000 Debs.			(includes £100,000 put to reserve)		

From this point, the accounts of the Company are not so informative as formerly. Two reserve funds were created, one of which was for the purpose of providing cover for Excess Profits Levy and other tax demands. The profit declared as 'available for distribution' was net of sums put to reserve in this way. By the end of 1921, the ordinary reserve fund totalled £198,200, whilst the special reserve fund totalled £252,711, making £450,911 in all. The total amount put to reserve in this period (1916 to 1921) was £584,319; the difference between the two figures of £133,408 being accounted for by payments to the Exchequer during the period of Government control.[33]

The profits during this period including sums put to reserve were as follows:

TABLE SHOWING PROFIT OF NEW HUCKNALL COLLY. CO., LTD. 1917–1921

1917	£194,573 (including £29,319 Reserves)
1918	£238,007 (including £65,000 Reserves)
1919	£302,211 (including £165,000 Reserves)
1920	£317,869 (including £225,000 Reserves)
1921	£14,617 (Results affected by Lockout)

In addition, some £40,800 of mortgage debenture loan was redeemed in this period leaving only £9,200 outstanding.[34]

The New Hucknall Company may have been more profitable than most. The indications are, however, that its results were not untypical. In the months of November and December 1917 four collieries in Nottinghamshire and North Derbyshire producing one million tons or more a year had an average profit of 3s. a ton; eight others with outputs of half-a-million to a million tons a year had an average profit of 2s. 10d. a ton; whilst fourteen collieries producing between 100,000 and 500,000 tons a year had an average profit of 2s. 5d. a ton. The average profit per ton for the district as a whole was 2s. 9d.; and this figure minimises the results of the newer Nottinghamshire pits, since the marginal enterprises in Derbyshire and West Nottinghamshire pulled down the average.[35] If we were able to study the accounts of all the new collieries in what we have loosely called the Mansfield area, it would without doubt be found that they were, on the whole, very profitable indeed.

3. LABOUR, HOUSING AND WELFARE

The new collieries of the Mansfield district were large ones, requiring many men. In 1945, in a survey made under the auspices of the Ministry of Fuel and Power, the Nottinghamshire-Derbyshire coalfield was divided into three parts: the exposed coalfield (lying roughly to the west of a straight line drawn from Chesterfield to Nottingham) the older concealed coalfield (lying to the east of the exposed coalfield and bounded on the east by a line drawn from Worksop to Nottingham, with Mansfield as its central point) and the newer concealed coalfield lying to the east of the older concealed coalfield. In the first of these areas, there were 66 collieries employing almost 40,000 men, with an average labour force per colliery of 603; in the second area (which includes the Leen Valley and the collieries sunk in the immediate vicinity of Mansfield, Sutton and Kirkby) there were 26 pits employing over 28,000 men, with an average labour force per colliery of 1,070; and in the third area (comprising the collieries sunk after the First World War) there were eight collieries only employing about 12,000 men, with an average labour force of 1,537.[36]

When the Barber Walker Company opened out their Bentley Colliery in South Yorkshire in 1908, they selected their 'early complement of underground workers . . . from men employed in the same seam at High Park and Watnall Collieries'.[37] No doubt other companies did much the same thing. Experienced miners were also attracted into the district from other areas by the comparatively high wages earned in Nottinghamshire and by the availability of colliers' houses. In the early 1920's for example, many miners moved from South Wales to the Kirkby district to fill vacancies advertised in the Labour Exchanges. These vacancies were presumably caused by the movement of men from the Kirkby district to the new colliery villages being built to the east of Mansfield like Blidworth and Bircotes (Harworth). There was evidently a general tendency for miners to move in an eastward direction away from the older, less productive, collieries of the exposed coalfield.[38] Nottinghamshire continued to gain men from Derbyshire.

Nottinghamshire's increased labour force was, then, partly provided by long-distance migrations from other coalfields and partly by short-distance migrations from the western, to the eastern, side of the Nottinghamshire-Derbyshire coalfield. The collieries sunk in what we have loosely termed the Mansfield district prior to 1920 were close to settled centres of population like Mansfield itself. Some of the miners coming in from other areas would, therefore, be able to find accommodation for themselves without much difficulty. Some houses would need to be built, particularly in order to attract and hold the skilled nucleus of miners necessary for heading out the workings and for establishing a satisfactory tempo of work. Later arrivals could be left to find their own houses.

Welbeck Colliery, opened out in the early years of the war and situated on the Northern outskirts of Mansfield, had some 543 colliery houses built between 1912 and 1922 and a further 334 built between 1924 and 1926,[39] sufficient for about half of its labour force of around 1,700 in 1916.[40] The Bolsover Company built Forest Town, a 'model village' suburb of Mansfield, to house a fair proportion of their employees at the new Crown Farm (or Mansfield) Colliery sunk in 1904–5.[41] These houses are incomparably better than those built some 30 years earlier at Newstead or Stanton Hill. The Company similarly built model villages near their new Derbyshire pits, Bolsover and Creswell 'which both in accommodation and layout compare not unfavourably with others built several decades later'.[42] The Bolsover Company, no doubt, believed that it was sound business to provide its employees with good houses in decent surroundings close to their work. The model villages of tied houses provided a stable labour force: they were, indeed, because of this, a factor in the 'Spencer' breakaway of 1926, which owed much of its early success to the support of Bolsover men.

The collieries sunk after 1920 were further away from existing centres of population and houses had to be built for a larger proportion of their men.

The Regional Survey Committee in 1945 concluded that 'In general, housing conditions are excellent and the colliery villages at Harworth, New Ollerton and the modern Bolsover pits are in many respects models of their kind.'[43] At Harworth, the new village of Bircotes was designed by a resident architect, and four assistants. They made 'the most of the ideal situation in laying out a small town of about eleven hundred houses, with wide well-paved roads (some tree-lined), modern drainage, electric lighting, and hot and cold water and a bath in every house. A large, substantially built, and attractive 'Institution' was incorporated in the plan, together with ample provision for every modern sport. A church, church hall and parsonage were built by the Company at their own expense, and £400 a year was provided towards the stipend of a curate-in-charge. . . .'[44] In this way, the Company hoped to 'ensure the necessary stable reserve of man-power at the site of the new colliery'.[45]

The Butterley Company had, as long ago as the late 1880's, set an example at their Kirkby Colliery by building colliers' cottages with baths.[46] Similarly, in the 1920's, the eight-hundred-odd houses built by them at New Ollerton set a high standard. The houses were:

'. . . of red-brick, and tiled, in small detached groups, lining the streets of the new village, each with a small lawn before it, and its garden at the back. . . . A supply of hot water, from exhaust steam from the colliery, and a supply of electricity, runs to every house.'[47]

The Regional Survey Committee of 1945 were 'very favourably impressed by the central system of hot-water supply from the colliery boiler house . . .' and recommended 'a wide adoption of this principal elsewhere.'[48]

The Butterley Company also built as part of their New Ollerton estate a factory rented by a hosiery firm, which provided employment for 600 people, mostly women and girls. Apart from this, there were 'virtually no secondary industries' in the new villages of the concealed coalfield.[49] At Ollerton, as at Harworth, facilities of various kinds—a new church, a clinic, an institute, sports grounds, and so on— were provided.[50]

Ollerton was grafted on to an existing village. So, too, was the nearby mining village of Edwinstowe.[51] Partly because of this, they settled down as integrated communities fairly quickly whilst Bircotes being more isolated, was still a raw place ten years after its construction. Both the new mining villages and the old benefited from the Welfare Levy imposed in the Mining Industry Act, 1920[52] as a result of a recommendation by the Sankey Commission of 1919.[53] The levy was at the rate of 1d. per ton of coal produced between 1920 and 1934 (and again after 1939) and at the rate of ½d. per ton between 1934 and 1939. The Miners' Welfare Fund was administered by the Miners' Welfare Committee (later called the Miners' Welfare Commission) which had equal representation from colliery owners and workers, plus a few people from outside the industry. It was appointed by the President of the Board of Trade. Similarly constituted committees were established at county and wages district levels.

Capital sums were made available from the Fund for the construction of pit head baths, canteens, medical centres, welfare institutes, reading rooms, sports grounds, swimming baths, children's recreation grounds, and so on. Money was also set aside for scholarships for miners and their families. Institutes and associated recreational facilities were soon to become a feature of all mining villages. They were open to non-mining families, too, and in some places local authorities gave them financial support on revenue account.

Pit head baths were not universally popular, however, and only a minority of collieries had them prior to 1938. Many miners alleged that coming out of a hot bath into the cool air caused pneumonia and that pit head baths were breeding-grounds for skin diseases. The opposition to the introduction of baths was, however, primarily caused by the innate conservatism of the older men. A new generation of young men who felt far more embarrassed at riding in buses in their pit dirt than they would at using a communal pit head baths building brought a change in the general attitude. From 1938 on, more and more pits voted for the erection of baths and every colliery in the district now has them.

One of the happiest innovations in the Nottinghamshire district was the establishment of day-release classes for miners organized by the Miners' Welfare Joint Adult Education Committee, representative of the Miners' Welfare Committee and of the University of Nottingham. Many men who were to take senior posts with the nationalized mining industry, one of them as a member of the National Board, owed their early education to this joint committee.[54] Quite a number obtained university degrees, latterly at the University of Nottingham.[55] The scheme was abandoned in 1953 in favour of a wider scheme of education bringing in more miners at a time, but aiming at a rather lower level of academic attainment.

4. WARTIME CONTROLS

The opening out of the Mansfield area was interrupted by the war years, when shortages of skilled labour and materials made it difficult to initiate large-scale development projects.

Up to the end of March 1916 some 282,200 miners, well over a quarter of the total labour force, had voluntarily joined the Armed Forces.[56] These were, in the main, the young men forming forty per cent, or more, of the 19–39 age-group. They were, as Redmayne says, 'the very pick of the manpower of the mining industry'.[57] Later, some miners were conscripted under the provisions of the Military Service Acts and altogether almost half-a-million miners saw military service.[58] On the other hand, men from other industries were attracted into mining, but being inexperienced, they were not so productive as the men they replaced. This accounts in part for the fall in productivity recorded in the table below:[59]

TABLE 14 SHOWING MANPOWER AND PRODUCTIVITY 1913–1920
(NATIONAL FIGURES)

Year	Manpower (thousands)	Output per man per year overall (Tons)
1913	1,107	260
1914	1,038	256
1915	935	271
1916	981	261
1917	1,002	248
1918	990	230
1919	1,170	196
1920	1,227	187

The fact that productivity was so well maintained down to 1917 indicates the success of appeals made to the patriotism of the miners who agreed, for example, to curtail their statutory holidays.[60]

The Home Secretary, the Rt. Hon. R. McKenna, M.P., appointed a Coal Mining Organization Committee in February 1915 'with a view to promoting such organization of work between employers and workmen as, having regard to the large number of miners who are enlisting for naval and military service, will secure the necessary production of coal during the war'.[61] The Committee, comprising three representatives of the Mining Association of Great Britain and three

Nottinghamshire Miners' Association

MINERS' OFFICES,
OLD BASFORD,
APRIL 10TH, 1918.

Instructions re Scheme for Recruiting 50,000 Grade 1 Men from Coal Mines.

1. Men on full compensation will not be accepted for military Service.
2. Men on part compensation must produce a certificate from Employer, or Insurance Company in proof thereof, as per Recruiting Code No. 341X, and they will not be called up for Military Service.
3. Men who on January 1st, 1918, were not 18 years and 8 months of age, or were 25 years of age, should not have been put in the ballot, and on supplying Major McGuire with birth certificates in proof thereof, they will be struck off the lists of those to be called up.
4. Men who on November 2nd, 1915, were married, or widowers with children dependent on them, should not have been put in the ballot, and on producing marriage certificate in proof thereof to Major McGuire, they will be struck off the lists of those to be called up.
5. Where lists of employees are proved to be seriously incomplete, the Military Authorities will carefully examine the case, and, if advisable, allow another ballot to be taken.
6. All who have voluntarily enlisted in any of His Majesty's forces since January 1st, 1918, and are Grade A Men, will be deducted from the quota required from that Colliery; if of a lower grade they will not be deducted, but will be allowed to return to the Colliery at their request.
7. Lists of Names already supplied by military authorities, and used for balloting purposes, will be returned to Lodge officials after the medical examinations have taken place, so that they may see what the medical category of every man is.
8. Class W. men are liable to be recalled for service; they should not be in the ballot; and if in the ballot will be passed over.
9. A Volunteer who was not in the ballot, and is over 24 years of age, can choose his regiment.
10. Every man has the right to appeal against being called up; but his appeal must be made to the Local Tribunal, and made within 7 days of him receiving the Calling Up Notice.

The Union as Recruiting Sergeant — 1918.

officials of the Miners' Federation of Great Britain (one of whom, Robert Smillie, belonged to the anti-war wing of the Labour Party,) met frequently under the chairmanship of the Chief Inspector of Mines, R. A. S. Redmayne. The suggestion as to the curtailment of holidays came from this Committee. They also examined the desirability of lengthening the working day, of bringing more women into the industry to do surface work, and of lowering the age at which boys could work underground. These suggestions did not commend themselves to the Unions, and were not pursued.[62] The Committee tried to reduce the incidence of voluntary absence from work, which amounted to about five per cent of possible attendance in the early days of war. They estimated that output could be increased by 13,882,141 tons a year if miners made every possible attendance. In 1916, absentee committees were set up at colliery and district level and these, according to Redmayne, 'undoubtedly contributed very materially to an improvement in the attendance of the workmen, though they did not achieve all that was hoped of them'.[63] The limitation of hours of opening of licensed premises was probably far more effective.[64]

The industry was plagued, too, by difficulties in obtaining supplies of materials. Some four-fifths of Britain's pitwood, valued at about £3½ millions at pre-war prices, was imported. By 1916, the price 'was fully 300 per cent higher than it was before the War and the supply from Norway, Sweden and Russia was uncertain. Further, supplies might at any time be cut off[65] On the initiative of the Coal-mining Organization Committee, a Central Joint Committee was established by the Government to organize the purchase and distribution of home-grown mining timber. This committee had compulsory purchase powers, although it used them sparingly. The War Office agreed to allocate a thousand prisoners-of-war for felling and sawing timber.[66]

Most other materials and plant used in coal-mining were home-produced, but because of war-time conditions, they were in short supply and their prices rose considerably.[67]

The tendency for the price of coal itself to rise considerably was held in check by the Price of Coal (Limitation) Act of 1915, which empowered the authorities to control the prices of inland coal, but not of export coal. At one period, the price of one quality of coal was 16s. 6d. per ton for inland consumption and from 60s. to 65s. per ton for export. After the Armistice, this coal was selling abroad for still higher prices, reaching £7 10s. in 1920.[68] The quantity and destination of export coal during the War were, however, under the control of a Committee established by the Board of Trade. The objects of this Coal Exports Committee were to ensure that sufficient coal was retained in the country for essential purposes; to ensure adequate supplies to our allies, and particularly France; and to encourage the free export of the remainder to neutral countries at the highest possible prices.[69]

Profits were also subject to Government control. In 1915 an Excess Profits Levy equal to 80 per cent of the difference between 'standard profits' (i.e. pre-war profits) and actual profits was imposed on all non-controlled industries, including mining.[70] In February 1917 the mining industry passed into the posession of the Board of Trade by a regulation made under the Defence of the Realm Act. Managers and owners of mines were thereafter subject to the directions of a Government official, the Coal Controller, who was assisted by an advisory committee of seven coal-owners and seven workmen's representatives. In practice, day-to-day control was in no way affected. The financial arrangements were now altered somewhat. The Government still took 80 per cent of excess profits, but the balance was now divided between the Coal Controller and the Company, the former taking 15 per cent, and the latter 5 per cent. The Coal Controller's share of the profit went into a pool from which deficiency payments were made to owners who failed to earn the guaranteed standard profits.[71] These financial controls did not, however, prevent colliery companies from amassing considerable reserves, as the New Hucknall Company did.[72] Other companies purchased capital equipment and undertook development work for future use out of revenue account. The financial control was, apparently, far less effective than has been supposed.[73]

The Coal Controller was a party to all wage negotiations during the period of control. Any increases in wages negotiated locally were subject to his approval, and he dealt with applications for general increases. Government Control of the mines came to an end on 31st March 1921, when the various increases in wages sanctioned by the Coal Controller lost their validity.

5. AFTER THE WAR

The high prosperity of the war, and the immediate post-war, period came to an end in 1921 when the demand for coal fell sharply. Faced with the possibility of making considerable losses, the Government decontrolled the mining industry on 31st March. The employers attempted to impose severe reductions in wage-rates but these were resisted by the men who were consequently locked-out until the end of July. The settlement then reached provided for a Government subsidy in aid of wages for the three months ended 31st October 1921 which mitigated the reductions in earnings.

Prices in 1922 were very much lower than for some time past: the national average pit head price of coal being 17s. 8d. against 26s. 2d. in 1921 and 34s. 7d. in 1920. The average declared value (Free on Board) of coal exported was 22s. 7d. in 1922 against 34s. 10d. in 1921 and 79s. 11d. in 1920.[74] These steep reductions in prices enabled British coal exporters to regain their pre-war level of exports; the 1922 figure, at 64·2 million tons, being only marginally less than the 1912 figure. In 1923, stimulated by the dislocation of the coal-mining industry in the U.S.A. and the Ruhr, exports rose to a record level of 79·4 million tons.[75] The average profit per ton during 1923 was 2s. 1d. compared with 10½d. in the previous year. According to a statement made by the mine owners to the Buckmaster court of Inquiry in 1924 (based upon returns from collieries producing 70 per cent of the total tonnage), during the period October 1922 to September 1923 inclusive, only 15·7 per cent of the total output from British mines was produced at a loss, against 37·4 per cent in the previous twelve months.[76]

In another statement presented to the Buckmaster Inquiry the M.F.G.B. alleged with some justification:[77]

'That the [wages] agreement of 1st July 1921, while giving the workmen wages less than the equivalent of pre-war earnings, allowed the owners profits substantially in excess of pre-war profits.'

It is possible to argue, therefore, that the improvement in the competitive position of the British coal industry in export markets in 1922 to 1924 was obtained largely at the expense of wage-earners.

Following the Buckmaster Inquiry, the 1921 Agreement was amended in the workmen's favour. But by this time, the level of exports was already falling. From 79·4 million tons in 1923 it fell to 61·6 million tons in 1924 and to 50·8 million tons in 1925.[78] The return to the Gold Standard at the pre-war parity intensified the already acute problems of Britain's coal exporters. These problems, it appeared, necessitated a further reduction in wages in order to bring export prices down to a competitive level.

Nottinghamshire's colliery proprietors were not affected nearly so badly by the industry's changed fortunes as the owners in high-cost districts, particularly where these were reliant upon the export trade. The Stanton Ironworks Company for example paid dividends on its ordinary shares of 14 per cent in 1920 and 1921, and 10 per cent in each of the succeeding three years.[79] The Digby Colliery Co. Ltd., which paid 14 per cent on its ordinary shares in 1924, however, found itself in difficulties in the first half of the following year, when its losses at Gedling Colliery were said to be running at the rate of £1,466 a week. The company suggested that the men should agree to bear one-half of this loss out of their wages, or that alternatively one pit should be closed and the other worked double shift. This latter proposal would have entailed a reduction in the labour force of nearly 1,700 men out of a total of around 3,800.[80] The difficulty was caused by a substantial fall in the price of coal due, among other things to the improvement in the exchange associated with the return to the Gold Standard.[81] Fortunately for the Company, a Government subvention in aid of wages was introduced at the end of July. How much this benefited the Digby Company one cannot say, but for the New Hucknall Company it amounted, in 1925, to £40,621—over a quarter of the firm's profits.[82]

The New Hucknall Company, indeed, made considerable profits

throughout this period. From the £14,617 of 1921 (when results were affected by the lock-out) the profit before tax rose to £160,271 in 1922 and £295,004 in 1923. There was a slight fall to £290,479 in 1924 during which year Annesley Colliery was taken over by the Company. In 1925 there was a falling off to £158,365 (which still represents about 18 per cent on the issued capital) but in 1926, the year of the great lock-out, the Company's profits reached the record level of £517,987. This astonishing result was brought about by sales of stock coal at famine prices, by the Government subvention during the early part of the year amounting to £27,000, but above all by the profitable trade conducted during the later stages of the dispute when many men were back at work and there was a ready sale for all grades of coal at prices greatly inflated by the continuing shortage. During the first half-year, the profits of the New Hucknall Company amounted to no more than £33,430 (including the £27,000 wages subvention) when coal sales totalled £477,146. During the second half of the year, however, profits of £484,557 were earned. Coal sales at £940,561 were almost double the corresponding figure for the first half-year whereas wages costs at £302,921 were £32,936 lower.[83] In the succeeding three years of industrial peace the Company was to earn only a fraction of this record profit: £53,734 in 1927; £33,616 in 1928 and £83,094 in 1929. There is no reason to doubt that other colliery proprietors in the county benefited similarly from the early return to work of the Nottinghamshire miners in 1926.

As the Samuel Commission demonstrated, it was the very small undertakings on the whole which suffered heavy losses in the period 1921–25.[84] Most of the medium and large-scale producers managed to continue to work at a profit.[85] Even in the quarter ended December 1925 the coal-owners of Nottinghamshire and Derbyshire, most of whose collieries were of at least a fair size, made an average loss per ton of coal sold commercially (before taking the wage subsidy into account) of only 0·02 of a shilling as compared with an average for South Wales of 3·20 shillings, and for the country as a whole of 1·47 shillings.[86] This is not merely a question of the relative sizes of undertakings: all the exporting districts had substantial net losses. Nevertheless, within each district the small inefficient concerns depressed the general standards. Tawney expressed the view that the Samuel Commission did not

'. . . lay as much emphasis as was desirable upon the fact that the industry was overstaffed, upon the improbability that it could, in view of the changed world-situation, be carried on upon the same scale as in the past while offering a decent livelihood to those engaged upon it, or upon the importance of concentrating production in the best areas, and of offering inducements to the older men to retire from the industry.'[87]

The Nottinghamshire colliery undertakings were, on the whole comparatively efficient, and they were to a large extent sheltered from the vagaries of international trade. The largest of them, whose development has been described in this chapter, were working virgin top hard coal with a skilled labour force and modern equipment. They were far better able to face the depression which was to become intensified from 1927 than the older concerns of the exposed coalfield. Some colliery closures were desirable even in the relatively prosperous Nottinghamshire-Derbyshire coalfield, but the pits which were to close under the impact of economic adversity were on the Western side of the coalfield. There were to be no closures in the Leen Valley proper until 1945 (when Bulwell went out of production); whilst at the time of writing all the collieries of the newer concealed coalfield (which we have loosely labelled the Mansfield District) still have many years of life in them and their levels of output continue to rise.

REFERENCES

1 The dates of sinkings, etc., given in this section are supplied by the N.C.B. Survey Dept. Most of them will be found in *The Concealed Coalfield of Yorkshire and Nottinghamshire* (H.M.S.O.) 1951.

2 Indenture dated 15th October 1880 between William Gregory Dawkins and others and the Stanton Ironworks Co. Ltd. Dodsley was, of course, the chief member of the Skegby partnership.

3 ibid., typewritten copy, p. 4.

4 *N.M.A. Minute Book*, 31st October 1896, 26th June 1897 and 28th April 1898.

5 Memorandum of Agreement made the 18th May 1898 between J. F. Thirlby and Peter Howard and the Crompton and Evans' Union Bank Ltd. Crompton, the banker, was also the major shareholder in the Stanton Ironworks Co.

6 Memorandum of Agreement made the 30th June 1902 between the same parties. The Boer War years were highly profitable for coal mining firms. The South Normanton Company for example made a net profit of £7,158 in half-year ending 28th February 1901 on an issued capital of £11,280. This was, however, a new colliery and the workings were very close to the pit bottom. See Company's *Annual Report and Accounts. 1900–01.*

7 Report of Manager, James Wroe, to Board of Directors dated 16th May 1896.

8 *Sutton Colliery Company's Balance Sheet* dated 31st December 1896.

9 *Sutton Colliery Company's Revenue Account* dated 31st December 1896.

10 *New Hucknall Colly. Co., Balance Sheets, Book 2*, and *South Normanton Colliery Co. Ltd., Accounts 1897.*

11 Report of Manager to Directors dated 16th May 1896. Mechanical coal cutters had been tried in Nottinghamshire before this by, for example, Barber Walker, but without much success. See, e.g. evidence of R. Harrison regarding a Winstanley Holing Machine tried out in the Deep Hard Seam at Eastwood— *Royal Commission on Accidents in Mines, Preliminary Report, 1881,* Q, 9495–9598.

12 Loc. cit.
13 Griffin, op. cit., I, p. 199. Because profits were low, ruthless economies were practised and Sutton acquired the nick-name 'The Bread and Herring pit.'
14 J. E. Williams, op. cit., p. 176.
15 ibid., p. 177.
16 *M.F.G.B. Minute Book*, 10th July 1923.
17 J. E. Williams, op. cit., p. 572.
18 ibid., p. 176.
19 ibid., p. 572.
20 Mr. J. Ball.
21 Mottram and Coote, op. cit., pp. 23–24, 116–120.
22 Whitelock, op. cit., p. 79.
23 ibid., p. 88. The shaft was 1847 ft. deep.
24 ibid., p. 163.
25 ibid., p. 166.
26 At least until very recently—ibid., pp. 167–8.
27 ibid., p. 175.
28 ibid., pp. 175–7.
29 Source: *New Hucknall Colly. Co., Ltd., Balance Sheets, Book 2*.
30 ibid., Book 3.
31 This apparent increase in share capital was, in fact, a conversion of half the Debenture Stock of £100,000 into Shares.
32 *New Hucknall Colly. Co., Ltd., Balance Sheets, Books 3 and 4*.
33 ibid., Books 3 and 4.
34 ibid., Book 4.
35 *Coal Industry Commission Report*, Vol. III, Cmd. 361, 1919, pp. 12–13. The profits are net.
36 *North Midland Coalfield—Regional Survey Report*, H.M.S.O., 1945, p. 22.
37 Whitelock, op. cit., p. 91.
38 This view is based on discussions with members of the staff of the National Coal Board's Manpower Branch.
39 *New Hucknall Colly. Co., Ltd., Balance Sheets, Book 4* and N.C.B. Estates Dept. Records. The 543 houses are at Warsop and the 334 at Welbeck Village.
40 *N.M.A. Minute Books*, Welbeck's manpower rose to over 2,000 in 1919, and over 2,200 in 1921.
41 There are 320 colliery houses at Forest Town. Mansfield Colliery had a labour force of about 2,200 in 1917—N.M.A. Minute Book, 1917 and N.C.B. Estates Dept.
42 *North Midland Coalfield, Regional Survey Report*, H.M.S.O., 1945, p. 22.
43 Loc. cit.
44 Whitelock, op. cit., p. 169.
45 ibid., pp. 168–9.
46 Mottram and Coote, op. cit., p. 95.
47 ibid., p. 121.
48 *North Midland Coalfield, Regional Survey Report*, H.M.S.O., 1945, p. 22.
49 ibid., p. 23.
50 Mottram and Coote, op. cit., pp. 116–117.
51 *North Midland Coalfield, Regional Survey Report*, H.M.S.O., 1945, p. 22.
52 10 and 11 Geo. 5, cap. 50.
53 *Coal Industry Commission Reports, Vol. I*, Cmd. 359, 1919, p. ix.
54 Mr. W. H. Sale was Labour Relations Director of the N.C.B.
55 A. H. Thornton, 'Day Release for Liberal Studies', *Adult Education*, XXIX (1956), p. 197 et seq.

56 R. A. S. Redmayne, *The British Coal-Mining Industry During the War*, Oxford, 1923, p. 257.
57 ibid., pp. 13 and 257.
58 ibid., p. 258.
59 Source: F. A. Gibson, op. cit., p. 11.
60 Redmayne, op. cit., p. 17. The mines were also working more regularly than pre-war.
61 ibid., p. 13.
62 ibid., pp. 18–20 and Griffin, op. cit., II, p. 23 based on N.M.A. Minute Book (e.g. 4th August 1917).
63 ibid., pp. 16–17 and 69.
64 Though offset to some extent by drinking at home.
65 Redmayne, op. cit., p. 45.
66 ibid., pp. 47–9.
67 ibid., p. 43.
68 ibid., pp. 34–35, 245 and 263.
69 ibid., pp. 25–28. The price of coal sold to Britain's Allies during the war was controlled in the same way as domestic coal.
70 ibid., pp. 64–66.
71 ibid., pp. 268, 94–9.
72 The New Hucknall Company appears to have succeeded in using one definition of profit pre-war and a different definition (profit net of sums put to reserve) during the war.
73 By Redmayne (op. cit., passim) and others following Redmayne.
74 *Colly. Year Book and Coal Trades Directory, 1951 edn.*, p. 559. (Figures to nearest 1d.)
75 ibid., p. 532 and *Report of (Buckmaster), Court of Inquiry, Concerning the Wage Position in the Coal Mining Industry*, London, H.M.S.O. 1924, Cmd. 2129, p. 9.
76 *Report of (Buckmaster) Court of Inquiry, 1924 Cmd. 2129*, p. 9 and Report of Royal Commission on the Coal Industry (1925) Cmd. 2600, I, p. 259.
77 *Report of (Buckmaster) Court of Inquiry, 1924*, p. 15.
78 *Colly. Year Book and Coal Trades Directory, 1951 edn.*, p. 532. See also Part III, Chapter II below. The export figures here given are exports to foreign countries, exclusive of coal consumed by ships trading to foreign parts. The figures quoted by Tawney ('The Problem of the Coal Industry', *Encyclopaedia of the Labour Movement*, London, 1927, p. 125) are inclusive of coal consumed by such ships.
79 *M.F.G.B. Minute Book, 1925*, p. 949.
80 Confidential letter from the Digby Colly. Co. to Frank Varley M.P. dated 18th May 1925. The losses were computed over a six week period as follows:

Week ending		Selling prices 1925		Selling prices (Corresponding weeks in 1924)		Losses per ton (1925)	
		s.	d.	s.	d.	s.	d.
12th	May	13	3	Not given		2	3·67
5th	May	13	3	Not given		2	3·16
28th	April	13	6	17	7·21	1	11·52
21st	April	13	6	17	4·83	2	3·99
14th	April	13	5	17	6·92	1	8·85
7th	April	14	9	17	1·53	2	4·49

Figures from the Cost Accounts Book of the Annesley Colliery similarly show a fall in prices in 1925 compared with 1924. The average monthly proceeds are as follows:

Average Pithead Prices of Coal from Annesley (to nearest 1d.)

	1924		1925	
	s.	d.	s.	d.
January	19	2		
February	19	8	17	5
March	21	0	17	3
April	21	8	17	3
May	19	1	15	11
June	18	3	14	5
July	17	10	15	2
August	17	10	15	8
September	18	3	15	0

81 Report of (Macmillan) Court of Inquiry Concerning the Coal Mining Industry Dispute (1925); Addendum to paragraph 14 by Sir Josiah Stamp. See also A. C. Pigou, Aspects of British Economic History, 1918–1925, London, 1948. pp. 148–51.
82 New Hucknall Colly, Co. Ltd., Balance Sheets, Book 5.
83 ibid. The New Hucknall Company had by this time acquired Annesley Colliery, the one Leen Valley mine which had never been particularly profitable. Development work was put in hand to improve productivity, but meantime Annesley was a disappointment. Results were as follows:

Half-year ending		Total profit or loss		Profit + or loss − per ton	
				s.	d.
31st March	1922	£9796	(L)	− 2	4·35
30th September	1922	£5622	(L)	− 1	2·93
31st March	1923	£6618	(P)	+ 1	0·95
30th September	1923	£5476	(P)	+ 0	10·84
31st March	1924	£15156	(P)	+ 2	4·16
30th September	1924	£7805	(P)	+ 1	1·21

With the collapse of the mild boom referred to in the text, Annesley's financial results worsened gradually until the Spring of 1925 when Britain's return to the Gold Standard made an already unsatisfactory position worse.

Period		Profit or loss			Profit + or loss − per ton	
				£	s.	d.
Month	October	1924	3494	(P)	+ 2	9·09
Month	November	1924	1351	(P)	+ 1	3·44
Month	December	1924	853	(P)	+ 0	8·91
2 wks. endg. 16th	February	1925	1304	(P)	+ 1	9·6
2 wks. endg. 2nd	March	1925	74	(P)	+ 0	1·9
2 wks. endg. 16th	March	1925	177	(P)	+ 0	4·5
2 wks. endg. 30th	March	1925	196	(L)	− 0	4·9
2 wks. endg. 13th	April	1925	337	(L)	− 0	10·0
2 wks. endg. 27th	April	1925	695	(L)	− 1	9·7
2 wks. endg. 11th	May	1925	619	(L)	− 1	2·8
2 wks endg. 25th	May	1925	933	(L)	− 2	6·5
2 wks. endg. 8th	June	1925	1498	(L)	− 5	10·5

2 wks. endg. 22nd	June	1925	1070	(L)	— 2	8·4
2 wks. endg. 7th	July	1925	923	(L)	— 2	4·9
2 wks. endg. 21st	July	1925	624	(L)	— 1	9·4
2 wks. endg. 4th	August	1925	602	(L)	— 2	4·1
2 wks. endg. 18th	August	1925	291	(L)	— 0	11
2 wks. endg. 1st	September	1925	476	(L)	— 1	6·4
2 wks. end. 15th	September	1925	464	(L)	— 1	4

Source: Annesley Colliery Cost Accounts Book.

84   Tawney, art. cit., p. 137.
85   See, for example, the table relating to 1923 in the *Report of the (Samuel) Commission, Cmd. 2600,* p. 259.
86   ibid., p. 293.
87   Tawney, art. cit., p. 128.

The Nottinghamshire Miners' Association: Its Period of Maturity and Growth 1893—1920

1. INTRODUCTION

By the opening of the twentieth century the Nottinghamshire Miners' Association had settled down into a humdrum existence. All colliery owners in the county gave it full recognition. Its full-time officials were recognized as persons of importance. Membership was gradually rising and its income was assured. In 1900, it became a landowner when its new offices, together with three adjacent houses for its officials, were opened.[1] The total worth of the Union at the end of June 1900 at £63,156, equalled £3 8s. 2d. for each of its 18,520 members. Only £7 2s. 1d. had been spent on strike pay during the twelve months ending 30th June 1900 compared with £8,545 during the previous twelve months.[2] The Association had become firmly established, moderate and respectable. The period covered in this chapter saw the Association take hesitant leftward steps, becoming affiliated, through the Miners' Federation of Great Britain, to the Labour Party. Towards the end of the period, a militant wing became articulate and achieved considerable support among the rank-and-file, particularly in the Mansfield area.

During this period, there was dissension between the Leen Valley and the Erewash Valley: between the butties and the day wagemen: and between the Liberals and the Socialists. These dissensions may not have appeared to be particularly important at the time, but they were portents for the future. This period was for the Union a period of growth and development, but it contained within it the seed of decay and disruption.

2. THE MOVEMENT OF WAGE-RATES

J. W. F. Rowe points out that between 1888 and 1920 there was a general upward trend in coal prices. The average total costs of production also rose markedly because of the fall in productivity which is inevitable in mining unless the natural tendency towards diminishing returns to effort is offset by substantial technological improvements. Output per man employed underground in Nottinghamshire per year fell from 429 tons in 1888 to 414 tons in 1890 and 350 tons in 1895, rising to 401 tons in 1900 when the pits were making exceptionally good time as a result of the war-time demand for coal, then falling to 367 tons in 1905, 364 tons in 1910 and 288 tons in 1920.[3] Despite the increased cost of production and the increased prices, however, the quantity of coal demanded rose year by year throughout the period so that the output of coal from Britain's mines in 1920, at 229,503,435 tons, was 35 per cent higher than in 1888.[4] Writing in 1922, Rowe said:

'Hence demand has not only increased, but it has increased sufficiently to outweigh the increased cost of supply. Prices have risen, principally because of the increase in the value of coal compared with other goods and services. Demand has been the predominant factor in the equation of exchange through the period. . . . This predominance of demand explains the apparent paradox of rapidly increasing wages combined with a fall in the productivity of labour, and it has enabled the industry to pass on to the consumer the burden of that decreased productivity.'[5]

If the value of coal increased relative to that of other commodities, it seems intrinsically likely that miners' wages rose relative to those of other people. In fact, according to Rowe, the miners of Nottinghamshire and Derbyshire were enjoying shift rates in 1914 which were some 84 per cent higher in the case of skilled men and some 66 per cent higher in the case of unskilled men than the rates paid in 1888. The increases in some areas were even higher: the unskilled miners in Warwickshire, for example, enjoyed 1914 rates some 106 per cent higher than the 1888 rates.[6] The average time worked had not, taking one year with another, changed much over the period.[7]

Real wages rose both in absolute terms and in comparison with those of other workers. The Co-operative food prices index, which we used in an earlier chapter, indicates the trend: (see table overleaf.)

It will be seen that the tendency for the average family's grocery bill to fall which was so marked a feature of the 1870's and 80's was reversed from around 1895. It would, indeed, be roughly 31 per cent more in 1914 than in 1895. However, over the whole period 1888 to 1914 the difference is only marginal. The other main items of expenditure, rent and fuel cost little, if any, more in 1914 than in 1888.[9] The improved wage-rates which we have noted of 84 per cent for skilled miners and 66 per cent for unskilled miners in Nottinghamshire therefore reflect quite closely the actual improvement in the standards of living of these classes of people between 1888 and 1914. Miners were very considerably better off at the latter date than at the former.

TABLE 15 SHOWING THE COST OF 21½ LB. OF GROCERIES AND
PURCHASING POWER OF £1 STERLING ON THE SAME BASIS 1888–1914[8]

Year	Cost of 21½ lb. of groceries (d.)	Purchasing power of £1 Sterling (1 lb. of groceries)	Index (1914 = 100)
1888	70·81	72·87	92·38
1895	58·38	88·39	76·16
1896	59·48	86·75	77·60
1897	61·47	83·94	80·19
1898	63·85	80·81	83·30
1899	61·00	84·59	79·58
1900	63·69	81·02	83·09
1901	65·18	79·16	85·03
1902	66·50	77·60	86·75
1903	65·37	78·94	85·28
1904	65·39	78·91	85·31
1905	67·56	76·37	88·14
1906	67·28	76·69	87·77
1907	67·82	76·09	88·48
1908	70·21	73·49	91·59
1909	71·79	71·88	93·65
1910	72·38	71·29	94·43
1911	71·00	72·67	92·62
1912	74·28	69·46	96·90
1913	72·45	71·22	94·52
1914	76·65	67·32	100·00

Let us now consider how this compares with workers in other industries. According to Phelps-Brown, in the twenty years to 1907
industrial wage-rates generally had risen by a quarter. This rise was
not universal, however. The railway men in particular had lagged
behind with increased rates of only 5 per cent.[10] From 1909 until 1913
money wages lagged behind the rise in the cost-of-living (which
Phelps-Brown estimates at 9 per cent between 1909 and 1913) catching
it up in 1914. Similarly, Bowley's (admittedly rough) 'real wage quo-
tient' for all industries (taking 1914 as 100) moves from 84 in 1887
to 101 in 1907 and then sags to 97 in 1911, rising to 100 in 1914.[11]
This indicates that the rise in the miners' real wage between 1888 and
1914 was substantially greater than that of workers generally. This is
one reason why colliery owners had little difficulty in recruiting inexperienced labour in this period.

3. ORGANIZATION AND LEADERSHIP

The principal constitutional innovation in this period was the introduction in 1906 of pensions for retired members. In the 1906 Rules
these payments were to be paid for 26 weeks only.[12] By 1912, however, the Association was able to afford a permanent pension of 5s. a

week for all financial members of fifteen years standing who were rendered unemployed after their 60th birthday.[13] This provision was symptomatic of the Association's maturity. In the early rules, the only benefits paid were to men on strike, locked-out or victimized. The introduction in this period of other benefits like old-age pensions and scholarships for general education reflects the decreasing need for a purely fighting organization. Disputes were now settled peacefully more often than not. Price-lists were invariably negotiated and not imposed by the management as they had been in the early days of the Union's existence. The Association enjoyed full recognition and its officials were treated with respect. This is in marked contrast to the refusal of officials of the Hucknall Collieries to deal with William Bailey in 1888 because he was the 'paid agent' of the men,[14] and to the dismissal of William Mellors, the union delegate, from Linby Colliery in 1886.[15]

Because strikes were infrequent, the Association was able to build up its funds, to pay pensions to its retired members (which helped to retain their loyalty, the union contribution of 6d. a week being now a valuable insurance against poverty in old age,) and to employ additional officials as the membership grew.

Throughout this period, there was a steady growth in membership resulting very largely from the increasing size of the labour force. The membership totals fluctuated, however, with the state of trade, now as formerly—and for the same reasons. This tendency is indicated in the table overleaf.

Upon the death of the Agent, William Bailey, in 1896, J. G. Hancock, the other permanent official, took his place. Aaron Stewart, who had been the President since 1887, then became a full-time official with the title of Secretary. Hancock came from Pinxton. Most of the Association's leaders prior to 1910 came from the Leen Valley, however. Thus, five Leen Valley men filled the office of President for a total of twenty-five years between 1881 and December 1906. The only successful Erewash Valley candidate, William Hardy (a veteran of the Derbyshire and Nottinghamshire Association, who lived at Codnor) held the office for one year only from midsummer 1897.[17]

The Association's Registered Office was located at Basford from the formation of the Union until 1959, and its permanent officials lived there. All the original branches of the Nottinghamshire Miners' Federation were in the Leen Valley and even so late as 1893, some 60 per cent of the men voting in an important ballot belonged to Leen Valley branches.[18]

It will be remembered that certain colliery owners broke away from the Federated Colliery owners during the 1893 lockout and formed a new Association called the Nottingham and Erewash Valley Colliery

TABLE 16 SHOWING FLUCTUATIONS IN MEMBERSHIP AND THE STATE OF TRADE
FROM 1893–1910[16]

Year	Membership	Avg. national pit-head price of coal (per ton)		Price of coal from Midland pits	
		s.	d.	s.	d.
1893	18,835	6	9·51	7	7·56
1894	16,550	6	7·43	6	9·84
1895	13,363	6	0·41	6	1·56
1896	14,642	5	10·26	5	9·84
1897	14.609	5	11·00	6	0·00
1898	15,287	6	4·22	6	2·00
1899	16,766	7	7·03	6	11·05
1900	19,968	10	9·66	10	2·76
1901	20,839	9	4·29	9	1·78
1902	21,338	8	2·84	8	0·72
1903	21,043	7	7·93	7	6·86
1904	20,982	7	2·59	7	2·67
1905	20,305	6	11·39	6	10·26
1906	23,774	7	3·50	6	0·23
1907	28,415	9	0·70	8	7·77
1908	30,753	8	11·00	8	2·89
1909	33,112	8	0·37	7	7·33
1910	31,252	8	2·37	7	2·34

Owners' Association which, despite its name, was based on the Leen Valley, and the pits belonging to this Association may now be referred to, for wages purposes, as Leen Valley pits. The Leen Valley Collieries were: Linby, Hucknall, Wollaton,[19] Annesley, Newstead, Cinderhill,[19] Newcastle,[19] Bestwood, Stapleford,[19] Clifton,[19] Kimberley,[19] New London,[19] Bulwell, Broxtowe,[19] Digby,[19] Watnall. From time to time, meetings of representatives of the Leen Valley branches of the N.M.A. were held at the Y.M.C.A. Hucknall ostensibly to discuss questions under negotiation with the Leen Valley owners. They also discussed other matters, and decided on nominations for the Presidency and Vice-Presidency of the Association.[20] They were determined to maintain the privileged position which they had hitherto held. Wages in the Leen Valley were higher than those in the Erewash Valley, since the Leen Valley pits were more profitable on the whole. The new Mansfield district in which, as in the Leen Valley, the profitable top hard seam was being exploited, became increasingly important from the beginning of the twentieth century. The supremacy of the Leen Valley was therefore threatened.

Charles Bunfield of Kirkby, the nominee of the Erewash Valley was elected Vice-President in 1902, and he held this office until 1907 when he defeated the Leen Valley's retiring President, John E. Whyatt, who had held that office since 1899. William Carter, of Mansfield, followed Bunfield into the Vice-Presidency.

In 1908, Bunfield was elected to the newly-created full-time office of Assistant Secretary by a handsome majority. The Leen Valley's nominee, John E. Whyatt, polled less votes than any of the other four candidates in the second ballot.[21] Carter then became President for a year after which he in his turn was elected to a full-time post made vacant by the death of Aaron Stewart. J. Whyatt then had a final spell in the office of President until, in 1912, he was defeated by George Spencer of Sutton.[22]

Spencer soon proved to be a much more effective leader than any of his colleagues. The full-time officials left Spencer (at this time merely a spare-time official) to undertake the major negotiations. He also drafted and presented cases before arbitrators.[23] Spencer won wide popularity because he possessed qualities of leadership which his colleagues lacked. He was a reasonably good speaker (although not by any means an orator), and what he had to say usually carried conviction. He was a well-read man, a W.E.A. student, with a flair for arithmetic. He commanded respect as a Wesleyan Methodist local preacher, his fondness for gambling not having so far manifested itself; and his membership of the Independent Labour Party brought him support from the more radical section of the membership. When a fifth full-time office was created in 1918, Spencer was elected to fill it and his place as President was taken by Frank Varley of Welbeck, who in his turn, became a full-time official in 1919.[24]

Much of Spencer's early popularity derived from his largely successful campaign to bring the Erewash Valley rates into line with the more favourable Leen Valley rates and to obtain higher wages for day wage men and surface workers.[25]

A certain amount of rivalry grew between Spencer and Varley.[26] They were both fairly young, energetic, intelligent, and ambitious. Neither man liked to be beaten in an argument and Spencer in particular would go to great lengths to get his own way. Varley, a more likeable character than Spencer, was a fine public speaker with a commanding presence and a well-modulated voice.

By 1920 there were six full-time officials: J. G. Hancock, W. Carter, C. Bunfield, G. A. Spencer, F. B. Varley and Lewis Spencer who had been the Treasurer since 1889. Lewis Spencer was a colourless individual, who had never acted as Agent.[27] He combined the duties of Treasurer and caretaker until 1922, when he was demoted to caretaker.[28] In 1920, Hancock, the senior official, was called the General Secretary, Bunfield was called the Secretary, whilst Carter, Spencer and Varley were simply called Agents. Bunfield, Varley and Lewis Spencer were each paid £7 10s. per week whilst the other three, who were Members of Parliament, were each paid £4 16s. 3d. a week.[29]

Each agent had a particular group of branches under his charge, and each one stuck rigidly to his own branches. Office accommodation was somewhat restricted: Hancock and Spencer shared one room whilst Varley, Carter and Bunfield shared another. They had no clerical assistance.[30]

Had the administrative and leadership structure been properly planned, the six officials could have worked together as a team. In practice, the team spirit was lacking and the administration was patchy because each official handled 'his own' business, and it was no-one's job to co-ordinate. Hancock, as the senior official, should probably have done so but his parliamentary duties made this impracticable; and by 1920 he was held in such scant regard that repeated attempts were being made to secure his resignation.[31] These attempts were unsuccessful because Hancock was protected by his service agreement. However, in 1921 it was decided that Spencer should become the General Secretary and Varley the Financial Secretary, Hancock being downgraded to Agent. At the same time Bunfield was downgraded to Treasurer. The two new men, Spencer and Varley, were thus recognized as the effective leaders of the Association.[32]

4. LOCAL DISPUTES

From the conclusion of the 1893 lock-out percentage additions to basis wage-rates (which were called 1888 Basis Rates until 1915 when a new basis—called the 1911 Basis—was formed by merging 50 per cent of the percentage addition into the basis), were fixed by the Conciliation Board of the Federated District. This applied even in the Leen Valley, although the owners there had broken away from the Federated Coal-Owners to form their own Association.[33] Because of this, the officials of the miners' district associations concentrated on improving the basis rates themselves. The owners often accused them of trying to obtain larger increases than the Federated District Conciliation Board had agreed by coercing owners to lift basis rates. Thus in November 1898 the owners complained because the N.M.A. were demanding an increase in basis rates at Kirkby Colliery in addition to the $2\frac{1}{2}$ per cent general advance negotiated through the Conciliation Board. Aaron Stewart admitted that an increase in the basis rate for coal getting was being sought because 'The company are not paying the district price.' The Pinxton Company similarly complained that the Union had forced them, by bringing the men out for six weeks, to concede an advance which was 'practically three times $2\frac{1}{2}$ per cent over again'. Mr. Stewart insisted that this again was a case where the basis rate for getting had been below the district price. The owners questioned the notion of a district price, but the Association made it clear that they were determined to bring the rates paid at the less well-paid collieries up to the general level.[34] In practice, this involved bringing other pits up to the Leen Valley standards whereas the owners tried to tie rates at the new pits (e.g. Warsop) to the lower Derbyshire rates.[35] For daily-paid people, in particular, a good case can be made out for uniform basis rates throughout the district and the Association endeavoured to achieve this with a fair measure of success. In 1908 the Association was successful in securing a banksmen's agreement for the whole of the Leen Valley proper. This provided a basis rate of 3s. 6d. a shift, plus the current percentage fixed by the Conciliation Board for underground workmen.[36] The Association then pressed the other owners to apply the same terms to their workmen. The Digby and Babbington Companies agreed to do so almost immediately,[37] but the Erewash Valley Association Owners refused to make a district agreement until 1912, when a basis wage was fixed for banksmen of 3s. 4d.: 2d. less than the Leen Valley rate. The actual increase secured by the men (including the 50 per cent advance then current) averaged 3d. or 4d. at most pits, but was about 1s. per shift at Trowell Moor.[38]

Similarly, after a strike at Newstead which kept the pit idle for a week at the height of the Boer War boom, a wage-scale for boys was agreed with the Leen Valley owners in December 1900.[39] In July 1901 the boys at Kirkby came out on strike for a fortnight. Their employers were allegedly trying to enforce a reduction of 3d. a day whilst the boys demanded the same rates as those in the Leen Valley. A year later a wave of unofficial strikes among boys spread through Yorkshire, Derbyshire and Nottinghamshire. The Leen Valley boys, whose strike in July 1902 cost the Union over £8,000 in relief pay to the men, secured an improved agreement and subsequently similar agreements were negotiated with James Oakes and Company (Pye Hill, Selston, Cotes Park, Stoneyford and Pollington Collieries): at Kirkby and other pits belonging to the Butterley Company: at Pinxton, Bentinck, New Hucknall and Brierley Hill.[40] In 1912 the Erewash Valley owners agreed with the Association on a wage-scale for boys employed on the surface.[41]

Winding enginemen, stokers, and tradesmen of various kinds were organised partly by the Association and partly by the Enginemen and Firemen's union (E. and F.U.). There was some rivalry between the two unions, but a joint board (of the N.M.A., the Derbyshire Miners Association and the E. and F.U.) helped to bring those employed outside the Leen Valley up to the Leen Valley standards in wages and hours.[42] However, a strike called unilaterally by the E. and F.U. at Clifton in 1908 evoked a spirited protest from the N.M.A.[43]

The introduction of coal cutting machines in this period was responsible for a series of disputes over rates of pay. Sutton was probably the first colliery in the district to use these machines successfully.

The first, electrically driven, was put into operation on Thursday 14th May 1896.[44] and contributed to the unrest which caused the pit to be idle for the better part of two years.[45] Similarly, the introduction of cutters at Radford created a dispute which was settled in November 1908;[46] whilst at Clifton and Eastwood, strikes over the prices to be paid for machine-holed coal lasted for over a year and six months respectively. These two disputes were settled by arbitration in 1910.[47] The Eastwood dispute involved in total about 3,650 men.[48]

Another cause of disputes during this period was the flame safety lamp. Miners, generally speaking, preferred to work with candles which provided them with much better illumination. Where the use of flame safety lamps was made compulsory, the men demanded higher pay because their output was reduced. The Pinxton price-list signed in 1903, for example, provided that 'Where lamps are used in stalls 1d. per ton, and in heads 5d. per yard extra shall be paid.'[49] At Trowell Moor, the men struck work in 1906 for a similar concession. The principle was so well established by that time that the arbitrator to whom the dispute was referred awarded the men an extra 1d. per ton as at most other pits.[50]

Ultimately, this particular difficulty was solved by the introduction of electric lamps. In 1917 and 1918, the men at New Hucknall and Bentinck demanded that electric safety lamps should be provided by the Company, and after a short strike in November, 1918, which cost the Association over £5,000 in strike pay, they won their point.[51] Subsequently, Council asked that all companies should buy electric lamps, and many of them did so fairly quickly since they realized that efficient lighting was a good investment.[52]

The war years saw the culmination of the campaign for district agreements for day-wage men. An agreement covering surface workers of all kinds, and underground tradesmen was made with the Erewash Valley owners in 1915.[53] The Association also attempted to make an Agreement with the Leen Valley owners, but the two sides could not agree upon its terms,[54] although an agreement for banksmen was made on 27th November 1915.[55]

Subsequently, arbitrations in 1916,[56] 1918,[57] and 1920[58] (The MacKenzie and Stoker Awards) fixed county-wide rates for all classes of surface workers despite the protestations of the Erewash Valley owners that they could not afford to pay the same rates as pits in the Leen Valley. During sittings of the 1920 arbitration court, the owners' and workmen's representatives agreed on a basis rate for underground haulage workers of 6s. 8d. a shift.[59]

By 1920, then, the principle of county-wide wage-rates for day-wage workers was firmly established. Stoker had pointed to the advisability of district rather than pit negotiations for such rates, and the acceptance of this advice made inevitable the ending of the division between the Erewash and Leen Valley colliery owners. In 1922, when the owners successfully demanded a reduction in the basis rates of men employed at non-top hard collieries, the separate owners' associations were not mentioned at all.[60] The owners acted then and thereafter as one body. The Nottingham and Erewash Association maintained its separate existence until the mid-1930's, but it was an existence without significance. For all practical purposes, by 1922, the 1893 coal-owners' split was healed; and it was no longer possible for the Notts. Miners' Association to play one district off against the other.

During the war years, there were two rather special local disputes over the demand of the rank-and-file for an end to filling coal with forks instead of shovels; and an end to the 'butty' system.[61] These two demands were part of the programme of a left-wing Independent Labour Party (I.L.P.) group led by Herbert Booth whose activities will be described in a future section.

Colliery owners insisted that coal sent to bank should be free from slack and dirt. In some cases, slack could be sent up separately to be paid for at half or less of the price of coal. In the Pinxton price list of 1902 it is provided that slack passing a $2\frac{1}{2}$ in screen would be paid for at 9d. a ton from stalls and 10d. a ton from headings against 2s. 1d. for lump coal. If more than 12 lb. of slack was present in a hundredweight of coal, twice the excess was to be deducted and paid for as slack.[62] A persistent offender could expect to be dismissed. Where there was no sale for slack it was generally made an offence to send it up the pit at all.[63]

The men were opposed to filling with screens because it reduced their output and therefore their earnings, and because small coal left in the waste can cause spontaneous combustion.[64] The campaign to abolish screen-filling reached its height in 1919 when the N.M.A. called an official strike which lasted from 19th March to 2nd April. The owners then agreed to accept shovel filling.[65]

Various colliery owners, (the Sherwood Colliery Company, for example), once more began to introduce screens in place of shovels early in 1921, when the post-war boom was coming to an end. Council protested at this violation of the agreement.[66] In April 1921 a national lock-out commenced because the M.F.G.B. refused to countenance massive wage cuts. When the lock-out was in its fourth week, Council resolved:

'That it be an instruction to all our members that they do not use in any seam or pit, for the purpose of filling coal, either fork or screen.'[67]

However, when the men resumed work at the beginning of July with their organization greatly weakened, many of them found that shovel-filling was no longer allowed. After abortive negotiations the owners gave formal notice that shovel filling would not be allowed at any pit in Nottinghamshire and Derbyshire after 25th October 1921.[68] At the Bolsover Company's pits, a joint committee with German Abbott and Tom Pembleton of Rufford as its leaders eventually forced the owners to agree to use the shovels.[69] Elsewhere, screen filling continued until the widespread introduction of conveyors necessitated a quicker tempo of work.

The campaign for the abolition of the butty system followed a parallel course. A ballot vote of members taken in 1918 showed a large majority against the butty system.[70] Discussions between the Owners' Associations and the Derbyshire and Nottinghamshire Miners' Associations resulted in an agreement to operate the 'all-throw-in' system under which all the adults in a particular stall share equally in the contract earnings.[71] At many pits where the leading butties had control of the branches the agreement was not implemented, or was implemented for only a short time, however. This was the case at Eastwood, where Joseph Birkin formed a Central Committee of checkweigh committee men from the Barber Walker pits, (Moor Green, High Park, Brinsley and Underwood) together with Lodge, belonging to the Ilkeston Colliery Company.[72] The 'butty' system was still in force there when the mines were nationalized in 1947, although it had long been abolished at most collieries.[73]

At the Babbington Collieries, the men struck work in February 1920, to force the Company to abandon piece-work coal getting altogether. They were temporarily successful. The company alleged that this change resulted in a reduction in the output per coal getter per day from 2 tons 6 cwt. to 1 ton 15 cwt.[74] Charles Bunfield, Secretary of the N.M.A. pleaded powerfully at a conference of the M.F.G.B., held in January 1921 for a national campaign to secure the abolition of piece-work in the interests of safety.[75]

However, after the 1921 lock-out, most local colliery owners forced the men to accept the 'butty' system. In December 1921 Council resolved that:

> 'We recommend the members to continue to throw-in, and share equally in the earnings.'[76]

The Association held meetings at Mansfield and elsewhere to oppose the re-introduction of the butty system, but by 1923, the agreement to work 'all-throw-in' was being 'honoured mainly in the breach' according to officials of the Nottinghamshire and Derbyshire Miners' Associations.[77]

Here again, the introduction of face conveyors, rather than the activities of the unions, brought about the change which the men desired. A longwall conveyor face with twenty or more men on it could be worked more efficiently by the 'all-thrown-in' system than the butty system. The Bestwood Coal and Iron Company, for example, tried 'all-throw-in' when they introduced conveyors in the 1920's and they found that it paid to do so. As time went on, more companies learnt the same lesson.

5. EIGHT-HOUR DAY AND MINIMUM WAGE AGITATIONS

After the 1893 lock-out as before it, the M.F.G.B. campaigned for a legal eight-hour day, whilst the leaders of Northumberland and Durham opposed it. The N.M.A. secured an eight-hour day by negotiation at the Hucknall Collieries of J. E. Ellis in 1895, but this proved to be an isolated victory: the 'movement in the Leen Valley' which William Bailey expected to follow from Ellis's gesture was abortive.[78]

Attempts by the M.F.G.B. to obtain an eight-hour day by Act of Parliament were similarly unsuccessful until 1908 when a Liberal Parliament passed the Coal Mines Regulation Act which provided that:

'. . . a workman shall not be below ground in a mine for the purpose of his work, and of going to and from his work, for more than eight hours during any consecutive twenty-four hours.'[79]

In effect, the length of the day was, however, eight hours plus one winding time (of approximately half-an-hour), whilst on not more than sixty days in a year the owner, agent or manager had power to extend the working day by one hour. The 1908 Act, as amended from time to time, has been widely evaded and complaints have been made persistently by miners' unions about illegal overtime working,[80] but with little effect. However, the Act was applied fairly strictly in the early days.

The Act came into force on 1st July 1909. During the previous six months, discussions had taken place between the N.M.A. and the owners regarding the detailed administrative arrangements necessitated by the change in working hours. The owners wanted to wind coal throughout the whole of the eight hours, allowing only 'reasonable facilities for obtaining food', whilst the men demanded a thirty-minute meal break. The boys, who feared that if the pits wound coal throughout the shift, they would have no break at all, came out on strike at many places. In Nottinghamshire: Clifton, Newstead, Bestwood, Broxtowe, Wollaton, Radford and Gedling were all at a standstill by 8th July and Watnall's output was also badly affected. In South Yorkshire, the boys were rioting,[81] but the only riot in Nottinghamshire was at Clifton, where boys ran a train of empty trams into the Trent.[82]

In the Leen Valley, the owners conceded a twenty-minute meal break against fifteen minutes in the Erewash Valley.[83] This difference caused much ill-feeling. On the whole, however, the change in working hours was put into operation without too much difficulty. There was a tendency for the wages of day-men employed by the butties to be reduced somewhat, but this caused little trouble.[84]

The second great national question which came to a head in this period was the demand for a statutory minimum wage. This arose out of a resolution adopted by the M.F.G.B. in October 1910 that:

'The miners of Scotland, England and Wales be requested to meet their respective employers and demand a fair living wage to be paid to all miners working in abnormal places.'[85]

A contract worker may be prevented from earning a reasonable wage through bad geological conditions or mechanical breakdowns which are outside the control of anyone; or by bad management typified by, for example, a shortage of timber or an uneven flow of trams; or by his own or his workmates' idleness or lack of intelligence. Arguments over the amount of abnormality payments to be made in particular circumstances occurred regularly at all collieries. In Nottinghamshire, most contract price lists of the early 1900's included abnormality or make-up clauses. The Pinxton Waterloo Price List of 1903, for example, provided that:

'In case of difficulties arising through bad coal, bunkies, faults, water, etc., preventing men getting wage as per list, this to be made up to 4s. 6d. per day, or equal to rates prevailing at that time.'

Provision is made, too, for allowance payments for falls, running gates, filling water and taking short end stalls. Contractors brought out of stalls to work on main roads were to be paid 4s. 6d. per day.[86] These clauses provided a considerable degree of protection.

In South Wales, where the prices of coal fluctuated wildly in this period[87] a manager's readiness to pay generous allowances would vary with the state of trade, whilst the men expected 'consideration' irrespective of the actual degree of abnormality. Neither side was faultless. Resentment over abnormality payments in South Wales sparked off one dispute after another in the period 1908 to 1911.[88]

The major dispute began in September 1910 at the Ely Colliery belonging to the Cambrian combine whose chairman was D. A. Thomas.[89] Thomas was masterful and stubborn, and he shared the latter quality with many of his workpeople. The dispute over payments for abnormal work spread throughout the Rhondda Valley, and at the year's end, there were some 12,800 men on strike.[90] The M.F.G.B. raised a national levy of 3d. a week to finance the strike, but the militants of South Wales demanded 'action not finance'.[91] A compromise settlement arranged by the M.F.G.B. leaders was rejected by a South Wales Conference of 288 delegates who wanted instead 'a general stoppage throughout the Federation for the purpose of securing for all colliery workmen a definite guaranteed minimum wage'.[92] The M.F.G.B. was split into two warring camps over this issue. The new leaders of South Wales with their syndicalist notions were on one side, whilst the older leaders of the Federation, liberals and socialists alike, were on the other. Ashton accused the South Wales militants of having 'only one weapon to fight with, that of "force", which alone means "anarchy" '.[93] At a national conference held on 13th June, bitter things were said on both sides. Ashton's view that there should be a return to work on the terms negotiated was supported by all districts except South Wales. The Federation therefore withdrew its support from the strikers, but they remained out until the end of August. Even on the evidence presented by Arnot, their intransigeance was without justification.[94]

Discussions on this question took place in the districts. The coal-owners of the Federated Area accepted the principle of a district minimum wage, but coal-owners in the 'outside' districts opposed it.[96] In January 1912 the Federation decided to take a ballot vote to determine whether the men were in favour of a national stoppage to secure minimum rates, and this resulted in a huge majority in favour of striking.[97]

The M.F.G.B. accepted that minimum rates should be fixed on a district basis but it stipulated that the district minima should be at least 5s. a day for men and 2s. a day for boys. Negotiations with the coal-owners continued, but without success. The Prime Minister, Asquith, put forward compromise proposals which recognized the principle of district minima, but these were rejected by the Federation and by the Northumberland, Scottish and Welsh coal-owners. Under these circumstances, a national strike was inevitable and on Tuesday 27th February 1912 it commenced. By the following Monday over one million men were out and every colliery in the Kingdom was at a standstill.[98]

The strike enabled the colliery owners to dispose of their stocks at good prices. The Digby Company, for example, cleared the Gedling pit bank of smudge, normally unsaleable, of which 20,000 tons had been sold by 25th March.[99] In Nottinghamshire the strike was characterized by the newspapers as a 'friendly strike'; with 'no militant spirit'. The Leen Valley men had 'no quarrel with the owners . . . but work must be suspended in accordance with the general movement'. George Spencer, the newly elected President of the N.M.A. appealed to the men to act peaceably so as not to alienate public sympathy.[100] Throughout the dispute, negotiations on local issues continued as though there were no strike on at all.[101]

Nationally, negotiations between the two sides, with Asquith acting as chairman, came to nothing, and the Government therefore decided to introduce a Minimum Wage Bill, which would provide for minimum wages to be settled in each district by a joint board with an independent chairman. The Government's Bill became law on 29th March 1912.[102]

The M.F.G.B. then balloted its members on the question:

'Are you in favour of resuming work pending settlement of the minimum rates of wages in the various grades by the district boards to be appointed under the Mines Minimum Wage Act?' A majority of those voting: 244,011 against 201,013, voted in favour of continuing the strike. In Nottinghamshire, the result was similar: 8,213 for continuing the strike and 8,187 for resuming work. The M.F.G.B. Conference on 6th April decided that, since the majority for continuing the strike was less than two-thirds, work should be resumed.[103] Many of the men felt cheated. Councillor A. Beswick, one of the Hucknall delegates, expressed a common view when he deplored the appointment of chairmen of district boards who would, in effect, be arbitrators. Another miner at the same meeting declared that 'We came out for nothing, and we are going in for the same.'[104]

The Joint District Board for Nottinghamshire held sessions between 29th April and 12th June 1912. It was unable to agree on the minimum rates, which were therefore fixed by the Chairman, County Court Judge, Henry Yorke Stanger, K.C. and issued as an Award on 25th June 1912. To meet the owners' contention that top hard pits were more profitable than others, there were two schedules of wages, one for pits working the top hard seam, but excluding Gedling; and the other for pits working other seams, but including Gedling. According to the *Nottingham Daily Guardian*, the Award gave the Leen Valley men nothing although some Erewash Valley men stood to gain from it.[105] According to Rowe, in Nottinghamshire and Derbyshire:

'Existing agreed "make-up" rates for coal-getters in both counties were higher than the minimum, which was therefore inoperative, but the Act did probably raise the rates of a number of unskilled workers.'[106]

Information submitted to the Nottinghamshire Joint District Board does suggest that quite a number of day-wage men benefited slightly,[107] but subsequent negotiations leading to improved wage agreements (e.g. the Stoker Awards) carried the rates of even the lowest paid men in the County above the legal minima. In some districts, the position was very different. The South Wales men in particular benefited greatly,[108] but most districts had been on strike for six weeks for 'what was in reality next to nothing'.[109]

6. POLITICAL DEVELOPMENTS

In its early days, the Nottinghamshire Miners' Association supported the Liberal Party, and this accounts in part for the support which the Ellis, Bailey and Seely families gave to it. The close relationship between Bailey and J. E. Ellis is well illustrated by the correspondence between them in 1895 on the subject of introducing an eight-hour day at the Hucknall Collieries.[110] The same subject had, however, caused the Association to abandon its allegiance temporarily in 1892 when the M.F.G.B. had decided to support only candidates who would agree to vote for the Mines Eight Hours Bill.[111] Henry Broadhurst, the Liberal M.P. for Nottingham West, was opposed to any Parliamentary interference with hours and he therefore refused to vote for the Bill.[112] The N.M.A. therefore decided to support the Liberal-Unionist candidate, Col. C. Seely; and William Bailey, although a Liberal councillor, moved a resolution welcoming Seely's candidature and urging miners to vote for him, at a public meeting at Bulwell.[113] Col. Seely won the election by a narrow majority.

To support a Liberal-Unionist candidate was very much against the normal run of things. Under Bailey's leadership, the Association tended to be Radical. During the 1885 General Election, which followed the extension of the franchise to workingmen in county constituencies, Bailey had acted as election agent to James Haslam in the Chesterfield Division. Haslam stood as a Radical/Liberal in opposition to the official Liberal Party candidate because of the Party's failure to nominate a representative of the working class for any of the Derbyshire constituencies. Haslam's programme included reform of the House of Lords, the payment of a fixed allowance to the Royal family, the payment of M.P.s, Free Trade and free education.[114]

Bailey campaigned for the adoption of working men as Liberal candidates. He joined T. R. Threlfall's Labour Electoral Association (L.E.A.), which was established for that purpose. When the first Nottinghamshire County Council elections were held in 1889, William Mellors contested the Byron Division as a L.E.A. candidate against three Liberals and two Conservatives. His nomination was endorsed by the N.M.A. and William Bailey acted as his election agent. Mellors topped the poll, and two Conservatives won the other seats. The Liberals accused Mellors of splitting the vote.[115]

In March 1891 the Council of the N.M.A. requested all branches to give financial support to the L.E.A., and in 1892 Bailey was elected National President of the Association.[116] Although the L.E.A. had a radical programme (payment of M.P.s; nationalization of the land; an eight-hours bill for miners, etc.), its chief concern was to secure greater working class representation on public bodies. It was in no sense a socialist organization. W. E. Harvey of the Derbyshire Miners' Association, who was elected Vice-President of the L.E.A. in 1894, refused to speak from the same platform as Keir Hardie at a miners' demonstration held in Durham in 1897; and in the same year he supported the Liberal candidate at the Barnsley by-election in opposition to Pete Curran, the I.L.P. candidate.[117]

Whilst William Bailey lived, Nottinghamshire was very much less antagonistic to socialism than Derbyshire. At the 1892 N.M.A. Demonstration held at Eastwood Keir Hardie (then Independent Labour M.P. for West Ham South) spoke, his rousing Socialist speech being enthusiastically welcomed despite an isolated interjection from a member of the audience about splitting the Liberal vote.[118] John Burns was also a regular speaker at Annual Demonstrations.[119]

Again, at one public meeting organized by the N.M.A. in 1889 Tom Mann, socialist member of the Amalgamated Society of Engineers, was one of the principal speakers.[120]

Bailey's successor, J. G. Hancock, was cast in a different mould. Superficially, his background resembled Bailey's: both came from humble Nonconformist homes; they were both country-bred; they were both Methodist local preachers; they were both members of the Liberal Party; but their personal qualities were quite different. Bailey was a passionate speaker, with a commanding personality. Hancock, on the other hand, was an unimpressive platform performer, but whilst Bailey was capable of doing rash things, Hancock went about his business deliberately. His first act on being appointed assistant secretary of the Association was to take instruction in book-keeping with an accountant in Nottingham.[121] Politically, he was well to the right of Bailey.

In April 1904 Council decided to sponsor J. G. Hancock for either West Nottingham, Rushcliffe or Mansfield Parliamentary Division, whichever became vacant.[122] In the event, none of the local seats became vacant so that when the 1906 General Election came round, Council asked all members to vote for the middle and upper-class Liberal candidates. Of these, only Richardson, a wealthy wholesale grocer, could be considered a Lib-Lab.[123]

Hancock had to be content for the time being with election to the Nottingham City Council as a Councillor for the Broxtowe Ward. He was first elected in 1904. Five years later, when seeking re-election, he declared that he was not a Socialist; and he asked the *Nottingham Guardian* to stop calling him one. He described himself as a champion of 'Labour reform and religion'.[124]

So far, the M.F.G.B. had kept clear of connection with the Labour Representation Committee (which adopted the title 'Labour Party' in 1906).[125] Following the General Election of 1906, the M.F.G.B. decided to ballot its members on whether to affiliate to the L.R.C. In addition to the twenty-nine Labour M.P.'s there were also twenty-five Lib,-Labs. of whom thirteen were miners.[126] The socialists inside the M.F.G.B. wanted the miners' M.P.'s to take the Labour Whip: under the Federation's Election Fund Rules, a candidate could run 'under any name he may assume'.[127] In consequence, some ran as Liberals and others as I.L.P. candidates.[128] Provided that their candidature was properly endorsed by the Federation they could claim their election expenses plus £350 a year and a first-class railway pass.[129]

The ballot was held in July 1906 and the N.M.A. Council advised members to vote against affiliation.[130] Nationally, there was a majority of 9,492 against affiliating to the L.R.C. (101,714 to 92,222): but in Nottinghamshire the majority against was overwhelming (9,471 to 1,671 according to the N.M.A. Minute Book; 11,292 to 1,806 according to Arnot).[131]

Two years later, this decision was reversed and the M.F.G.B. joined the Labour Party in the early months of 1909.[132] In July, 1909, Hancock was invited to fight a by-election in Mid-Derbyshire by the Divisional Liberal Association on the recommendation of the Derbyshire Miners' Association. Since he had signed the Labour Party constitution he was regarded by the M.F.G.B. as a Labour candidate. One of his strongest supporters was the Liberal coal-owner M.P. for Mansfield, A. B. (later Sir Arthur) Markham. According to J. E. Williams

'Both Markham and Hancock attempted to obscure any distinction between Socialism and Liberalism which might have existed in the minds of the electors.'[133]

However, as we have seen, in October 1909 Hancock specifically denied being a Socialist, and asked the papers not to refer to him as such.[134] Hancock was elected by 6,735 votes to 4,392.[135] His election cost the M.F.G.B. £1,362 and the N.M.A. a further £180.[136]

Earlier in 1909, the N.M.A. had been asked to affiliate to the Nottingham Borough Labour Party but it refused to do so.[137] Its national affiliation was soon to be brought into question, too. In June 1910 G. R. Pearson, a member of the N.M.A. living at Pinxton obtained an injunction restraining the Association from using any of its income for political purposes.[138] Council therefore decided to appeal to members to pay voluntary subscriptions for political purposes of at least 1d. per month, but this did not bring in enough money to pay national and local government election expenses.[139] Payment of expenses to people engaged in local government work had to be suspended until the enactment of the Trade Union Act, 1913,[140] which allowed a union to set up a political fund separately administered, provided that a majority of its members decided by ballot to have one. Any dissenting members had the right to 'contract out' of contributing to the Fund.

Meantime, Hancock's continued adherence to the Liberal cause brought him increasingly into disfavour with the Labour Party. The secretary of the Mid-Derbyshire Labour Party complained in 1913 that Hancock had 'subscribed £50 to the Liberal agent, attended Liberal Party meetings and voted in Parliament with the Liberal Party'.[141] In the previous year when Mr. F. Shaw, the Basford Branch delegate, had submitted a notice of motion which sought to invite Bob Smillie, the Socialist Vice-President of the M.F.G.B., to become the prospective Parliamentary Candidate for West Nottingham, the officials, at Hancock's instigation, had ruled that the motion was frivolous and should therefore be excluded from the agenda. According to the *Nottingham Guardian*, the rebels expected that the newly-elected President, George Spencer 'who represents the advanced section and is a member of the I.L.P., would back up the resolution, but he inclined towards Mr. Hancock's view'.[142] It would appear, therefore, that Council was still overwhelmingly Liberal. When the Labour Whip was withdrawn from Hancock owing to his continued membership of the Liberal Party, Council accepted, subject to confirmation, a motion that the N.M.A. should withdraw from the M.F.G.B. Political Fund and form one of its own:

> '. . . so that the N.M.A. may itself become a political unit, frame its own policy and rules, and completely control its own fund and political interests both Imperially and locally.'[143]

Hancock's move to take the N.M.A. out of the M.F.G.B. Political Fund was supported by Spencer and had the question been left to Council to settle, Hancock would undoubtedly have had his way. However, Herbert Booth, a young miner from Hucknall who had been a student at the Central Labour College in the two years prior to August 1914 brought the matter fully into the open. In the late autumn of 1914, Booth and a fellow I.L.P. member, William Askew (a checkweighman at Newstead Colliery) held meetings all over the County on Sunday mornings at which they exposed the attempt to secede from the M.F.G.B. politically. They were helped by a ruling from the Registrar of Friendly Societies that the move to establish a separate political fund for the N.M.A. could only succeed if it had the support of a majority of the members voting in a secret ballot.[144] When the ballot was held, a substantial majority voted against withdrawal from the M.F.G.B. political Fund.[145] From Booth's campaign, a left-wing group of I.L.P. members emerged. Their programme included the abolition of the butty system, abolition of fork filling, the institution of pit head ballots for the election of branch officials (in place of voting by show of hands at an Annual General Meeting) and a demand that full-time officials should be subject to re-election at three-yearly intervals instead of holding permanent appointments. Booth's group were attacked strongly by Spencer and the butties. They also aroused the opposition of the non-conformist churches because of their Sunday meetings. The Hucknall Urban District Council, which was dominated by Liberal Nonconformists, forbad them to use Hucknall market place for Sunday meetings.

From the left, Booth's group were attacked by the Socialist Labour Party (S.L.P.) branch established in the Mansfield area by Jack Lavin, an Irishman employed at Welbeck Colliery. Lavin had lived in the U.S.A. where he had been influenced by Eugene Debs and Daniel de Leon. He joined the Socialist Labour Party of America and its trade union affiliate, the Industrial Workers of the World; and when he came over to England shortly before the first World War, he advocated the establishment of militant industrial unions catering for all the workers in an industry.[146] Lavin had a persuasive tongue and a likeable personality combined with the feverish energy which so often accompanies the early stages of tuberculosis and before long he had built up a small group of supporters who formed a branch of the S.L.P. of Great Britain. This group held meetings throughout the Mansfield area at which the doctrine 'that all trade union leaders are corrupt and traitors to the working class'[147] found wide acceptance. Although this branch of the S.L.P. had no more than nineteen members at any time, it had an influence out of all proportion to its numerical strength, an influence which played a powerful part in the dissensions of the 1920's.

To the S.L.P., Booth and his colleagues were reformers tinkering with an obsolete institution. This is how Harvey, the S.L.P. propagandist, begins his denunciation of the old trade unions:

'The present form of organization is played out. Not only has it fulfilled its mission and outlived its usefulness, but it has become reactionary and is maintained, not in our interest, but in that of our masters.[148]

The industrial unionist aimed not at reform but at the abolition of the capitalist system.

'Clear in the knowledge that THE WORKING CLASS REVOLUTION MUST MOVE IN THE LIGHT OF ITS OWN LEGALITY, and not in that of the capitalist class, the Industrial Union by its tactics develops the revolutionary spirit of the workers, and trains them for the Social Revolution. . . . Its purpose is to PARALYSE THE STATE—the engine of class rule, and the organ for the maintenance of status quo—by gaining power over the substance whose shadow it is.' [149]

Lavin refused to accept trade union office and so did his supporters until after his death. Whilst Booth's group sought to break the grip of the butties and the Liberals by rousing the rank-and-file, Lavin's group was essentially destructive. Booth wished to increase the Union's effectiveness by stimulating member-participation whilst Lavin sought to discredit it. After Lavin's death in 1919 the members of his S.L.P. branch began to enter into day-to-day struggles of the Association. (Owen Ford, for example, became a checkweighman at Welbeck Colliery.) For the Association this had a debit side as well as a credit since the left-wing militants continued their intemperate attacks on the leadership from within the organization.[150]

Because of the popularity of Booth's left-wing group, Spencer trimmed his sails to the wind, and for a time adopted radical postures himself. Fortunately for Spencer, Booth was elected full-time Agent of the Forest of Dean miners in 1918, so that when, shortly afterwards, Spencer stood for election to full-time office, his principal opponent was out of the running. Booth was out of the County until April 1922 when he was elected checkweighman at Annesley Colliery.[151] He never quite regained the popularity he had enjoyed during the war years.

At the so-called coupon election of 1918, Hancock was once more returned as Liberal M.P. for Belper (formerly the Mid-Derbyshire Constituency) whilst Spencer and Carter were elected as Labour M.P.s for Broxtowe and Mansfield respectively. At its meeting on Monday 30th December 1918 Council congratulated Spencer and Carter, who were official M.F.G.B. nominees, but said nothing about Hancock.[152] This indicates the extent of the leftward swing over the previous decade.

The Association now had three of its permanent officials in Parliament. Urgent business apart, the branches for which the three Members of Parliament acted had to wait until the weekend for contact with their Agents. This state of affairs was totally unsatisfactory. The left-wing extremists in the coalfield were able to strengthen their positions in the absence of the permanent officials whose leadership was, of necessity, spasmodic.

In May 1919 Frank Varley was elected as a sixth permanent official.[153] Varley had shown qualities of leadership of a high order during his occupancy of the Presidency, and largely because of his ability to dress up moderate opinions in militant verbiage he exercised a moderating influence on the men in the Mansfield district.

7. BREAK-UP OF THE FEDERATED AREA

The Federated District first came into existence in 1888. Its constituent areas, Yorkshire, Derbyshire, Nottinghamshire, Leicestershire, South Derbyshire, the Midland Federation, Lancashire, Cheshire and North Wales, which formed the nucleus of the M.F.G.B., produced the bulk of their output for the home market and were, therefore, insulated from the vagaries of international trade which kept Northumberland, Durham and South Wales tied to sliding scales.

For a long time, these outside districts refused to join the M.F.G.B., and when, eventually, they did so, the inland coalfields forming the Federated District maintained their old organization, which formed a federation within a federation, so to speak.

The Conciliation Board for the Federated Area, consisting of representatives of owners and unions, held quarterly meetings to discuss general issues affecting the District, besides special meetings to discuss applications for alterations in the percentage addition to basis wages.

The men's representatives on the Conciliation Board held regular meetings to formulate policy and arranged annual and special conferences for delegates from the constituent district unions. At the 1917 Special Conference of the Federated District the Chairman, S. Walsh, emphasized that the purpose of the meeting was to strengthen the position of the inland districts within the M.F.G.B. Conference by formulating common policies.[154] This point of view met with general approval. Indeed, George Spencer moved a resolution to the effect that the Federated Area should affiliate as one body to the M.F.G.B. 'with a view to obtaining united action on all questions which come before that body'. He made it clear that he wished to counteract the influence of the South Wales Miners' Federation which was now controlled by the syndicalists. His motion was adopted unanimously, but nothing came of it.[155]

But by 1918 the approval was not nearly so general. South Wales had put down a motion for consideration at the M.F.G.B. Conference, asking that 'the machinery for dealing with the general wage rate be centralized in the National Federation'.[156] This would have put paid to the Federated Area. Area conferences were divided on whether to support this motion. W. Latham of the Midland Federation and both George Spencer and Frank Varley of Nottinghamshire urged the inland districts to vote against the South Wales motion.

Spencer considered that once the wartime controls were removed the owners would refuse to negotiate nationally. He continued:

'The principle of centralization can only be desirable or effective on the assumption that after the war, when we return to normal conditions, we have secured permanently control or nationalization of the mines. . . . We have no guarantee that anything approaching that will take place. I think the whole of the evidence from the employers of this Area and the Federation . . . is, *that they are not disposed to come together to form a National Wages Board*. They themselves will do all they possibly can to hinder that. I think, until we have secured a permanent central authority so far as the mines are concerned . . . it would be a very unwise thing indeed to disband an institution which has been so effective and so favourable *to our own particular interests.*[157]

During these debates, several speakers showed their suspicion of the South Wales 'extremists'.

On the other hand, the South Wales position was strongly supported inside the Federated District by Herbert Smith, of Yorkshire. At the London Conference, held on 4th June 1918 he said:

'Some of our friends say, "What shall we do in the Conciliation area; cannot we get it extended?" I am not anxious to get it extended. I have had quite plenty with this. I want on the 31st July to shake off the chains. . . . As to the question of the control of mines, I am rather surprised at some of the speeches made, and I do not think we ought to say we are going to be satisfied with the control of mines, but to nationalize them—that we ought not to play with this thing. Every district should stand for nationalization, we ought not to assume that the control of the mines is going to cease. . . .'

The divergent attitudes of George Spencer and Herbert Smith, the one supporting district negotiations and the other advocating national action, foreshadowed the division to come in 1926.

At the end of 1918, owners' and workmen's representatives were still meeting to discuss the possibility of resuscitating the Conciliation Board but to no avail. In the event, instead of securing the National Board and National wages pool for which they were asking, the Left were instrumental in breaking up the Federated Area into its constituent districts, thereby doing incalculable harm to the miners of the Midlands without doing any good to anyone else.[158]

8. CONCLUSION

The period covered by this chapter was the mining industry's heyday. The demand for coal was rising almost continuously, and the price of coal relative to that of other goods was rising similarly. The standard of living of the miner and his family was improving steadily throughout the period and at the end of it was considerably higher, both in absolute terms, and relative to that of other workers, than at its beginning.

This improved standard of living may account for the comparative peace in the mining industry outside South Wales in the period 1909–1914 when industrial strife was perhaps more intense than at any previous time.[159] Phelps-Brown, whose general analysis is sound, nevertheless exaggerates the relative importance of mining disputes in this period. He proceeds from the unjustified assertion that:

'the miners' average output had been falling, whereas the value of coal in terms of raw materials and foodstuffs generally had not risen.'[160]

In fact, the national average pit head price of coal rose by about 25 per cent between 1909 and 1914[161] whilst foodstuffs increased in price by no more than 8 or 9 per cent.[162] In the Federated District, where wages were regulated largely according to price variations, there were seven 5 per cent advances between 1907 and 1913, and two 5 per cent reductions.[163] There was, besides, constant pressure to increase basis rates. Clearly, Rowe's view that the value of coal (compared with that of other goods and services) rose is the correct one.[164]

Phelps-Brown then asserts that 'disputes were concentrated in these particular sectors': general labour, the mines and the railways.[165] In fact, mining disputes outside South Wales were notable neither for their incidence, nor their duration, nor their violence. Of the stoppages important enough to be listed in the *Colliery Year Book* occurring between 1908 and 1914, thirteen were in South Wales, two were in Nottinghamshire, one was in Warwickshire, four were in Yorkshire, one in each of Northumberland, Durham, Bristol and North Staffordshire and two were in Lancashire. In addition, one dispute affecting the whole country, the 1912 Minimum Wage Strike, resulted from agitation by the South Wales syndicalists.[166] Of these disputes, those in Nottinghamshire, Warwickshire, Yorkshire, North Staffordshire and South Wales in July 1909 involving some 129,000 men; and those in Durham and Northumberland in 1910 involving a further 115,000 men, were due to difficulties over the application of the legal eight-hour day and not to any general atmosphere of industrial unrest. Of the remaining disputes outside South Wales, only one involved really large numbers of men: the Yorkshire stoppage of 1914 involving 150,000. In the others (at Eastwood, Notts. in 1908 over the introduction of coal cutters, Burnley in 1910, Wigan and Bristol in 1911) only 10,873 men were involved altogether. The South Wales disputes, other than the 1909 one, on the other hand, involved 111,002 men and one of these, that in the Rhondda Valley in 1910, lasted for almost a year, some 2,985,000 working days being lost.[167]

Why should South Wales have been so badly affected by disputes? The answer lies partly in the marked drop in output per man shift following on the introduction of the legal eight-hour day. This drop was said to be as large as 13 per cent at the Cambrian Combine pits,[168] so that the men do not appear to have exerted themselves to keep up their output: they still worked at the same steady pace as before. Colliery managers were, it is said, tightening up on payments for abnormal conditions, particularly at the Cambrian Combine pits. Abnormality payments, which are meant to compensate for temporary difficulties, were used in South Wales to make up wages to what the men regarded as satisfactory levels. There was pressure from the men to obtain a regular level of 'consideration payments', irrespective of the actual degree of abnormality, whilst managers were under pressure to reduce such payments. This was the economic cause of the South Wales disputes.[169]

There was however, a political cause. In the South Wales coalfield the syndicalists gained wide support. There developed, as Phelps-Brown says, 'a new temper in the younger men, a blazing anger, a bitter determination to enforce new claims. For their established leadership and its traditional methods the new militants showed a withering contempt.'[170] An unofficial reform committee, whose members included A. J. Cook, Noah Ablett and George Barker, was established in 1911. Its manifesto *The Miners' Next Step* advocated direct industrial action in place of conciliation; and all-inclusive industrial unions with no benefit except strike benefit in place of the district and sectional unions with friendly society as well as trade functions which then existed. The pamphlet called for 'a policy of open hostility', the adoption of 'ca' canny' (that is, a deliberate restriction of effort) to make collieries where the men were in dispute with the owners unremunerative, a continual agitation for increased minimum wages and reductions in hours of work so as to extract 'the whole of the employers' profits'; and the building up of an organization to take over the mining industry 'and carry it on in the interests of the workers'.[171]

The Syndicalists succeeded in winning over the South Wales Miners' Federation: what was originally an unofficial movement became an official one. Cook, Ablett and Barker all became full-time Union officials. Outside South Wales, however, the Syndicalists remained a small though vocal minority. In Nottinghamshire, the S.L.P. group founded by Jack Lavin had considerable support in the Mansfield Area, but the constitutional left-wing movement of I.L.P. members led by Herbert Booth was a far more effective pressure group appealing to much wider sections of the miners.

At National Conferences of the M.F.G.B. the South Wales militants were opposed by delegates from the old Federated District, and particularly by George Spencer. However, their policy of demanding a national wages agreement in place of district agreements was eventually adopted by the M.F.G.B. despite the opposition of delegates from the Midland coalfields.

The practical measures demanded by the Syndicalists met with much wider support than the philosophical basis of the Syndicalist programme. First, the demand for a legal minimum wage, then the demand for a national wage agreement and then the demand for nationalization of the mining industry were all endorsed by a majority of miners.

The right wing, who saw where all this was leading, nevertheless had to give some support to the agitation in order to avoid being swamped by it; but the struggle between left-wing and right-wing in the M.F.G.B. was on. On the one side were the advocates of the complete abolition of the capitalist system to be achieved by direct industrial action and on the other were those who sought the amelioration of the miners' lot within the framework of the capitalist system. Herbert Booth represented a broad middle group of Socialists who believed in fighting for their left-wing programme by constitutional means.

The attempt by J. G. Hancock and George Spencer to secede from the M.F.G.B. politically can be seen as a harbinger of future disunity. The fact is that the lib.-labs. at one extreme and the Syndicalists at the other held completely irreconcileable views of the purposes of trade unions. They disagreed on aims; and they disagreed on methods. These disagreements were to play a dominant part in the development of industrial relations in the years ahead.

APPENDIX A

MEMBERSHIP OF N.M.A. COMPARED WITH NUMBERS
EMPLOYED IN THE NOTTS. COALFIELD
1883–1910

Year	Persons employed above and below ground (a)	N.M.A. Membership (b)	Col. (b) expressed as a percentage of col. (a)	Pit head price of coal from Midland districts (to nearest 1d.) (d) s. d.
1883	15,286	2,167	14·2	6 0
1884	15,333	1,041	6·8	6 0
1885	15,974	1,067	6·7	5 9
1886	16,147	350	2·2	5 6
1887	17,018	1,633	9·6	5 8
1888	17,380	1,959	11·3	5 6
1889	18,853	7,549	40·0	6 7
1890	20,390	10,888	53·4	7 6
1891	21,512	18,341	85·3	7 5
1892	22,295	17,011	76·3	7 4
1893	23,121	18,835	81·4	7 8
1894	23,271	16,550	71·1	6 10
1895	23,534	13,363	56·8	6 2
1896	22,759	14,642	64·3	5 10
1897	23,024	14,609	63·5	6 0
1898	24,499	15,287	62·3	6 2
1899	25,276	16,766	66·3	6 11
1900	26,982	19,968	74·0	10 3

APPENDIX A—*continued*

1901	27,783	20,839	75·1	9	2
1902	29,510	21,338	72·3	8	1
1903	30,169	21,043	69·8	7	7
1904	31,075	20,982	67·5	7	3
1905	31,687	20,305	64·1	6	10
1906	33,164	23,774	71·7	6	0
1907	35,415	28,415	80·8	8	8
1908	36,573	30,753	84·1	8	3
1909	37,851	33,112	87·5	7	7
1910	37,863	31,252	82·5	7	2

Sources:

Col. (a): Gibson, op. cit., p. 24.

Col. (b): Figures for 1884–1898 (except 1887–1890 inclusive). Letter from Chief Registrar of Friendly Societies dated 2.2.1955 giving extracts from his records; 1883—N.M.A. Minute Book; for 1887–1890 a printed report of W. Bailey cited Griffin, *The Miners of Nottinghamshire*, Vol. I, Nottm. 1956, p. 56; and for 1898–1910, 'Thirteenth Abstract of Labour Statistics', Cmd. 5041 and 'Report of Trade Unions in 1908–10' Cmd. 6109, cited R. P. Arnot, *The Miners*, Vol. I, London, 1948, p. 393.

Col. (d): Gibson, op. cit., p. 157.

N.B. For 1887, the Registrar General of Friendly Societies gives membership of the N.M.A. as 2,506 as against the 1,633 reported by Bailey.

APPENDIX B

N.M.A.: DISPUTE AND UNEMPLOYMENT PAY 1914–1926

	Members at December		Strike and lockout pay	Out-of-work pay	Total receipts
Year	Total	Financial			
1914	33,915	32,028	251	2,127	36,934
1915	35,315	33,434	—	1,801	34,957
1916			NOT AVAILABLE		
1917	37,907	36,259	4,628	728	39,726
1918	37,611	36,169	2,767	1,154	36,813
1919	42,892	41,859	64,951	21,666	58,723
1920	45,155	44,171	133,791	3,975	102,178
1921	43,206	34,199	153,199	46,737	130,954
1922	38,236	23,713	446	8,501	89,290
1923	34,687	24,910	73	355	54,731
1924	33,384	25,137		378	56,458
1925	34,767	27,477		2,335	60,102
1926	10,055	8,663	65,961	1,167	27,101
			426,284	90,024	727,967

Source: N.M.A. Minutes Books, 1914–26.

REFERENCES

1 *Nottingham Daily Guardian*, 18th November 1900.
2 ibid., 13th August 1900.
3 F. A. Gibson, op. cit., p. 24.
4 ibid., p. 11. The 1888 output was 169,935,219 tons.
5 J. W. F. Rowe, *Wages in the Coal Industry*, London, 1922, pp. 126–7. See also A. J. Taylor, 'Labour Productivity and Technological Innovation in the British Coal Industry', *Ec.H.R.*, XIV, No. 1, 1961, p. 55 where the author argues that difficulties in supply, rather than increasing demand, caused prices to rise. The emphasis is curious. Difficulties in supply only arose because of increasing demand.
6 ibid., p. 85.
7 *Colliery Year Book and Coal Trades Directory*, 1951 edn., p. 500.
8 *Peoples Year Book*, 1926 edn., pp. 194–5 (see note 3 to Part II, Chapter II, p. 144 supra).
9 The rents of colliery houses are rarely altered, and charges for concessionary coal are much the same now as they were seventy years ago.
10 E. H. Phelps-Brown, op. cit., pp. 298–9.
11 ibid., p. 337. The evidence in the text may be supplemented by reference to A. L. Bowley, *Wages and Income in the United Kingdom since 1860*, Cambridge, 1937, pp. 6, 8 and 30.
12 Rule 45, 1906 Set.
13 Rule 45, 1912 Set.
14 *Nottingham Daily Express*, 2nd January 1888.
15 *Hucknall Star and Advertiser*, 14th December 1888.
16 Sources: Records of Chief Registrar of Friendly Societies and Gibson, op. cit., p. 157.
17 *N.M.A. Minute Books*, cited Griffin, op. cit., I, pp. 181–2.
18 *N.M.A. Minute Book*, cited Griffin, op. cit., I, p. 99.
19 Watnall belonged to the Leen Valley geographically, but its owners (Barber Walker) maintained their allegiance to the old Colliery Owners' Association. On the other hand, the collieries marked (19) were geographically outside the Leen Valley. The Digby and Babbington Companies appear to have rejoined the old Association before 1918—see Stoker Award dated 5th September 1918.
20 Herbert Booth, in a letter to the writer.
21 N.M.A. Minute Book, cited Griffin, op. cit., I, p. 155.
22 ibid., p. 181.
23 See, for example, *Minutes of Joint District Board for Nottinghamshire*, passim, cited: Griffin, op. cit., I, pp. 190–200.
24 *N.M.A. Minute Book*, 26th May 1919.
25 This information was supplied by Mr. Herbert Booth.
26 Though Arnot probably exaggerates—op. cit., III, p. 201.
27 According to Mr. Albert Bailey, the previous Treasurer, John Jackson, was a sympathetic milkman and William Bailey thought that it was improper to have an outsider in this post. He had become friendly with Lewis Spencer, who was a class leader at the Percy Street Primitive Methodist Chapel of which Bailey became a member in 1887, and he induced him to take the treasurership—originally on a part-time basis.
28 *N.M.A. Minute Book*, 25th July 1921.
29 These were the payments made in the early months of 1920. In July, it was

P

agreed that full-time officials should be paid £255 10s. per annum plus current percentage, war wage and Sankey money, but this was not to apply to Lewis Spencer who subsequently received a smaller salary than the Agents—*N.M.A. Minute Book*, 26th July 1920.

30 I have this information from Mr. Herbert Booth.

31 *N.M.A. Minute Book*, 25th October 1920, 29th November 1920 and 31st January 1921.

32 *N.M.A. Minute Book*, 31st January 1921; 28th February 1921; 21st March 1921; 25th April 1921; 30th May 1921; 27th June 1921 and 25th July 1921.

33 *Nottingham Daily Express*, 6th April 1894; Griffin, op. cit., I, p. 106, Rowe, op. cit., pp. 46–8.

34 *Minutes of Federated District Conciliation Board*, 17th November 1898: Griffin, op. cit., I, pp. 132–135.

35 *Derbyshire Times*, 10th July 1897, Griffin, op. cit., I, p. 122.

36 *N.M.A. Minute Book*, 29th February 1908.

37 ibid., 27th March 1908.

38 ibid., 6th April 1912.

39 ibid., 15th December 1890.

40 Griffin, op. cit., I, pp. 147–8; and 139–141; *N.M.A. Minute Book*, 1901–2 passim.

41 *Nottingham Daily Guardian*, 30th March 1912 cited Griffin, op. cit., I, p. 168.

42 e.g. *N.M.A. Minute Book*, 24th April 1908. The full name of the E. and F. U. was: The Derbyshire, Nottinghamshire and Midland Counties Enginemen, Motormen and Firemen's Union.

43 *N.M.A. Minute Book*, 10th April 1909.

44 Report of James Wroe, Manager, to the Directors of the Sutton Colly. Co. Ltd., dated 16th May 1896. Mechanical cutters had been tried out earlier than this at, e.g., Eastwood Collieries, but with little success.

45 Griffin, op. cit., I, pp. 111, 121 and 124.

46 *N.M.A. Minute Book*, 28th November 1908; *Nottingham Daily Express*, 30th November 1908.

47 *N.M.A. Minute Book* (especially 30th July 1910 and 27th August 1910). *Nottingham Daily Guardian*, 28th November 1910, 27th and 28th September 1911.

48 See also *Minutes of Joint District Board for Nottinghamshire*, 1912, cited Griffin, op. cit., I, p. 198.

49 Cited Griffin, op. cit., I, p. 141.

50 *N.M.A. Minute Book*, 24th November 1906; 29th December 1906; 26th January 1907; and 2nd March 1907. The reference to arbitration was agreed to by the owners in order to end a strike over this issue. It will be seen from the text that A. J. Taylor's suggestion that technical innovation met with little opposition from the men is unjustified.—A. J. Taylor, 'The Coal Industry', *The Development of British Industry and Foreign Competition 1875–1914*, London, 1968, p. 58.

51 ibid., 1917 and 1918 passim, especially 16th November 1918.

52 ibid., 1st January 1919.

53 ibid., 29th May 1915.

54 ibid., 30th October 1915.

55 *Award* of W. H. Stoker, dated 5th September 1918.

56 *Award* of W. W. Mackenzie, K.C., dated 9th December 1916.

57 *Award* of W. H. Stoker, dated 5th September 1918.

58 *Award* of W. H. Stoker, dated 16th June 1920.

59 Loc. cit.

60 *Agreement Concerning All Seams Other Than Top Hard* dated 8th May 1922.
61 Griffin, op. cit., II, pp. 51–5 and 97–100.
62 ibid., I, p. 140.
63 As at Butterley in 1874, see *Nottingham Daily Journal*, 27th April 1874.
64 F. Hodges, *Nationalisation of the Mines*, London, 1920, pp. 31–35.
65 *N.M.A. Minute Book*, 11th January 1919.
66 ibid., 28th February 1921.
67 ibid., 25th April 1921.
68 ibid., 29th August, 26th September and 15th October 1921. *M.F.G.B. Minute Book*, 1921, p. 489.
69 According to German Abbott.
70 *N.M.A. Minute Book*, 1918, (end paper). A majority favoured day-wage payments.
71 ibid., 27th and 28th January, 24th February, 26th May 1919.
72 *Minute Book of the Eastwood Central Committee* (in the possession of Mr. A. A. Booth).
73 The 'butty' system remained in force at the Bolsover Co. pits until the Second World War.
74 Letter from E. C. Fowler to J. G. Hancock dated 12th March 1920 cited Griffin, op. cit., II, p. 63.
75 *M.F.G.B. Minute Book*, 1921, p. 61.
76 *M.F.G.B. Minute Book*, 31st December 1921.
77 J. W. F. Rowe, op. cit., p. 67 n.
78 Griffin, op. cit., Vol. I, pp. 108–9.
79 8 Edw. 7. Cap. 57.
80 E.g. *Minutes of Derbyshire Miners' Association*, 29th July 1918, cited J. E. Williams, op. cit., p. 534.
81 *Nottingham Daily Guardian*, 9th July 1909.
82 ibid., 10th July 1909.
83 ibid., 9th July and 30th August 1909.
84 ibid., 5th July 1909 and information supplied by G. A. Spencer.
85 Arnot, op. cit., II, p. 57.
86 Griffin, op. cit., I, pp. 140–1.
87 Rowe, op. cit., p. 47.
88 Arnot, op. cit., II, pp. 57–77. *Colliery Year Book and Coal Trades Directory*, 1951 edn., p. 502.
89 Arnot, op. cit., Vol. II, p. 59.
90 *Colliery Year Book and Coal Trades Directory*, 1951 edn., p. 502.
91 Arnot, op. cit., Vol. II, p. 69 and G. Harvey, *Industrial Unionism and the Mining Industry*, Pelaw-on-Tyne, 1917, p. 33.
92 Arnot, op. cit., Vol. II, pp. 71–72.
93 ibid., p. 73.
94 ibid., pp. 76–7.
95 ibid., p. 80.
96 ibid., p. 82.
97 ibid., pp. 86–91.
98 ibid., pp. 96–102.
99 *N.M.A. Minute Book*, 25th March 1912.
100 *Nottingham Daily Guardian*, 28th February 1912.
101 *N.M.A. Minute Book*.
102 Arnot, op. cit., Vol. II, pp. 101–7.
103 ibid., pp. 109–110.
104 *Nottingham Daily Guardian*, 1st April 1912.
105 *Nottingham Daily Guardian*, 1st July 1912.

106 Rowe, op. cit., pp. 108–9.
107 Griffin, op. cit., I, p. 200.
108 Rowe, op. cit., pp. 107–8.
109 ibid., p. 110.
110 Griffin, op. cit., I, pp. 108–9.
111 Election Manifesto dated July 9th 1895—Griffin, op. cit., I, illustration preceding p. 107.
112 *Nottingham Daily Guardian*, 30th June 1891.
113 ibid., 20th June 1892; Griffin, op. cit., I, pp. 79–80.
114 J. E. Williams, op. cit., pp. 489–90.
115 *Hucknall Star and Advertiser*, 14th and 21st December 1888.
116 *Nottingham Daily Guardian*, 20th May 1891, and Bailey's private papers.
117 J. E. Williams, op. cit., pp. 494–5.
118 *Nottingham Daily Express*, 8th August 1892.
119 See, e.g., *Nottingham Daily Guardian*, 12th August 1894.
120 *Nottingham Daily Guardian*, 20th May 1889.
121 Hancock gave Herbert Booth to understand that he served articles with a Chartered Accountant. This can hardly be true.
122 N.M.A. *Minute Book*, 30th April 1904. The N.M.A. in common with the other district unions, paid 1s. per member per year into the M.F.G.B. Labour Election Fund. It was entitled to nominate one Parliamentary candidate for each 10,000 members.
123 ibid., 6th January 1906.
124 *Nottingham Daily Guardian*, 1st November 1909.
125 F. Williams, *Fifty Years March—The Rise of the Labour Party*, London, 1950, p. 149.
126 ibid.
127 M.F.G.B. *Labour Election Fund*, Rule 4 (1901 set) cited Arnot op. cit., I, p. 361.
128 Arnot, op. cit., I, pp. 363–4.
129 ibid., I, p. 361.
130 N.M.A. *Minute Book*, 7th July 1906.
131 N.M.A. *Minute Book*, 25th August 1906; Arnot, op. cit., I, p. 364. The proportion of membership voting was very low.
132 Arnot, op. cit., I, pp. 366–8. The M.F.G.B. had to pay an affiliation fee of 15s. per thousand members to the Labour Party.
133 J. E. Williams, op. cit., pp. 498–500.
134 See note 127 above.
135 J. E. Williams, op. cit., p. 500.
136 Arnot, op. cit., I, p. 368, and N.M.A. *Minute Book*, 4th December 1909.
137 N.M.A. *Minute Book*, 6th February 1909.
138 ibid., 2nd July, 1910; M.F.G.B. *Minute Book*, 8th and 9th June 1910. This followed the Osborne judgment of 1908.
139 N.M.A. *Minute Book*, 3rd September 1910.
140 2 and 3 Geo. V. cap. 30.
141 J. E. Williams, op. cit., pp. 504–5.
142 *Nottingham Daily Guardian*, 3rd June 1912.
143 N.M.A. *Minute Book*, 30th January 1915.
144 ibid., 27th February 1915.
145 Herbert Booth: letter of 6th January 1959.
146 See H. Pelling, *America and the British Left*, London, 1956, passim.
147 Herbert Booth's phrase. The S.L.P. programme in relation to the mining industry is set out in: G. Harvey, *Industrial Unionism and the Mining Industry*, Pelaw-on-Tyne, 1917.

148 Harvey, op. cit., p. 3.
149 ibid., pp. 128–9.
150 Based on conversations with Spencer, Booth and Ford.
151 Based mainly on correspondence and conversations with Booth. Spencer secured 8,125 votes out of 14,349 cast in the ballot for a full-time official— *N.M.A. Minute Book*, 27th May 1918.
152 *N.M.A. Minute Book*, 30th December 1918. Had finance been forthcoming Varley would have opposed Hancock for Labour.
153 *N.M.A. Minute Book*, 26th May 1919.
154 Minutes of Federated District, 17th July 1917.
155 ibid., 18th July 1917.
156 The South Wales resolution envisaged the continuance of wage and price regulation after the war, which rather begged the question.
157 *Minutes of Federated District*, ibid., 23rd August 1918. (Emphasis supplied).
158 The scrapping of the Conciliation Board for the Federated District was a necessary pre-requisite for the development of the class struggle along classical Marxist lines. The Conciliation Board at times presented a united front of owners and men in defence of the privileged position of the Federated Area, and this blurred the class division.
159 Phelps-Brown, op. cit., pp. 294–343.
160 ibid., p. 334.
161 Gibson, op. cit., p. 157.
162 *People's Year Book, 1926*, edn., pp. 194–5.
163 *M.F.G.B. Minute Books*, 1907–1913.
164 Rowe, op. cit., p. 126. See also A. J. Taylor, 'Labour Productivity and Technological Innovation in the British Coal Industry, 1850–1914', *Economic History Review*, XIV, No. 1, 1961, pp. 54–5.
165 Phelps-Brown, op. cit., p. 335.
166 *Colly. Year Book and Coal Trades Directory*, 1951 edn., p. 502.
167 *Colly. Year Book and Coal Trades Directory*, 1951 edn., pp. 502 and 504.
168 Phelps-Brown, op. cit., p. 318.
169 Phelps-Brown, op. cit., p. 319; Arnot, op. cit., II, pp. 57–81.
170 Phelps-Brown, op. cit., pp. 319–20.
171 *The Miners Next Step*, Tonypandy, 1912, cap. 5.

PART III

CHAPTER I

The Uneasy Peace 1919—1924

1. INTRODUCTION

The post-war years saw a pronounced leftward swing in the political pendulum which was to carry the Labour Party into office in 1924. For a time, too, the advocates of 'direct industrial action' enjoyed considerable support. A Triple Alliance of miners, transport workers and railwaymen had been formed in 1915. This was in practice a consultative body which left the individual unions with full autonomy but which was intended, in theory, to secure united action whenever one of the three partners was involved in a trade dispute.[1]

In the post-war period, the Alliance was pressed to take direct action to enforce the lifting of the blockade of Germany, the ending of the war of intervention in Russia, the withdrawal of the British garrison in Ireland and the nationalization of the mines.[2] This programme was, for a time, widely supported in Nottinghamshire; so much so that even George Spencer and Frank Varley for a short time expressed near-revolutionary views. In July 1919 Spencer was 'in favour of taking action . . . in reference to the blockade, conscription and to Russia in particular'.[3] By September, however, Spencer had changed his opinions. The industrial weapon should now, he thought, be reserved for use in connection with the demand for nationalization of the mines. In the intervening period, Nottinghamshire had taken a ballot on the question of striking in support of direct action to end conscription, intervention in Russia, and so on, and it appeared that the rank-and-file were not nearly so militant as the minority who attended meetings and passed resolutions. As Spencer explained:

'We have taken our ballot. At one district there was actually a majority against intervention or direct action. At one colliery it was not so good as one might have anticipated, and especially at one pit in particular where we looked upon it as probably where we had men of the most advanced views, the result from that quarter was nothing like satisfactory on the question of direct action.'[4]

The N.M.A. Council, which now had a predominance of left-wing delegates, continued to pass militant resolutions, but Spencer no longer felt any particular obligation to support them. Similarly, J. R. Clynes of the Transport Workers' Federation was opposed to a strike for political purposes, which would lead to 'a state of starvation and certainly a state of riot'.[5]

The division of opinion between those who supported, and those who opposed, direct industrial action for political ends is at the root of the split which developed in the N.M.A. On the one hand, the Mansfield District Committee, a body established originally to administer the Berry Hill Hall Miners' Convalescent Home, became an organizing centre for the left; whilst on the other hand an organization calling itself the British Workers' League (B.W.L.) campaigned in favour of 'non political' trade unionism, and became the organizing centre for the right. It was supported by prominent representatives of the butties like William Holland and Joseph Birkin and its strongholds were the Bolsover and Barber Walker collieries. It was to form the nucleus of Spencer's 'non-political' union. The B.W.L. was an offshoot of the British Commonwealth Union, a right wing pressure group formed towards the end of the war by a group of provincial industrialists.[6]

On the right, too, was J. G. Hancock, who wrote secretly to the Babbington Coal Company expressing his opposition to 'Mine Nationalization and also to the Day Work System'.[7] But on mines nationalization at least, the left-wing view was the popular one: The vast majority of miners were in favour of permanent national ownership of the industry, and in the first half of 1919, they seemed to have a fair chance of getting it.[8]

2. THE SANKEY REPORTS

In January 1919 the M.F.G.B. claimed a substantial increase in pay, a six-hour day, protection for demobilized ex-miners who were unemployed and nationalization of the mines.[9]

In order to avoid a strike,[10] the Government set up a Royal Commission to enquire into the organization of the industry, miners' pay and conditions of employment and similar questions.[11] The M.F.G.B. Conference refused to participate in the work of the Commission unless they were given adequate representation on it. In the event, six Commissioners were members or supporters of the Federation, three were representatives of Coal-Owners and the other three were independent Government nominees. The Chairman was Mr. Justice Sankey.

The Commission was to issue an interim report by 20 March but instead it issued three interim reports. One was signed only by the M.F.G.B. side of the Commission, another was signed by the Coal-

Owners' representatives, and a third was signed by the Chairman and the three Government nominees. This third report (usually referred to as the Sankey Report), recommended a seven-hour day with effect from 16th July 1919, a six-hour day (depending on the economic conditions of the industry) with effect from 13th July 1921,[12] a 46½-hour working week for surface men, an increase of 2s. a day in wages and, most important of all to the miners, a radical reorganization of the industry ('either nationalization or a method of unification by national purchase and/or by joint control').[13]

Bonar Law, speaking for the Government in the absence of the Prime Minister, said that the Government accepted the (interim) Sankey Report 'in spirit and in letter'. This was taken by the M.F.G.B. Conference to be a promise of nationalization, but George Spencer pointed out, quite correctly, that it was nothing of the sort.[14] A ballot vote showed an overwhelming majority in favour of accepting the Government's terms—which were the same as the Sankey recommendations—and the strike was called off.[15] To pay for the increased wage and the reduction in hours, the Government increased coal prices. This cost the miners much of the public sympathy they had previously enjoyed.

The Sankey Commission sat again from 24th April to 23rd June and then issued four final reports. The Chairman and the six M.F.G.B. sympathizers advocated nationalization of the mines,[16] but the other members opposed it.[16] The Government refused to adopt any plan of nationalization[17] but offered the establishment of large trusts some of whose directors would represent the workers.[18]

The leaders of the M.F.G.B. felt that the Prime Minister was breaking a solemn promise, but Bonar Law and Lloyd George insisted that the interim Sankey Report, which they had agreed to implement, did not commit them to nationalization. For their part, the M.F.G.B. made it clear that they would not co-operate in the management of privately-owned trusts.[19]

The M.F.G.B. tried to induce the T.U.C. to take direct industrial action to secure mines nationalization, but by a large majority the Special Trades Union Congress meeting on 11th March 1920 decided against a general strike and in favour of an intensive propaganda campaign.[20] This campaign proved totally ineffective.

The Government increased the price of coal after agreeing to the Sankey Commission's recommendations for increased pay and shorter hours. This increase, of 6s. per ton, was strongly criticized by the M.F.G.B. and the militants felt that a national strike should be organized in order to make the Government remove the increase.[21] The M.F.G.B. also demanded that piece-workers should receive higher contract prices to compensate them for the fall in output brought about by the reduction in hours from eight to seven per day. This claim was eventually conceded, and in Nottinghamshire piece-rates were increased by 14·17 per cent.[22]

3. THE DATUM LINE STRIKE

During the period of the post-war boom, miners' leaders expressed concern at the steeply rising cost of living. The official cost-of-living index (taking July 1914 as 100) moved from 200 at June 1918 to 220 at January 1919, 225 a year later, and 250 in June 1920.[23] The leaders of the Miners' Federation therefore decided in 1920 to press for a reduction in the selling price of coal so as to initiate a fall in the cost of living. The mines were, at this time, producing large profits of which a substantial proportion went to the Treasury. The M.F.G.B. insisted that, if profit levels were not reduced by bringing down the price of coal, then miners should be given substantially higher wages to offset the increasing cost-of-living. Indeed, at times, the M.F.G.B. demanded both a reduction in coal prices and a wage increase also; but the emphasis given to these two demands varied from one leader to another. Generally speaking the left-wing militants of South Wales pressed for increased wages whilst Bob Smillie, M.F.G.B. President, and his moderate colleagues stressed the importance of bringing prices down.[24]

The Government refused to consider reducing the price of coal, but did concede an increase of 20 per cent on gross earnings (excluding War Wage). This was accepted after a ballot vote of the men and came into effect on 12th March 1920.[25] Almost immediately, the Government increased the price of household coal by 14s. 2d. per ton and of industrial coal by 4s. 2d. per ton.[26] Bob Smillie was not alone in thinking that this was another attempt to turn public opinion against the miners and to facilitate the de-control of the industry.[27] The Prime Minister made no secret of the enormous profits the Government were making from exported coal.[28]

The M.F.G.B. demanded that this price increase should be taken off, and that miners' wages should be raised by a further 2s. a day. This led to a curious situation. At the National Conference of the M.F.G.B. held at Leamington in July 1920 Frank Varley of Nottingham, normally regarded as a right-winger, moved for an advance in wages of 4s. a day instead of 2s. and for the dropping of the demand for a reduction in the price of coal. He was seconded by the left-wing A. J. Cook of South Wales, but opposed by his colleague George Spencer who considered the reduction in price to be far more important than the proposed wage increase.[29] After a ballot vote in which a large majority voted in favour of striking to obtain the increase in wages and reduction in price,[30] the M.F.G.B. asked the Triple Alliance for support.

The Alliance joined the M.F.G.B. in an approach to the Government but were unwilling to strike in sympathy. The Government offered to refer the wage question to arbitration and suggested as an alternative that the miners and owners should negotiate an output bonus. After negotiations, which proved abortive, a national strike commenced on October 18th. The N.U.R. then decided to strike in sympathy with the miners unless their 'reasonable and just' claims were granted, or negotiations resumed, by 23rd October.[31] This resolution was the undoubted cause of the quickening of the Prime Minister's interest in the dispute. He invited the M.F.G.B. officials to re-open negotiations and after four days the Government conceded the immediate advance of 2s. a shift demanded by the miners. In addition, further increases were to be paid if output exceeded a given level (the 'Datum Line') and a National Wages Board with a permanent scheme for the regulation of wages was to be established on terms to be negotiated between owners and Unions by 31st March 1921. The 2s. a shift advance was to be guaranteed by the Government until the end of December.[32]

This offer was the subject of another ballot vote in which a small majority voted to reject the terms. However, at the resumed M.F.G.B. Conference Bob Smillie ruled that a two-thirds majority was necessary to continue a strike so that the result of the ballot was tantamount to acceptance of the offer. This ruling was attacked by A. J. Cook, S. O. Davies and Noah Ablett of South Wales, and Tom Greenall of Lancashire, but it was accepted by Conference. Accordingly, the men went back to work (after being out for just over a fortnight) on 4th November 1920.[33]

For the N.M.A. the strike had been disastrous. The funds were drained of £132,000 in strike pay. The strike had similarly weakened the other Areas financially. Many miners' leaders believed that they could have achieved just as much through arbitration as they did through striking; and it would appear that even left-wing leaders came to recognize that the strike was a tactical error.[34]

To what extent the 'Datum Line' strike depressed the whole economy of the country it would be impossible to say, but it occurred at a time when unemployment was rising and when commodity prices were falling from their high post-war levels. Of this trend Prof. Pigou says: '. . . the collapse of prices led, as it was bound to do, to an attack, among other wages, upon those of coal miners, and so was ultimately responsible for the disastrous coal strike of April-June, 1921, which, of course, in turn inflicted heavy damage on industry.' The level of unemployment among trade unions making returns, which had risen gradually from 0·9 per cent in April 1920 to 2·2 per cent in

September, jumped to 5·3 per cent in October (the month of the Datum Line Strike) and after falling back to 3·7 per cent in November, continued to rise steeply to 10·2 per cent in March 1921.[35]

4. THE 1921 LOCKOUT

Following the conclusion of the Datum Line Agreement, the Mining Association and the M.F.G.B. held interminable discussions on a permanent settlement to come into effect when the mines were decontrolled. All agreements negotiated with the Government would then come to an end in any case.

The M.F.G.B. wanted to perpetuate the life of the National Wages Pool and of National Agreements, but the owners insisted on returning to district agreements. It was not even proposed to re-create the Federated Area.[36]

The negotiations were rudely interrupted by the Government who decided to decontrol the mines on 31st March 1921—five months earlier than expected. This decision was taken because the bottom had dropped out of the export market and the mines were making substantial losses. This came as a shock to both owners and men. Frank Hodges, General Secretary of the M.F.G.B. expressed the view that only Nottinghamshire, Derbyshire and Yorkshire could work at a profit at the prices then ruling, whilst Frank Varley pointed out that Cumberland was producing coal at a loss of 14s. a ton, and he asked how the men could possibly be expected to bear this out of their wages.[37]

Clearly, even with wage reductions, some of the grossly uneconomic collieries would be unable to keep open with the removal of subsidies. But the Government went ahead with its plans and the Coal Mines (Decontrol) Act became law on 24th March 1921. By this time all the miners were under notice to terminate their existing contracts of employment. The owners had presented their terms for a new wage settlement which provided that the wages paid in each district should depend on the financial position of such district.

The 1914 wage was to be regarded as a minimum, and pieceworkers were to retain the addition paid as a result of the reduction in hours from eight to seven. The owners were to have a standard profit equal to 17 per cent of the aggregate wage so calculated. Any surplus was to be divided between wages and profits in proportions 75 to 25.[38]

It was calculated that the reductions in gross wages would range from 1·03 per cent in Derbyshire, Nottinghamshire and Leicestershire, to 47·55 per cent in Cumberland and Westmorland; with an average reduction for all districts around 22 per cent.[39]

The Executive Committee tentatively suggested that the policy of a National Wages Board and national pool should be temporarily dropped so that district associations could be free to negotiate the best terms possible for their members.[40] This suggestion was strongly opposed by the South Wales militants. S. O. Davies, for example, wanted to 'throw down the gauntlet' to bring capitalism to an end.[41] Of the large districts, only Yorkshire and Northumberland voted in favour of district negotiations and the temporary abandonment of the demand for a National Pool. Nottinghamshire, which had the most to gain from such abandonment nevertheless voted against the idea, along with eleven other districts. The E.C.'s suggestion was defeated at National Conference by 727 votes to 241 (each vote representing a thousand members).

On 30th March the M.F.G.B. Executive met Sir Robert Horne, the President of the Board of Trade to report that negotiations with the owners had proved fruitless and to ask for Government assistance to help the industry to pay a living wage. Sir Robert made it clear that a subsidy in aid of wages was out of the question.

In answer to a question from Sir Robert, the deputation complained about the total inadequacy of the offers made by the Owners relating to the various districts. Frank Varley pointed out that the operating results for Nottinghamshire and Derbyshire for February justified a reduction of only 1d. a day in the existing wage (using the principles laid down by the Mining Association) but the owners proposed a reduction of 2s. 6d. a day, the extra 2s. 5d. being to meet contingencies.[42]

The lock-out began on 1st April. The M.F.G.B. insisted that all the men should come out including 'safety men' (e.g. pump-men, winders, and ostlers). This was a mistake because it enabled the owners and the Government to castigate the miners as irresponsible. When the Triple Alliance sent a deputation to see the Government on 9th April they were told that negotiations could not take place until the safety-men were allowed back to work. Accordingly, the M.F.G.B. instructed Districts to let the safety men return.[43]

The Railwaymen and Transport Workers had called a sympathetic strike to start on Friday 15th April, and the miners hoped that this would induce the Government to arrange suitable terms for a settlement. However, the sympathetic strike did not take place and the day on which it should have started became known as 'Black Friday'. The excuse for calling off the strike was provided by Frank Hodges on 14th April when he was understood to say that the M.F.G.B. would be prepared to abandon temporarily the National pool. On the following day, the Prime Minister invited the M.F.G.B. to meet the Owners at the Board of Trade to negotiate on this new basis, but the M.F.G.B. Executive made it clear that they could not abandon the demand for a National Wages Board and a National Pool.[44] The Triple Alliance leaders were then able to say that the miners were being unreasonable.

The lock-out lasted from the beginning of April until the beginning of July. The terms on which a settlement was finally reached were within the Federation's grasp from the end of April when the Government offered a subsidy of £10 million in aid of wages conditional on a durable settlement. Further, whilst the Government were opposed to a National Pool they were in favour of a National Wages Board to determine the general principles on which district agreements should be based.

This offer was turned down by the National Conference, Northumberland being the only district to vote in favour of acceptance.[45] A similar offer was made on 27th May and was referred to districts. All the districts voted against. The Prime Minister then made it clear that his offer of a £10 million subsidy would remain open only for another fortnight. This warning induced the Mining Association to suggest a resumption of negotiations.[46]

The two sides met on 6th June and the owners presented a revised offer taking the Government subsidy into account. The M.F.G.B. decided to put these terms to the men by ballot vote: and the National Conference agreed that the members should not be advised on which way to vote.[47] The owners' terms involved district negotiations although there would be a National Wages Board to fix general principles for districts to follow. The Government's £10 millions would be used to ensure that the immediate reductions in wages would not exceed 2s. a day. There would be no further reductions until August. The final reductions likely to result varied from district to district, and in one proposed arrangement the Leen Valley men actually stood to get a small increase.[48]

When the votes were counted, all districts (except the Cokemen and Enginemen) were found to have voted in favour of continuing the strike.[49] In Nottinghamshire, less than a third of the members troubled to vote. Other districts with only a small majority for continuing the struggle, were the ones who had little to lose from the proposed terms of settlement: Derbyshire, Leicester, Midlands, Nottingham and South Derby (plus Northumberland, which did stand to suffer a substantial reduction, but where labour relations were traditionally good).

South Wales, Scotland, Lancashire and Forest of Dean, the 'militant' districts with large majorities for continuing the strike, on the other hand, had a great deal to lose under the proposed terms of settlement.[50] When the M.F.G.B. officials informed him of the result of the ballot, the Prime Minister said that the Government's offer would remain open only until the following night.[51]

The M.F.G.B. Executive then sought to widen the conflict by inviting other unions to take 'national action with the miners to secure their mutual demands'.[52] However, nothing came of this; and the following week, on 24th June, the Executive asked for a further meeting with the Government and the Owners. This meeting took place on 27th June, following which the E.C. recommended the districts to accept terms substantially the same as those the men had so recently rejected. The district vote was reported to the E.C. on 1st July. Thirteen districts had voted in favour whilst five (Lancashire and four small districts which stood to lose heavily under the district settlement: Bristol, Forest of Dean, Kent and Somerset) had voted against.[53] An immediate return to work was ordered.

Lancashire protested at the unconstitutional action of the E.C. which had called for a district vote on a matter already decided by ballot: but this protest was brushed aside.[54] Undoubtedly, it would have been foolish to prolong the dispute any longer. The funds of the districts had been drained dry by lock-out pay: Nottinghamshire, which had paid out £153,416, had plunged very heavily into debt.[55] Further, suffering was intense in many areas. It was not so bad for miners with large gardens. Those who had neither gardens nor secondary sources of income, however, relied largely on soup kitchens.

Looking back over a space of five decades, it seems obvious that the miners should have settled at the end of April. The extra two months of suffering weakened their organization immeasurably with no compensating advantages. Nottinghamshire, which had nothing to gain from the dispute, was particularly badly hit, and it took five years to clear off the debt arising from the lock-out. Meantime, members were called upon to pay steep levies and partly for this reason many dropped out of the Association.

5. THE MINERS' INDIAN SUMMER

The economic position of the miners worsened following the 1921 lock-out. Commodity prices were falling, but the miners' real wage-level fell much further and much faster. Increasing unemployment affected all industries to a greater or lesser extent; but the fall in real wages was greater in mining than in almost all other occupations.

Taking August 1914 as 100, the average weekly wage rate in mining fell from 223 at the end of February 1920 to 130 in March 1923. The rate for railway porters, by contrast, fell from 310 to 260. The cost-of-living index (again taking 1914 as 100) stood at 174.[56] Since industrial action did not seem, for the moment, to be productive of much good, miners' leaders became more active politically. The left-wing, Communist-led, sought opportunities for sharpening the class conflict, believing that capitalism had been so shaken by the War and the post-war dislocation of markets that it could not last much longer in the face of determined opposition by the organized working class. In 1922, South Wales sought to secure the affiliation of the M.F.G.B. to the industrial auxiliary of International Communism, the Red International of Labour Unions, which sought the 'international over-throw of capital'.[57]

The moderates, on the other hand, looked to the ballot box for salvation. People must be taught to vote Labour at future elections.[58] Still further to the right was the so-called British Workers' League which advocated non-political trade unionism. This body was active in Nottinghamshire and Derbyshire and was thought to be inspired by the Bolsover Colliery Company.[59] Many butties supported it.

Mansfield, by now the centre of the coalfield, was a battleground fought over by the left-wing militants of the Mansfield District Committee (who appealed to the many miners who had dropped out of the Union during the 1921 Dispute to rejoin it on a left-wing programme) and the B.W.L. who hoped to gain adherents for their 'non-political' trade union movement.

During 1923, the French occupation of the Ruhr and a coal strike in the U.S.A. brought much-needed relief to the British mining industry whose coal exports rose from 87,351,530 tons in 1922 to 102,817,570 tons in 1923.[60] Inland consumption rose also in response to a quickening tempo of industrial activity. The percentage of unemployment for all industries, revealed by the figures compiled from Trade Union returns, fell from 13·6 in January 1923 to 7·0 in May 1924.[61] Total output of coal in Great Britain rose from 249,606,864 tons in 1922 to 276,000,560 in 1923, falling back slightly to 267,118,167 tons in 1924.

Because of the improvement in trading conditions, the M.F.G.B. sought an improved wages agreement and to this end a special conference was held in March 1923. Varley and Spencer were opposed to any move to amend the 1921 settlement since it was doubtful if this could be done peacefully, and they feared that another dispute would wreck the Union. As Varley said:

> 'I am as confident as I stand here, having regard to the fact that the last stoppage so strained the loyalty of our men, if we attempt to strain that loyalty again, it will smash us.'[62]

Towards the end of the year, a ballot vote revealed a substantial majority in favour of abrogating the old agreement: 510,303 to 114,558 nationally and 11,392 to 5,059 in Nottinghamshire.[63] The Nottinghamshire total demonstrates the luke-warmness of the rank-and-file, being equal to about one-third of the labour force, and less than a half of the 34,000-odd membership.[64] Spencer and Varley continued their public opposition to terminating the Agreement, and for this they were criticised by left-wing members of the Council.[65]

On 17th January 1924 the M.F.G.B. gave three months' notice to terminate the Agreement. With an improved state of trade and with the remarkable effect on the climate of working-class opinion of the formation of the first Labour Government, the chances of securing an improved agreement seemed bright. The advent of Ramsay Macdonald's Government (of which Frank Hodges, formerly Secretary of the M.F.G.B., was a junior member) worked a remarkable transformation in Frank Varley's attitude. When the owners offered terms which would have produced, according to Varley's own computation, an extra 3¾d. a shift in Nottinghamshire and as much as 11½d. a shift in North Wales, Varley opposed their acceptance. He wanted 'something to take back to Notts.', not an agreement which favoured the poorer districts. He supported an E.C. recommendation that there should be an inquiry into miners' wages sponsored by the Government from which the miners could 'hope in the present psychology of the British public' for something better than the owners' offer.[66]

The owners' offer went to a ballot of the men, when it was rejected by 338,650 votes to 322,392. The left-wing districts: South Wales and Lancashire recorded huge majorities against the offer, despite the fact that they stood to gain by it; whilst Nottinghamshire, which would benefit very little, recorded a majority (7,909 to 7,506) in favour of acceptance. Subsequently, a Court of Inquiry set up by the Secretary for Mines, largely supported the miners' case and 'concluded with the recommendation that negotiations should continue with a view to a modification of the terms of the agreement of 1921'.[67]

On 29th May 1924 the new secretary of the M.F.G.B., A. J. Cook, reported to a special conference on the subsequent negotiations with the owners which had secured a slight improvement in the terms offered. The terms finally accepted by the conference were: that standard profits should be 15 per cent of standard wages: that any surplus should be divided between wages and profits in the proportions 88 to 12 and that the general minimum should be 30 per cent on standard wages.[68] The revised agreement was to run for twelve months. Unfortunately, the mild boom of 1923–4 was, for the miners, no more than an Indian summer. Before the revised agreement had run its course the owners were once more seeking wage reductions.

6. CONCLUSION

The end of the First World War saw the mining industry booming. Europe's demand for British coal was apparently insatiable. The labour force, at 1,200,000, was double what it had been thirty years or so before, but productivity had fallen from an average of 308 tons per man employed above and below ground in the period 1883–92 to 196 tons in 1919 and 187 tons in 1920.[69] This was partly due to shorter hours, partly to the influx of inexperienced adults during the war years, partly to the increased attention given to coal preparation, and partly to the ageing of the industry.[70] Bearing in mind, however, that on the other hand the pits were working full-time in 1919 and something less than full-time in the earlier period and that various technological improvements had also been introduced in the meantime, it is difficult to escape the conclusion that the tempo of work had slowed down considerably.

The harsh discipline to which miners had been subject before the war was now relaxed by reason of the excess of demand for, over supply of, coal. In relation to the demand for their services, therefore, miners were themselves in short supply. A near-revolutionary situation developed in the early months of 1919, when the demand for mines nationalization became insistent, and when direct action to secure it and various other political ends (like the abandonment of the war of intervention in Russia) was advocated even by men like G. A. Spencer. It developed not because miners were desperate and hungry, but rather because comparative prosperity and security of employment had so far freed their minds from a constant pre-occupation with scraping a living as to leave room for the consideration of wider questions. Two years later the market had collapsed: coal was no longer in short supply. The threat of a stoppage of supplies could no longer be used to force the Government to take action. But the left-wing leaders failed to realize the extent to which conditions had changed, and so they sought victory in 1921 in circumstances that were bound to lead to defeat. In so doing they brought some of the district associations to the point of collapse. The Nottinghamshire Association found itself crippled with debts that took five years to liquidate; and its membership dropped from something over 45,000 in early 1921 to around 33,000 in 1923 of whom only about 25,000 were less than three months in arrears with their subscriptions.[71]

No account of this period which fails to take fully into account the apathy of a considerable section of the rank-and-file—in Nottinghamshire amounting to about half of the labour force—can be considered satisfactory. The government of a trade union may rest in the hands of an articulate minority as Mr. Allen argues[72] but the ultimate sanction of withdrawing from the union still rests with the individual however inarticulate he may be.[73] The 1920 Dispute could have been settled by arbitration, as the M.F.G.B. President, Robert Smillie, advised. Smillie warned his colleagues that a strike would seriously weaken the organization and was not worthwhile in the circumstances of the time; but his advice was ignored.

Similarly, the 1921 lock-out could have been ended within four weeks instead of being allowed to drag on for twelve. Once the Government had agreed to their subsidy of £10 millions, the miners had achieved all that they were likely to achieve. The prolongation of the dispute put the loyalty and unity of the men to an unnecessary strain. It achieved nothing. The principle of a National Wages Pool, in the circumstances of 1921, was indeed impossible of achievement, however desirable it may have been.

Because of the disastrous effects on its organization and finances of the disputes of 1920 and 1921, the Miners' Federation of Great Britain in general, and the N.M.A. in particular, was already half-defeated when the next great dispute began. Had it preserved its strength instead of dissipating it purposely, it would have been in a far better position to oppose the wage-cutting policy which followed the return to the gold standard in 1925.

REFERENCES

1 Phelps-Brown, op. cit., p. 330.
2 ibid., p. 349; M.F.G.B. Minute Book, 1919, pp. 260–1 et seq.
3 M.F.G.B. Minute Book, 1919, p. 378.
4 ibid., p. 508.
5 Triple Alliance Conference Minutes, 23rd July 1919.
6 J. E. Williams, op. cit., pp. 547 and 676–7, Griffin, op. cit., II, pp. 116–7.
7 Griffin, op. cit., II, p. 63. I am indebted to Peter Lowe, a Ph.D. candidate at Sheffield University for information on the British Commonwealth Union.
8 Arnot, op. cit., II, p. 186.
9 ibid., p. 185.
10 ibid., p. 187. The voting figures were: In favour of stoppage 615,164, against stoppage 105,082. The corresponding Notts. figures were 25,949 to 1,944.
11 ibid., p. 188.
12 To these hours should be added one winding time of 30 to 45 minutes.
13 Arnot, op. cit., II, pp. 198–200.
14 I repeat this with some trepidation because when I made the point in my last book, I was accused (by Prof. S. Pollard, who appears to be no more capable of understanding plain English than was the M.F.G.B. Conference) of crediting Spencer with miraculous powers of foresight. See Economic History Review, Vol. XV No. 3, April 1963, p. 564.
   A. R. Griffin, op. cit., II, p. 46, M.F.G.B. Minute Book, 1919, p. 184.
15 M.F.G.B. Minute Book, 1919, p. 235.
16 Arnot, op. cit., II, pp. 206–9.
17 Arnot, op. cit., II, pp. 206–9.
18 M.F.G.B. Minute Book, 1919, p. 560, Arnot, op. cit., p. 211.
19 ibid., pp. 560–2.
20 Arnot, op. cit., II, p. 218.

21 *M.F.G.B. Minute Book, 1919*, pp. 302 et seq.
22 *N.M.A. Minute Book*, 28th July 1919 and *M.F.G.B. Minute Book, 1919*, p. 470.
23 *Ministry of Labour Gazette.*
24 Arnot, op. cit., p. 233.
25 *N.M.A. Minute Book, 1920.* There was a guaranteed increase of at least 2s. per shift for those of 18 years and over, 1s. for the 16 to 18-years-old and 9d. for boys under 16, where the 20 per cent gross earnings fell short of those amounts.
26 The reason for the difference of 10s. is that household coal prices had been reduced by 10s. in 1919.
27 Arnot, op. cit., II, pp. 236–7.
28 *M.F.G.B. Minute Book, 1920*, pp. 807–10. The average pit head price per ton was, at this time, 33s. 3d. for the domestic market and 75s. for the export market.
29 ibid., p. 839.
30 The national majority in favour was 71·75 per cent; the figure for Notts. was 55·05 per cent and that for Lancashire (a left-wing district) 89 per cent.
31 *M.F.G.B. Minute Book, 1920*, pp. 937–959; 1033–1258. Spencer together with Bob Smillie, M.F.G.B. President; Hough of Yorkshire and Hogg of Northumberland, advocated arbitration throughout.
32 Arnot, op. cit., II, pp. 273–4.
33 *M.F.G.B. Minute Book, 1920*, pp. 1422–35.
34 Arnot, op. cit., II, pp. 231–2.
35 A. G. Pigou, *Aspects of British Economic History, 1918–1925*, London, 1948, p. 39 et seq., esp. pp. 195 and 236.
36 For the arguments, recorded verbatim, see *M.F.G.B. Minute Book*, 1920 and 1921 (passim).
37 *M.F.G.B. Minute Book, 1921*, pp. 116–133; Mining Association: *One Hundred Questions and Answers on Coal*, circa 1936, p. 113, Arnot, op. cit., II, p. 290.
38 *M.F.G.B. Minute Book, 1921*, p. 134.
39 ibid., p. 135.
40 ibid., p. 136.
41 ibid., p. 177.
42 ibid., pp. 199–201.
43 Arnot, op. cit., II, pp. 310–1.
44 ibid., p. 212.
45 *M.F.G.B. Minute Book, 1921*, p. 353.
46 ibid., p. 360.
47 ibid., pp. 387–8.
48 ibid., pp. 361–364 and A. R. Griffin, op. cit., II, pp. 91 and 101.
49 ibid., pp. 390–1.
50 Griffin, op. cit., II, pp. 102–104.
51 *M.F.G.B. Minute Book, 1921*, p. 392.
52 Loc. cit.
53 ibid., pp. 393–4.
54 ibid., p. 396.
55 *N.M.A. Minute Books*, Monthly Accounts.
56 Source: *Manchester Guardian Commercial, European Construction*, Section 16, p. 867, cited Pigou, op. cit., p. 233 and A. R. Griffin, op. cit., II, p. 114.
57 *M.F.G.B. Minute Book, 1922*, pp. 463–7.
58 See, e.g. speech of G. A. Spencer at Hucknall, *Nottingham Daily Guardian*, 4th July 1921.
59 J. E. Williams, op. cit., p. 677.
60 *Colly. Year Book and Coal Trades Directory*, 1951 edn., p. 576.

61 Pigou, op. cit., p. 40.
62 *M.F.G.B. Minute Book*, 1923, pp. 143–4.
63 Arnot, op. cit., II, p. 344.
64 *N.M.A. Minute Book*, January 1924. Only 25,000-odd members had paid their full dues.
65 ibid., 26th January 1924 and 23rd February 1924.
66 *M.F.G.B. Minute Book*, 1924, pp. 211–2.
67 Arnot, op. cit., II, p. 348.
68 *M.F.G.B. Minute Book*, 1924, p. 345 et seq.
69 Ministry of Fuel and Power, Statistical Digest, 1951.
70 Cf. A. J. Taylor, 'The Coal Industry', *The Development of British Industry and Foreign Competition, 1875–1914*, London, 1968, pp. 50–55.
71 *N.M.A. Minute Book* (Monthly Accounts).
72 V. L. Allen, *Power in Trade Unions*, London, 1954, passim.
73 This 'ultimate sanction' may nowadays be circumscribed by the closed shop.

CHAPTER II

The 1926 Lockout: Causes and Consequences

1. INTRODUCTION

Between the end of 1924 and the end of 1925 unemployment among members of trade unions making returns rose from 9·2 to 11 per cent.[1] Heavy industry suffered more than other occupations. Unemployment amongst coal-miners rose from 5·7 per cent in 1924 to 15·8 per cent in 1925.[2] Coal output fell from 276 million tons in 1923 to 243 millions in 1925,[3] and many inefficient collieries had to close. Contrary to the assertions of the coal-owners, Britain slightly increased her share of the total world export trade in coal (with 51·2 per cent in 1924 against 49·8 per cent in 1913) but in absolute terms our coal exports fell from an average of 88·37 million tons in the years 1909–13 to 68·97 million tons in 1925.[4] Coal was feeling the effects of competition from oil, lignite and hydro-electricity, in addition to which coal-burning equipment was becoming steadily more efficient.

The Government did nothing to stimulate the economy, because it was preparing for a return to the gold standard. When at the end of February 1925 the New York re-discount rate was raised from 3 to 3½ per cent, the Bank of England responded by raising Bank rate to 5 per cent; and on 27th April the Chancellor of the Exchequer, Winston Churchill, announced Britain's return to the gold standard.[5] Sir Josiah Stamp and J. M. Keynes both warned that the considerable degree of deflation involved in a return to the gold standard would cause industrial unrest, particularly in the mining industry.[6]

Keynes pointed out that whilst Britain's economy was stagnating, other countries were enjoying a period of prosperity. Our exports were too highly priced, and consequently we were being outsold by our competitors. This was not due to the allegedly high wages and low productivity of British workmen. Instead, '. . . the explanation can be found for certain in another direction. For we know as a fact that the value of sterling money abroad has been raised by 10 per cent, whilst its purchasing power over British labour is unchanged. This alteration in the external value of sterling money has been the deliberate act of the Government and the Chancellor of the Exchequer, and the present troubles of our export industries are the inevitable and predictable consequences of it.' The Government's policy would necessitate a reduction of ten per cent in our wages bill. In due course, price levels in Britain could be expected to fall in compensation, but meanwhile some workers would have to face a steep reduction in their standards of living.

Coal exports had been particularly badly affected and had been priced out of the South American, Canadian and European markets. It would be necessary to cut prices by 1s. 9d. a ton if we were to regain our export markets: '. . . sufficient to turn a net profit of 6d. a ton, which was what the Coal Industry earned in the first quarter of this year, into a loss of 1s. 3d. a ton.'[7] Coal mining being a labour-intensive industry, large wage reductions were inevitable. And so the miners were to be made to suffer the consequences of a policy over which they had no control and for which they were in no way responsible.[8]

Keynes's analysis has recently been criticized by Professor Sayers who doubts whether

'. . . a choice of $4·40 as the 1925 parity instead of $4·86 avoiding Keynes's 10 per cent adjustment, would have made very much difference in any but the very short run.'

because, from the end of 1926 onwards, the French and Belgians stabilized their currencies at artificially low values in order to help their export industries and had Britain stabilized sterling at $4·40, an even lower level would have been fixed for the French and Belgian francs.[9] This argument makes the rather large assumption that the French would have been prepared to impose an extremely heavy additional burden upon their economy merely in order to offset a realistic valuation of sterling, and that the Belgians would have followed suit automatically. Further, it has no relevance to the question with which we are here concerned (namely, the immediate effects on the coalmining industry of a return to the gold standard at the pre-war parity) since the French and Belgian stabilization did not take place until the end of 1926 and since, in any case, both countries are net importers of coal. Professor Sayers mentions Stamp's criticism of the return to gold at the pre-war parity, but he does not really address himself to it. Nor does he show any awareness of the effects of the Government's action on industrial relations which so concerned Keynes and Stamp.

The coal industry's difficulties were not attributable solely to the return to the gold standard. The industry had failed to modernize and it was suffering the effects of competition from other fuels and the coal mines of other countries.[10] But it is because the industry was already making heavy weather that the return to the gold standard was felt so severely.

2. PRELIMINARY SKIRMISHES

The industry's serious economic position, and possible remedies, were discussed between the Mining Association and the M.F.G.B. during the first half of 1925. The Federation suggested improvements in efficiency but for the owners the prime need was a substantial reduction in wages.[11] Then, on 30th June 1925 the Mining Association brought the discussions to an end in a letter to the M.F.G.B. announcing their intention to terminate the Agreement of 18th June 1924 and to hand back to the district colliery owners' associations the responsibility for wage negotiations.[12]

It was now proposed that the division of the proceeds of the industry should be done on a new basis which the miners could not possibly accept. Under the 1924 Agreement wages were a first charge on the industry and the owners could not claim a profit until after the minimum wage had been met. The Mining Association now proposed, however, that the owners should take their profit in any case. As Herbert Smith, President of the M.F.G.B. put it: 'What it means is you have 87 per cent after the owners have taken 13 per cent, after costs other than wages have been met, to divide between you as you like as to amounts on certain base rates.'

According to the Federation's auditors, the owners' terms would have had the effect of reducing the percentages on base rates as follows:

Scotland	47·91%
Northumberland	47·40%
Durham	47·66%
Eastern Area (including Notts.)	9·08%
North Wales	30·14%
Forest of Dean	33·47%
Kent	14·18%[13]

The M.F.G.B. Conference rejected these terms unanimously. The Government then appointed another Court of Inquiry under the Industrial Courts Act, 1919, but the M.F.G.B. refused to have anything to do with it.[14]

The Chairman of the Court of Inquiry was the Rt. Hon. H. P. Macmillan, K.C., and the other members were W. Sherwood (a trade union official) and Sir Josiah Stamp, C.B.E. George Spencer thought that the refusal to co-operate with the Inquiry was a mistake which would alienate public opinion.[15] Spencer was undoubtedly right. The Macmillan Inquiry was in no way unsympathetic to the miners. Indeed, its report, issued on 13th July 1925 was very critical of the owners' case. For example, dealing with the proposal that hours should be increased in order to reduce the unit labour cost the report says:

> 'The argument of the Mining Association involves a large assumption namely that such a saving in costs and reduction in price would enable the industry to dispose of its whole increased output, notwithstanding the depressed and disturbed market conditions at home and abroad, and notwithstanding the large stocks of coal known to exist at present in foreign countries.'[16]

Increasing the hours for the same pay would, in the demand situation then existing, depress prices still further; and foreign mine owners would probably retaliate by increasing the hours of their men also. The Court also insisted '. . . that the workers are justified in claiming that any wages agreement which they can be asked to accept should provide for a mimimum wage'.[17] and it expressed the view that 'The present crisis in the industry, unlike other crises which have arisen in the past, is to a large extent the creation of neither party to the dispute,'[18] Sir Josiah Stamp considered that the Government in restoring the Gold Standard were largely to blame.

Lock-out notices were due to expire on Friday 31st July. During the preceding week, inconclusive discussions took place between the Government, the owners and the Federation; and Stanley Baldwin, the Prime Minister, stated that there could be no question of a Government subsidy.[19] However, because the transport unions had promised to strike in sympathy with the miners,[20] the Government changed their minds and agreed, 'to render assistance to the industry until the spring'.[21] In the meantime, the miners were to continue to work to the 1924 agreement; and a full-scale Inquiry into the industry was to take place.

The temporary settlement was seen by the militants as a victory for drastic action. Indeed J. Williams, of the left-wing Forest of Dean, thought they had let the Government off too lightly: 'We have had the chance to wrest ourselves free from capitalism, we had more than that, we have had the chance to bring about a real genuine revolution.' Extremists in the Government made it clear that the struggle was not over for them, either.

Thus, early in August 1925 Sir William Joynson Hicks, the Home Secretary, announced at Northampton:

> 'This thing is not finished. The danger is not over. Sooner or later this question has got to be fought out by the people of this land. Is England to be governed by Parliament and by the Cabinet or by a handful of trade-union leaders?'[22]

Most trade unionists saw the struggle as an ordinary industrial dispute in defence of the standards of the miners. The Prime Minister had made it clear that other workers must also expect to suffer a reduction in wages 'to put industry on its feet'.[23] If the attack on the miners' standards succeeded then the workers in other industries could expect the same treatment. The trade union movement therefore rallied to the miners' support.

For the extreme left-wing, however, this was a 'revolutionary situation' calling for measures designed to sharpen the class conflict and they drew the moral, as Francis Williams says, that '. . . the power to overthrow the Government by direct action and carry through a social revolution now lay in the hands of the trade unions if only they would have the courage to use it.'[24]

3. THE SAMUEL COMMISSION

The new Inquiry into miners' wages took the form of a Royal Commission with Sir Herbert (later Lord) Samuel as chairman. After some preliminary hesitation, the M.F.G.B. decided to present evidence to the Commission.[25] The Samuel Commission opposed the nationalization of the mines and considered that the economic difficulties of the industry warranted an immediate reduction in earnings; and they opposed any further subsidy which 'would constitute in many cases a dole to the inefficient, to the disadvantage of the efficient'.[26] However, on other questions they were sympathetic to the miners' case. They opposed any lengthening of the working day, and they said that wage Agreements should be National ones so as to avoid excessive competition between districts at the expense of wages. They urged the need for increasing efficiency by closing uneconomic pits by amalgamations, by research into methods of mining and using coal and by the setting up of co-operative selling agencies. They recommended (like Sankey) the nationalization of mineral rights and they suggested that an impartial body should determine the transfer price of coal sold to a subsidiary (e.g. an iron works.) They also recommended the establishment of joint consultative committees. Contrary to the usual extreme left-wing view[27] the Commission made it clear that no sacrifices should be asked for until steps had been taken to ensure improved efficiency.[28]

The Commission's Report, subsequently endorsed by the Government, contained much that was useful; but neither the owners nor the M.F.G.B. would accept it.

4. THE GENERAL STRIKE

On 24th March 1926 the Prime Minister announced that the Government were prepared to accept the Samuel Commission's report, provided that the owners and miners did so too.[29] However, the

M.F.G.B. supported by the T.U.C. insisted that there should be 'no reduction in the wages, no increase in working hours, and no interference with the principle of National Agreements';[30] but the Mining Association, whilst reluctantly agreeing to negotiate a National agreement[31] insisted on the necessity for an immediate reduction in pay and an increase in hours of work.

In the middle of April, the owners in most districts gave notice to terminate contracts at the month's end. In those districts where, as in Nottinghamshire, the owners did not give notice, the unions handed in strike notices to expire at the same time.[32] The terms on which the owners were prepared to re-employ their men after 1st May were so severe as to invite rejection. The average reductions were estimated at 2s. 1d. a day for Scotland; 2s. 4d. for Northumberland; 2s. 9d. for Durham; 2s. 10d. for South Wales; 1s. for Yorkshire; 1s. 7d. for Lancashire; 1s. 8d. for North Wales; 1s. 7d. for South Staffordshire and Shropshire; 2s. 7d. for Cumberland and 1s. 3d. for the Forest of Dean.[33]

At a special meeting of the Executive Committee of unions affiliated to the T.U.C. including the M.F.G.B. held on 29th April, it was decided that the General Council should take over the conduct of the negotiations.[34] A sub-committee of the General Council met the Prime Minister on 1st and 2nd May, when the following formula was agreed:

> 'The Prime Minister has satisfied himself as a result of the conversations he has had with the representatives of the T.U.C. that, if negotiations are continued (it being understood that the notices cease to be operative), the representatives of the T.U.C. are confident that a settlement can be reached on the lines of the (Samuel) report within a fortnight.'[35]

The T.U.C. representatives recognized that this formula might involve wage reductions;[36] and because of this, A. J. Cook, on behalf of the M.F.G.B. entered a strong protest against the irregularity of accepting the formula without consulting the miners.[37]

At this stage, when a settlement seemed likely despite the leaders of the Miners' Federation, the Prime Minister refused to continue the negotiations unless the General Strike notices sent out by the T.U.C. were unconditionally retracted; a demand to which he knew the General Council could not accede.[38] His action was precipitated by the refusal of printers employed by the *Daily Mail* to print the paper unless a strongly anti-union leading article were withdrawn.[39] The right-wing leaders of the T.U.C., like Bevin and J. H. Thomas were appalled: they would have preferred the General Strike call to remain a gesture. The situation gave satisfaction only to the militants on both sides, although 'On the Government side there was a determination, even on the part of those who had once favoured conciliation, that the struggle once begun must be fought to an end.'[40]

The T.U.C.'s strike arrangements showed signs of hurried improvisation; the Government's emergency arrangements, on the other hand, had been well prepared and were put into effect with the precision of a military operation.[41] The strike started on Tuesday 4th May when transport workers, printers, iron and steel workers, builders, electricity supply and gas workers and a few other categories were called out. The response to the strike call was overwhelming: indeed, the real difficulty of the General Council was to restrain those trades not called out from withdrawing their labour.[42]

From the start, the right-wing leaders of the T.U.C. were looking for a way to bring the strike to an end. Sir Herbert Samuel, who came hurrying back from Italy in order to offer his services as a mediator, provided the way. After discussions with the T.U.C., the colliery owners, the M.F.G.B., and the Government, he suggested terms for a settlement of the dispute similar to those embodied in the Samuel Report.[43] Samuel made it clear to the T.U.C. that he was not authorized to speak on behalf of the Government but they nevertheless decided to regard his proposals as a satisfactory basis for further negotiations and accordingly, on 12th May, the Prime Minister was informed that the strike was over. The General Council's claim that they had 'obtained assurances that a settlement of the mining problem can be secured which justifies them in bringing the general stoppage to an end' was false.[44] No assurances, beyond the Prime Minister's promise to 'use every endeavour to ensure a just and lasting settlement', were obtained. The Miners' Federation felt that they had been betrayed. And so the lock-out continued in an atmosphere made bitter by misunderstanding and intrigue.[45]

5. THE COURSE OF THE LOCKOUT

The M.F.G.B. Conference on 15th May received an outline of proposals for the settlement of the dispute from the Prime Minister. These proposals, following closely the recommendations of the Samuel Commission, provided for legislation to secure amalgamations of mining companies, restrictions on the recruitment of mineworkers and a National Wages Board to consider general wages questions: suggested that committees should be set up to examine such questions as the possibility of establishing selling syndicates, profit-sharing schemes and family allowances; undertook to prepare a scheme for the introduction of pit committees with workers' representation and promised a further subvention in aid of wages of approximately £3 millions to help the industry over its immediate difficulties. At the same time, the Government expected the miners to accept a reduction in minimum wage-rates; made it clear that wage-rates should be ascertained in each district separately (the proposed National Wages Board having power merely to establish the principles which should govern the district settlement); and offered to give immediate legal effect to any agreed 'temporary modification' in the hours of work.[46] These proposals were rejected both by the Federation and by the owners.[47]

The majority of opinion inside the M.F.G.B. was clearly opposed to any reduction in wages, any increase in hours and any suggestion of district negotiations with varying minimum percentages. A few leaders right at the start, however, feared that intransigence must bring defeat, and advocated a negotiated settlement. These included Fred Swift of Somerset, who felt that the miners were likely to be in a weaker bargaining position the longer they held out;[48] Frank Hall of Derbyshire, who advocated the adoption of the 1893 policy of allowing men to work at any pit where the owners were prepared to pay the pre-stoppage wages;[49] and Frank Hodges, secretary of the Miners' International and ex-secretary of the M.F.G.B. who said at a public meeting in Nottingham that 'the miners would be prepared to accept longer hours in preference to lower wages'.[50] The main advocates of a negotiated settlement, however, were Nottinghamshire's F. B. Varley and George Spencer. Speaking at Mansfield on Sunday 16th May Varley attacked the T.U.C. for letting the miners down and then went on to advocate a return to work on the best terms obtainable whilst the Unions renewed their strength preparatory to fighting again on some future occasion.[51] Subsequently, in an article in the *New Leader*, he expressed the view that the men would be well advised to accept some reductions in wages in return for the continuation of a National Wages Board and further Government subsidies.[52] Spencer expressed his opposition to a strike on 1st May before the stoppage started[53]—and thereafter ceaselessly advocated a compromise settlement.

Nottinghamshire entered the stoppage practically penniless, the debts incurred during the 1921 Dispute having been liquidated only a short time before. This is one reason why the N.M.A. Council, alone of the district organizations, was urging the Federation to negotiate terms for a settlement as early as the middle of May.[54] A gift of £10,000 from the Derbyshire Miners' Association together with £7,500 from the central relief fund of the M.F.G.B. enabled the N.M.A. to pay its members one week's strike pay.[55] Thereafter, members received no more than a few shillings a month—mainly contributed by the Russian Trade Unions.

Right from the beginning of the dispute, three Nottinghamshire pits, Blidworth, Clipstone, and Ollerton, where coal had not long been reached, worked normally, supposedly by arrangement with officials of the N.M.A.[56] There was also a great deal of outcrop working, some of it organized on a commercial scale.[57]

The Executive Committee of the M.F.G.B. took a tentative step towards negotiating a settlement when, early in July, it adopted suggestions for a settlement proposed by the Industrial Christian Fellowship suggesting a resumption of work on the April wages and conditions and for a permanent national settlement to be reached, by arbitration if necessary, within four months. These proposals were rejected out of hand by the owners and the Government. Inside the M.F.G.B. the so-called 'Bishop's proposals' brought out clearly the conflict between moderates and militants. The left-wing opposition to arbitration was expressed by Arthur Horner thus:

> 'Industries where there is a known amount of division can perhaps afford the luxury of an Independent Chairman, but when we are dealing with an industry which is utterly incapable of providing except by outside assistance a decent standard of living for the workmen, and when we know an independent Chairman is bound to be determined in any judgement he makes by the prevailing facts of the industry on any particular point, then our case will not stand an Independent Chairman who is bound to decide upon the economic facts. . . . I say that the first thing that we are bound to have in the circumstances is, perhaps not in Yorkshire, but in South Wales, in Durham, a considerable reduction in wages, and we will not be in a position to defend ourselves.'[58]

For the extreme left-wing, the correct policy was to refuse to compromise, to exert a strangle-hold on the economy by starving it of coal in order to enforce a political settlement providing for the pre-stoppage conditions (the *status quo*). Spencer, who represented the right-wing, demonstrated the illogicality of Horner's argument. The industry could not afford to pay the pre-stoppage wages: each district should therefore extract the best terms it could for its own members. For once, A. J. Cook, the left-wing General Secretary of the M.F.G.B. was in agreement with Spencer. He believed that the Federation's bargaining position was so weak that a compromise settlement would have to be sought. Nationalization, at that stage was out of the question. He asked his colleagues to

> 'face the facts, and come out of the struggle not demoralized, but to retain confidence in each other and not tell everybody that Labour is dead.'[59]

Horner was supported by J. Williams of the Forest of Dean, Pearson of Durham and Aneurin Bevan, who thought that

> 'it would be better for our men to be defeated as a consequence of their own physical exhaustion than it would be to be defeated as a consequence of any moves we are taking.'[60]

Cook's appeal to 'face the facts' was turned down by the districts: on a district vote 367,750 votes (from five districts) were recorded against the proposals and 333,036 (from thirteen districts) in favour.[61] The intransigent districts were:

Lancashire	75,000
South Wales	129,150
Forest of Dean	8,500
Yorkshire	150,000
Cumberland	8,500

This vote was not a ballot of the membership.

The M.F.G.B. was now committed by the intransigence of a vocal minority in the three large left-wing districts to a barren fight for the pre-stoppage conditions. A. J. Cook, whose advocacy of a compromise solution had been unsuccessful, toured the country in an attempt to stem the flow of men returning to work.[62] In Nottinghamshire, there were some 700 men working underground in the early part of August and in addition at least 1,700 men were working on outcrops.[63] This was straining the loyalty of the men still out and in consequence, in William Carter's revealing words, the N.M.A. Council gave the county's delegates to national conference

'every possible latitude to give almost every possible licence to the Executive Committee to do everything they possibly can in the negotiations with a view to getting the maximum offer from the powers that be, and that when they think the time has arrived when they can get no further concessions, these proposals to be submitted to the men for acceptance or rejection.'[64]

On 28th August the N.M.A. applied to the M.F.G.B. Executive for authority to conduct district negotiations but this was rejected as being contrary to Conference policy.[65]

By the beginning of September, on the Association's own calculations, 7,000 to 8,000 men were back at work in Nottinghamshire in addition to about 1,500 outcroppers. Sixty five per cent of the men at the Bolsover group of pits had returned to work on terms negotiated by a 'breakaway' organization.[66] One delegate estimated that a further 10,000 men would be back at work within a week.[67]

The M.F.G.B. was now prepared to negotiate 'for a new national agreement with a view to a reduction in labour costs to meet the immediate necessities of the mining industry'.[68] But the Mining Association refused to re-open national negotiations on the ground that national agreements led to political interference with the industry.[69] A fortnight later the Government suggested that the men should return to work on district agreements, but that, following a general resumption of work, a National Arbitration Tribunal (with power to review any matters to do with wages and conditions of employment submitted to it by a district where more than seven hours a day was being worked) would be established by Statute.[70] This suggestion was rejected by a national conference on 29th September, George Spencer alone advocating its adoption.[71]

The delegates to the N.M.A. Council meeting on 1st October estimated the number of men at work at between 32,000 and 33,000. Roughly 70 per cent of the N.M.A.'s 34,000 members were working so that Nottinghamshire was virtually out of the fight.[72] On 6th October, George Spencer led a deputation of men from the Digby and New London pits to the colliery management. Already, the bulk of the men were back at work, and the purpose of the deputation was to arrange for the minority who had so far remained loyal to the Federation to go back to their old jobs. The management acceded to Spencer's request. Because of this incident, Spencer was ordered out of the M.F.G.B. Conference where he was castigated as a traitor.[73]

On the motion of South Wales the M.F.G.B. decided, on 7th October, to intensify the fight for the *status quo*.[74] But the militant gestures no longer carried conviction. The M.F.G.B. was unable to bring out the safety men, because the safety men would not come out; and it was unable to enforce an embargo on the transport of imported coal because the transport unions no longer had the power or even the will to help.[75] The numbers of miners back at work was steadily rising, despite the energetic campaigning of miners' leaders: especially A. J. Cook who was touring the country with a new slogan: 'Back to work we go on the *status quo*.'[76]

In this situation, the T.U.C. once more played an intermediary role. A sub-committee of the General Council met the Prime Minister on 26th October and ascertained that

'the position of the Government was, that it was prepared to set up a National Tribunal for co-ordinating district settlements providing that the Federation agreed to recommend to its constituents that negotiations for such settlements should be opened up in the districts without delay.'[77]

The M.F.G.B. Executive then called a national conference which took place on 4th and 5th November. At this Conference, Fred Swift of Somerset felt that an immediate return to work should be arranged on the most favourable terms obtainable. He was supported by Thomas Richards of South Wales, W. Straker of Northumberland, Carter of Nottingham, P. Chambers of Scotland and even Aneurin Bevan all of whom recognized that in the absence of an organized resumption of work, the Federation would lose control of the men completely and be ruined as an organization.[78] Arthur Horner, on the other hand, believed that the more militant policy pursued since the last Conference was proving effective and should be maintained.[79]

On 5th November the E.C. of the Federation met the Prime Minister and on the following day received from the Secretary for Mines a letter explaining

'the general principles which the Government understands the owners in each district are prepared to follow in negotiating district settlements.'

These general principles provided for wages to be determined in each district according to its financial results, the ratio for the division of net proceeds between wages and profits to be within the range 87–13 to 85–15. There would also be a minimum basis rate equivalent to 20 per cent on standard[80] 'subject to district settlements of hours and working conditions'.[81]

At the re-convened national conference held on 10th November, Herbert Smith, the President, advocated the continuance of negotiations despite the harshness of the terms.[82] By now, on the Federation's own estimates,[83] there were 237,547 men back at work.[84] This led Bob Smillie to warn his colleagues that, in the absence of a speedy settlement, the organization might be wrecked.[85] Conference decided to recommend that the owners' terms should be accepted as a basis for negotiation, but a subsequent district vote produced a large majority (460,806 to 313,200) against acceptance.[86] This curious result was attributed by some to a Communist Party campaign (to which A. J. Cook was said to have lent his support) to 'Stand by Cook and reject the terms'.[87]

Despite the district vote, however, Conference realized that the situation was hopeless, and on 19th November, it advised districts to enter into negotiations locally; and within a fortnight most districts were back at work on terms dictated by the owners.[88] The 1926 lockout seriously weakened the M.F.G.B. The district settlements finally reached were less favourable than any which they might have negotiated early in the dispute whilst the Government subsidy was still available and whilst the Government were prepared to maintain the seven-hour day. The Federation's organizational weakness following 1926 left the men unprotected for almost a decade.

However sound the miners' case may have been morally, they had no chance of winning; and the longer they held out the more likely it was that their ultimate surrender would be unconditional. This probability was clearly seen by many right at the outset and it helps to explain the actions of George Spencer to which we must now turn our attention.

6. THE 'BREAKAWAY'

At Eastwood, Joseph Birkin, a member of the Association's Executive Committee, organized and profited from outcrop workings as he had done in 1921. He was one of the leaders of the so-called British Workers' League, an organization of 'butties' supported by some colliery owners and in particular, by the Bolsover Company. This organization formed the nucleus of the 'breakaway'.

An 6th August 1926, the Owners' Association wrote to the N.M.A. suggesting a joint meeting to discuss terms on which employment could be resumed.[89] This approach was rejected.[90] Then, on 19th August, the owners of Derbyshire and Nottinghamshire decided to offer terms for the resumption of work providing for a $7\frac{1}{2}$-hour day and roughly the pre-stoppage wage-rates.[91] On the day following the Digby Company reported that their employees who were returning to work did not appear to take much notice of the details of the terms offered: they were, presumably, too demoralized to care.[92] At the Bolsover pits, on the other hand, there was an organized return to work. A hundred delegates met the directors of the Company at Edwinstowe on 19th August when the terms agreed upon by the Owners' Association were conveyed to them.[93] This was the culmination of meetings held over a period of three weeks between colliery proprietors and 'unofficial deputations', which consisted, said Spencer, of 'active Trade Union members'. They were, in fact, adherents of the B.W.L. whose leaders, William Holland and Harry Willett, for example, also held office in the N.M.A.[94] Within a fortnight, 65 per cent of the Bolsover Company's employees were said to be back at work.[95]

Varley and Spencer had tried, unsuccessfully, to secure the Federation's permission to meet the District Owners' Association in order to receive their offer officially and then to report on it to the Federation Conference. Spencer and Varley were afraid that if they refused to meet the owners, the Association would lose control of the situation.[96] On 2nd September, Spencer promised that he and his colleagues would do 'everything possible in the next fortnight to keep the Association intact', but a rank-and-file delegate warned the national conference that a further 10,000 men (in addition to the six or seven thousand already back) were likely to resume work within a week.[97]

By 1st October, some 32,000 to 33,000 men were back at work in the county.[98] George Spencer appealed to the Federation to accept proposals providing for district agreements made by the Government on 17th September. He warned Conference that to continue the struggle would inevitably weaken their organization as more and more men went back to work. He continued:

'You may say "Be loyal to the Federation". We have endeavoured against strong pressure to be loyal to the Federation. . . . Whilst we have a duty to the Federation, we have a duty to the men we immediately represent.'

He felt that they should admit defeat and organize a return to work on the Government's terms.[99]

On the following day, Spencer undertook that Nottinghamshire would endeavour to remain loyal to the Federation, but this was dependent on the men. The N.M.A. might be forced to make a district agreement if a large majority of the men were back at work.[100] Both Spencer and Varley deplored the speeches made by A. J. Cook and others in the Mansfield district in which they had been attacked because of their advocacy of a negotiated settlement. These speeches, according to Spencer, had induced some men to return to work, whilst Varley feared that the activities of the left-wing Mansfield District Committee would break up the Association.[101]

Within a day or two, it became clear that the vast majority of the men—including 70 per cent of the Association's members, were back at work,[102] and the officials were concerned about the remaining 30 per cent. Ought they to go back now that the struggle was virtually over, or ought they to stay out and risk losing their jobs?

This was the problem with which Spencer was faced on 5th October at a meeting of the Digby and New London men held at Hill Top. The bulk of the men were back at work, and those who were still out had been told by the management that they would only be allowed to go back to their old jobs where these had not been taken by strike-breakers. The branch appealed to Spencer to lead a deputation to the management to try to get all the men taken back on their old jobs. As the branch delegate, a Communist named C. A. Pugh, explained to the national conference:

'I have been quite as extreme as any of the elements in South Wales, but when men come to me as their representative, as their delegate, and say: "For God's sake do something for us . . . or we are going to be thrown on the streets. . . ." We asked the men who were at work if they were prepared to come out again . . . and we asked the other men who were standing solid if they were prepared to still stand solid. There was a hesitancy which meant probably the next morning the majority would have been at work. As a last resort the Committee asked Mr. Spencer to go on a deputation to see the management to obtain the right for these men to be set on again and not victimized.'[103]

Spencer deplored the action the men had taken,[104] but he agreed to accompany a deputation to see the management. Spencer explained to the national conference that:

'. . . if they had not gone to work, it meant men who have been loyal to the Federation would have been victimized. There were men in that district who were nine and twelve months after 1921 before they got back again to work. So I went. . . . The delegate at that particular pit had been one of the most ardent supporters of the Federation policy, but he has had to take up this position . . . because he saw as far as that locality was concerned, it was hopeless, and they had to solve their own particular position. Under the circumstances, I went with them. I don't regret it and I do not plead extenuating circumstances. I believe I did the best day's work in my life for these men, and you can pass your sentence.'[105]

In reply Herbert Smith, the President of the Federation, accused Spencer of cowardice in departing from Federation policy and A. J. Cook called upon Conference to 'excommunicate' Spencer as a 'blackleg of the worst order'. By 759 votes to four, Spencer was ordered to leave the Conference.[106]

Next, Spencer was summoned to a meeting of the N.M.A. Council. According to Spencer himself, the letter calling him to the meeting from the General Secretary (William Carter) stated that Spencer 'should be exonerated from all blame' and that what he had done 'had been in the interests of the men themselves'.[107] The meeting was held on 16th October under the chairmanship of William Bayliss who refused to read Carter's letter which Spencer regarded as a 'vindication'. Council decided that Spencer, together with the twenty-eight delegates who were back at work, should be excluded from Council meetings; and that he should be suspended from office pending the re-constitution of Council.[108]

Three days later the officials of the Federation met the N.M.A. Council, and an attempt was made to heal the split. The resolution excluding delegates who had gone back to, or signed on for, work was rescinded.[109] A. J. Cook, in a speech at Eastwood, invited Spencer to 'admit the error of his ways and come back'.[110] Herbert Smith, full of confidence, undertook to see Spencer at his home on Langtry Grove and induce him to return to his allegiance; but Spencer refused to open the door to him.[111]

The Federation leaders also tried to bring the Nottinghamshire men out again and A. J. Cook's oratory certainly had some effect but it was no more than temporary.[112] By 4th November there were 40,000 men and boys back at work, and many who were still out would have liked to return, but had been refused employment.[113] By 10th November, of a total labour force of 51,000, some 44,000 were at work.[114]

On 30th October, Council once again expelled the nineteen delegates who had returned to work, and these people had a meeting of their own in the Miners' Offices. They decided to hold a further meeting there on 1st November. This meeting took place with Ben Smith in the chair.[115] Spencer was present throughout the meeting and Varley, Bunfield and Hancock attended for part of the time.[116] This meeting decided to ask the officials to fix a meeting with the owners. Spencer undertook to make the arrangements, but the meeting was not held until a week later. William Carter then called a Special Council Meeting for Tuesday 2nd November to which all delegates were invited but the Spencer Group did not attend. Serious negotiations between the Nottinghamshire Coal Owners and the Spencer Group opened on 16th November and the Agreement, which was made four days later provided for the setting up of a District Wages Board on which the two sides were to be equally represented and which had power to appoint an independent chairman to settle unresolved disputes. The surplus of proceeds over standard costs were to be divided between wages and profits in the proportions 85:15, with a minimum percentage on basis rates of 38 per cent. Hours of coal manipulators above and below ground were to be 7½ a day against seven before the stoppage, and eight (the new legal maximum) in many other districts. The Agreement was to last for five years in the first instance, and it virtually guaranteed freedom from strikes during that period.[117]

Under this new Agreement, earnings were initially quite high because of the high prices caused by the coal shortage. Thus a coal face worker with a basis rate of 8s. 9d. a shift would receive, in December 1926, 16s. 7d. against 12s. 10d. before the stoppage and 13s. 9d. in November 1926.[118] The N.M.A. Council at a meeting held on 22nd November was of the opinion 'that no useful purpose can now be served by further continuing the Stoppage, and request its members to sign on at the earliest opportunity'.[119]

On 22nd November, the Spencer group decided to form the 'Nottinghamshire and District Miners' Industrial Union'. Ben Smith was elected President, with William Evans Vice-President and Richard Gascoyne Secretary. George Spencer was elected 'leader of the men at work represented'.[120] The colliery owners undertook to support the new Union by giving it sole negotiating rights; by agreeing to deduct the Union contribution from wages; by contributing £12,500 to the Union's pension fund and by harrying known members of the N.M.A.[121] Many N.M.A. branch officials were refused employment anywhere in the coalfield. Some owners went so far as to force their checkweighmen out of office. This happened, for example, at Welbeck, Rufford and New Hucknall. Only one colliery proprietor in the County—James Oakes—would allow the N.M.A. to collect union contributions on the premises. Elsewhere, collectors had to stand on street corners, or go round from door to door.

Despite its advantages, however, the Industrial Union made very slow headway. According to Frank Varley, the membership of the N.M.A. rose from 7,000 to 12,000 during the first fortnight of 1927, whilst the membership of the N.M.I.U. was estimated at 4,000 to 5,000.[122] The Industrial Union still had a mere 14,000 members in 1936,[123] less than a third of the men employed; and this number included many members of the N.M.A. who paid into the N.M.I.U. so as to insure against dismissal.

7. CONCLUSION

Even without a return to the gold standard at the pre-war parity, the industry would have been in a difficult position in the 1920's. But it was this return to the gold standard which led almost inevitably to the conflict of 1926, since it forced upon colliery owners the necessity of reducing wages in order to keep the prices of their exported coals down to a competitive level.

The support given to the miners by workers in other trades in 1926 reflected great credit on the Trade Union movement. Most trade union leaders recognized that a successful attack upon miners' wages would be followed by wage reductions in other employments: to support the miners was therefore strategically sound as well as morally right. The T.U.C. leaders were, however, constitutionalists, not revolutionaries. They had no wish to take over the government of the country. Having embarked upon the General Strike, their chief desire was to bring it to a speedy conclusion. The Samuel memorandum provided them with their pretext for ending the Strike. The miners felt, with some justification, that they had been let down. It must be admitted, however, that nothing short of a substantial Government subsidy enabling the Owners to maintain the pre-stoppage wages and hours, together with the acceptance of a National Board and a National minimum percentage, would have satisfied the Miners' Federation. It was some time before the M.F.G.B. would contemplate a compromise settlement. The discussions which took place, with the Government's knowledge, between A. J. Cook, Seebohm Rowntree and W. T. Layton in July 1926 offered a basis for a compromise settlement, but nothing came of them.[124] Cook, despite his revolutionary oratory on open-air platforms, appealed to the Federation conference to 'face the facts' and try for a compromise settlement; but his policy was turned down. Instead, the left-wing policy advocated by Arthur Horner of starving the economy of coal, thus forcing the Government to guarantee the pre-stoppage conditions (the *status quo*) was endorsed by the districts. For the right-wing, represented by Spencer, defeat was inevitable and the only sensible policy was to return to work on negotiated terms whilst the organization renewed its strength, whilst for the left-wing the only policy was to insist on the pre-stoppage conditions and to refuse to acknowledge the possibility of defeat.

And what of the rank-and-file? It is all very well to picture miners on strike as soldiers in the class war, as does Professor Pollard,[125] but there is a limit to the extent to which the ordinary miner was prepared to sacrifice the health of his family for the sake of a hopeless cause. Many miners' wives in areas like the North-East coast with its closely-knit mining villages and the ready availability of relief from Labour-dominated local authorities, gave their locked-out husbands active encouragement.[126] But in the urban areas of Nottinghamshire, where mining families formed a minority of the population and where the local authorities were unhelpful, there were many miners' wives who urged their men to return to work. To see the children go hungry, the furniture and Sunday clothes put into pawn, the insurance policies surrendered for cash, then to be threatened with eviction for non-payment of rent was more than many women could bear without protest.

For many men, to return to work required a certain amount of courage. To be called a 'blackleg' was abhorrent to the average miner, but eventually a point was reached at which the unpleasantness of home outweighed this fear. By the middle of August 1926 many men were completely demoralized. Pulled this way by the desire to 'stand solid' as they were continually exhorted to do, and that way by the pressing needs of their families, they developed symptoms of neurosis. Rumours spread apace. It was widely believed, for example, that many of the policemen imported into the county were Grenadier Guardsmen in police uniforms. Fear of the police, fear of eviction, fear of losing their jobs permanently to strangers, fear and privation unrelieved by hope drove many loyal trade unionists back to work. Those who did not want their friends to think badly of them found jobs in other counties: Nottinghamshire men moved to Leicestershire, Leicestershire men moved to Nottinghamshire; and in so doing increased the fear of permanent unemployment among local men who were still out.

By the middle of August not one man in five had any real hope of a successful conclusion to the stoppage. The Nottinghamshire leaders, who tried to find some formula which would enable their members to get back to work, did so not merely because of their own beliefs, but also in response to the general feeling in the district. And the longer the dispute lasted, the worse matters became until even William Carter, as loyal a leader as one could hope to have, exclaimed in relation to a visit of the Federation Executive to Nottinghamshire '. . . it is not propaganda we want, it is food we want, and it is starvation we are faced with. I know as good Trade Unionists as I am who have had to return to work, and had we been able to give money hundreds and thousands would have refrained from going back to work'.[127] This is the reality behind Professor Pollard's military analogy.

The 1926 stoppage continued for far too long. In the end, the Miners' Federation suffered a humiliating defeat. The long struggle had weakened the organization; had destroyed the fighting spirit of its members; and left it a sadly divided body. In consequence, it was in no position to protect its members properly in the difficult years which were to come. The miners continued to suffer for the militancy of the extreme left and the stubbornness of their President for almost a decade.

In the present writer's view, once the General Strike was over the Miners' Federation should have recognized the weakness of its position and should have formulated minimum demands which were possible of achievement. In particular, it should have been prepared to accept wage reductions in return for the maintenance of a seven-hour day. Both the Macmillan Inquiry and the Samuel Commission opposed the Owners' proposal of an extended working day, but the Federation's intransigence enabled the Owners to have their own way with the Government. A. J. Cook made several attempts to induce his colleagues to pursue a negotiated settlement and this despite his open-air performances. On the other hand, the President, Herbert Smith, was informed throughout by mulish stubbornness (at least, until near the end of the dispute when he and Cook exchanged roles)[128] whilst Arthur Horner and the other left-wing extremists insisted throughout that there must be no reductions in wages, no increase in hours, and no district settlements. In the event, the miners had to accept all three. In trying to achieve too much, in refusing to recognize the necessity for compromise and in failing to appreciate the weakness of its bargaining position, the Miners' Federation dictated its own defeat.

APPENDIX

MANPOWER AND OUTPUT IN THE NOTTINGHAMSHIRE COALFIELD 1921–1938

Year	Manpower under-ground	Total manpower	Saleable output
1921	40,350	50,645	8,291,384
1922	41,630	52,074	12,627,485
1923	44,026	55,364	14,217,351
1924	45,140	57,360	14,190,313
1925	45,024	57,223	14,022,436
1926	45,285	56,316	9,007,901
1927	45,245	57,955	13,646,895
1928	40,914	52,114	13,194,406
1929	41,894	52,702	14,738,255
1930	42,036	52,393	14,576,000
1931	40,545	51,307	14,483,415
1932	38,396	49,499	13,549,964
1933	36,761	46,969	13,638,408
1934	36,126	46,852	14,308,552
1935	35,576	45,923	14,015,308
1936	34,510	45,538	15,059,284
1937	35,193	45,579	16,400,410
1938	35,617	46,477	15,468,357

Source: Annual Reports of Secretary for Mines and H.M. Chief Inspector of Mines 1921–1938.

Notes: The 'Underground manpower' figure is at mid-December and is derived from e.g. Table 14 (1934) Table 17 (1938) and equivalent tables for other years. The 'Total manpower' figure prior to 1925 relates to persons 'ordinarily employed'. Subsequently, the number of persons on colliery books is the average of figures taken at four selected dates. This is derived mainly from Table 11 (1934) and Table 13 (1938).

The output figure is derived from Table 2 (1934 and 1938) and equivalent table for other years.

REFERENCES

1   i.e. May 1924: Pigou, op. cit., p. 219.
2   ibid., p. 50.
3   Report of First Secretary for Mines and Chief Inspector of Mines for 1934, p. 122.
4   R. H. Tawney, 'The Coal Industry', Encyclopaedia of the Labour Movement, London, n.d., I, pp. 125–6.
5   Pigou, op. cit., pp. 148–151.
6   Sir Josiah Stamp, Addendum to the Report of the Court of Inquiry Concerning the Coal Mining Industry Dispute, 1925 (the Macmillan Report.)
J. M. Keynes, The Economic Consequences of Mr. Churchill, London, 1925 passim.
7   The financial results of Gedling and Annesley Collieries referred to earlier bear out this analysis.
8   W. Ashworth (An Economic History of England, 1870–1939, London, 1960, p. 387, esp. fn. 3) believes that Keynes's 10 per cent was an exaggeration. A. J. Youngson (The British Economy, 1920–1957, London, 1959, pp. 234 et seq.) believes that '. . . no responsible statesman or banker could possibly have taken the gamble of accepting Keynes's advice . . . to go back at a lower parity, or not to go back at all, carried as much risk of industrial troubles (through inflation instead of deflation) as did the policy actually adopted. . . .'
Whatever validity these arguments may have, they do not really deal with what is, for us, the central question. The policy adopted by the Government led inevitably to an immediate attack upon the already low living standards of the miners. This in turn was bound to lead to general industrial unrest. If 'adjustments' were necessary, why should those least able to bear them be made to do so?
9   R. S. Sayers, 'The Return to Gold, 1925', Studies in the Industrial Revolution, ed. L. S. Pressnell, London, 1960, p. 321.
10 Ministry of Fuel and Power: Coal Mining—Report of the Technical Advisory Committee (the Reid Report), Cmd. 6610, London, 1945, pp. 29 and 141.
11 The talks are recorded verbatim in the M.F.G.B. Minute Book, 1925.
12 ibid., pp. 311–2.
13 ibid., p. 415.
14 ibid., p. 480.
15 ibid., pp. 493–4.
16 Macmillan Report, para. 22.
17 ibid., para. 34.
18 ibid., para. 36.
19 M.F.G.B. Minute Book, 1925, p. 676.

20 ibid., p. 678.
21 ibid., p. 680.
22 Cited F. Williams, *Magnificent Journey*, London, 1954, p. 372.
23 Cited ibid., p. 369 and Arnot, op. cit., II, p. 377.
24 F. Williams, op. cit., p. 373, see also Griffin, op. cit., II, pp. 143–4.
25 *M.F.G.B. Minute Book*, pp. 822, 827 and 842.
26 *Report of the (Samuel) Commission, Cmd. 2600*, I, p. 39.
27 E.g. Arnot, II, 404, and A. Hutt, *British Trade Unionism*, London, p. 107.
28 *Report of the (Samuel) Commission*, p. 229.
29 *M.F.G.B. Minute Book, 1926*, p. 97.
30 ibid., p. 44.
31 This is contrary to the popular view expressed by Arnot (op. cit., II, p. 408,) and F. Williams (op. cit., p. 376) but see *M.F.G.B Minute Book, 1926*, pp. 183 and 179.
32 *N.M.A. Minute Book*, 20th April 1926.
33 *M.F.G.B. Minute Book, 1926*, p. 339.
34 ibid., p. 204.
35 loc. cit.
36 F. Williams, op. cit., p. 379.
37 *M.F.G.B. Minute Book, 1926*, p. 205.
38 ibid., p. 297; Arnot, op. cit., II, pp. 426–7; C. L. Mowat, *Britain Between the Wars 1918–1940*, London, 1946, pp. 308–10.
39 J. Symons, *The General Strike*, London, 1959, pp. 55–8.
40 ibid., p. 60 and F. Williams, op. cit., p. 388.
41 Symons, op. cit., p. 60 et seq., C. L. Mowat, op. cit., pp. 303–4.
42 Symons, op. cit., pp. 60, 68–71.
43 ibid., pp. 188–191, 199–207, 241–247.
44 ibid., p. 212, pp. 235–240.
45 ibid., pp. 221–5.
46 *M.F.G.B. Minute Book, 1926*, pp. 471–2.
47 ibid., p. 457 et seq., Arnot, op. cit., II, p. 462.
48 *M.F.G.B. Minute Book, 1926*, p. 457.
49 *Nottingham Journal*, 29th May 1926.
50 *N.M.A. Minute Book*, 24th April 1926; *M.F.G.B. Minute Book, 1926*, pp. 227, 909.
51 *Nottingham Journal*, 17th May 1926.
52 ibid., 28th May 1926, Dickie, op. cit., p. 75.
53 *M.F.G.B. Minute Book, 1926*, pp. 381–2.
54 *N.M.A. Minute Book*, 17th May 1926.
55 ibid., 25th May 1926.
56 My informant is Mr. H. W. Booth. See also *M.F.G.B. Minute Book, 1926*, p. 562 and *N.M.A. Minute Book*, 1st October 1926.
57 *N.M.A. Minute Book, 1926*, passim (E.g. 5th July 1926 when an appeal was made to the Mines Inspectorate, the police and local councils to prevent outcropping).
58 ibid., p. 580.
59 ibid., pp. 582–6.
60 ibid., pp. 588–9.
61 ibid., p. 606.
62 ibid., passim.
63 ibid., pp. 562 and 615.
64 ibid., p. 616 and *N.M.A. Minute Book*, 12th August 1926.
65 *N.M.A. Minute Book*, 28th August 1926 and *M.F.G.B. Minute Book, 1926*, p. 234.

66 ibid., p. 724.
67 ibid., pp. 743–4.
68 A. J. Cook to Winston Churchill (Chancellor of the Exchequer) 3rd September 1926—*M.F.G.B. Minute Book, 1926* pp. 235–6.
69 *M.F.G.B. Minute Book,* p. 765.
70 ibid., pp. 240–1 and 246.
71 ibid., pp. 828–9.
72 *N.M.A. Minute Book,* 1st October 1926.
73 *M.F.G.B. Minute Book, 1926,* pp. 855–905.
74 ibid., pp. 864–893.
75 The National Union of Seamen, led by the right-wing Havelock Wilson had been opposed even to the General Strike, and it now sponsored 'non-political' miners' unions. Many railwaymen had suffered victimization following the General Strike, and there was now much under-employment on the railways because of the miners' lock-out. They were in no position to risk being locked-out by refusing to transport coal.
76 Symons, op. cit., p. 224.
77 *M.F.G.B. Minute Book, 1926,* pp. 253–4.
78 ibid., pp. 499–512.
79 ibid., p. 501–2.
80 'Standard' was defined as basis rates, plus the percentage paid on basis rates in 1914, plus any piecework addition for working (as in Notts.) less than an eight-hour day.
81 *M.F.G.B. Minute Book, 1926,* pp. 536–544 and p. 257.
82 ibid., pp. 932–6.
83 ibid., pp. 952–5.
84 ibid., pp. 941–2.
85 ibid., pp. 966–7.
86 ibid., pp. 1027 and 1040.
87 ibid., p. 1041. Cook denied complicity in the campaign—see ibid., p. 1063.
88 For details of the terms see ibid., pp. 1431–83.
89 *N.M.A. Minute Book,* 12th August 1926.
90 ibid., 21st August 1926.
91 Griffin, op. cit., II, p. 201.
92 ibid., p. 202.
93 J. E. Williams, op. cit., p. 715.
94 *M.F.G.B. Minute Book, 1926,* pp. 663–4.
95 ibid., p. 724.
96 ibid., pp. 663–4. See also Carter's speech, ibid., p. 724.
97 ibid., pp. 743–4.
98 *N.M.A. Minute Book,* 1st October 1926.
99 *M.F.G.B. Minute Book, 1926,* p. 829.
100 ibid., pp. 838–9.
101 Loc. cit.
102 *N.M.A. Minute Book,* 1st October 1926.
103 *M.F.G.B. Minute Book, 1926,* p. 901.
104 ibid., p. 855. By ignoring Pugh's evidence, and distorting Spencer's, Arnot (op. cit., II, p. 494) and Williams (op. cit., pp. 721–2) give a totally misleading impression.
106 ibid., pp. 899–901. Spencer was not a paid servant of the Federation, as Herbert Smith alleged, but of the N.M.A.
107 G. A. Spencer, *The Trade Unions Bill Vindicated by a Labour M.P.,* London, 1927, p. 9.
108 *N.M.A. Minute Book,* 16th October 1926.

109   ibid., 19th October 1926.
110   *Nottingham Journal*, 20th October 1926.
111   According to Spencer, Booth, and Albert Shaw.
112   *M.F.G.B. Minute Book, 1926*, p. 507. Carter's speech explains this.
113   ibid., p. 509.
114   ibid., p. 941.
115   *Nottingham Journal*, 1st November 1926.
116   ibid., 2nd November 1926 and 3rd November 1926 and *M.F.G.B. Minute Book, 1926*, p. 513.
117   Report of G. Burlinson to Digby Colly. Co. dated 16th November 1926 and Agreement dated 20th November 1926.
118   However, in September 1927 the percentage came down to the minimum (38 per cent) and remained there until April 1936—H. W. Booth, *Wages in the Nottinghamshire Coalfield 1916–1949*, Nottm., 1950.
119   *N.M.A. Minute Book*, 22nd November 1926.
120   *N.M.I.U. Minute Book*, 22nd November 1926.
121   ibid., 1926, passim. See also Griffin, op. cit., II, pp. 207–11.
122   *M.F.G.B. Minute Book, 1927*, p. 6.
123   Griffin, op. cit., II, p. 283. The figure of 7,000 members suggested there is a miscalculation. The contributions in 1936 were 6d. per week and the average amount collected was (approximately) £350 per week.
124   Griffin, op. cit., II, pp. 241–5. This episode has been ignored, or minimized, by most left-wing writers. For example, Page Arnot mentioned it only in the following oblique reference:

> 'Within the Miners' Federation this struggle took various forms, including the development of a sort of vendetta against Arthur Cook, who in the course of 1926 had made some mistakes of which his opponents now sought at this later date [1928] to take advantage.' (Arnot, op. cit., II, p. 540). Dr. Williams (The Derbyshire Miners) does not mention the incident at all.

Arthur Horner has this to say:

> '. . . Joseph Jones who was leading the Yorkshire delegation to the M.F.G.B., launched a bitter attack on Arthur Cook. He accused Cook of having, during the lock-out, received proposals to end the dispute from Sir Walter Layton. Jones alleged that Cook never reported these proposals to the Executive Committee. I know from my personal experience during the strike that Cook had proposals from all over the place and most of them involved some form of capitulation. Sir Walter Layton's proposals were apparently on similar lines. Cook never even told me about them and did not regard them as serious but two years afterwards everyone was looking for a scapegoat and Jones brought this one out of the bag' (A. Horner, *Incorrigible Rebel*, London, 1960, p. 99.)

This will not do. Cook did in fact negotiate with Rowntree and Layton knowing that they had access to the Government. Further he signed a document suggesting concessions to be made by the miners and he appended to it both a note at the foot of the document and also a fairly lengthy covering letter.

His real offence in relation to the negotiations with Rowntree and Layton was in keeping his Executive Committee completely in the dark and there is little doubt that he did that precisely because he feared the reaction of people like Horner. See A. R. Griffin, op. cit., II, pp. 240–245.

For an example of the way in which Communists made use of Cook's name for their own (disruptive) ends, see *M.F.G.B. Minute Book*, 1928, p.

642 and p. 1157. And for all their friendship, Communists did not hesitate to attack Cook fiercely whenever he took an independent line, (see e.g. A Horner, op. cit., pp. 104–107; *M.F.G.B. Minute Book, 1926*, pp. 579 et seq. Apparently, Cook was himself a member of the Communist Party in 1920, but according to the *Daily Worker* obituary he was expelled 'at the end of the 1921 stoppage because of his vacillation'. See W. G. Quine, *A. J. Cook— Miners' Leader in the General Strike*, (unpublished M.A. Thesis), Manchester, 1964, p. 16.

125 *Economic History Review*, 2nd Series, Vol. XV, No. 3, April 1963, p. 564.

126 *M.F.G.B. Minute Book, 1926*, p. 653.

127 ibid., pp. 507 and 859.

128 *M.F.G.B. Minute Book, 1926*, pp. 932–6 and 955. Smith now (10 November 1926) saw no point in struggling on, whilst Cook thought that the terms on which a settlement was then being suggested were unacceptable, since they involved surrendering everything for which the men had fought.

CHAPTER III

The Nottinghamshire Coalfield Stagnates 1927—1939

1. INTRODUCTION

The number of mines producing coal in Great Britain, according to the Ministry of Fuel and Power's Statistical Digest, rose from 2,563 in 1926 to 2,569 in 1927 and then fell to 1,782 in 1933: rising to 1,841 in 1934 and then falling in the two succeeding years to 1,758. Under the stimulus of re-armament this number rose to 1,807 in 1937 and 1,860 in 1938. Since then each year has seen a diminution in the number of mines producing coal. In 1945, there were 1,570.

In 1927 again, 998 thousand men (above and below ground) produced 251 million tons of coal: in 1945, 709 thousand men produced 175 million tons. There is, however, this difference between the 1927 and 1945 situations: at the earlier date, the owners were fighting for markets in competition with each other, foreign producers and suppliers of alternative fuels, whilst at the later date they could not produce enough to meet the demand and in consequence supplies were rationed and prices controlled.

Nottinghamshire's coalmines stagnated with the rest. There were, it is true, two new collieries opened early in the period (Thoresby and Bilsthorpe in 1928) but not until the war years was the next new one (Calverton) projected and in the meantime, several old pits had been deliberately closed so as to reduce the coalfield's productive capacity. We must now see how this came about.

2. OUTPUT RESTRICTION

After the 1926 dispute the owners in various districts discussed schemes of output restriction, and cartels were formed in South Wales, Scotland and the Midlands. The Central Collieries Commercial Association (popularly known as the 'Five Counties Scheme') covered Yorkshire, Derbyshire, Nottinghamshire, Lancashire, and Cheshire, Cannock Chase, Leicestershire, South Derbyshire, North Staffordshire and

Warwickshire.[1] It came into operation on 1st April 1928 and it controlled a yearly output of about 100 million tons. The Scheme was designed to regulate output by fixing quotas, and to stimulate exports by giving subsidies varying between 1s. 6d. and 4s. per ton. These subsidies were financed by a levy on each ton of coal raised by members: the maximum levy being 3d. per ton.

Each colliery had a basic tonnage, which was calculated from the actual output for any one of the previous 15 years selected by the colliery owner. Naturally the highest yearly output was invariably selected. Each month, a Quota Committee decided how much coal was to be produced, and this was then expressed as a percentage of the aggregate of the basic tonnages. This percentage was then called the Quota, and each owner could produce up to the permitted percentage of his basic tonnage without incurring a penalty. Should he exceed his quota by more than 1 per cent, he was fined 3s. per ton. Quotas could, however, be bought and sold with the permission of the Quota Committee. Special arrangements were made for developing collieries.

Since the scheme was voluntary, some owners, with about 10 per cent of the productive capacity, remained outside. By fixing prices slightly lower than members of the scheme (as did Palmer Morewood of Swanwick) an independent producer could expand his sales considerably, thereby clearing his stocks. It was widely believed that these people benefited far more from the scheme than those who belonged to it.

The export subsidy stimulated exports from the Midlands largely at the expense of the traditional exporting districts for whom a subsidy scheme would have been impractical. During the year ended 31st March 1929 the C.C.C.A. districts exported 5 million tons against 2·2 million tons in the previous year[2] Total exports for the country were 51 million tons in 1927 and 50 million in 1928. There was a great improvement—to 60 million tons in the following year, but this was not sustained and by 1932 exports were down to just under 39 million tons.[3]

By this time, the voluntary scheme had been replaced by a compulsory one embodied in the Coal Mines Act, 1930. This Act established Central and District Schemes for regulating output; and encouraged amalgamation of producers. The colliery owners were left to arrange the Rules of the schemes, although these were subject to the approval of the Board of Trade. The members of the Central and District Boards were colliery owners appointed by the general body of owners.

Each district Board had power to fix minimum prices from time to time. The Northern districts fixed low minimum prices, and thus con-

S

tinued the policy of undercutting the Midland districts which had led to an increase in waterborne coal's share of the London market from 42·3 per cent in 1923 to 57·7 per cent in 1931 at the expense of rail-borne coal largely from the inland districts.[4] As with the 'Five Counties' scheme, quotas could be bought and sold, but only within districts.

The Act did nothing to regulate the chaotic state of the coal distributive trade which had been criticized by various official bodies including the Sankey Commission. In commenting on this omission, Neuman points out that whilst pit head prices had risen by only 27 per cent above the pre-war level by 1930; retail prices had risen by 100 per cent.[5]

The Act created a Coal Mines National Industrial Board, which was to enquire into labour relations questions; but the owners refused to nominate members to this body or to recognize its competence. The Act also reduced the legal maximum hours of work underground from eight hours to $7\frac{1}{2}$ per day. This did not directly affect Nottinghamshire, since the shift length in this county was already $7\frac{1}{2}$ hours; but it was indirectly helpful in that it reduced the effective productive capacity of the industry nationally, and raised slightly the unit costs of production of those districts which had imposed an eight-hour day in 1926.

At the apex of the cartel arrangements introduced by the Act was a National Council representative of the District Boards. Each district had power to elect at least one member of the National body and the larger districts could nominate members in proportion to output. The National Council had the duty of fixing the district allocations: that is, the maximum permitted outputs for the several districts; and it levied a fine of 2s. 6d. per ton on all output in excess of a district's allocation. The National Council also had general oversight of the operation of the district schemes.

Each district board had to re-distribute its allocation amongst all the undertakings in its district and to fix minimum prices for each class of coal produced in the district. The biggest of the district schemes: the Midland (Amalgamated) District, was based on the Five Counties Scheme and it covered Yorkshire, Derbyshire, South Derbyshire, Nottinghamshire and Leicestershire.[6] Each section (i.e. 1 South Yorkshire, 2 West Yorkshire, 3 Derbys. and Notts., 4 South Derbys., and 5 Leicestershire) and each colliery within the section was given a standard tonnage based on the average outputs of the years 1923, 1924, 1925 and 1927, although changes in these standard tonnages could be made where circumstances changed. The actual permitted output of a colliery during a particular period was calculated from its standard tonnage in much the same way as with the earlier (Five Counties) scheme. The district's allocation fixed by the National Council was shared between the collieries in proportion to their respective standard tonnages.

In the Midland (Amalgamated) District, colliery undertakings were grouped for trading purposes, and a Selling Agency was set up for each group. The Selling Agent had the sole right to sell all the coal available for the market (i.e. exclusive of the Owners' internal use) of all the Owners in his group; and he was responsible to the Executive Board of the district scheme.[7] In 1936, statutory Selling Schemes of various kinds, but all designed to restrict competition, were introduced in all districts.

The imposition of output quotas caused particular difficulties for certain classes of colliery owners. Thus, the owners of new, relatively capital-intensive collieries (like those to the East of Mansfield) had to put up with a high fixed cost per unit of output. The Quota prevented them from spreading their fixed costs over as large a tonnage as possible.[8] Making generous allowances for dirt (as at Bestwood and Harworth) was marginally helpful. Again, those colliery owners who had to pay high minimum royalty rents had cause to complain about output restriction. To take Linby as an example, the Consolidated Mining Lease of 8th October 1927 (having a 100 year term) provided for a rent of 4½d. per ton raised and weighed, less an allowance of 5 per cent; or, if the High Main Seam only proved workable, 3½d. per ton and no allowance. There was, however, a minimum rent of £5,100 per year until 1st July 1936 when it was due to fall to £4,000. On the 1934 output, the minimum rent was equal to 9·8d. per ton.[9]

Output restriction also inhibited further capital investment. To take the case of Linby again, in the mid-1930's they were prevented from exploiting the deep soft, deep hard and low main seams because to do so it would be necessary either to sink a new shaft and to widen and deepen an existing one, or to widen and deepen both of the existing shafts to a depth of about 680 yards. This expenditure could only be justified if output could subsequently be expanded substantially; but the Company were advised that they were unlikely to obtain a suitable addition to their standard tonnage.[10]

Yet another drawback was that a colliery might have a surplus of one or more classes of coal; and yet be unable to meet orders for another class because its output quota had been used up. Where there was a surplus of orders for small coal, they could be met by crushing large coal but where there was a surplus of orders for large coal then no matter how much small coal the owner might have stacked up, he could do nothing to fulfil the orders. At times, indeed, there was a positive shortage of certain classes of coal whilst considerable stocks of other classes were going begging.[11] In the Midland (Amalgamated) District there was some attempt made to meet part of this problem by fixing separate standard tonnages for Coking Supply and Low Temperature Coking Supply for owners who had carbonization plants.[12]

Perhaps the worst drawback of the quota system, however, was that it helped to keep the inefficient producer in existence whilst penalising the more efficient producer. What the industry needed was to concentrate production on the more efficient units so as to ensure the maximum utilization of modern plant and so as to encourage further investment in improved capital works (e.g. drifts) machinery and techniques. In the event, the Coal Mines Re-organization Commission, established under the 1930 Coal Mines Act to encourage amalgamations of mining enterprises proved to be largely ineffective. There was little incentive for voluntary amalgamations, and the Commission's powers were insufficient to force amalgamations on unwilling owners.[13] The operation of the Commission was suspended in 1935; and in 1938 it was replaced by a Coal Commission established by Act of Parliament to acquire all freehold coal royalties on behalf of the Nation and to stimulate the rationalization of the industry. Apart from voluntary amalgamations, nothing came of the desire for rationalization. The Commission did, however, complete its work of acquiring all freehold coal royalties by the middle of 1942, the old owners being compensated with some £66,450,000-worth of Coal Commission Stock.

When Britain came off the gold standard on 21st September 1931 coal exports were stimulated, but only for a short time. The effective depreciation of the £ sterling had a deflationary effect on the economies of other countries which wiped out this temporary advantage.[14]

Of more permanent importance was the Coal Utilization Council, formed by coal owners and traders in October 1932 for the purpose of encouraging the public to use coal-burning equipment by designing improved fires, stoves and furnaces and by publicizing the advantages of coal as opposed to other fuels and particularly oil.[15]

3. CAPITAL AND ENTERPRISE

In this period the mining industry, considered nationally, was unprofitable. Table 18 illustrates the position.

As always, however, some areas were more profitable than others, and the owners of the most efficient collieries made substantial profits. Nottinghamshire's comparatively favourable position may be illustrated by table 19 for 1934.

The New Hucknall Company has, in earlier chapters, been presented as a reasonably typical undertaking. In our period, it was operating

TABLE 18

COSTS OF PRODUCTION, PROCEEDS AND PROFIT (OR LOSS)
PER TON OF COAL DISPOSABLE COMMERCIALLY IN
GREAT BRITAIN FROM 1924–1939

Year	Total costs of production		Proceeds		Balance Credit		Debit
	Per ton of coal disposable commercially (to nearest penny)						
	s.	d.	s.	d.	s.	d.	d.
1924	18	7	19	9	1	2	
1925	16	10	17	1		3	
1926	14	6	15	9	1	3	
(January to April)							
1927	15	7	15	1			6
1928	14	2	13	3			11
1929	13	7	13	11	0	4	
1930	13	9	14	1	0	4	
1931	13	9	14	0	0	3	
1932	13	8	13	10	0	2	
1933	13	4	13	7	0	3	
1934	13	0	13	5	0	5	
1935	13	0	13	6		6	
1936	13	8	14	7		11	
1937	14	8	15	11	1	3	
1938	16	0	17	4	1	4	
1939	16	4	17	11	1	7	

N.B. (1) Proceeds of miners' coal have been deducted from costs of production (col. 2.) (2) Results for 1925 and 1926 include Govt. Subsidy. (3) For a true profit, interest on loans (app. 3d. per ton) should be subtracted from the Credit column.

Source: Coalmining—Report of Technical Advisory Committee (Reid Report) Cmd. 6610, London, 1945, p. 142, see also J. P. Dickie, *The Coal Problem*, London, 1936, p. 363.

four collieries: New Hucknall (sunk 1876–9) and Bentinck (opened 1896) which may be thought of as fairly modern Erewash Valley mines; Welbeck (opened 1915) a larger, more heavily capitalized mine in the Mansfield area, and Annesley (sunk 1865) perhaps the most disappointing of the Leen Valley collieries. As we have seen, Annesley was sunk by the Worswick family from Leicestershire, but they had only a short lease. Possibly for this reason, the colliery was under-capitalized and the Worswicks did not renew their lease when it expired in 1904. The colliery was then taken over by a company of which Mr. F. Chambers (of the Hardwick Colliery Co.) was managing director; and finally came into the hands of the New Hucknall Company some twenty years later by which time the profitable top hard seam was exhausted.[16] Its plant was then valued at £238,287; but even so a great deal of money needed spending on the colliery which had been badly mis-managed for years. The New Hucknall Company's Chief Agent expressed considerable concern over the high costs of

TABLE 19

PROFIT (OR LOSS) PRODUCTIVITY AND EARNINGS FOR 1934

District	*Profit (+) or Loss (−)* s. d.	*Percentage of wages costs to net proceeds*	*O.M.S. (Cwt.)*	*E.M.S.* s. d.	*Avg. of manshifts worked*
Scotland	+ 5¾	94·0	25·22	8 9¼	304
Northumberland	− 1	101·2	23·74	7 9½	282
Durham	− 3	103·3	22·12	8 0½	261
S. Wales and Mon.	− 1¼	101·1	19·83	9 0½	264
Yorks	+ 10¾	90·4	26·08	10 2	225
N. Derbys and Notts	+ 1 0¼	89·0	27·38	10 5¼	216
S. Derbys, Leics. Cannock Chase and Warwicks	+ 1 3¾	87·8	22·13	9 8	228
Lancs. Cheshire and N. Staffs	+ 5¼	95·9	19·62	9 2½	249
Cumberland, N. Wales, S. Staffs., Shropshire, Bristol, Forest of Dean Somerset and Kent	0 0	100·0	19·32	8 8	278
Avg. for all districts	+ 5	95·4	22·94	9 1¾	253

N.B. (1) Profit or Loss is on revenue account only. Deduct 3d. from Gross profit to give approximate nett position. (2) 'Net Proceeds' means gross proceeds per ton minus costs per ton of all items other than wages. (3) O.M.S. is output per manshift of saleable coal. (4) E.M.S. is average earnings per shift of all employed. (5) Note the degree of underemployment in the more efficient districts.

Source: Report of the Secretary for Mines, 1934, p. 30.

production at Annesley in 1925. At one stage, the Deep Hard Seam was losing 4s. 6d. per ton. The colliery manager insisted that underground development and 'new work' on the surface were largely responsible for the increasing costs.[17] An unidentified newspaper article of late-1931 speaks of the 'transformation' both of Annesley Colliery and of the village since the New Hucknall Company took over. In particular, new coal preparation and dirt-tipping plants had been installed.

As we saw in an earlier chapter, 1926 was a good year for the New Hucknall Company, a profit of £517,987 being earned. The profit for 1927, at £53,734 was little more than a tenth of this record figure, and in 1928 it fell still lower to £33,616. The following year saw a marked improvement which was sustained in the succeeding years as the table shows:

TABLE 20

PROFIT OF NEW HUCKNALL COLLY. CO. LTD. 1929–1939

Year	Profit	Reserves (additional to profit)	Remarks
	£	£	
1929	83,094	—	
1930	92,080	20,000	
1931	86,982	40,000	
1932	80,514	20,000	
1933	110,562	—	
1934	102,110	—	
1935	113,306	—	
1936	140,126	—	
1937	154,018	—	
1938	71,566	35,000	
1939	76,951	35,000	Plus National Defence Cont. £5,700 and Income Tax £57,754

The Issued Capital of the Company throughout the period remained as follows:

5 per cent Preference Stock	—	£187,500
Ordinary Stock	—	£1,250,000

At 31st December 1939 the Company's Balance Sheet showed reserves for general purposes of £310,975 and reserves for depreciation, bad debts and other contingencies, of £595,884 besides provision for taxation and contingencies of £100,000.[18] This indicates the strength of the Company, despite the depression and is a tribute to the soundness of its management. If the collieries belonging to the New Hucknall Company may be regarded as a fair cross-section of the coalfield, the Pinxton and Linby companies may be taken as representative of the Erewash and Leen Valley owners respectively.[19]

The Pinxton Collieries Ltd. was at this date a public company, but its Board of Directors still included two members of the Coke family. The Directors, and their shareholdings in 1936, were as follows:

TABLE 21

Name of director	Ordinary Shares (£1 each, fully paid)	6% Prefs.
Col. E. C. Brierley, D.S.O., O.B.E.	1,250	
Gen. E. S. D'Ewes Coke, C.M.G., D.S.O.	10,500	25,005
Charles H. Spencer	1,800	585
Col. Basil E. Coke, M.A., O.B.E.	1,085	
Percy F. Day	600	

There were eleven other major shareholdings accounting for 116,497 Ordinary and 64,123 6% Preference Shares; and a further 146

Ordinary shareholdings accounting for £23,122. The total authorized Share Capital was:

100,000	6 per cent Preference Shares of £1, fully paid	=	£100,000
200,000	Ordinary Shares of £1, fully paid	=	£200,000
			£300,000

The profits earned over the period 1932 to 1935 were modest, although 1936 saw a marked improvement, due partly to an increase of about a shilling a ton in proceeds, and partly to the sale of marginal output.

TABLE 22

PINXTON COLLIERIES LTD.—TRADING RESULTS 1932–1937

Year (endg. 30th Sept.)	Output (thousand tons)	Proceeds per ton	Wages costs per ton	Profits per ton
		s. d.	s. d.	s. d.
1932	534	12 11	9 3	6·21
1933	508	12 7	9 4	0·99
1934	554	12 5	9 1	4·35
1935	548	12 4	8 9	5·45
1936	599	13 4	8 10	1 5·90
1937 (first half year)	324	14 6	8 11	2 3·21

Linby was owned by a private company which included the Worswick family among its major shareholders: they held just over one-seventh of the authorized and issued share capital of £70,750. Eight families of whom the Walters, Machins, Worswicks and Skinners were chief, held almost six-sevenths of the share capital, the remaining £11,725-worth being divided among 17 other shareholders.

Like other Leen Valley collieries, Linby had undoubtedly been highly profitable up to the 1920's, but the exhaustion of the top hard seam in 1931 and the obsolescence of much of its plant coupled with the unfortunate economic climate of the 1930's produced a very much less favourable position.

TABLE 23

LINBY COLLIERY CO. LTD.—COLLY. TRADING RESULTS 1933–37

Year (endg. 30th June)	Output (thousand tons)	Proceeds per ton	Wages costs per ton	Profits per ton
		s. d.	s. d.	d.
1933	130	14 7	9 10	6·88 (Loss)
1934	132	14 0	9 4	3·59
1935	124	13 7	9 4	5·94 (Loss)
1936	143	14 0	9 2	0·03
1937	163	14 10	9 4	11·62

Nottinghamshire as a whole came through the worst years of the depression reasonably well as these figures show:

TABLE 24

OUTPUT AND PROFITS, NOTTINGHAMSHIRE, 1928–1933

Year	Output (tons)	Proceeds (per ton)		Wages costs (per ton)		Operating profit (per ton)	
		s.	d.	s.	d.	s.	d.
1928	12,343,577	11	10	8	9		5·95 (Loss)
1929	13,665,880	12	6	8	5		8·73
1930	13,398,423	12	4	8	5		7·32
1931	13,321,458	12	7	8	1	1	2·71
1932	12,702,719	12	7	7	11	1	1·24
1933	13,638,408	12	5	7	9*		10·82*

* First ten months of year only.

However, many customers in Southern and Eastern England had switched from rail-borne coal supplied by Nottinghamshire and other Midland districts to sea-borne coal from Scotland, Northumberland and Durham some of whose delivered prices were said to be 4s. to 7s. a ton lower than coal from the Midlands.[21]

Nottinghamshire's prosperity owed much to the comparatively favourable geological conditions and the fact that the average size of the undertaking was bigger than in many other counties. This holds good, for example, as between Nottinghamshire and Derbyshire. Derbyshire's pits were generally older and smaller than Nottinghamshire's and they were, on the whole, working less rewarding seams because the best ones were exhausted. In 1928 Nottinghamshire's output exceeded Derbyshire's for the first time, and by 1930 the 46 collieries of Nottinghamshire were producing 800,000 tons more than the 108 collieries of Derbyshire.[22]

However, very considerable material investment was being undertaken in Nottinghamshire both to improve productivity and to improve the quality, and therefore the saleability, of the product.

The New Hucknall Company, for example, erected a new power house at Annesley in 1928 and this supplied electricity for underground and surface use for Annesley, Bentinck and New Hucknall Collieries. Fans were converted from steam to electricity whilst underground electricity replaced compressed air for conveyors, coal-cutters and haulages.[23]

By 1938 some 70 per cent of Nottinghamshire's output was cut by machine against a National (i.e. England and Wales) average of 56 per cent; whilst in mechanical conveying Nottinghamshire led the field. Of its total output of 15,468,000 tons, no less than 12,687,000 tons was mechanically conveyed. Only two districts (South Yorkshire which had 121 collieries and South Wales with 424 collieries as against 46 for Nottinghamshire) had greater tonnages mechanically conveyed. Further, Nottinghamshire had a greater number of gate-end loaders in use than any other district—97 out of a total of 766 for Great Britain as a whole. Nottinghamshire also led in the provision of electric safety lamps of which there were 34,533 in use in 1938 compared with 9,167 flame safety lamps. At the other end of the scale, Durham had almost as many flame-lamps as electric ones: 40,663 compared with 44,793.[24]

Virtually a new system of mining had evolved. This was a cyclic system where, on one shift the coal was undercut by machine, on the next it was hand-loaded on to a face conveyor and on the third shift the conveyor was moved over to the new face line and supporting packs were built. Now, all the fillers on a face were members of one team, but they were so spaced out along the face—each man in his eight or ten or twelve-yard stint—as to have no close contact with each other. This system is in contrast with hand-getting where the long-wall face was divided up into sections (the so-called 'stalls') each section being the responsibility of a small team of men who undertook all the work with the possible exception of holing (i.e. undercutting the coal) on a non-cyclic basis.

This new system produced record outputs. Thus, in 1933 the Bolsover Company's Rufford Colliery achieved a record output from a double-unit conveyor of 1,093 tons in a day; and shortly afterwards beat its own record by turning 1,147 tons from one conveyor face in a day. The filling tasks at the Bolsover Company's modern collieries in the Mansfield district were notoriously large: well over 20 tons a shift; but throughout the County fifteen to eighteen tons was usual. Such tasks would have been unthinkable in most counties outside the Midlands.[25] Even at New Selston, belonging to J. Oakes and Company and situated on the exposed coalfield, an overall O.M.S. of 33·9 cwts. was achieved in 1938. This was well above the national average.

The progress in mechanization over the whole country was, however, manifestly unsatisfactory. The output per manshift in Britain increased by only 14 per cent between 1927 and 1936 whilst in Poland it increased by 54 per cent. The increase in the Ruhr between 1925 and 1936 was 81 per cent whilst in Holland over the same period, it was no less than 118 per cent. In terms of actual output per manshift Britain's position deteriorated as follows:

TABLE 25

COMPARATIVE PRODUCTIVITIES 1925–1936[26]

Place	Basic year	O.M.S. in basic year	O.M.S. in 1936
Poland	1927	23·44 cwt.	36·20
Holland	1925	16·48 cwt.	35·94
The Ruhr	1925	18·62 cwt.	33·66
Britain	1927	20·62 cwt.	23·54

The output per man-shift in the Midlands (around 28½ cwts. in 1938) was artificially depressed by the working of short shifts but over the country as a whole improvements in efficiency were going ahead at much too slow a pace.

One special kind of investment going forward in the 1920's and 1930's was investment in by-products plants of various kinds. Coke ovens (producing metallurgical coke as their main product) and tar distilleries (like the one at Pinxton) were fairly common prior to this time. Now, however, new smokeless fuels were being developed. The most successful of these was Coalite (manufactured by Low Temperature Carbonisation Ltd.,) a re-active fuel suitable for open fires and much more pleasant to burn than ordinary gas coke. This firm opened its third plant (at Bolsover) in 1936.[27]

The New Hucknall Company invested considerable sums in a subsidiary company which erected at Welbeck Colliery a plant for the production of petrol from coal. The plant started operations in 1927 when it was designed to produce oil from cannel coal for re-sale to tar distillers for blending with creosote oils. However, when the price of creosote fell from 9d. to 3d. a gallon it was decided to try to produce petrol. After two years research a workable system was developed and 'Welbeck English Spirit' was put on the market at 1s. 2½d. per gallon. Some twenty-six gallons of petrol were obtained from one ton of cannel coal. Petrol stations were opened at the four pits of the New Hucknall group.[28]

At about the same time a new enterprise for the direct distillation of oil from coal was promoted in Leicestershire. The original partners, called their undertaking L and N Coal Distillation, Ltd. Unfortunately, before their process was perfected, the price of natural oil fell so drastically as to make coal distillation uneconomic and the project languished for a time. Then the company concentrated on perfecting a smokeless fuel with oil as a by-product and considerable sums of new capital were injected into the enterprise. The new Company, which came to be called the British Coal Distillation Ltd., had its pilot plant at Newbold, Leicestershire. The chairman of the company,

Mr. R. D. Hardy, was a director of the Leicestershire Colliery and Pipe Company Ltd., the owners of New Lount Colliery.

The pilot plant which had a capacity of 100 tons of coal a day eventually proved successful and a joint subsidiary was then formed with B. A. Collieries Ltd. under the title Suncole (Nottingham) Ltd. and a large plant, called the Suncole Plant, was erected at Cinderhill. This plant came on stream just before the outbreak of war but technical problems dogged it from the start and it never came fully into production.[29] The plant was designed to consume 220,000 tons of coal a year, but it closed down in 1940.

A few voluntary amalgamations took place in this period. The Babbington Colliery Company, for example, went into liquidation, its Nottinghamshire collieries (Cinderhill, Babbington and Bulwell) being taken over in 1938 by the Bestwood Coal and Iron Company (which was re-styled B. A. Collieries Ltd.) whilst its Derbyshire collieries Tibshelf and Birchwood were taken over in 1939 and closed down by the Sheepbridge Company. Similarly, the Digby Colliery Company was taken over by B. A. Collieries who closed the fairly old New London Colliery whilst retaining the more modern Gedling Colliery. During its final eleven months of life New London produced 159,979 tons. The 'Quotas' of the closed collieries were automatically allocated to the new owners. The Sheepbridge and Bestwood Companies were thus able to increase the outputs of their more efficient mines. Another merger proposed at about the same time (1938), that between the Pinxton and Linby companies, fell through owing to the last minute doubts of some of the principals involved. The Linby Company stood to gain a short-term advantage from the proposed merger in that some of the Pinxton Quota would have been transferred to Linby thus bringing down the royalty rent per ton and reducing the fixed cost per unit of output. The Pinxton Company, on the other hand, stood to gain a long-term advantage in that their own reserves were expected to last for a comparatively short time whilst the Linby Company had 90 years of a 100 year lease outstanding.

On the eve of the War, the Coal Commission suggested that the collieries of Nottinghamshire and Derbyshire should be grouped into three combines: one combine, for example, was to consist principally of B. A. Collieries Ltd; the Cossall Colliery Company Ltd; the Nottingham and Clifton Colliery Company Ltd; the Shipley Collieries Ltd; the Ilkeston Collieries Ltd. and the Wollaton Collieries Ltd.[30] There is little doubt that compulsion would have been exercised had the country remained at peace. But the War imposed new needs (in particular, the need to extract the last ton of coal, however inefficiently produced) and once the War was over, the nationalization of the industry was seen to be inevitable.

4. LABOUR

In earlier chapters, we have discussed problems connected with the supply of labour. In this period, however, there was a very considerable surplus of labour. The degree of actual unemployment can be gauged from the following table:

TABLE 26

NUMBERS INSURED AND UNEMPLOYED IN THE COAL-MINING INDUSTRY

Year	Persons insured (thousands)	Total unemployed (thousands)	Unemployment rate (%)
1923	1267	39	3
1924	1259	72	6
1925	1233	198	16
1926	1226	—	—
1927	1199	221	18
1928	1116	252	23
1929	1075	177	16
1930	1069	219	20
1931	1047	298	28
1932	1045	355	34
1933	1024	339	33
1934	982	281	28
1935	939	241	25
1936	896	199	22
1937	868	130	15
1938	858	133	16

Source: H. Wilson, *New Deal for Coal*, London, 1945.

In addition, there was a considerable degree of underemployment. Over the year as a whole, collieries in Nottinghamshire in this period rarely worked an average of more than four days a week. 'Market men' (i.e. men without regular places in a team) were in a particularly unenviable position. At some collieries the market man had to go down the pit to find out whether there was work for him that day or not. If he was lucky he would be chosen to make up a team; but if the regular men had all turned up for work then he might have to return to the surface without having earned a penny.

Further, there were lengthy periods when the men worked short shifts. The pit would start up in the morning and would carry on working until that day's orders had been fulfilled. Then 'loose-all' would be shouted, and work for the day would be at an end. In some cases, the men would have made half or three-quarters of a shift, but there were times when they made only two hours. This would still involve them in getting up at five o'clock in the morning, in paying full bus or train fares, in spending the same amount of time travelling to work, riding the shaft and walking to the face as for a full shift. To make matters worse, it debarred a man from 'signing on' at the Labour Exchange. Very often, men attended work five times in a week for two or two and a half shifts' pay and they were unable to claim unemployment pay to supplement their earnings.

Managements did not arrange work like this in order to rob men of their 'dole' (although it must have seemed like that to the men). Rather, they worked short shifts so as to fulfil current orders only, thus saving handling and stocking costs. The pressure put upon colliery managers by their employers made callous indifference to their workmen's difficulties inevitable. And there were always plenty of unemployed men available to fill the places of any who found their grievances insupportable.

It is hardly surprising that good colliers drifted into other occupations, particularly in areas like Nottingham where, very often, there was alternative work available. Nor is it surprising that many miners discouraged their sons from entering the industry. The manpower in the Nottinghamshire coalfield fell from an annual average of 56,911 in 1927 to 45,270 in 1938.[31]

The high productivities at the coal face achieved at Nottinghamshire collieries has already been noted. Labour was also more productively employed outbye the face in Nottinghamshire and Derbyshire than in other districts. The Reid Committee reported that, in October 1944 the average amount of saleable coal handled per haulage and tub loading worker in Nottinghamshire and Derbyshire was 7·81 tons against a national average of 4·90 tons. The only district with a better performance was the comparatively small Leicestershire and South Derbyshire district with 8·24 tons. The third best performance was 6·60 tons by Fife and Clackmannan. At the bottom of the table was Bristol with 2·19 tons. Lancashire and Durham among the big counties showed poor performances and even South Yorkshire, with its modern mines, was far behind Nottinghamshire and Derbyshire with 4·93 tons per man.[32]

The efficiency of Nottinghamshire's labour force is reflected in a low wages cost per ton. In 1932, for example, the Wages Cost per ton for Nottinghamshire at 7s. 11½d. was 1s. 1¼d. below the national average (to the nearest farthing). It was, however, slightly above the figures for Scotland (7s. 10¾d.), Northumberland (7s. 1½d.) and Durham (7s. 9¾d.). South Wales and Monmouthshire, on the other hand, had a wages cost of 10s. a ton, and in Lancashire, Cheshire and North Wales it was 11s. 2½d. a ton. The figure for Nottinghamshire and North Derbyshire together was 8s. 10½d.[33] The picture for 1936 was similar:

TABLE 27

WAGES COSTS PER TON 1936[34]

District	Proceeds		Wages cost per ton		Other cost per ton		Profit or Loss	
	s.	d.	s.	d.	s.	d.	s.	d.
Notts. and N. Derbys.	14	5	8	7	3	10	+ 1	11·62
Scotland	13	9	8	5	4	0	+ 1	4·64
Northumberland	12	8	7	7	4	6	+ 0	6·37
Durham	13	3	8	3	4	10	+ 0	0·89
S. Wales	15	7	10	0	5	8	− 0	0·58
Lancs., Cheshire Staffs	17	3	11	0	5	1	+ 1	2·64
Great Britain	14	8	9	2	4	6	+ 0	11·46

There is no evidence of wages cost per unit of output being held at an abnormally low level by reason of the activities of the Spencer Union, as was often alleged by opponents of Spencer. There is, on the other hand, a very clear indication of general managerial efficiency in the low 'costs other than wages' figures which were consistently well below the national average.

The earnings per man-shift in Nottinghamshire were considerably above the national average, but unfortunately short time depressed the yearly wage. Thus, in 1932, E.M.S. in Nottinghamshire and North Derbyshire at 10s. 4¼d. was higher than in any other district and 1s. 2¼d. higher than the national average. On the other hand, the Earnings for the year at £108 19s. 9d. were only 7s. 11d. above the national average.[35] One Nottinghamshire company, the Bestwood Coal and Iron Company, claimed to have paid earnings far higher than the national average however. They used this assertion in an appeal to their employees not to join in a projected national stoppage in 1936. They quoted the following figures:

TABLE 28

	Annual average earnings									Weekly average earnings								
	Bestwood			Notts.			Gt. Britain			Bestwood			Notts.			Gt. Britain		
	£	s.	d.	£	s.	d.	£	s.	d.	£	s.	d.	£	s.	d.	£	s.	d.
1928	121	16	9	112	19	5	113	6	7	2	6	10	2	3	5	2	3	7
1929	138	8	8	119	18	5	118	6	4	2	13	3	2	6	2	2	5	6
1930	130	19	1	117	13	0	113	8	2	2	10	4	2	5	3	2	3	7
1931	130	13	2	114	2	4	111	10	9	2	10	3	2	3	11	2	2	10
1932	137	8	7	108	19	9	109	8	5	2	12	10	2	1	11	2	2	1
1933	164	5	3	109	4	6	110	5	10	3	3	2	2	2	1	2	2	5
1934	171	17	6	112	16	3	115	11	6	3	6	1	2	3	4	2	4	5
1935	177	17	8							3	8	5						

The Bestwood Company pursued a vigorous policy in this period. They invested heavily in equipment; and recognized that to get the most out of the equipment they had to provide the men with incentives. They installed face conveyors and mechanical loaders earlier than most companies and they stimulated individual effort by scrapping the butty system and substituting an 'all-throw-in' system of payment.

To squeeze the most out of the permitted output, they devised a generous dirt deduction agreement which enabled the men to make fuller time than they would otherwise have done. This agreement reads as follows:

Dirt Agreement—All Mines 1930

'We, the undersigned do hereby agree on behalf of the men concerned, that the percentage of dirt from the Screens and Washery shall be deducted from the output, but rectified to the men concerned by a proportionate increase on the wages. The same to be determined monthly, i.e. if the dirt percentage comes to 8 per cent, then the wages (all on rate) shall be increased by 8 per cent, this shall not interfere with any existing dirt agreement.'

James Hunt
H. Skinner
M. Stone
R. Fletcher
A. Pearce

During the period of partial Government control of the industry in the Second World War, it became apparent that evasions of the Quota restrictions had been fairly widespread. Thus, when a member of the North Midlands Regional Coal Board asked in November 1943 why some colliery owners returned more saleable coal than coal weighed at the pit-head, the Chairman said that he thought that the practice dated from the pre-War selling scheme. At another meeting of the Board held in May 1944 the Regional Services Director said that 'he had been approached by a member of the personnel of a Department of Weights and Measures, who had raised the question of colliery weights. He had stated that the weights entered into the books were often 25 per cent lower than the actual weights shown on the colliery weighbridges'.[36]

B. A. Collieries also built up a large retail business so as to retain the profit otherwise taken by merchants, and they encouraged the workmen to act as Agents in securing retail orders. A leaflet headed 'Help Us—Help Yourself' issued to all workmen offered commission of 4d. per ton for workmen securing orders of five tons or less per month, 6d. per ton for those securing orders of from six to eleven tons per month and 8d. per ton for those securing orders of twelve tons per month and over.

This Company also practised personnel management of a kind. It set up a Labour Department to handle all personnel questions including wages and workmen's compensation. During the early 1930's there was a great deal of dissension over the Bestwood Colliery Check Weigh Fund. There were allegations of corruption, threats of libel actions, and attempts to unseat checkweighmen. The Company's Labour Department (although it was not then officially called that) appears to have fished in these troubled waters: at any rate, one of the protagonists reported on his activities to the head of the Department. For example, in connection with a leaflet addressed to members of the Notts. Miners Association containing allegations of corruption, he writes:

20th April 1933

'Dear Mr. Sale,

I am forwarding you leaflet as stated in my previous letter to you. I shall also distribute same throughout the Notts. Coalfield as soon as printers order is completed.

Yours

A. Winn.'

Among other things, this leaflet invited members of the N.M.A. to withhold their subscriptions pending an investigation of the allegations.

The head of the B.A. Collieries' Labour Dept. (Mr. F. Sale) at a later date (1940) advised that Branch officials of the Union should be 'buttered up'. Reporting to Mr. R. C. Lancaster (General Manager) he said:

'. . . the various Colliery Branch officials should come in for attention of a certain kind, to encourage them to bring in good time news of any trouble spot, so that this may be investigated, and where possible, dealt with.'[37]

There is, of course, nothing new in workmen reporting on Union matters to members of the management. Nor was the practice confined to one company. The circumstances following the 'split' in the ranks of the men encouraged tale-bearing and this intensified the suspicion and mistrust between man and man which existed throughout the Nottinghamshire coalfield in this period.

In the 1920's the Leen Valley men lost the Five-Day Week which they had enjoyed since 1892. They agreed to work six-days a week for the duration of the War in 1915, and they continued to do so during the post War boom. After the boom collapsed, the men at individual pits agreed to abandon the five-day week so as to be able to claim unemployment pay for Saturdays. The position was formalized at Annesley, for example, by an Agreement which reads as follows:

'We, the undersigned agree and have always recognised that the Annesley Colliery has been considered a six-day week pit from the time that the New Hucknall Colliery Company Ltd. took over the Annesley Colliery, the Saturday work being conditioned on the Pits working full time during the remainder of the week.

For the workmen (Sgd.)   J. Walker
For the Company (Sgd.)   H. Holt
(Manager)

April 26th 1927.'

Similar understandings were reached at the other Leen Valley collieries.

Migrations of labour continued in this period. The collieries working the 'new' concealed coalfield attracted men from the Erewash and Leen Valleys; whilst Harworth in particular relied on immigrants from the Northern coalfields.

One exceptionally regrettable feature of coalmining employment in the 1920's and 1930's was the failure to achieve any significant improvement in the accident rate. For Britain as a whole, the fatal accident rate per 100,000 Man-shifts worked increased from 0·39 in 1922 to 0·53 in 1934 and the serious accident rate improved only very slightly. The details are given in this table:

TABLE 29

PERSONS KILLED AND INJURED
PER 100,000 MAN-SHIFTS WORKED
1922–1934[38]

Year	Killed	Seriously injured	Total injured
1922	0·39	1·68	65·9
1923	0·41	1·64	66·9
1924	0·38	1·53	62·5
1925	0·40	1·54	63·4
1926	0·42	1·67	66·9
1927	0·45	1·85	68·5
1928	0·42	1·77	69·0
1929	0·43	1·70	70·9
1930	0·43	1·62	70·8
1931	0·41	1·57	66·9
1932	0·45	1·63	63·7
1933	0·43	1·52	63·7
1934	0·53	1·60	66·1

The position did not greatly improve until after the War. In 1938, the fatal accident rate was still 0·41 per 100,000 manshifts. In 1943 the rate was down to 0·36 and further improvements followed. The rate for 1948 and 1949 was 0·25. Similarly, the serious injury rate was 1·52 per 100,000 manshifts in 1938—little better than the 1924 figure, but again steady improvements followed during and after the War. The rate was 1·31 in 1943, 1·36 in 1947 and 1·20 in 1949.[39]

In the 1930's the colliery companies, with the encouragement of their insurers, made safety equipment available at concessionary prices. The most notable advance in this direction was the introduction in 1930 of the safety helmet—an American idea—by Major Hudspeth, Chief Mining Engineer to the Safety in Mines Research Board. At some collieries, these had become quite widely used by 1934.[40] The wearing of safety gloves and reliable boots and knee pads was also encouraged.

5. CONCLUSION

The period 1927 to 1939 was an extremely difficult period for the mining industry. During the greater part of the period the demand for coal was sluggish although towards the end re-armament brought about a marked improvement.

Marketing schemes were developed to restrict output, stimulate sales (particularly in export markets) and control prices. These schemes had the effect of sharing out the market between all producers, efficient and inefficient alike, and were inconsistent with the Government's desire to rationalize the industry by concentrating production on the more efficient units. The controls were, in any case, subject to considerable evasion. Profits in Nottinghamshire, whilst modest in comparison with earlier—and later—periods, were much more satisfactory than in other districts.

In this period, hand-filling on to a face-conveyor coupled with the use of gate-end loaders, replaced the earlier system of hand-getting and loading into tubs over most of the coalfield. The use of electricity, for coal-cutters, haulages, lighting, and so on, also spread. Considerable sums were invested in oil-from-coal and other by-product plants. Some projects proved unprofitable, and the most potentially promising one, a coal distillation plant, proved a failure.

APPENDIX

MIDLAND (AMALGAMATED) DISTRICT (COAL MINES) SCHEME, 1930
(DERBYSHIRE AND NOTTINGHAMSHIRE SECTION)
OUTPUTS IN 1937 AND 1938, STANDARD TONNAGES, ETC.
(INFORMATION COMPILED IN JANUARY 1939)

	Output 1937	1938	Standard Tonnage 1938	Proceeds 1938 Compared with 1937		Cost per Ton 1938 Compared with 1937		Profits Per Ton Compared with 1937		O.M.S. 1938 Compd. with 1937
				s.	d.	s.	d.	s.	d.	cwt
Bolsover Colly. Co.	4,057,384	3,616,064	5,710,962	+1	2	+1	4	−0	2	−0·64
Butterley	2,473,703	2,181,558	3,426,514	+1	3	+2	0	−0	9	−1·53
Blackwell	1,004,995	1,008,276	1,352,928	+1	0	+0	5	+0	7	+1·02
Sherwood	1,107,402	1,008,617	1,530,450	+1	5	+1	10	−0	6	−0·52
Barber Walker	728,548	748,051	1,000,947	+0	6	+0	8	−0	3	−0·33
S. Normanton	120,581	131,219	202,636	+0	7	−0	1	+0	8	+0·39
Babbington (Tibshelf and Birchwood* Colls. only)	247,925	267,493	360,000	+1	5	+0	10	(Losses)		+1·19
New Hucknall	1,500,550	1,354,399	2,042,497	+1	0	+1	3	−0	3	−0·55
J. Oakes	450,039	428,073	653,276	+0	9	+1	0	−0	2	+0·05
Palmer-Morewood	314,147	271,648	425,000	+0	9	+0	11	−0	2	+0.57
B. A. Colls†	1,904,105	1,771,246	2,703,774	+0	8	−0	0	+0	9	
Individual colly. outputs										
Babbington (Deep Soft)	158,908	154,600								
Bulwell (Main Bright)	172,480	181,928		+1	2	+0	2	+1	0	+1·04
Cinderhill (Main Bright)	160,892	181,851								
Bestwood (Top Hard and High) Main	707,917	736,781		−0	1	+0	1	−0	2	+2·24
Gedling (High and Low Hazel)	543,929	516,087		+1	6	+0	3	+1	2	+0·98
	Jan.-Nov. 159,979									
New London	159,979	—								
Newstead	1,093,336	1,022,737	1,600,000	+1	2	+0	9	+0	5	+0·68
Stanton	1,730,308	1,555,618	2,537,784	+1	3	+0	11	+0	4	−0·46
Linby	174,070	165,514	255,759	+0	11	+1	2	−0	3	−1·38
Nottm. and Clifton	173,000	130,000	250,000							
Pinxton‡	627,851	615,613	855,000	+0	9	+1	0	−0	3	−0·24

* By this time (January 1939) Babbington, Cinderhill and Bulwell had been acquired by B. A. Collieries, and shortly afterwards (April 1939) Tibshelf and Birchwood were absorbed by Sheepbridge who closed them down, despite considerable sums invested by the Seelys to make them economic.

For example, F. J. W. Seely in January 1939 said that £16,000 had been spent on electrification and a further £9,000 on a dry cleaning plant at Tibshelf. However, a major fault (24 ft.) had been encountered in the Low Main Seam. At Birchwood, forty acres of Blackshale had been exchanged with James Oakes and Co. (Cotes Park Colly.) for similar reserves in the Threequarter Seam which the Company proposed to develop over the succeeding three years at a cost of £25,000 to be charged to Revenue Account. The estimated life of the Threequarter at 700 tons per day was twenty-two years.

The company asked for a 50 per cent increase in its Standard Tonnage (540,000 tons against 360,000) to make these developments worthwhile. Presumably, its application was turned down.

† For B. A. Collieries, G. J. S. Chalmers stated that £313,658 had been expended on capital account (in addition to expenditure on the Suncole venture) over the previous few years. It was said that the B.A. pits had worked more fully than those of other companies. In 1938, days worked were as follows:

Bestwood Top Hard	275	
Bestwood High Main	216	(worked double shift in 1938— first time since 1931)
Babbington	232	
Bulwell	244	
Cinderhill	247	
Gedling	249	

(It was noted that New London closed in November 1937 and that its permitted output, spread over the other collieries, provided them with twenty-seven extra working days each (included in above total).) New London's output had been:

1935—168,353 tons
1936—187,831 tons
1937—159,979 tons (ten full months)

By contrast, the average number of days worked by five other undertakings in the Section were given as 197 in 1938. The small Doe Lea Colliery (Derbyshire), on the other hand, had worked on 278 days, but its output was so small that this did not worry anyone.

The output per manshift for the B.A. pits may be compared with the district average as follows:

(Year ending 30th September 1938)

B.A. Colls.	Nottinghamshire	Notts. and Derbys.
28·27 cwt.	30·08 cwt.	28·09 cwt.

Detailed profit, etc. figures for B.A. Collieries for year ending 30th September 1938 compare with the district as follows:

	B.A. Colls.		Notts. and Derbys.	
	s.	d.	s.	d.
Proceeds (per ton)	16	10·10	16	0·25
Costs (per ton)	14	10·53	14	3·60
Profits (per ton)	1	11·57	1	8·65
O.M.S.	28·27 cwt.		28·09 cwt.	

‡ For the Pinxton Colls. Ltd., it was stated that proceeds were held down by an old contract with the Notts. and Derby Coke and By-Product Co. Ltd., whereby the transfer price of slack was governed by the prevailing prices of coke.

The Company had spent £25,039 up to the end of 1938 on widening and deepening the Langton shaft to 487 yards (including cost of winding engine headgear and screening plant.)

Source: Notes of Sub-Committee Meetings of Notts. and Derbyshire Section of Midland (Amalgamated) District. Dated 19th January 1939, 23rd-26th January 1939, and 6th February 1939.

REFERENCES

1 For a good account of the operation of the Five Counties Scheme see A. M. Neuman, *Economic Organisation of the British Coal Industry*, London, 1934, pp. 161–5. See also: *The Derbyshire and Nottinghamshire District Collieries Commercial Association—Deed of Constitution and Trust Deed (including Rules and Regulations of the C.C.A.)*, Leeds, 31st March 1928.

2 Neuman, op. cit., p. 164.

3 ibid., p. 123.

4 ibid., p. 384.

5 ibid., p. 396.

6 *Midland (Amalgamated) District (Coal Mines) Scheme 1930, Rules* (approved 29th October 1930 and subsequently amended on various dates to 1940). Reference should also be made to the *Coal Mines Act 1930*.

7 *M.A.D. Scheme, 1930 Rules*, Clauses 17–20.

8 Neuman, op. cit., p. 435.

9 Report on Linby Colliery by P. F. Day, October 1936.

10 Report of G. P. Hyslop and H. W. Naish, 1936, Scheme A, p. 3.

11 Neuman, op. cit., p. 433.

12 *M.A.D. Scheme 1930, Rules*, Clauses 15 and 16.

13 H. Wilson, *New Deal for Coal*, London, 1945, pp. 24–6, J. P. Dickie, *The Coal Problem*, London, 1938, pp. 147–154.

14 Neuman, op. cit., p. 437.

15 ibid., pp. 439–440.

16 *Nottinghamshire Guardian*, 7th October 1904, *Nottinghamshire Daily Express*, 1st October 1906, and *Report of the Royal Commission on Coal, 1871*, Vol. III, Appendix 27, pp. 27–8.

17 Letters from P. Muschamp, Chief Agent to W. Waplington, Colliery Manager,

dated 19th May and 9th September 1925 and Letter from Waplington to
Muschamp dated 15th September 1925.

18   *New Hucknall Colly. Co. Ltd., Balance Sheet Book*, No. 5.

19   Report of G. P. Hyslop and H. W. Naish to the Pinxton and Linby Companies
     dated 26th November 1937.

20   *Nottinghamshire Guardian*, 2nd January 1934.

21   loc. cit.

22   *Mines Inspector's Report (North Mid. Divn.)* for 1930. Actual outputs for
     1930 were: Notts. 14,576,000 tons, N. Derbys. 13,787,822 tons.

23   Unidentified newspaper article of late 1931. Strangely, at Welbeck electricity
     did not replace compressed air at the face until about 1945.

24   *Annual Report of Secretary for Mines, 1938*, cited *Colly. Year Book and
     Coal Trades Directory, 1951 edn.*, p. 510. It should be remembered that some
     men carry flame lamps as gas detectors in addition to electric lamps.

25   *Coal-Mining—Report of the Technical Advisory Committee* (hereafter cited
     as *the Reid Report*) 1945, Cmd. 6610, p. 11.

26   ibid., p. 29. See also ibid., p. 141.

27   J. E. Williams, op. cit., p. 574.

28   Unidentified newspaper article, 1931.

29   For a summary of the various processes see J. P. Dickie, op. cit., pp. 325–337.
        The original 'Suncole' plant at Newbold had one retort of 100 tons capac-
     ity. One of the main technical problems was to overcome the tendency of the
     retort linings to buckle owing to the different rates of expansion of the
     inner and outer casing. This problem was eventually solved at the pilot plant.
        The Cinderhill plant was originally intended to have six 100-ton capacity
     retorts, of which five should have been working at any one time whilst the
     other was being serviced. However, in order to achieve marginal economies,
     the plan was altered and three retorts, of 200-ton capacity, were built in-
     stead. Immediately, the difficulties overcome at the pilot plant were repeated
     and considerable sums were spent on trying to build a retort lining which
     would not buckle.
        The plant closed when B.A. Collieries refused to sink more capital into
     the enterprise.

30   *Derbyshire Times* 16th June 1939, cited J. E. Williams, op. cit., p. 576.

31   Reports of H.M. Chief Inspector of Mines and Secretary for Mines. These
     reports contain several sets of manpower figures collected on different bases.
     The figures given in the text are averages of four dates in each year.

32   *Reid Report*, p. 12.

33   *Report of Secretary for Mines*, 1934, p. 30.

34   *Annual Statistical Summary for 1936*, London, (Mines Dept.) Cmd. 5427, 1937.

35   *Report of Secretary for Mines and Chief Inspector of Mines* for 1934,
     pp. 142–4.

36   *Minutes of North Midland Regional Coal Board*, 1st November 1943 and
     8th May 1944.

37   Report of Labour Department dated 28th March 1940.

38   *Report of Secretary for Mines and Chief Inspector of Mines* for 1934, p. 175.

39   *Ministry of Fuel and Power Statistical Digest*, 1951, p. 76.

40   *Sheffield Daily Telegraph*, 7th February 1934.

CHAPTER IV

The Second World War and After, 1939—1947

1. INTRODUCTION

The mining industry of 1939 was organized very differently from that of 1914. At the earlier date, there were hundreds of separate undertakings in fierce competition with each other; whilst at the later date the controls established in accordance with the 1930 Coal Mines Act were in operation.

In 1939, therefore, there was not the same need for a rigid Government control as existed in the first World War. Instead, the Government decided to make use as far as possible of the district schemes established under the 1930 Act to ensure that the industry was so run as to serve the national interest. It is true that the Emergency Powers Act gave the Government power to impose virtually any sort of control it liked over the industry, but the controls actually proposed at the outset of war were, to echo the official historian of the mining industry in wartime, 'modest compared with the emergency powers actually possessed by the Government'.[1]

Government control of some kind was necessary to ensure that the nation's essential needs were met and that prices were not allowed to get out of hand.

The system of control actually devised was a decentralized one. In each coalfield a Coal Supplies Officer was appointed 'to see that the distribution of coal from the pit head was effected in accordance with public policy'.[2] It was agreed between the Government and the coal owners' Cartel that the independent chairmen of the District Executive Boards (e.g. the Midlands (Amalgamated) District) should be appointed as Coal Supplies Officers receiving instructions as to priorities of consumer needs and similar matters from the Government's Coal Supplies Committee, but paid by the District Executive Boards. In other words, he was the employee of the Cartel which therefore became a Government agency.

Divisional Coal Officers whose areas coincided with the Civil Defence Regions, were appointed 'to keep an eye on the difficulties of the consuming areas'[3] making sure, for example, that adequate stocks were held, that transport problems—including those created by the bombing of railways—were overcome, and that essential users were given priority. They looked to the Coal Supplies Officers to ensure that their needs were met.

Coal exports were subject to Government licensing, the actual work of controlling exports being in the hands of Coal Export Officers who, like the Divisional Coal Officers, made their requirements known to the Coal Supplies Officers. In 1939 it was anticipated that France would need considerable quantities of British coal; but with the fall of France in 1940, our only substantial export market disappeared.

In addition to these officers of the Control, there were also Local Fuel Overseers appointed and paid by local authorities to operate whatever system of rationing of retail customers might be decided upon.[4] Customers had to be registered with a coal merchant, and were subject to a maximum allocation which was not guaranteed.

The fall of France caused considerable under-employment in the exporting coalfields and as their coal was diverted to the home market other coalfields became under-employed too. For this reason, miners were allowed to join the Forces, indeed many were actually called up. Altogether, some 80,000 mineworkers joined the Forces between July 1939 and July 1941 (when the call-up of miners was ended) and these were mainly in the 21–25 age-group. In addition, approximately 7,000 miners left the industry for other employments prior to May 1941 when such movements were restricted. They were sadly missed as the war progressed.[5] Quite apart from the actual numbers involved, the age-structure of the industry was seriously disturbed.

From the middle of 1941, contraction of supply, accompanied by the increasing demands of war industries, changed the situation from one where resources were under-employed to one where there was a positive and gradually worsening shortage of coal. The production of deep-mined coal fell as follows:

> 1939—231,337,900
> 1940—224,298,800
> 1941—206,344,300
> 1942—203,633,400

By 1945 it had fallen still further—to 174,657,900 tons.[6]

In April 1940 the Government established an advisory body consisting of representatives of the Mining Association and the Miners' Federation with officials of the Mines Department. This was called the Coal Production Council. District and pit production committees, with representatives of owners and miners, were similarly established. The pit committees in fact spent much of their time in dealing with absenteeism. It is doubtful whether any of these bodies had more than a marginal effect on output.[7]

The developing shortage of coal gave rise to a series of Government measures. First, the Essential Works (Coalmining Industry) Order 1941 made it illegal for a mineworker to leave his employment, or for a coal-owner to discharge an employee, without the approval of the National Service Officer (a civil servant belonging to the Ministry of Labour and National Service). The National Service Officer was also given power to discipline absentees referred to him by employers. A third provision of the Essential Works Order was the guaranteed wage to be paid where a miner was prevented from earning wages by circumstances outside his control except where he was involved in an industrial dispute.[8] This was followed by the compulsory registration of all civilians who had been employed as miners at any time. Those who were physically fit could be drafted back into the pits.[9]

Then, in June 1942, the Government decided to tighten its control over the industry. The Mines Dept. of the Home Office was replaced by a new ministry—the Ministry of Fuel and Power—with Major Lloyd George as its first head. The country was divided into twelve regions of which eight covered colliery districts whilst four covered districts away from the coalfields. In each region was a Regional Controller who had power (in the eight regions centred on coalfields) to give directions to colliery undertakings. At each colliery there had to be an individual—usually the manager—nominated to receive and apply such directions. A manager could, however, object to any direction which, in his view, might affect the safety of the mine. The Regional Controller was assisted by a Production Director and Labour Director, a Services Director and a joint committee representative of colliery owners and mineworkers in the region. There was a complementary body at national level (called the National Coal Board) but this had a purely advisory function: the centre of gravity lay in the regions.[10] This system of control left intact the private ownership of the mines, and in practice left most colliery undertakings substantially in control of their own affairs.[11] The Government had power, however, to take over the management of individual undertakings which were being inefficiently run.

Retail coal prices were controlled from the outbreak of war; although the actual machinery of control changed several times. In brief, prices could not be increased without Government permission.[12] In 1940, a levy of 2d. a ton was instituted to form a pool administered by the Cartel (i.e. the Central Council of Colliery Owners) from which payments could be made to owners whose pits had to work short time because of the loss of export orders. The levy was later widened in scope to assist 'necessitous undertakings', that is, undertakings working at a loss but whose output was needed for the war effort.[13] The arrangement could be justified by the restriction of prices: in a free market coal prices would have risen considerably from the middle of 1941 and even inefficient collieries could have expected to make profits.

2. PRODUCTION IN WARTIME

The first Regional Controller for the North Midland Region (which covered the Nottinghamshire, Derbyshire, Leicestershire and South Derbyshire coalfields) was Mr. Raymond Evershed, K.C. He held this office from August 1942 until April 1944 when he was replaced by another barrister, Mr. Theodore Turner, K.C.[14]

The first Production Director, Mr. H. Watson-Smith, held office only until the 1st February 1943 when he resigned because he found it difficult to 'serve two masters'. The Regional Board expressed the opinion that a Regional Production Director should be paid wholly by the State and should be required to sever his connection with his old employer; and that his future should be assured.[15] Since no-one could be found to replace Watson-Smith, it was decided that several Board members who were mining engineers should be asked to share the duties of the post by each supervising a group of collieries. This system worked reasonably well, and in consequence it became national policy to appoint Group Production Directors.[16] Full-time Group Production Directors were appointed early in 1944. In April 1944 Mr. T. E. B. Young was appointed full-time Production Director and he was succeeded in July of the same year by Mr. J. J. Torrance.[17]

Right from the outset of the 1942 control two Nottinghamshire undertakings, Clifton and South Normanton, required special supervision. In November 1942 a control order was made by the Minister in respect of Clifton and Mr. Dixon was appointed General Manager. Later, in February 1943, it was announced that Mr. R. Ringham had agreed to take the chairmanship of this controlled undertaking.[18]

In 1942 also, South Normanton was receiving help under the 'Necessitous Undertakings' Scheme. The output in October-November, 1942 at 500 tons a day was slightly better than it had been earlier. Output per man-shift (23·36 overall and 41·33 at the face) was, however, low by Nottinghamshire standards.[19] A year later the overall O.M.S. was about 25½ cwts. but the Company was still running at a loss. Of the 350 underground men, one in seven was said to be incapable of a full week's work; the electrician in charge was over seventy years of age, whilst the managing director was almost eighty. The direction of the Company was considered inadequate; and mechanical breakdowns over-frequent. It was also alleged that some of the men on books were dead and that payments were being made to their relatives.[20] It was therefore decided that a Technical Supervisor and a Financial Adviser should be installed by the Regional Control.[21]

The war gave impetus to mechanization. R. C. Lancaster, who was the Region's mechanization specialist, reported in September 1943 on the first two Meco-Moore Power Loaders which had been tried out at the Rufford and Thoresby Collieries of the Bolsover Company. These were unable to match the output of conventional hand-filling at these collieries of over twenty tons per day.

R. C. Lancaster's company, B. A. Collieries, were using three 12 B.U. Joy Loaders in room and pillar work in the Bestwood High Main, whilst an 8 B.U. Joy Loader was in use at Langwith (Derbyshire) for the partial extraction of a Top Hard pillar.[22] It was unfortunate, perhaps, that American-style room and pillar mechanization schemes were taken up with such avidity in the later stages of the War and in the immediate post-war period. On the whole, these schemes provided a very poor return on capital invested because they were not suited to the physical conditions in British mines.

In this early stage of power-loading, Nottinghamshire's performance lagged behind that of the country as a whole as these figures for 1943 indicate:

TABLE 30

POWER LOADED OUTPUT

	Nottinghamshire	Gt. Britain
Output of Power Loaded Coal (Tons)	37,285	1,150,483
No. of Power Loaders in use	11	110
Avg. Output per Power Loader (Tons)	3,389	10,459
Power Loaded Output as a Percentage of Total Output	0·22	0·85

The proportion of coal *cut* by machinery continued to rise, however, although in retrospect the amount of hand-holing still being done in 1943 seems surprisingly high. These figures indicate the trend:

TABLE 31

NOTTINGHAMSHIRE (COUNTY, NOT WAGES DISTRICT)
COAL CUT BY MACHINE

	1938	1943
(a) No. of pits using coal cutters	41	45
(b) Total number of cutters in use	340	397
(c) Quantity of coal cut	10,839,000	14,350,000
(d) Percentage of total output represented by (c)	70	82

Compared with the rest of the North Midlands Region, Nottinghamshire's war-time performance seems disappointing. The 1943 outputs of the various districts, expressed as a percentage of the 1938 outputs, were as follows:

Leicestershire and South Derbyshire   162
Derbyshire   111
Nottinghamshire   106·5

This trend is accounted for in part by the increase in Leicestershire and South Derbyshire's labour force. Manpower employed in 1943, again expressed as a percentage of the 1938 manpower, was as follows: [23]

Leicestershire and South Derbyshire   111
Derbyshire   98
Nottinghamshire   96·5

Perhaps we should defer any further discussion on manpower to our next section in order to avoid repetition. There is, however, one further point which needs to be made on mechanization. There was a tendency to think of this in terms of face mechanization, whereas the greatest weakness in British mining practice was its hopelessly inefficient use of labour outbye the face. In American mines, one haulage worker was used for every fifty tons or so of coal produced; in Britain the average in October 1944 was one man for 4·90 tons. The two best and two worst districts in this respect were: [24]

TABLE 32

District	Tonnage of saleable coal per tub loading and haulage worker
Leics. and Derbys.	8·24
N. Derbys. and Notts	7·81
Bristol	2·29
Cumberland and Westmorland	2·49

3. LABOUR IN WARTIME

As we have seen, the call-up of miners was ended in July 1941, and thereafter some ex-miners who had joined the forces were allowed to return to the mines; whilst men called up were allowed to opt for underground employment as an alternative to military service. [25]

However, voluntary recruitment proved inadequate and compulsion was therefore used. At the outset this applied only to young colliery surface workers and it caused considerable resentment. Indeed, the most serious strike in Nottinghamshire during the war years was over this issue. A surface worker at Newstead Colliery, Sidney Page, was imprisoned for refusing to go underground. Page was well liked at Newstead, where all the men came out on strike on Monday 13th September 1943.

The Regional Controller, Mr. Evershed, attended a meeting at Newstead on the following day with Herbert Booth, the Notts. Miners'

Agent. The leader of the men's deputation was Booth's old colleague William Askew, checkweighman who, besides being a branch delegate, was also a member of the E.C. of the Notts. Miners' Federated Union (N.M.F.U.). The delegation made it clear that the men would stay out whilst Page was in prison. By this time, all the Leen Valley pits—and some others—were out in sympathy.

Joe Birkin the Vice-President of the N.M.F.U. and Mr. A. H. M. Jackson of the Newstead Company saw Page in prison later that day and told him that he could resume surface work after the war. On this understanding, Page agreed to go underground and on the following day he signed an undertaking to this effect. The Home Secretary then agreed to release Page from Prison.

However, Askew and a deputation of four men met Mr. Evershed on Thursday 16th September and demanded (a) that Page should be released unconditionally; (b) that there should be no further prosecutions of a like kind; and (c) that the word 'direction' should be taken out of the Order relating to surface workers being sent to underground work. In reply, Evershed observed (a) that Page had already been released; (b) that he would need guidance from London on any future cases and (c) that the argument that surface workers should have the same option to go into the forces as other young men subject to call-up had already been made to him.

Later in the day, Askew asked Evershed to attend a meeting at Hucknall to discuss the demand for an undertaking that there would be no further prosecutions. Arrived at the meeting, Evershed found that whilst those he met were (to the best of his knowledge) union branch officials, they were acting as an unofficial Strike Committee. This Committee asked for an assurance that there would be no victimization of strike leaders, and this they were given in general terms. They then adopted the following resolution:

> 'Resolve that we, the Strike Committee conducting the dispute in the Nottinghamshire coalfield, having been assured that Page is released, and further being of the opinion that outstanding cases are not likely to be brought into the Court pending the Government's considering the points brought forward by the Strike Committee and conveyed to Mr. Evershed, are prepared to recommend return to work having been given a guarantee against any victimisation.'

This resolution was subsequently endorsed by a general meeting of men held at Hucknall on Friday 17th September and by the Newstead Branch Committee of the Union, and was broadcast by the B.B.C. at the Regional Controller's request. The men accordingly went back.

It has been said (by, for example, Mr. Herbert Booth) that the Communists engineered this dispute, but this is not so. On the contrary, the Communist Party at this time were opposed to all strikes. They advocated the maximum war effort, including the opening of a Second Front in Europe and the production of every possible ton of coal.

There may have been some Trotskyist participation; but the present writer knows of only one Marxist of any type who was involved: Jock Finnegan, Bulwell Branch delegate, who was an adherent of the Socialist Party of Great Britain.

George Spencer, supported by W. C. Phillips of Barber Walker, criticized Evershed for meeting an unofficial strike committee. This sort of action, he believed, would undermine the Union. However, it is difficult to see what alternative Evershed had. The Union had no control of the situation at all so that it was no use negotiating with them.

After the strike, the Regional Coal Board unanimously agreed that pending the introduction of general conscription for underground work, surface workers should be given the option of going in the Services instead of being 'directed' underground.[26]

General conscription for underground work did, in fact follow fairly quickly. In December 1943 the 'Bevin Boy' scheme was introduced: all boys who were due to be called up participated in a ballot and those whose names 'came out of the hat' had to go into the mines. The Bevin Boy scheme was designed to produce 50,000 mining entrants in 1944 but it produced only 15,000 in that year and 5,900 in the next. The scheme was abandoned with the end of the war.[27]

The introduction of 'optants' and 'Bevin Boys' stimulated the introduction of training schemes for new entrants. Before this time it was common for boys to work first on the surface or in the pit bottom and then to progress towards the coal face as they became experienced in mining conditions. But there were few collieries offering any sort of conscious training. Now, training officers were appointed at collieries and special preliminary training centres were established for groups of collieries.

Provisional training schemes for 'optants' were introduced on 23rd November 1942.[28] The first central training establishment for Nottinghamshire, at Creswell Colliery, released its first intake of 137 boys on 21st February 1944.[29] Shortly after this, a coal face fully reserved for training was opened at Gedling Colliery—one of the first two such faces in the country.[30]

A specialized kind of training establishment was necessitated by the new mining machinery being introduced from America. This was opened at Sheffield early in 1944 and it offered courses for skilled craftsmen on new types of machines; and courses lasting six months for unskilled production workers to fit them for semi-skilled maintenance work. At the outset, these courses were not very well supported by colliery owners.[31]

The introduction of volunteers, 'optants' and 'Bevin Boys' did not solve the industry's manpower problems. Whilst the total manpower rose substantially, the face manpower did not. Further, the absence rate went up. In the four weeks ended 12th December 1942 the average number of men on books in Nottinghamshire was 41,750. Six months later (17th July 1943) this number had fallen to 41,528. The influx of recruits raised the figure by 7th October 1944 to 42,467 but this fell to 42,445 by 17th February 1945.[32]

However, on 9th October 1944 the Regional Production Director pointed out that there were 1,148 more men on books in Nottingham-shire in September 1944 than in the corresponding period of 1943, but that there were fifty-six fewer at the coal face. The attendance and output per man-shift (O.M.S.) figures were also down as this table shows:[33]

TABLE 33
NOTTINGHAMSHIRE
FACE MANPOWER PERFORMANCE

	Wk. ended 25.9.43	Wk. ended 23.9.44	Difference
Men engaged on the Coal Face	17,511	17,455	−56
Shifts worked at the Coal Face	82,223	77,362	−4871
O.M.S. at the Face	78·26 cwt.	77·94 cwt.	−0·22 cwt.

Because they were unwilling miners. 'Bevin Boys' were, on the whole, more prone to excessive absenteeism than others.[34] There was, however, a high absence rate throughout the war; and the tendency for the rate to rise as the war progressed was put down variously to war-weariness, malnutrition, the beer shortage and high earnings.[35]

To meet the charge that miners were not getting sufficient food canteens were erected. However, only a small minority of miners took main meals in the canteen: it was impossible for them to come up the pit for a meal in the middle of the shift; and at the end of the shift they were usually impatient to get home. The extra cheese ration which miners enjoyed was probably of more use to most of them than canteen meals.[36]

The shortage of beer is said to have induced a mild neurosis in men who were used to having it on tap. In consequence when the public-houses were open there was a tendency to 'swill': a pheno-menon encountered in countries like Australia with rigid licensing laws. To what extent men took time off work to look for beer (or cigarettes which were also in short supply) it would be difficult to say.

Many miners were undoubtedly better able to afford to take time off than before the War. In October 1944 it was stated in Parliament that out of a list of ninety-six to one hundred industrial employments, arranged in descending order of wages paid, miners stood fourteenth whereas in 1938 they had been eighty-first.[37] The only industries higher on the list than coalmining owed their high earnings largely to considerable overtime, carrying premium rates of pay. Representative examples illustrate this:

TABLE 34
AVERAGE EARNINGS AT JANUARY 1944[38]

Trade	Av. Weekly earnings			Av. no. of hours worked	Avg. pay per hour	
	£	s.	d.		s.	d.
Motor Vehicles, Cycles and Aircraft	8	6	1	52·8	3	2
Shipbuilding and Repairs	7	2	9	54·6	2	7
Coal Mining	6	9	5	45·9 (estimated bank to bank)	2	10

Until August 1942 Pit Production Committees dealt with individual persistent absentees—levying fines, issuing warnings, and, in particularly bad cases, referring to the National Service Officer. Thereafter, they were relieved of the odium of sitting in judgment on fellow workmen; and Regional Investigation Officers were employed to deal with offenders. Absentees considered incorrigible were prosecuted under a wartime regulation, with imprisonment as the ultimate sanction. The Investigation Officers were usually ex-branch officials of miners' unions; and the nature of their work made them very unpopular.[39]

The causes of high absence rates in the mining industry are many and various: bad working conditions, awkward hours of work, shift working, trouble with officials, minor indispositions which would not keep a factory or office worker off work, but which disable a miner,[40] among others. Perhaps it should also be remembered that miners were unused to working six days a week throughout the year. They were accustomed to taking two or three days a week off during the summer months, and sometimes in winter too. Further, the men throwing over twenty tons of coal a day on to a belt at pits in the Mansfield area must sometimes have been physically exhausted, particularly after a night on firewatching or Home Guard duty.[41]

High absenteeism and falling output in the later years of the war produced exhortation for the many as well as punishment for the few. In the North Midlands Region, the Labour Director, Harry Hicken (ex-Secretary of the Derbyshire Miners' Association) addressed meetings of miners in various localities appealing for everyone to make the maximum effort. The Communist Party, in the period following the entry of Russia into the war, conducted a sustained production campaign. At public meetings, in leaflets handed out at pit gates and in broadsheets they called for the maximization of production. Absentees were urged to go to work regularly, strikers to return to work, colliers to take bigger stints and trade union officials to co-operate fully with management. Unfortunately for the Communists, they were treated with the deepest suspicion by many senior management officials who were unable to understand that in advocating close co-operation with capitalists, the Communist Party line was consistent with the Party's over-riding purpose of fostering the interests of the Soviet Union.

One curious development of this period was the formation by B. A. Collieries, Ltd. of the 'Miners' Second Front Movement' whose programme was closely similar to that of the Communist Party. It even issued a badge (with crossed tools) reminiscent of the hammer and sickle. Typical of its output is a leaflet headed 'Here-and-There' which reads:

'If you could look into the homes of people living in those parts of Europe which are occupied by the Nazis, you would see scenes of misery which would horrify you. Add to this the misery of Russia in towns and villages, which have been almost entirely destroyed.

'This all means that probably never since the World began have so many people suffered so much in so short a time—and yet we in this country, living just outside this suffering, are leading, more or less, our ordinary peace-time lives.

'Some of us have failed to realize this. At a time when men and women are dying daily in thousands, and millions are slowly being starved or tortured to death, we are remembering wrongs and injustices of the past.

'What are our injustices and hardships compared to those of all those millions which cry aloud to Heaven for redress? Let us forget our wrongs. They come between us and our work and so hinder us in our efforts to put an end to all this misery in Europe.

'Forget the Past! Help to build a better future for mankind! '

Members of the Communist Party working at pits of the B.A. Company were instructed to join, and give every support to, this movement.[42]

Of marginal importance were meetings arranged in co-operation with the Ministry of Information in colliery canteens addressed by European refugees, experts on Russia, and others. Concerts were also provided in canteens by the Council for the Encouragement of Music and the Arts (which were not greatly appreciated) and by the Entertainers National Service Association (which were, despite the ghastly nature of much of the entertainment).

Except for the Page dispute, there were few strikes of note in Nottinghamshire until 1944. In 1944, however, there was a great deal of unrest. On 21st August the Regional Controller reported to the Regional Board that there had been no fewer than six strikes in the

U

previous six weeks and five of these were at Nottinghamshire pits: Clifton, Watnall, Sutton, Cinderhill and Teversal.

The national tendency was much the same as this table shows:

TABLE 35
ESTIMATED LOSS OF OUTPUT THROUGH DISPUTES
(GREAT BRITAIN)

		Tons
1940		500,600
1941		341,900
1942		833,200
1943		1,090,700
1944:	1st Quarter	2,032,900
	2nd Quarter	587,400
	3rd Quarter	170,900
	4th Quarter	210,500

Source: J. Harold Wilson, New Deal for Coal, London, 1945, p. 121.

Most of the disputes in 1944 were over trivial local issues. For example, of the strikes referred to above, the one at Cinderhill was caused by pieceworkers who claimed that their wages had been depressed by a high attendance of men during 'bull' week (i.e. the week before a holiday); that at Clifton arose from the refusal of a few men to change shifts when told to do so; that at Sutton was a protest at the late payment of holiday money from the joint savings scheme; whilst that at Teversal was caused by dissatisfaction over rates of pay for week-end work.

There was undoubtedly a general malaise which can be best described as war-weariness. Morale improved tremendously following the invasion of France which pretty well coincided—happily for the industry—with the implementation of the Porter Award of April 1944 which lifted and consolidated miners' wages.

4. WAGES AND PROFITS IN WARTIME

The method of district wages ascertainment, with net proceeds being shared by masters and men in agreed proportions, remained intact during the early war years. However, by restricting prices, the Government held both profits and wages down. Accordingly, as the cost of living rose, various bonuses were awarded as follows:

Cost of living increases:

1st November 1939	8d. per shift
1st January 1940	5d. per shift
1st April 1940	4d. per shift
1st October 1940	5d. per shift
1st January 1941	6d. per shift
1st July 1941	4d. per shift

Attendance bonus:

1st June 1941	1s. per shift

The Mining Association had always opposed national wages negotiations. The first tentative step in the direction of such national negotiations was taken with the establishment of the Joint Standing Consultative Committee in January 1936. In March 1940, this body agreed that increases in wages necessitated by the special circumstances of the war should be negotiated nationally; but that the district ascertainments should continue to be made as usual.

The percentage additions to basis rates arrived at in Nottinghamshire were as follows:

TABLE 36

NOTTS. WAGES DISTRICT
PERCENTAGE ADDITIONS TO BASE RATES[43]

	1939	1940	1941	1942
January		80·00	104·00	110·00
February		80·00	104·00	110·00
March		80·00	104·00	110·00
April		86·00	104·00	110·00
May		87·00	104·00	108·00
June		89·00	104·00	
July		91·00	108·00	
August		93.00	108.00	
September	55·27	95·00	108·00	
October	74·35	100·00	108·00	
November	75·35	100·00	108·00	
December	75·00	100·00	110·00	

The Greene Award of 1942 'froze' all district percentages, so that the Nottinghamshire percentage remained at 108 until April 1944 when percentages were consolidated into basis wages.

Had it not been for the Greene Award, the percentage would have dropped quite sharply because costs other than wages were rising whilst coal prices were stable thereby leaving a decreasing surplus to be shared between owners and miners. This tendency is brought out in table 37.[44]

Both miners and owners were dissatisfied. The M.F.G.B. applied for a national minimum wage of 85s. for a week's work for those aged 18 and over, a 4s. per shift increase for all over 18 years and a 2s. per shift increase for boys under eighteen. The Mining Association resisted this claim in the Joint Standing Consultative Committee. They insisted that any wage increase should be tied to production and attendance.[45] The Government, recognizing the wide unrest in the industry, established a special Board of Investigation, with Lord Greene as its chairman, to examine the whole question and to report.[46]

On the immediate wages issue, the Greene Board substantially conceded the miners' Claim. They awarded a flat rate increase of 2s. 6d. a shift for underground workers of 18 years and over and

TABLE 37
NOTTS. WAGES DISTRICT
ASCERTAINMENT 1941 AND JANUARY—MAY 1942

Date	Output	Proceeds			Cost of production other than wages			Wages at 85% of Surplus			Total wages per shift (AVG.)		Owners' credit Balance			Owners' credit balance as % of surplus
	tons	£	per ton s.	d.	£	per ton s.	d.	£	per ton s.	d.	s.	d.	£	s.	d.	
1941	16,860,485	17,086,342	20	3·21	4,249,582	5	0·49	10,765,738	12	9·24	19	6·23	2,071,022	2	5·48	16¼
Jan. 1942	1,461,444	1,495,022	20	5·52	376,303	5	1·80	987,841	13	6·23	20	7·06	130,878	1	9·49	11¼
Feb. 1942	1,316,623	1,333,761	20	3·13	297,206	4	6·18	887,996	13	5·87	20	7·70	148,559	2	3·08	14¼
Mar. 1942	1,463,780	1,503,113	20	6·45	391,064	5	4·12	974,560	13	3·79	20	5·81	137,489	1	10·54	12¼
Apr. 1942	1,333,703	1,351,374	20	3·18	366,051	5	5·87	911,849	13	8·09	20	11·15	73,474	1	1·22	7½
May 1942	1,375,683	1,399,128	20	4·09	375,436	5	5·50	922,449	13	4·93	20	7·51	101,243	1	5·66	9·89

surface workers of 21 years and over, with lesser amounts for younger men; and a national minimum wage for adults of 83s. a week for underground workers and 78s. for surface workers.[47]

The Greene Board also recommended the adoption of an output bonus scheme. This provided for the payment of a bonus on a sliding scale calculated separately for each district. For each district, a monthly standard tonnage was calculated on the basis of past performance and the bonus was then proportioned to outputs in excess of the standard tonnage.[48] George Spencer, in a brilliantly-argued paper, attacked the basis of calculation of the standard tonnage for Nottinghamshire. He pointed out that productivities in Nottinghamshire had improved year by year both absolutely and in comparison with other counties, and that further improvements would therefore be more difficult of achievement than in counties which had so much leeway to make up. To use his own words:

'The task of achieving a definite percentage increase in production varies both relatively and absolutely with the integer on which it is calculated, and the higher such integer is, and the closer it approximates to the limit of capacity so does the task become more difficult of achievement.'[49]

In any event, Nottinghamshire gained very little from the arrangement, although Spencer's advocacy succeeded in obtaining a reduction in the 'Standard Tonnage' from 345,500 tons to 337,600 tons. This was reckoned as 100 per cent and for each 1 per cent addition a bonus of 3d. per shift was payable.

Only on three occasions was a bonus earned: for the four week periods ending 3rd October 1942 (output 101·2 per cent of Standard) 28th November 1942 (101·1 per cent) and 26th December 1942 (103·2 per cent). The scheme was abandoned following the review of August 1943.[50]

A more permanent achievement of the Greene Board was the establishment of Conciliation machinery. This provided for disputes to be categorized as either National, district or pit questions. National questions were to be decided by a National Board consisting of two parts: a Joint National Negotiating Committee (having equal representation from either side—Mining Association and Miners' Federation) and a National Reference Tribunal composed of independent people to make binding awards where the J.N.N.C. was unable to agree. The first chairman of the N.R.T. was Lord Porter and their awards are usually known as 'Porter Awards'.

District questions were to be dealt with by a District Conciliation Board (again with equal representation) and in the event of disagreement reference was to be made to an independent District Referee having power to make binding awards. A similar scheme was later drawn up for dealing with pit questions.[51] This Conciliation Scheme has remained substantially unchanged.

One of the most important of the Porter Awards was the one of April 1944 which provided for the consolidation of wages of day-wage workers. The Attendance Bonus, the Greene Award, the 1936 Flat Rate and the District percentage were merged into the basis rate to give a consolidated rate to which was to be added the flat rate of 2s. 8d. cost-of-living bonus.

For the calculation of the consolidated piece-work prices, the 1911 basis rate was taken, but the percentage, frozen by the Greene Board at 108 per cent in Nottinghamshire was increased to 164·1166. This increase in the percentage was to absorb all the various flat rates (except the 2s. 8d.) which were thus consolidated as with day-wage workers. There were to be no further percentage additions to basis rates. The Award also provided for the payment of 1s. per shift to all skilled and many semi-skilled men (this was commonly called the 'skilled shilling').[52]

The Porter Award also guaranteed wages until the end of 1947 following which they could only be varied by the giving of six months' notice by either side. In effect, therefore, wages could not fall below the April 1944 levels until the middle of 1948 at the earliest.

Generally speaking, the cost of wage increases and certain other kinds of expenditure necessitated by war-time conditions were borne from a central fund fed by a levy on coal. This system evolved piecemeal, and the full story is much too complicated to be dealt with here.[53] Such levies obviously involve the subsidization of high-cost districts by low-cost districts, and for this reason the whole system was criticized time and again by George Spencer. For example, he provided the following 'balance sheet' in 1942:

TABLE 38

STATEMENT SHOWING CHARGES FOR
SPECIAL LEVIES INCLUDED IN THE ASCERTAINMENT
TOGETHER WITH NOTE OF AMOUNTS RECOVERABLE BY
COLLIERIES IN THE DISTRICT[54]

Nottinghamshire

	Period	Amt.
1. *Levies Included in Ascertainment*		
Timber Levy	May 1940-August 1942	£401,964
War Emergency Assistance Scheme Levy	January 1941-May 1942	£248,420
Guaranteed Wage Levy	August 1941-May 1942	£115,767
Coal (Charges) Order Levy 1942	June-August 1942	£448,063
		£1,214,214

2. *Amounts Recoverable from Central Funds*
War Emergency Assistance Scheme
    (Credited in Ascertainment) to August 1942   £2,116
Guaranteed Wage Payments
    (Lists supplied by Central Council) June
    1941–July 1942   £67,717
Greene Report Additions
    June–August 1942 (provisional)   £356,985

                                      £426,818

Balance showing amount by which Nottinghamshire subsidised other districts in the period = £787,396.

The Coal Charges Fund levy eventually (in August 1944) reached 12s. a ton. Nottinghamshire made net contributions to the Fund each year whilst South Wales, to take a contrary example, enjoyed net drawings from the Fund year by year. The comparative figures are as follows: [55]

TABLE 39

Year	Nottinghamshire (net contributions)		S. Wales and Monmouth (net recoveries)	
	s.	d.	s.	d.
1942		4 per ton	2	4 per ton
1943		7 per ton	3	3 per ton
1944	1	6 per ton	7	10 per ton
1945	5	2 per ton	8	7 per ton

The Fund itself went into deficit, and in addition to financing this deficit the Government gave assistance to the industry with capital expenditure.[56] It will be seen therefore that the Government had moved much further towards financial control of the industry than had seemed likely in the early days of the war.

5. THE NATIONALIZATION ISSUE

The Miners' Federation of Great Britain and the Labour Party were committed to a policy of nationalization of the coal mining industry. Labour M.P.'s. in a famous Parliamentary debate on the industry in October 1943 advocated immediate nationalization, but the Prime Minister, Winston Churchill, said that he 'could not take the responsibility of making far-reaching controversial changes which I am not convinced are directly needed for the war effort without a Parliament refreshed by contact with the electorate.'[57]

Various leaders of the M.F.G.B. made clear their intention to pursue the nationalization issue vigorously once the war was over, and indeed the National Union of Mineworkers (N.U.M.), which came into being on 1st January 1945, had as one of its objects: 'To seek the establishment of Public ownership and Control of the mining industry.'[58]

The colliery owners did not allow the argument to go all one way. A. K. McCosh, the Chairman of the Scottish Colliery Owners, issued a hard-hitting pamphlet in January 1944 which begins:

'It is deplorable that, whilst the country is engaged in the greatest struggle in its history, any effort should be diverted to political controversy at home.

'Unfortunately there are those who seem to regard the war as a heaven-sent opportunity of furthering their own political aims.

'Amongst these are the protagonists for the nationalization of the coal mines.'[59]

However, even the colliery owners recognized that something drastic had to be done to improve the industry's efficiency. The authors of the Reid Report, who were leading mining engineers, came to the conclusion that it was

'not enough simply to recommend technical changes which we believe to be fully practicable, when it is evident to us, as mining engineers, that they cannot be satisfactorily carried through by the Industry organized as it is today.[60]

The Mining Association decided to issue its own Report. The author of this document was Robert Foot, Chairman of the Association and his Report: *A Plan for Coal*, is usually referred to as the Foot Plan. This document advocated the creation of a Central Coal Board with powers to ensure 'the efficient management of the Industry in the interests of the Nation.'[61] The members of the Board were, however, to be representatives of colliery owners only. Neither the Government, nor miners, nor consumers were to share in the control of the industry.

In a reply to the Foot Plan the N.U.M. quoted with approval the opinion of the *Financial News* 'that Mr. Foot's Plan would not readily appeal to the City', implying that the industry, whilst in private ownership, was unlikely to attract large new capital investment. The Plan was also considered to be faulty in that it failed 'to take cognizance of the bad relations between miners and mine-owners which have developed over many years'.[62]

In the early days of the 1945 Labour Government, the N.U.M. responded to a Government appeal by appointing special officers in each district charged with the task of seeking increased production. Mr. Arthur Horner was seconded to the post of Production Officer at national level and Ald. William Bayliss was similarly seconded as the Nottinghamshire Production Officer.[63] These officers could do little beyond exhortation, but even if they were not very effective their appointment showed goodwill.

By this time it was clear that the mines would be nationalized. This may be one reason, indeed, why the N.U.M. decided to appoint Production Officers. It was widely believed among mining trade unionists that the colliery owners were at best lukewarm in their support of the Government's campaign to maximize output: it could hardly have been supposed that imminent nationalization would make them more kindly disposed towards the Government and its coal control staff.[64]

APPENDIX A

THE NEW HUCKNALL COMPANY IN WARTIME
(*Source:* New Hucknall Balance Sheet Book 5)

	1939 £	1940 £	1941 £	1942 £	1943 £	1944 £
Profits	76,951	53,924	43,510	42,156	61,219	55,690
Plus: Reserves	35,000	35,000	52,000	40,000	63,140	40,000
Plus: National Defence Cont.	5,700	549	—	—	—	—
Plus: Income Tax	47,754	68,990	98,876	80,747	79,642	85,084
Plus: Excess Profits Tax	—	35,157	121,370	38,854	37,650	—

N.B. E.P.T. of £36,766 entered as Revenue and ∴ included in Profit figure above.

1944 BLACKWELL COLLY. CO. LTD.
SUMMARY OF ACCOUNTS

		£
1.	Capital Issued: Ordinary Stock	900,000
2.	Operating Profits	197,263
3.	Net Profits	37,909
	Plus: Depreciation	30,000
	Plus: Provision for Taxation	130,062

N.H. AND B. COMPANY LTD.*

	1945	1946
Profits	£225,486	£431,500
Plus: Provision for Income Tax (est.)	£168,003 N.B. E.P.T. Recoverable (est.) of £185,464 entered as Revenue & ∴ included in profit above	(N.B. includes: Tax Recoverable and overprovided £176,209 and also: Refund from Ministry of Fuel and Power for Plant debited to Revenue 1945 £13,796

* N.H. & B. was an amalgamation of the two firms.

APPENDIX B

NOTTINGHAMSHIRE WAGES DISTRICT—SUMMARY OF RESULTS 1940–1944

	1940	1941	1942	1943	1944
Output (tons)	16,653,667	16,860,485	16,927,499	16,153,266	15,803,785
Proceeds (per ton)	17s. 6'40d.	20s. 3'21d.	21s. 7'87d.	24s. 0'37d.	27s. 7'64d.
Wages (per ton)	10s. 7'44d.	12s. 0'00d.	12s. 7'79d.	12s. 5'64d.	12s. 2'05d.
Pension Fund (per ton)		2'19d.	6'39d.	5'77d.	5'04d.	5'19d.
Allocation Fund (per ton)	0'41d.	0'62d.	0'65d.	0'69d.	0'71d.
Joint Savings (per ton)	2'51d.	2'23d.	2'20d.	2'25d.	2'31d.
Costs (other than Wages) (per ton)	4s. 2'58d.	5s. 0'49d.	6s. 8'91d.	8s. 10'50d.	12s. 9'88d.
Balance (profit) (per ton)	2s. 2'27d.	2s. 5'48d.	1s. 6'55d.	2s. 0'25d.	1s. 11'50d.

Source: Independent Accountants' Joint Report to the Notts. Wages Board dated 31st December 1945.

APPENDIX C

MEN EMPLOYED IN NOTTS. WAGES DISTRICT—1940–1945

	1940	1941	1942	1943	1944	1945
January	41,974	41,101	41,032	41,158	40,798	41,581
February	41,962	40,982	41,010	41,248	40,954	41,546
March	42,152	40,854	41,005	41,189	41,156	41,724
April	42,208	40,866	41,230	41,095	41,416	41,704
May	42,240	40,738	41,052	41,166	41,724	41,739
June	42,407	40,654	41,134	41,089	41,829	41,512
July	42,375	40,628	41,146	40,972	41,930	41,427
August	42,416	40,853	41,203	40,955	41,883	41,016
September	42,170	40,949	41,180	40,787	41,828	40,749
October	42,043	41,071	41,132	40,740	41,651	60,622
November	41,788	41,075	41,263	40,678	41,672	40,706
December	41,603	41,114	41,259	40,763	41,442	

Source: Independent Accountant's Joint Report to the Notts. Wages Board dated 31st December 1945.

APPENDIX D

SUMMARY OF SPECIAL LEVIES, SHOWING THE EXTENT TO WHICH
NOTTINGHAMSHIRE SUBSIDIZED HIGH-COST AREAS DURING THE WAR

Year	Levies (Excluding Timber Levy) £	Amounts recoverable by Notts. collieries £	Excess of Levies over amounts recoverable £
1941	259,447	23,473	235,974
1942	1,492,772	1,086,029	406,743
1943	2,945,980	2,436,037	509,943
1944	4,915,754	3,832,652	1,083,102
1945	7,247,879	4,007,777	3,240,102

N.B. 'Recoverable' amounts are provisional only.
Source: Independent Accountant's Joint Report to the Notts. Wages Board
dated 31st December 1945.

APPENDIX E

ABSENTEEISM 1943–1945

MANSHIFTS LOST EXPRESSED AS A PERCENTAGE OF POSSIBLE MANSHIFTS
IN NOVEMBER OF EACH YEAR

NOTTINGHAMSHIRE WAGES DISTRICT

	Coal face	Total
November 1943	22·40%	17·89%
November 1944	23·00%	18·23%
November 1945	25·38%	20·37%

REFERENCES

1 W. H. B. Court, *Coal (History of the Second World War, United Kingdom Civil Series)*, London, 1951, p. 38.
2 ibid., p. 40.
3 loc. cit.
4 ibid., pp. 41–2.
5 ibid., pp. 114–16 and 119.
6 ibid., p. 109.
7 ibid., pp. 130–131.
8 ibid., p. 140.
9 ibid., p. 144.
10 In addition to Production, Labour and Services Directors the National Board also had a Finance Director who was charged, among other things, with managing the Coal Charges Fund. The National Coal Board included the Vice-Chairmen of the Regional Boards, of whom one was a colliery owner and the other a trade union nominee. (ibid., pp. 206, 209–10, 219.)

11 ibid., pp. 174–5.
12 ibid., pp. 190–2.
13 ibid., pp. 188, 335, 347 and 350.
14 *Minutes of the North Midland Regional Coal Board* (Subsequently cited as *N.M.R.C.B. Minutes*).
15 ibid., 1st February 1943. The Board apparently had it in mind that a zealous Production Director might find difficulty in obtaining employment in the post-war period.
16 W. H. B. Court, op. cit., pp. 240–1.
17 *N.M.R.C.B. Minutes*, 17th Janury 1944, 5th April 1944, 25th April 1944 and 31st July 1944.
18 ibid., 9th November 1942, 15th February and 21st June 1943.
19 ibid., 9th November 1942.
20 This may be a reference to help given to relatives of men killed in the South Normanton explosion of 1937.
21 ibid., 1st November 1943, 15th November 1943 and 17th July 1944.
22 ibid., 6th September 1943.
23 ibid., 17th July 1944 and 21st August 1944.
24 *Reid Report*, p. 12; Court, op. cit., p. 282. T. E. B. Young, *Report on Visit to Coalfields of the U.S.A.*, 1947, pp. 14–16.
25 Court, op. cit., p. 303.
26 *N.M.R.C.B. Minutes* 20th September 1943.
27 Court, op. cit., p. 304.
28 *N.M.R.C.B. Minutes* 15th February 1943.
29 ibid., 7th February 1944.
30 The other being at Ashington—ibid., 22nd May 1944. The Gedling Training officer, J. B. Plummer, subsequently received the B.E.M.
31 ibid., 22nd May 1944.
32 ibid., 9th August 1943 and 26th February 1945.
33 ibid., 9th October 1944.
34 Court, op. cit.. pp. 306 and 308.
35 i.e. the backward-sloping supply curve of labour.
36 Court, op. cit., 244, 246, 315–16.
37 ibid., p. 266.
38 *N.M.R.C.B. Minutes*. 6th November 1944. It must be emphasized that the higher average hourly rate in motor engineering, etc. is due to premium overtime rates.
39 Court, op. cit., passim.
40 Diarrhoea, for example.
41 Some such men were prosecuted—and a few imprisoned—for refusing to do Home Guard duties.
42 Leaflet issued by the Second Front Miners' Organization, Bestwood Colliery, (n.d.). This passage is based on personal knowledge.
43 H. W. Booth. *Wages 1950*, Nottm. (printed for the N.U.M. Notts. Area), 1950, p. 4.
44 Wages Ascertainment—duplicated copy. See also Court, op. cit., p. 221.
45 The cases for the two sides are set out in: *Board of Investigation upon the Immediate Wages Issue in the Coalmining Industry*, London, June 1942.
46 Court, op. cit., pp. 220–2. Griffin, op. cit., II pp. 301–2.
47 Court, op. cit., pp. 223–4.
48 ibid., p. 48.
49 G. A. Spencer, *An Appeal by the N.M.F.U. against the 'Standard Tonnage'*, dated 28th October 1942.
50 loc cit., H. Booth, op. cit., p. 7 and Court op. cit., pp. 225–7.

51 Court, op. cit., pp. 234–5; see also the full constitution of the National Conciliation Scheme.
52 Court, op. cit., pp. 262–5. Booth, op. cit., pp. 7–8. See also Harold Wilson, *New Deal for Coal*, London, 1945, p. 105.
53 For a full discussion, see Court, op. cit., pp. 333–51.
54 G. A. Spencer, op. cit., Appendix 5. See also Griffin, op. cit., pp. 296–303.
55 Court, op. cit., pp. 343 and 346.
56 ibid., pp. 348–9.
57 *H. of C. Debs.* 13th October 1943, Col. 924., cited Court, op. cit., p. 248.
58 Rule 3(r). The 1948 set of Rules also call for the complete abolition of capitalism. (Rule 3s.)
59 A. K. McCosh, *The Case Against Nationalization of the Coal Mines,* Sheffield, 1944.
60 *Coal Mining—Report of the Technical Advisory Committee* (Chairman C. C. Reid) Cmnd 6610, 1945, p. 139.
61 Robert Foot, *A Plan for Coal*, London, 1945, pp. 61–2.
62 E. Edwards, *The Miners Case—An Answer to the Foot Plan*, London, 1945, p. 5.
   H. Wilson, op. cit., deals fully with the various pamphlets put out by the colliery owners in this period.
63 *N.M.R.C.B. Minutes*, 17th September 1945.
64 Cf. H. Wilson, op. cit., p. 122 et seq.

CHAPTER V

Spencerism

1. INTRODUCTION

George Alfred Spencer occupies a prominent place in the demonology of the extreme left.[1] Clearly, a less emotive, a more reasoned, criticism of Spencer and Spencerism is long overdue. What, then, did George Spencer believe? This is the way he put it himself in 1948:

> 'I have always made it a cardinal point of policy to show that by a joint effort with the Management material benefits will result to the worker. It is no exaggeration to say that in Nottinghamshire the employees fully accept this thesis and the consistent and good labour record exemplified as it is by the increasing output per man shift over the years, shows that the theories which I propounded in 1926 and which I acted upon, when put into practice with a co-operative management produces the best possible kind of results, both from a managerial and labour point of view.
>
> 'Once it has been accepted by the men that collaborative effort is justified in their own interests, once, in other words, on the lowest grounds of self-interest they have accepted the provision that better mutual results accrue from collaboration than from dissention (sic), important matters follow. The Owners have a confidence which exists in no other field. . . .
>
> 'In the first instance the Owners felt themselves more prepared to make substantial capital investments in machinery, [owing to] the stable labour relationship which was possible as a result of the new approach.'

He went on to speak of the Nottinghamshire Miners' Pension Fund and the generous Workmen's Compensation settlements which were attributable to 'this beneficial labour relationship'.[2]

Spencer believed, then, that close co-operation between Owners and workpeople was necessary. As he said following the 1926 dispute:

> 'In my view there can be no improvement in the lot of the worker unless and until there is co-operation between the two, but while I am co-operating with the Owners, I shall see to it that the workers get their share of the wealth that the joint efforts create.'[3]

He believed that the wages paid in a particular district necessarily depended on the profitability of that district. He therefore agreed with the system of sharing surplus revenue between labour and capital in agreed proportions district by district. A national minimum wage would either be so low as to be completely unacceptable to districts like Nottinghamshire or so high as to put the poorer districts out of production.[4]

There was nothing new about the views put forward by Spencer in 1926. He had advocated them fairly consistently for twenty years. Spencer was an advocate of arbitration and compromise. In particular, he disliked the idea of using the industrial weapon for political purposes.[5] In opposing a suggestion that strike action should be taken to force the Government to do something to reduce unemployment in 1921, Spencer felt that unemployment was the consequence 'of our own folly at the General Election, and the people will have to learn from experience, a very sad experience of this character'.[6] Political questions should be settled through the ballot box, and not by striking.

On the side of organization, it follows that Spencer preferred a substantial degree of local autonomy. Where wages are negotiated on a district basis, it is at district level that the power lies. The M.F.G.B. was a Federation of autonomous district associations. It had only one full-time officer, its general secretary; districts contributed to the General Fund 1½d. per member per quarter and to the national Political Fund 3d. per member per quarter. During the Financial Year ended 30th June 1925 clerical salaries cost the Federation £671 17s., enough to pay for a clerk, a typist and an office boy at the most.[7] During the first World War, however, the advent of partial Government control of the industry caused a shift in the locus of power from district to national level. This was welcomed by the militants of South Wales and elsewhere who wished to convert the Federation into a centralized industrial union operating within the framework of a nationalized industry where all important issues would be decided at national level.[8] It was this view which Spencer opposed so strongly. For Spencer, the Federation's purpose should be to co-ordinate the activities of the districts, but not to control them. It was in this sense that he wanted an effective Federation.[9] The welfare of Nottinghamshire was his concern, and he believed that national control would result in the subsidization of the poor districts by the profitable ones. This, as we shall see, is at the root of Spencerism.

2. THE ORIGINS OF SPENCERISM

The notion that Spencerism originated in the natural wickedness of George Spencer can satisfy no one except believers in the doctrine of original sin. The origins of Spencerism have to be sought elsewhere. As we have seen, a special relationship developed in the late nine-

teenth century between the Liberal coal-owners of the profitable Leen
Valley Collieries and officials of the N.M.A. One of these officials,
J. G. Hancock, was still in office in 1926.

During the 1926 dispute an arrangement along the lines of the Leen
Valley settlement of 1893 suggested itself to leaders in Nottinghamshire and Derbyshire. Frank Hall of Derbyshire, Varley, Spencer and
Hancock of Nottinghamshire were in favour of a resumption of work
in any area where the pre-stoppage conditions could be obtained.[10]

But the 1893 type of settlement did not commend itself to the
Federation in 1926. The latter dispute was not just about wages and
hours, it was also about national, as opposed to district, negotiations
and minimum wage-rates.

The demand for national negotiations was partly political and partly
economic. Those who advocated it were in favour of mines nationalization which was, indeed, its natural corollary. The various districts
operated under such varying conditions, both physical and competitive,
that a national wages structure could only operate if based upon a
national pooling of revenue, or, at least, the creation of a national
wages fund. The Owners refused to entertain the idea and what the
left-wing had therefore to attempt was to force the Government to
impose a political settlement on the industry to provide, as the M.F.G.B.
Executive said in 1921 'a National Wages Board and a National
Pool'.[11]

The differences in views which developed inside the M.F.G.B. went
even wider than this. Bob Smillie expressed one view when he said:

> 'In the interests of the community, it is vital that after the War, the
> co-operation of all classes, established during the War, should continue,
> and more especially with regard to the relations between employers and
> employed.'

George Harvey, an industrial unionist and a member of the Socialist
Labour Party, in attacking this point of view, said:

> The mineworkers can decide, they can either support Smillie and his
> co-operation of classes idea, or they can pursue the fighting policy of
> Industrial Unionism. . . .
>
> 'Labour is at the cross-roads—it can either co-operate with capital and
> be a National organization of patriots, or—it can manfully fight for its
> Right and line up Internationally for the abolition of Capitalism, which
> would end warfare and the subjection of Labour.'[12]

The first open manifestation of the developing discord between left
and right wings of the N.M.A. was J. G. Hancock's attempt in 1915
supported by Spencer, to form a political fund separate from that of
the M.F.G.B. which was defeated by Herbert Booth's committee of

I.L.P. members.[13] Further to the left Jack Lavin and his S.L.P. branch prepared their followers to expect the worst from men like Spencer, Varley and Hancock.[14] When A. J. Cook began his missionary campaign in the Mansfield area he found that the ground had been well prepared for him.

The activities of the left-wing in the post-war years provoked an inevitable reaction from the right. With the support of the Bolsover Colliery Company and prominent butties, a right-wing organization, which called itself the British Workers' League, advocated non-political trade unionism in the district.[15] Prior to the 1926 Lockout, Spencer and Varley opposed this body[16] which they saw as a challenge to their positions as Labour M.P.'s. One of the spokesmen of the B.W.L., Wilfred Stevenson, made personal attacks on the competence of the N.M.A.'s permanent officials, and offered himself, on the strength of a diploma which he obtained through a Trade Union scholarship to Ruskin College, as a more suitable leader.[17]

At the beginning of the 1926 dispute, the N.M.A. was at a low ebb, its paid-up membership of 27,593 representing less than a half of the labour force of about 56,000.[18] The huge debts accumulated in 1921 had only just been cleared so that there were no strike funds. From the beginning of the dispute, outcropping was being carried on on a commercial scale and men were working at Blidworth, Clipstone and Ollerton. As the dispute wore on the B.W.L. people acted as strike-breakers. Spencer warned the M.F.G.B. Conference on August 16th that, for three weeks, unofficial deputations had been meeting the Owners for the purpose of arriving at an agreement. Varley and Spencer were afraid that the initiative would be taken out of their hands by this breakaway movement.[19]

For Spencer and Varley the situation was slipping completely out of control from late August. Their members were returning to work in increasing numbers without any protection at all. There was no sense in protracting the strike because there was now nothing whatever to gain. On 30th September Spencer was still promising that they would 'endeavour still to be loyal to the Federation', if there was a chance of holding the men.[20] By this time, no less than 70 per cent of the Association's members were working.[21]

The problem which this created for Spencer and his colleagues (who were employed by the Nottinghamshire Miner's Association, and not by the M.F.G.B. as Professor Pollard supposes)[22] is illustrated by the happenings at Digby and New London. Whilst deploring the fact that the bulk of the men had returned to work. Spencer agreed to lead a deputation to the management to try to arrange a return to work without victimization for the (mainly left-wing) militants who had thus far remained loyal to the Federation.[23] Left-wing writers have put

x

the worst possible construction on Spencer's action. Spencer himself felt that he had done the right thing. As he said at the time:

'I don't regret it and I do not plead extenuating circumstances. I believe I did the best day's work in my life for those men, and you can pass your sentence.'

To say that to a Federation Conference required courage of a high order. Spencer had many faults but cowardice, surely, was not one of them.

After his expulsion from the M.F.G.B. Conference, Spencer agreed to lead the embryo union established by the (mainly) Bolsover men.[25]

In joining the breakaway body, Spencer knew that the career which he had hoped for as a labour leader was ruined. Why then did he join? He did so because of the ignominious way in which he was ordered out of the M.F.G.B. Conference. His detestation of Herbert Smith, the Federation President, and A. J. Cook, the Secretary, was, for the moment, pathological in its intensity. By the time that they had realized the wisdom of securing the return of Spencer to his allegiance, he had taken his decision. In future, he would fight the left-wing not from inside the Federation but from outside.

3. THE DEVELOPMENT OF THE SPENCER UNION

The Spencer Union soon received the backing of Havelock Wilson, leader of the National Union of Seamen (N.U.S.). Wilson's Union, for long unrecognized by the employers, entered into an arrangement with them during the world war which developed, in 1920, into the National Maritime Board. In return for virtually compulsory Union membership, the N.U.S. gave a guarantee of peaceful labour relations. It became, in short, a client Union anti-militant in policy and anti-labour in politics.[26]

Now, Wilson backed Spencer financially, and placed paid organizers at his disposal. Meetings were held in various coalfields for the purpose of forming branches of the Spencer Union, and the official journal of the 'Miners' Non-Political Union' was issued from N.U.S. Headquarters. Wilson and Spencer formed a body with the high-sounding title 'The Non-Political Trade Union Movement' with headquarters in the City, but it secured little support outside the mining industry. Spencer was taken up by bodies like the 'Anti-Socialist and Anti-Communist Union' and the Economic League, but he received much less backing from large employers than he and Wilson had expected.[27]

The reason for this is not far to seek. The T.U.C., under the leadership of Walter Citrine and Ernest Bevin, pursued a policy of industrial peace. Right-wing trade union leaders had found the General Strike a shattering experience.[28] On the employers' side there was, equally, a recognition of the potential power of the Trade Union Movement. Recognition disputes, which accounted for 30 per cent of strikes and lockouts even as late as 1923, accounted for less than 3 per cent in the seven years following the General Strike.[29]

At the 1927 Trade Union Congress, the President, George Hicks, inspired by Walter Citrine, suggested an exchange of views between the two sides of industry to see:

'how far, and upon what terms, co-operation is possible in a common endeavour to improve the efficiency of industry and to raise the workers' standard of life.'

This met with a favourable and speedy response from a group of employers led by Sir Alfred Mond (Later Lord Melchett) and a joint committee was established. The left-wing equated 'Mondism' with Spencerism. A. J. Cook alleged that Mondism involved the segregation of industrial and political activities which meant 'using your industrial machinery to re-establish capitalism on sound lines, stabilizing it'.[30] Horner, speaking in the same debate, said that rationalization produced massive unemployment and that its aim was to save capitalism by reducing labour costs still further. He equated this, as did George Spencer himself, with Spencerism.[31]

The Spencer Union was an anachronism, called into existence to meet the type of industrial unrest which culminated in the General Strike. The role which Spencer wished to play was played quite successfully by the T.U.C. General Council in the period which followed the General Strike. Peace within industry, rationalization, and the segregation of industrial from political activities provided a platform for Citrine and Bevin as well as for Spencer. Only within the mining industry was Spencer felt to have any special appeal; and only in Nottinghamshire did he have any lasting success.

It may be asked why it was that the Spencer Union thrived in Nottinghamshire and not elsewhere. The colliery owners in other districts certainly encouraged it,[32] some of them very actively, but with little success. In May 1928 a ballot vote organized by the T.U.C. among Nottinghamshire miners produced a vote of 32,277 men in favour of representation by the N.M.A. against 2,533 votes for the Industrial Union. But the N.M.A. had only 15,740 members. The others stayed outside.

It is true that victimization is partly to blame. At some collieries, to be known as a member of the N.M.A. was to invite dismissal despite an undertaking to the contrary given by the Coal-owners in 1928.[33]

However, having made all due allowance for victimization there was still a lack of resolution among the men. Even at collieries belonging to

James Oakes, who was favourably disposed to the N.M.A., the membership of the Association was deplorably low. Comparing January 1926 with January 1931 the membership was down from 728 to 330 at Pye Hill; from 435 to 140 at Cotes Park and from 450 to 170 at New Selston all belonging to James Oakes. At Kirkby, with its large proportion of migrants from South Wales, on the other hand, membership remained high with 2,000 in 1931 against 2,687 in 1926 despite the Butterley Company's opposition to the N.M.A. It was clear to men like Herbert Booth that the temper of the men generally ruled out the possibility of forcing the owners to abandon Spencer. Cook also had the sense to see this and he tried hard to bring about a fusion of the N.M.A. and the Industrial Union during the tenure of office of the second Labour Government, but the move was frustrated by the left-wing militants of the N.M.A. who would have no truck with Spencer.[34]

Spencer's membership did not grow as he had hoped. At some collieries, men were told that they must join the Industrial Union and some who refused to do so were dismissed. But in the main, the men pleased themselves whether they joined or not, and most of them preferred not to do so. The fact is, that Spencer was unpopular. Those who were victimized in some way on account of their opposition to the Industrial Union naturally detested him and his Union, but the present writer has met others who returned to work notoriously early in 1926 but who have been loud in their condemnation of Spencer ever since. Many, again, disliked Spencer because some of his local followers were dishonest and others were sycophants.

It is clear that, had the men at other collieries been as resolute as those at Kirkby, the Industrial Union could have been crushed before long, but most even of the N.M.A. members, let alone the non-unionists, were unprepared for further struggles. They had had enough of fighting. And so the Spencer Union continued without serious opposition for ten years.

4. THE END OF THE SPENCER UNION

The leaders of the N.M.A. were determined to secure recognition for their organization in place of the Industrial Union. However, whilst Herbert Booth saw the need to fuse with the Industrial Union, William Bayliss refused to have any dealings with Spencer at all. The Communists supported Bayliss, but it is wrong to see this as a dispute between left and right since Booth was himself a left-wing Socialist.

Booth heartily disliked Spencer, but unlike some, he did not see him as the personification of evil. Further, he was not afraid of Spencer. He had battled with Spencer inside the Association before, and was quite prepared to do so again. He also believed that some of the Spencer people were decent trade unionists at heart and would make loyal members once the old divisions were ended.

In 1935 the M.F.G.B. became seized once more of the necessity for finding a solution to the problem of non-recognition in Nottinghamshire. Accordingly, on 2nd February 1935 (when the membership of the N.M.A. was down to 8,500) the Executive Committee met the N.M.A. Council and made it clear that in its view a settlement could only be reached after negotiations with Spencer.

Nationally, a Joint Standing Consultative Committee came into existence at the beginning of 1936.[35] Evan Williams, the President of the Mining Association, indicated that his organization would like to bring the Nottinghamshire Owners on to the Joint Committee and the M.F.G.B. therefore made it clear to him that his organization was expected to arrange a meeting between the M.F.G.B. and Spencer aimed at the latter's eventual elimination.[36]

Unfortunately, the situation was complicated by a dispute at the Harworth Colliery of the Barber, Walker Company in which Union recognition became the main issue. The men at Harworth had, if anything, been more apathetic than the men in other new mining villages, and at the beginning of 1935 there were only seven members of the N.M.A. employed there out of a total labour force of 2,285.[37] One possible reason for this apathy was a high turnover of labour. The Harworth men were also much better paid than men at nearby South Yorkshire mines.

The economic basis of the Dispute, of which most commentators seem to be unaware, was a dirt deduction agreement negotiated by the Industrial Union. The tonnage prices were increased to take account of the high deduction for dirt, but this was extremely difficult to explain and according to Herbert Booth Spencer had to go to the Harworth Branch twice a year to try to convince the incoming North-countrymen that the arrangement was fair.[38]

During 1935 the membership of the N.M.A. at Harworth increased to 157 and a new branch was formed. Six months later this number had almost doubled (to 302) but the people responsible for re-starting the Branch had been voted out in favour of ultra left-wing militants. The President and General Secretary of the N.M.A. were particularly astounded at the defeat of J. Pickering, the President of the Branch who was ousted by Mick Kane, a member of the Communist Party.[39] By 29th August 1936 when the new Branch officials decided to seek recognition of their status from the colliery manager, they still had less than one-sixth of the men in membership with them; and not a majority as some left-wing writers claim.[40] Following a one-day strike on 2nd September, twenty-five N.M.A. members were dismissed. Later there was a strike by pieceworkers over the dirt deduction agreement, and the Company then announced that all the men who were not at work were considered to be in breach of contract and would only be re-engaged if they agreed to join the Industrial Union.[41]

Meantime, on 4th November, a ballot conducted by the M.F.G.B. to determine which Union the men wanted to represent them had resulted in an overwhelming vote for the N.M.A.—1,175 to 145 for the Industrial Union. That the Industrial Union received any votes at all, though, is surprising since Spencer had instructed his members that they were not to take part.[42] On 11th December the M.F.G.B. Executive advised the men still working at Harworth to give notice to terminate their employment, and this brought the number of men drawing strike pay up to 1,060, all of whom automatically became members of the N.M.A. if they were not already in.

On the other side, according to Spencer and the coal-owners, the number of men at work on any one day numbered 600 to 900 for the three shifts, later increasing to 1,100.[43]

The intensity of the dispute at Harworth gave a sense of urgency to the campaign for recognition of the N.M.A. throughout Nottinghamshire. A majority of the N.M.A.'s active members were still reluctant to negotiate with Spencer; and neither Spencer nor the Nottinghamshire Owners for their part entered into discussions with any show of enthusiasm. Much pressure was put on the parties by the Mines Department, who were anxious to avoid a national strike of miners in support of the N.M.A.'s demand for recognition. When the two sides were brought together at the Mines Department, Spencer insisted upon the adoption of certain basic principles involving a continuation of the existing Wages Agreement in the county for five years; a pledge that Nottinghamshire should be immune from strikes during the currency of the agreement; and that the rules of the amalgamated body should provide that political business could only be transacted at specially convened political meetings. In other words, he was not prepared to modify his principles or policies: the end of the Spencer Union would leave Spencerism intact.

Eventually, on 28th May, the fusion of the N.M.A. and the Industrial Union was approved by a special conference of the M.F.G.B.[44] It was to be carried through, despite an adverse ballot vote among the membership of the M.F.G.B., on Spencer's terms.

5. A NEW DISPENSATION

The Nottinghamshire and District Miners' Federated Union came into existence officially on 1st September 1937.[45] The appointment of its first permanent officials was provided for in its Rules as follows:

President:	G. A. Spencer	(N.M.I.U.)
General Secretary:	Val Coleman	(N.M.A.)
Financial Secretary:	Horace Cooper	(N.M.I.U.)
Agent:	Herbert Booth	(N.M.I.U.)
	William Bayliss	(N.M.A.)

Spencer ruled the Federated body, just as he had done the Industrial Union, not merely because of the power which his official position gave him, but also because he was by nature an effective leader. In comparison, Coleman and Cooper were pedestrian: only the subordinate officials Booth and Bayliss were anywhere near as able as Spencer. And whilst they had much local negotiating to do—this was their chief responsibility and it took them out of the Office a great deal—Spencer did not take part in pit negotiations at all. He handled the main district negotiations; he represented the County on national bodies; he settled constitutional questions; and he assumed responsibility for complicated workmen's compensation questions on which he was recognized as an expert.

Of one innovation Spencer was deservedly proud: this was a pension scheme financed out of the proceeds of the district ('out of the ascertainment').[46] Before long, the old argument inside the Federation between those who wanted a unified national organization, with a pooling of wages designed to subsidise the poorer districts by the richer; and Spencer, who wanted to retain local autonomy and district agreements, was resumed. During the Second World War, as during the first, national wage negotiations were superimposed on district negotiations. At each stage, Spencer protested.[47] Early in 1943, a Joint National Negotiating Committee for the industry was established, and George Spencer, its strongest critic, became one of its members. Next, left-wing members of the Federation urged upon their colleagues the necessity of converting their loose Federation into a strongly centralized body.[48] Spencer conducted a campaign inside Nottinghamshire against the formation of a National Union. He warned his members that they would lose by it financially, but few of them took much notice.

The decision to form a National Union of Mineworkers was taken—subject to confirmation—at a Conference held in Nottingham where Spencer's was the only voice raised in opposition.[49] Thereafter, he continued to campaign against the formation of the N.U.M. but he realized that he would be defeated. In the event, of 24,001 men voting in Nottinghamshire, only 2,836 opposed the formation of the N.U.M. and when the new Union came into existence on 1st January 1945 Spencer and Coleman had to go into retirement since they were over 65 years of age.[50]

Among the objects of the new Union were several to which Spencer took particular objection, including:

'To seek the establishment of Public ownership and Control of the mining industry' (Rule 3 (r))
'To negotiate a National Wages Agreement with a national ascertainment covering the whole of the British Coalfield.' (Rule 3 (t))

Even in retirement, Spencer continued to complain that the Nottinghamshire miner was subsidizing miners in other districts. Thus, in 1948: 'I do not exaggerate when I say that if the Nottinghamshire miner was today working on his own arrangement with the owners and not subsidizing less efficient or less fortunate fields, every workman in Nottinghamshire would be getting 40s. to 50s. a week more in wages.'[51]

Spencer's final blast was an article written in February 1950.[52] Thereafter, ill-health silenced him.

6. CONCLUSION

No study of Spencerism would be complete without a brief assessment of the character of Spencer.

Spencer was born into a mining family. He was the second of eighteen children and in his early years endured a grinding poverty. As a young man, he was a Wesleyan Methodist local preacher and he became interested in trade union and labour affairs. He took care to dress carefully and was looked upon as a very respectable, serious-minded, young man. He also became pompous and not a little conceited. Unlike most young colliers, he was abstemious (although his father kept a public house at one time). Instead, he did his best to educate himself, buying and reading books (Kropotkin was one of his early heroes) attending W.E.A. classes and saving money. Saving money, indeed, became something of an obsession with him as with many Puritans: in a word, he was inclined to be mean.

The Sutton district in which Spencer worked had lower wage-rates and less favourable conditions of employment than the Leen Valley. Spencer resented this on his own behalf, and decided that one way of advancing himself would be to campaign for higher wages for the Erewash Valley collieries. He was convinced that the officials of the N.M.A., being Leen Valley men, were not sufficiently concerned with the problems of their lower paid members. To try to correct this state of affairs was not merely the right thing to do; but it was also a popular thing to do.

Spencer joined the I.L.P., but he did not allow his political interest to deflect him from his immediate purpose, which was to achieve paid office in the Union. He was elected checkweighman at New Hucknall, then became President of the N.M.A., a spare-time office but one which became increasingly important during his occupancy of it.

Spencer sought a gradual improvement in the standards of living of his people, not a change in the whole order of society. He wanted miners to be respectable in appearance—cloth caps and mufflers were anathema to him—orderly in manner; conscientious in their work. He wanted them to enjoy better housing and welfare facilities; security of work and security in old age. And he wanted their children to have improved educational facilities. In all this, Spencer was in no way remarkable. He was, like many trade union officials, a reformer not a revolutionary. He felt a profound distaste for the violent language of left-wing leaders who, in return, regarded him as the worst type of careerist trade union official.

A careerist Spencer certainly was. He saw himself as a future cabinet minister in a Labour Government. Even after the breakaway he had hopes of being supported by moderate members of his Party, and of being rehabilitated. However, once he had accepted the 'non-political' label this was virtually ruled out. Spencer did re-join the Labour Party (as an affiliated member) in 1937, and some of his ex-members became quite active in the Party, but for him there was then no way back; and indeed, he eventually became a close friend and confidant of Sir Waldron Smithers who, as M.P. for Orpington, was something of a Whig. After the breakaway, Spencer became more of an autocrat than ever. The people who surrounded him were little more than puppets. Hancock he took with him as Treasurer because he could not trust his friends, some of whom were personally dishonest.

Spencer was always something of a cheat: to oppose him at cards was a hazardous occupation. He liked to gamble, but not to lose. He cultivated people who could give him useful stock exchange information, and his investments thereby prospered. Spencer always had his eye on the main chance; but he never regarded the pursuit of his own interests as being inimical to the interests of his members. His desire to win at every game he played applied to negotiations with the Owners and he did not always play fair even with them.[53]

Spencer had many faults; but he was not afraid to express his opinions frankly and fearlessly; he could use cunning as well as intelligence in trying to get the better of someone, and yet he could be helpful and sympathetic. He was a queer mixture of a man. He could express intense dislike of one man, (e.g. Herbert Smith) and admiration for another who had opposed him just as strongly (e.g. Arthur Horner).[54]

To suppose, as some have, that he was driven solely by selfish motives is without warrant. The turning point in Spencer's career was the New London settlement. Here, there is no doubt that he did what he thought was right. He was immediately accused of treachery and cowardice. The rest of his life was to be coloured by his treatment on that occasion, and not least by the fact that some of the men he had helped subsequently repudiated him.

Horner and Cook on one side and Spencer himself on the other saw Spencerism as no more than a special case of Mondism. Spencer himself had much the same outlook, philosophy and ambition as many another right-wing leader of labour. It is at least likely that had a J. R. Clynes or a C. T. Cramp been faced with the same situation as Spencer, he would have acted much as Spencer did. Had the move towards fusion in 1930–31 been successful Spencer could have played his part in the M.F.G.B. and in the wider trade union movement without modifying his policies at all save in one respect: he would have had to agree to the discussion of political matters at political meetings of the Union. This indeed, was exactly the position in 1937 when fusion was achieved. The Spencer Agreement providing for compulsory arbitration instead of strikes as the last stage of conciliation; the Spencer insistence on the importance of establishing good relations with the employers so as to maximise profitability as a prior condition of enhanced wages; the Spencer insistence on the importance of pension schemes, holiday savings, and things of that sort; the segregation of political from industrial matters, all these were unaffected by fusion. Spencer continued, but from inside the Federation instead of outside, to advocate district settlements and the importance of retaining local autonomy.

Even after nationalization, the Nottinghamshire area of the N.U.M. continued to pursue policies derived from the Spencer philosophy. A recent case illustrates this. In 1966 the N.C.B. and the N.U.M. decided that coal face mechanization had reached a stage where 'it is the machine . . . in the main that determines the amount of production that comes from a coal face' and that the old incentive systems of payment should therefore be replaced, on power loader faces, by a day-wage system. Mr. W. Paynter, General Secretary, in explaining the proposal to the N.U.M. Conference went on to say:

> 'The second important principle that is embodied in these proposals is that we are moving in relation to face workers towards the realization of a national uniform rate for the job.'[56]

Like his predecessors, A. J. Cook and Arthur Horner, Paynter comes from South Wales and, as in the past, opposition to the proposed national agreement came from Nottinghamshire.

The main speech in opposition to the agreement was made by Mr. Joe Whelan who pointed out that many Nottinghamshire miners would suffer a steep reduction in earnings. He continued:

'It is true to say that we accept that the principle of a set wage or a guaranteed rate is a desirable thing, and we accept that this offers some advance for some of our craftsmen—we are not disputing that—but even then we have got justifiable reasons to feel that it is at the expense of our pieceworkers in the Notts. coalfield.'

Later, he said:

'We do respect, Mr. Chairman, the efforts of the National Executive Committee, to resolve a difficult problem. We accept that there are areas who are going to gain from this agreement, and naturally they will want to accept this draft. I hope that the Conference will accept that our reasons, which I have quoted are valid reasons for our opposition to it.'[57]

Mr. Whelan was attacked by Mr. E. Allison of Derbyshire who alleged that: 'Every word he has said has emphasized pure selfishness.'[58] Whelan was supported by his colleague Mr. Bernard Savage (of the Blidworth Branch) who said:

'We shall probably not only vote against this this morning, but we shall probably actively resist its implementation on the basis of the fact of the feeling of the men in the coalfield.'[59]

Spencerism is, at bottom, an appeal to self interest. Miners' leaders, and miners themselves, have demonstrated that Spencer had no monopoly of whatever personal characteristics are required to pursue this end.[60]

REFERENCES

1 See, e.g., Arnot, op. cit., II, pp. 537–8. (where Spencerism is equated with Fascism). J. E. Williams, letter in *Society for the Study of Labour History Bulletin*, No. 5, Autumn, 1962, p. 51. (where Spencer is described as a scoundrel); and *Economic History Review*, Vol. XV, No. 3, April 1963, p. 564. (where Professor S. Pollard called Spencer a coward, which he manifestly was not.)

2 *Draft proof of 29th July 1948.*

3 ibid.

4 See, for example, Griffin, op. cit., II, pp. 125, 291–2.

5 Except for a very brief period following the 1914–18 war when militancy was fashionable—see *M.F.G.B. Minute Book*, 1919, p. 378 and Griffin, op. cit., II, p. 41.

6 *M.F.G.B. Minute Book*, 1921, p. 83, cited Griffin, op. cit., pp. 105–6. See also ibid., p. 125.

7 *M.F.G.B. Minute Book*, 1925, p. 607.

8 The syndicalist view is clearly expressed in G. Harvey, *Industrial Unionism and the Mining Industry*, Pelaw-on-Tyne, 1917.

9 *M.F.G.B. Minute Book*, 1944, p. 546. Griffin, op. cit., II, pp. 291–305.

10 See e.g., *M.F.G.B. Minute Book*, 1926, pp. 635–6. Dr. Williams (op. cit., p. 709. insists that Frank Hall 'stood loyally by the Federation's policy in all

his public utterances'; but see the *Nottingham Journal*, 29th May 1926, where Hall is reported as suggesting a settlement like the Leen Valley Settlement of 1893.

11   Those three collieries were Clipstone, Blidworth and Ollerton.

12   Harvey, op. cit., pp. 207–8. Cf. Griffin, op. cit., II, pp .114–6.

13   *N.M.A. Minute Book*, 30th January 1915, cited Griffin, op. cit., II, p. 22.

14   Griffin, op. cit., II, pp. 38–9, 116, 239.

15   Griffin, op. cit., II, pp. 116–7; J. E. Williams, op. cit., pp. 547, 631, 676 and 736.

16   *Derbyshire Times*, 19th May 1923. cited J. E. Williams, op. cit., p. 677; Griffin, op. cit., II, p. 117.

17   Herbert Booth is my main informant. Stevenson eventually made himself so unpopular that he had to leave Nottinghamshire, when the Grassmoor Company, Derbyshire, found him employment.

18   *N.M.A. Minute Book*; Accounts for 1920 and 1926.

19   *M.F.G.B. Minute Book*, 1926, pp. 666–7.

20   *M.F.G.B. Minute Book*, 1926, pp. 838–9.

21   *N.M.A. Minute Book*, 1st October 1926.

22   Art. cit., p. 564.

23   *M.F.G.B. Minute Book*, 1926, pp. 855–8 and 896–905.

24   S. Pollard, (*Ec.H.R.*, art. cit., p. 564) alleges cowardice.

25   Draft proof of 29th July 1948.

26   F. Taylor, *Havelock Wilson* (unpublished paper, c. 1958) W. Citrine, *The Truth about the Miners' Ballot*, (reprint of a speech at Kirkby on 28th May 1928) and Griffin, op. cit., II, pp. 221–3.

27   Griffin, op. cit., II. pp. 228–9.

28   E. Burns, *The General Strike. May 1926: Trades Councils in Action*, London (Labour Research Dept.) 1926, p. 7, A. Hutt. *British Trade Unionism*, London, 1945, p. 113, and Kingsley Martin, 'The General Strike', *Encyclopaedia of the Labour Movement*, London, c. 1927, II, pp. 26–7.

29   F. Williams, *Magnificent Journey: The Rise of the Trade Unions*, London, 1954. pp. 400–401.

30   *M.F.G.B. Minute Book*, 1927–8, p. 1,003. The whole of this speech is interesting.

31   ibid., p. 999 and *Derbyshire Times*, 28th April 1928, cited J. E. Williams, op. cit., pp. 740–1.

32   Especially in South Wales. *M.F.G.B. Minute Book*, 1927–8, pp. 1,004–6. J. E. Williams, op. cit., pp. 739–41. A. Horner, *Incorrigible Rebel*, London, 1960, pp. 130, et seq. The secretary of the Spencer Union in South Wales was William Gregory, formerly employed at Raglan Colliery where the first branch was formed. From there, Spencerism spread to Bedwas and then to many other collieries. The Industrial Union in South Wales was much more of a 'Company' union than the N.M.I.U. It was not finally liquidated until 1938 when its members were absorbed by the South Wales Miners' Federation.

33   *M.F.G.B. Minute Book*, 1935, p. 13.

34   Griffin, op. cit., II, pp. 246–7.

35   *M.F.G.B. Minute Book*, 1935, pp. 19 and 43.

36   *M.F.G.B. Minute Book*, 1936, p. 30.

37   Membership figures are from the *N.M.A. Minute Book*, and men employed are from a document prepared for Spencer by the Barber Walker Company. Whitelock (op. cit., p. 181) gives the labour force as 2,200 in 1936.

38   The Harworth Dirt Deduction Agreement was probably a bad bargain anyway. Herbert Booth secured its annulment in 1937.

39 *N.M.A. Minute Book*, 27th June 1936 and conversations with Val Coleman and Herbert Booth.

40 E.g. R. Page Arnot (op. cit., III, pp. 205–6) and J. E. Williams (op. cit., p. 764). There were then 356 members. Page Arnot's account is, indeed, full of inaccuracies. Here are a few of them:

On p. 200 he describes Spencer as 'President at first of the Nottingham "non political union" ' an office which Spencer never held. He also says that Spencer was expelled from the M.F.G.B. Conference in 1926 'on the order of the delegates acting unanimously' whereas the motion was carried by 759 to four, with some abstentions.

On p. 201 he implies without warrant that Varley opposed Spencer's Union merely because of his personal dislike of Spencer. On p. 208 he says, of a ballot at Harworth in which 1,320 men voted that: 'As far as the M.F.G.B. Chairman could calculate, 88 per cent of the men employed took part in the ballot.' In fact, 1,320 represents only 60 per cent of the labour force.

41 The pieceworkers tried to dismiss their checkweighman, but did not comply with the legal requirements.

42 This materially affects the validity of Dr. Williams' argument which implies that 145 votes fairly reflected the strength of the Industrial Union at Harworth—see *Society for the Study of Labour History Bulletin*, No. 5, Autumn 1962, p. 51 (final paragraph).

43 There were 665 at work on 14th December (N.M.I.U. Statement of 3rd February 1937), 900 on 18th January 1937 (letter from Spencer to the Press of 18th January 1937), and 1,100 in April 1937 (Press statement by Notts. coal-owners of 9th April 1937). According to the Colliery Manager (in a letter to the N.M.I.U. dated 4th March 1937) there were 1,147 men-on-books at that date. The following table gives the men-on-books position prior to 14th December 1936:

HARWORTH COLLIERY—NUMBER OF MEN ON BOOKS

Week-ending 1936	Surface	Underground	Total
Oct. 3	395	1,787	2,182
Oct. 10	395	1,772	2,167
Oct. 17	393	1,739	2,132
Oct. 24	394	1,730	2,124
Oct. 31	393	1,695	2,088
Nov. 7	393	1,691	2,084
Nov. 14	395	1,691	2,086
Nov. 21	391	964	1,355
Nov. 28	391	980	1,371
Dec. 5	391	992	1,393
Dec. 12	391	972	1,363

Source: G. A. Spencer's files.

(N.B. The names of men who had tendered strike notices would be taken off books when their notices expired).

44 *M.F.G.B. Conference Report*, 1937, p. 365.

45 Griffin, op. cit., II, pp. 275–6.

46 The principles of this will be understood by reference to the document at Griffin, op. cit., II, pp. 284–6.

47 See, e.g. *M.F.G.B. Special Conference Report* (May 8th 1941) pp. 48–9. For the debate between Spencer and the left during the Second World War, reference may also be made to the following:
M.F.G.B. Annual Conference Report, (15th July 1940), pp. 73–81.

M.F.G.B. *Special Conference Report*, (8th May 1941), pp. 4, 47–9, 61, 64–74.

M.F.G.B. *Annual Conference Report*, (14th July 1941, pp. 107–35.

See also M.F.G.B. *Minute Book*, 1939, pp. 237–240; 404–437.

M.F.G.B. *Minute Book*, 1943, pp. 67–82, 116, 174–5, 387–402.

These are summarized in Griffin, op. cit., II, pp. 290–304.

48 See, e.g. M.F.G.B. *Minute Book*, 1943, p. 39.

49 M.F.G.B. *Minute Book*, 1944, pp. 467, et seq.

50 N.M.F.U. *Minute Book*, 1944. They were compensated for loss of office.

51 *Draft proof of 29th July, 1948*.

52 This deals, among other things, with the subsidization of other coalfields by Nottinghamshire.

53 Griffin, op. cit., II, pp. 286–8, pp. 251–2.

54 In later life, Spencer and Horner seem to have got on very well.

55 *Report of N.U.M. Special Conference held Friday 15th April 1966*, p. 7. (speech of W. Paynter.)

56 ibid.

57 ibid., p. 35.

58 ibid., p. 36. Mr. Whelan's understandable retort was: 'If he wants to insult me, he can do it outside.'

59 ibid., p. 44. Paynter, Whelan and Savage were all members of the Communist Party at this time.

60 As evidenced by the widening earnings gap between the lower paid day wagemen, (whose wages were fixed nationally) and the highly paid piece-workers (whose rates were negotiated locally) in the period preceding the introduction of the National Power Loading Agreement. See, in particular, Notts. arbitration award dated 21st May 1962; N.U.M. Special Conference Report, (10th October 1958,) esp. pp. 8–9; and 1962 letter from Mr. W. Paynter to branches of the N.U.M. calling attention to the widening gap: 'It is not in the interests of the Union that this should continue uncontrolled, and the National Executive Committee therefore urge Areas and Branches to keep this in mind when dealing with piecework contracts.'

BIBLIOGRAPHY

1. Primary Sources (Manuscript including Plans)

Blackwell Collieries—*Notices to Workmen Book.**

J. Boot, *Report on the Dunsil Ancient Workings in the Parish of Teversal*, dated 14th December 1869. (N.C.B.)*

Butterley Co's. Sales and Output Book. Butterley Co's. Archives.

Butterley Statistical Survey, 1856. Butterley Co's. Archives.

H. W. Booth: Letters to A. R. Griffin.*

Chatsworth Estate Plans.*

Denby Drury Lowe correspondence book, 1884–7.*

Eastwood Central Committee, Minute Book, (Mr. A. A. Booth).

Edge Manuscripts, (Notts. County Archives).

Ellis—Bailey correspondence, (1895) (Mr. Albert Bailey).

Harpur Hill Mine Plans, (N.C.B.).

J. Haslam and others, *A Logue Book of Miners and Mining Information* (Ilkeston Public Library).

New Hucknall Colliery Co. Ltd., Balance Sheet Books and Journals, (now in Notts. County Archives).

New Hucknall Colliery Co. Ltd., Annesley Colliery, Cost Accounts Book for 1920–6.*

New Hucknall Colliery Co. Ltd., Fenwick-Day correspondence.

New Hucknall Colliery Co. Ltd., Letters from P. Muschamp (Chief Agent New Hucknall Co.) to Waplington (Manager, Annesley Colly.) 19th May 1925 and 9th September 1925 and Waplington's reply of 15th September 1925.*

New Hucknall Colliery Co. Ltd., *Hucknall Colly. (Huthwaite) Plans* (N.C.B.).

Memoranda of Agreements between J. F. Thirlby and Peter Howard and Crompton Evans Union Bank, 18 May 1898 and 30 June 1902.*

Nottm. Trades Council Minute Books.

Notts. Miners' Association *Minute Book* (later ones printed).

Notts. Miners' Industrial Union, Minute Book 1926–7.*

Selston Enclosure Commission Report, 1819.

Skegby Colliery Account Book of John Dodsley for 1847–8. (Sutton-in-Ashfield Library).

Sleights and Langton Colliery Map, 1869.*

South Normanton Colliery Correspondence Books, various dates.*

South Normanton Colly. Co. Ltd., *Annual Reports and Accounts*, 1892–1904.*

Sutton Colly. Co.: Report of Manager, James Wroe, to Directors dated 16th May 1896.*

Sutton Colly. Co.: Revenue Account for 1896 (Year ending 31st December.)*

Rev. F. V. Walker: Letters to A. R. Griffin and Miss Walvin.*

Various papers, (some manuscript and some typed) of G. A. Spencer and O. B. Lewis and odd note books of Val. Coleman and Job Smith (of the Pinxton Colly. Co.).*

Miners' Bond of 1848 (see illustration).*

Miscellaneous notes of Colliery Owners' meetings, together with correspondence.

2. *Primary Sources, typescript*

Pinxton Pottery Account Book (typewritten abstract) 1795.*

Pinxton Tithe Apportionment Register, 1839 (typed copy).*

Indenture dated 15th October 1880 between William Gregory Dawkins and Stanton Ironworks Co. Ltd., regarding sale of land at Stanton Hill (typewritten copy).*

Agreement between N.M.A., Derbys. Miners' Asscn. and National Asscn. of Colly. Deputies, 1918.*

Letter from E. C. Fowler of the Babbington Coal Company to J. S. Hancock of the N.M.A. dated 12th March 1920.*

Letter from Digby Colly. Co. Ltd. to F. B. Varley 18 May 1925 (with enclosure).*

Reports of G. Burlinson to Digby Colliery Company on the negotiations between the colliery owners and Spencer, 1926.*

G. P. Hyslop and H. W. Naish, *Report on Linby and Pinxton Merger Proposals*, 1936.*

P. F. Day, *Report on Linby Colliery to Directors of Pinxton Colliery Co.*, October 1936.*

M.A.D. Scheme—Notts. and Derby Section, Minutes, 1939.*

B. A. Collieries, Ltd.—Report of Labour Dept. 28th March 1940.*

G. A. Spencer, An Appeal by the N.M.F.U. against the *Standard Tonnage*, 28th October 1942.*

North Midland Regional Coal Board, Minutes, 1942–6.*

G. A. Spencer, Draft proof of 29th July 1948.*

Miscellaneous papers (some manuscript, some typewritten) from G. A. Spencer, O. B. Lewis and others including, for example, documents relating to the Bestwood Checkweigh Dispute of the 1930's.*

3. *Primary Sources, printed: Royal Commissions, Etc.*

Children's Employment Commission (Mines) 1842.

Reports of H.M. Inspectors of Mines and Secretary for Mines; various dates from 1851.

The 1851 Census, Ages, Civil Condition and Occupations, London, 1854.

Royal Commission on Trade Unions, 1867–9.

Royal Commission on Coal, 1871.

Select Committee on the Causes of the Present Scarcity and Dearness of Coal, 1873.

Royal Commission on Accidents in Coal Mines, 1881.

The 1891 Census, *Area, Houses and Population*, London 1893.

Coal Industry Commission (Sankey) 1919.

Court of Inquiry Concerning the Wage Position in the Coal Mining Industry (Buckmaster) 1924.

Court of Inquiry Concerning the Coal Mining Industry Dispute (Macmillan) 1925.

Royal Commission on the Coal Industry (Samuel) 1925.

Board of Investigation upon the Immediate Wages Issue in the Coalmining Industry (Greene) 1942.

Coal Mining—Report of the Technical Advisory Committee (the Reid Report) 1945.

Coal Mines Acts, various dates, (see References).

N.B. In addition, the author has made use of the 1851 Census Enumerators' Returns (Manuscript) of which there is a microfilm copy in the Nottingham City Reference Library.

4. *Primary Sources, printed—Wages Agreements and Awards.*

Joint District Board for Nottinghamshire, 1912, Minutes and Award (also amended Award of 1928).

Mackenzie Award 9th December 1916.*

Agreement Concerning all Seams Other than Top Hard (Notts.) 8th May 1922.*

Stoker Awards (Notts.) 5th September 1918 and 16th June 1920.*

H. W. Booth, *Wages in the Nottinghamshire Coalfield, 1916 to 1949*, Nottm. 1950.*

Bestwood Dirt Agreement, 1930.*

Greene Award, 1942.*

Five-Day Week Agreement 18th April 1947 (National).

N.C.B.: *Revision of the Wages Structure Handbook* 1955 (with subsequent amendments).

Nottinghamshire Power Loader Agreement, 19th August 1957.*

Colliery Price Lists (various).*

5. *Other Primary Sources, printed.*

T. Bailey, *Annals of Nottinghamshire*, London, 1855.*

T. Bulmer and Co., *History, Topography and Directory of Derbyshire*, Preston, 1895.

Catalogues of Plans of Abandoned Mines, London (H.M.S.O.).

Major John Talbot Coke and Others to the Pinxton Coal Co. Ltd., Conveyances and Assignments of Freehold and Leasehold Properties in the Counties of Nottm. & Derby, Wigan 1901.*

Derbyshire & Notts. Dist. Collieries Commercial Association—Deed of Constitution and Trust Deed (including Rules of the Central Collieries Commercial Association) Leeds, 31st March 1928.*

D.S.I.R., *The Concealed Coalfield of Yorkshire and Nottinghamshire*, London, 1951.

Federated District Conciliation Board and Conferences: Minutes.*

Wm. Harrison, 'Description of England', *Life in Shakespeare's England* (ed. J. D. Wilson) Harmondsworth, 1944.*

Hist. Manuscripts Commission Report on the Manuscripts of Lord Middleton, London (Cmd. 5567, 1911).

K. Tweedale Meaby, *Extracts from the County Records of the Eighteenth Century*, Nottm. 1947.*

Midland (Amalgamated) District Coal Mines Scheme (1930) Rules (approved 29th October 1930 and subsequent amendments at various dates to 1940).

Midland Counties Colly. Owners' Association, *Rules*, 8th July 1914.*

Mines Dept., *Annual Statistical Summary for 1936*, London 1937.*

Miners' Federation of Great Britain: Minutes. (Minute Books contain verbatim reports of conferences; E.C. Minutes, Govt. Reports, etc.).*

Ministry of Fuel and Power, *Statistical Digest 1951*, London, 1952.*

C. Morris (Ed.) *The Journeys of Celia Finnes*, London, 1947.

Fynes Moryson, 'Itinerary', 1617, *Life in Shakespeare's England* (ed. J. D. Wilson) Harmondsworth, 1944.*

National Union of Mineworkers, Rules.*

North Midland Coalfield Regional Survey Report, London (H.M.S.O.) 1945.*

Notts. Miners' Association: Rule Books (various dates) and Minutes.*

People's Year Book, 1926, Manchester 1925.*

M. Wheeler, Life of Matthew Hayes, Nottm., 1899.

White's *History, Gazeteer and Directory of the County of Nottingham*, (various editions).

Y

T. E. B. Young, *Report on Visit to Coalfields of the U.S.A.*, London, 1947.*

Newspaper files: Nottingham *Review*, Nottingham *Journal*, Nottingham *Guardian*, Nottingham *Express*, Hucknall *Star and Advertiser*, and Press cuttings of the late Ald. E. Mellors, the late G. A. Spencer, Miss Walvin (from *Alfreton and Belper Journal*) and others.

Butterley Company's Archives (include posters and handbills issued by Sir John Alleyne addressed to workmen, 1871–2).*

* Copies of items marked with an asterisk are in the author's possession.

Secondary Sources

A. V. Alexander, 'The Co-operative Movement', *Encyclopaedia of the Labour Movement*, London, c. 1927.

V. L. Allen, *Power in Trade Unions*, London, 1954.

R. P. Arnot, *The Miners*, (3 vols.) London, 1948–61.

T. Ashton, Three Big Strikes in the Coal Industry, Manchester, (n.d.).

T. S. Ashton, 'The Coalminers of the Eighteenth Century,' *Economic History*, I (1928).

T. S. Ashton, *The Industrial Revolution, 1760–1830*, Oxford, 1947.

T. S. Ashton and J. Sykes, *The Coal Industry of the Eighteenth Century*, Manchester, 1929.

W. Ashworth, *An Economic History of England*, London, 1960.

J. A. Birks and P. Coxon, *An Account of Railway Development in the Nottttinghamshire Coalfield*, Mansfield, 1949 (duplicated).

A. L. Bowley, *Wages and Income in the United Kingdom since 1860*, Cambridge, 1937.

E. Burns, *The General Strike, May 1926: Trades Councils in Action*, London (L.R.D.) 1926.

J. D. Chambers, *Modern Nottingham in the Making*, Nottm., 1945.

W. Citrine, *The Truth About the Miners' Ballot (Reprint of a Speech at Kirkby—28th May 1928)*.

Cole and Postgate, *The Common People, 1746–1938*, London, 1938.

Colliery Year Book and Coal Trades Directory, 1951 edn. (Statistical Tables based on Govt. Reports).

J. H. Collins, *Principles of Coal Mining*, London 1876.

Communist Party, *Harworth Men Make History*—A Story of the Fight Against Spencerism, Nottm. 1936.

W. H. B. Court, *Coal* (History of the Second World War, United Kingdom, Civil Series) London, 1951.

Daniel de Leon, *The Preamble of the Industrial Workers of the World*, Glasgow, edn. 1905.

J. P. Dickie, *The Coal Problem*, London, 1938.

J. C. Drummond and Anne Wilbraham, *The Englishman's Food*, London, 1959.

Ebby Edwards, *The Miners' Case—An Answer to the Foot Plan*, London, 1945.

J. Farey (Senr.), *General View of the Agriculture and Minerals of Derbyshire*, London, 1811 (3 vols.) (Partly Primary).

Robert Foot, *A Plan for Coal*, London, 1945.

Dorothy M. George, *England in Transition*, London, 1953.

F. A. Gibson, *A Compilation of Statistics of the Coal-Mining Industry*, Cardiff, 1922.

A. R. Griffin, *The Miners of Nottinghamshire*, 2 vols., Nottm., 1956 and London, 1962.

C. P. Griffin, Robert Harrison: *The Development of the Managerial Function in a Coal-Mining Partnership*, (Unpublished B.A. Dissertation) Nottm., 1965.

W. Hallam, *Miners' Leaders*, London, 1894.

J. L. and B. Hammond, *The Town Labourer, 1760–1832*, London, 1949.

G. Harvey, *Industrial Unionism and the Mining Industry*, Pelaw-on-Tyne, 1917.

John Haslem, *The Old Derby China Factory: The Workmen and Their Production*, London, 1876.

F. A. Henson and R. S. Smith, 'Detecting Early Coal Workings from the Air', *Colliery Engineering*, June 1955.

G. W. Hilton, *The Truck System*, Cambridge, 1960.

E. J. Hobsbawm, *Primitive Rebels*, Manchester, 1959.

F. Hodges, *Nationalisation of the Mines*, London, 1920.

G. G. Hopkinson, 'Inland Navigations of the Derbyshire & Notts. Coalfield, 1777–1856', *Journal of Derbyshire Archaelogical Society*, 1959.

A. Horner, *Incorrigible Rebel*, London, 1960.

A. Hutt, *British Trade Unionism*, London, 1945.

J. M. Keynes, *The Economic Consequences of Mr. Churchill*, London, 1925.

R. Kidd, *The Harworth Colliery Strike, (National Council for Civil Liberties)*, London, 1937.

K. G. J. C. Knowles, *Strikes—A Study in Industrial Conflict*, Oxford, 1952.

F. W. Leeman, *Co-operation in Nottingham*, Nottm. 1963.

E. D. Lewis, *The Rhondda Valleys*, London, 1959.

Liberal Party, *Coal and Power: The Report of an Enquiry presided over by the Rt. Hon. D. Lloyd George*, London, 1924.

A. K. McKosh, *The Case Against Nationalization of the Coal Mines*, Sheffield, 1944.

E. A. Martin, *A Piece of Coal*, London, 1896.

Kingsley Martin, 'The General Strike', *Encyclopaedia of the Labour Movement*, London, c. 1927.

E. Mason, *Practical Coal Mining for Miners*, London, 1951.

Mechanical Engineers, Proceedings of the Institution of, October-December 1903.

Mining Association, *Historical Review of Coal Mining*, London, 1924.

Mining Association, *One Hundred Questions and Answers on Coal*, circa 1936.

R. H. Mottram and Colin Coote, *Through Five Generations; The History of the Butterley Company*, London, 1950.

C. L. Mowat, *Britain Between the Wars 1918–1940*, London, 1946.

J. U. Nef, *The Rise of the British Coal Industry* (2 vols.) London, 1932, reprinted by Frank Cass, 1966.

A. M. Neuman, *Economic Organization of the British Coal Industry*, London, 1934.

F. Nixon, 'The Early Steam Engine in Derbyshire', *Transactions of the Newcomen Society*, Vol. XXXI, 1957–8 and 1958–9.

F. Nixon, *Notes on the Engineering History of Derbyshire*, Derby, 1956.

G. Parkinson, *True Stories of Durham Pit Life*, London, 1912.

H. Pelling, *America and the British Left*, London, 1956.

E. H. Phelps-Brown and S. V. Hopkins, 'Wage-Rates and Prices: Evidence for Population Pressure in the Sixteenth Century', *Economica*, November 1957.

E. H. Phelps-Brown, *The Growth of British Industrial Relations*, London, 1959.

A. C. Pigou, *Aspects of British Economic History, 1918–1925*, London, 1948.

S. Pollard, Book Review in *Economic History Review*, Vol. XV, No. 3, 1963.

W. Purdy, *Colliery Explosions and Their Prevention*, Eastwood, 1912.

R. A. S. Redmayne, *The British Coal-Mining Industry During the War*, Oxford, 1923.

Wemyss Reid, *Memoirs and Correspondence of Lyon Playfair*, London, 1899.

Y.*

W. W. Rostow, *British Economy of the Nineteenth Century*, Oxford, 1944.

J. W. F. Rowe, *Wages in the Coal Industry*, London, 1923.

R. S. Sayers, 'The Return to Gold, 1925', *Studies in the Industrial Revolution*, London, 1960.

H. A. Shannon, 'Brick—A Trade Index', *Economica*, New Series, No. 1, 1934.

Percy Byshe Shelley, (1792–1822) *Peter Bell The Third*.

Adam Smith, *The Wealth of Nations*, (Everyman Edn.), London, 1910.

R. S. Smith, 'Huntingdon Beaumont: Adventurer in Coalmines' *Renaissance and Modern Studies*, (I) Nottm., 1957.

R. S. Smith, *The Willoughbys of Wollaton* (Unpublished Ph.D. Thesis), Nottingham, 1964.

R. S. Smith, 'Britain's First Rails: A Reconsideration', *Renaissance and Modern Studies*, Nottm., 1960.

F. Smith, *History of Pinxton* (Typescript, n.d.).

G. A. Spencer, *The Trades Union Bill Vindicated by a Labour M.P.*, London, 1927.

D. Spring, *English Landed Estate in the Nineteenth Century*, London, 1963.

I. C. F. Statham, *Winning and Working*, London, 1929.

P. Stevenson, *Introductory Course Notes* (typescript) 1964.

Julian Symons, *The General Strike*, London, 1959.

R. H. Tawney, 'The Problem of the Coal Industry', *Encyclopaedia of the Labour Movement*, London, 1927.

A. J. Taylor, 'The Sub-contract System in the British Coal Industry', *Studies in the Industrial Revolution*, London, 1960.

A. J. Taylor, 'Labour Productivity and Technical Innovation in the British Coal Industry', *Econ. Hist. Review*, XIV, No. 1, 1961.

F. Taylor, *Havelock Wilson* (Unpublished paper prepared at Ruskin College), 1958.

A. H. Thornton, 'Day Release for Liberal Studies', *Adult Education*, XXIX, 1956.

Victoria History of the County of Nottinghamshire (2 vols.), London.

Henry Walker, *Pinxton Old and New*, Alfreton, 1886 (A collection of articles written for the *Alfreton and Belper Journal*).

S. and B. Webb, *History of Trade Unionism, 1666–1920*, London, 1920.

H. F. West (Ed.) *The Autobiography of Robt. Watchorn*, Oklahoma, 1948.

G. C. H. Whitelock, *250 Years in Coal*, Eastwood, 1956.

F. S. Williams, *The Midland Railway: Its Rise and Progress*, London, 1878.

Francis Williams, *Fifty Years March—The Rise of the Labour Party*, London, 1950.

Francis Williams, *Magnificent Journey—The Rise of the Trade Unions*, London, 1954.

J. E. Williams, *The Derbyshire Miners*, London, 1962.

J. E. Williams, 'Labour in the Coalfields: A Critical Bibliography', *Soc. for the Study of Labour History*, Bulletin, No. 4, 1962.

J. E. Williams, Letter in *Society for the Study of Labour History*, Bulletin No. 5, 1962.

H. Wilson, *New Deal for Coal*, London, 1945.

Sir Arnold Wilson and H. Levy, *Workmen's Compensation*, 2 vols., Oxford, 1939.

A. C. Wood, 'Chartism in Nottingham', *Transactions of the Thoroton Society*, LIX, 1955.

A. C. Wood, *A History of Nottinghamshire*, Nottm., 1947.

C. H. Wood (ed.) *Hardwick Hall*, Derby (n.d.).

A. J. Youngson, *The British Economy, 1920–1957*, London, 1959.

Note: This Bibliography lists the main sources; but it is by no means exhaustive.

INDEX